D0857112

KATRINA

KATRINA

A HISTORY, 1915–2015

ANDY HOROWITZ

Harvard University Press

CAMBRIDGE, MASSACHUSETTS & LONDON, ENGLAND

2020

Publication of this book has been supported through the generous
provisions of the Maurice and Lula Bradley Smith Memorial Fund

First printing

Library of Congress Cataloging-in-Publication Data
Names: Horowitz, Andy (Andrew Deutsch), author.
Title: Katrina : a history, 1915–2015 / Andy Horowitz.
Description: Cambridge, Massachusetts : Harvard University Press,
    2020. | Includes index. |
Identifiers: LCCN 2019049275 | ISBN 9780674971714 (cloth)
Subjects: LCSH: Hurricanes—Louisiana—New Orleans—History. |
    Hurricane Katrina, 2005. | New Orleans (La.)—Economic
    conditions. | New Orleans (La.)—History. | New Orleans (La.)—
    Politics and government.
Classification: LCC HV636 2005 .N4 H67 2020 |
    DDC 363.34/9220976335—dc23
LC record available at https://lccn.loc.gov/2019049275

CONTENTS

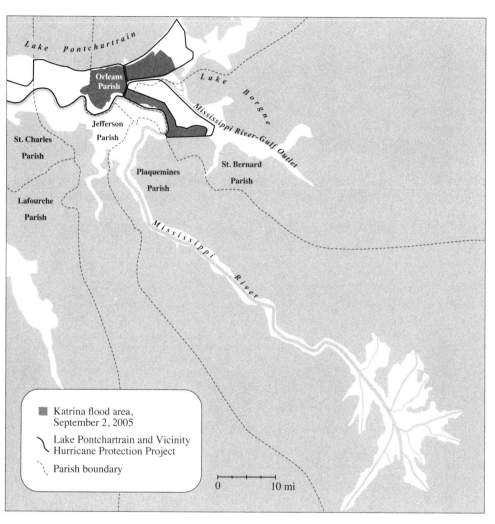

Katrina flood area, September 2, 2005.

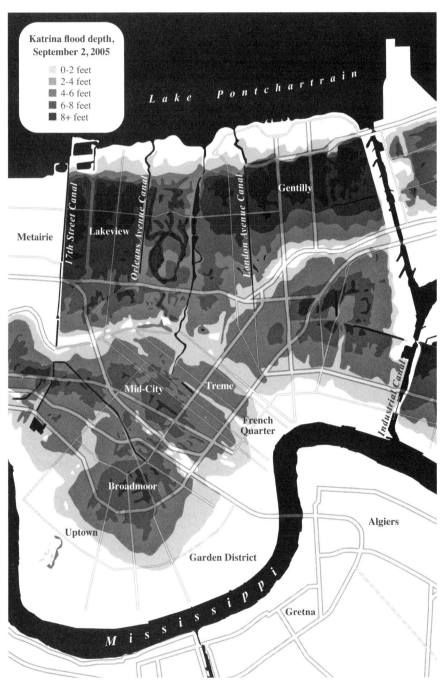

Katrina flood depth, September 2, 2005.

New Orleans
East

Gulf Intracoastal Waterway

Mississippi River–Gulf Outlet

Bayou Bienvenue

Lower
Ninth
Ward

Arabi

Chalmette

River

0   1 mi

KATRINA

INTRODUCTION

O N SEPTEMBER 29, 1915, AT THE MUDDY END OF THE MISSISSIPPI'S farthest reach into the Gulf of Mexico, one hundred miles downriver from New Orleans, an unnamed hurricane made landfall. An anemometer recorded wind gusts of 140 miles per hour there, at the town of Burrwood, Louisiana, where on easier days several hundred members of the Army Corps of Engineers lived in orderly cottages and worked to keep the shipping canal at the river's mouth clear of sediment.[1] As the storm moved upriver, the aneroid barometer at Tulane University plummeted to 28.10 inches. The rain gauge filled with 8.36 inches of precipitation in twenty-one hours. Even in a region accustomed to hurricanes, these were extraordinary measurements. Isaac Cline, the chief meteorologist at the United States Weather Bureau in New Orleans, reported that the storm was "the most intense hurricane of which we have record in the history of the Mexican Gulf coast, and probably in the United States."[2]

But meteorology is not meaning. On their own, these data reveal little about how the storm might have mattered to people, or how they might have responded to it. These precise metrics of wind speed, rainfall, and barometric pressure do not trace the shape of life in places that seem, repeatedly, to come under assault from the forces of nature. We need different tools to gauge those times when coincidences of earth, wind, and water upset the course of human events in ways so overwhelming that we name them with a word whose basic meaning suggests that the entire universe is out of joint: disaster.

Consider that during the 1915 hurricane, across the state of Louisiana, 275 people died. Property damage estimates ran to $12 million ($280 million in 2015 dollars). Upriver from Burrwood, only four houses remained standing in the town called Empire. East of New Orleans, in St. Bernard Parish, the settlement of Saint Malo was washed from the map entirely. That village bore the name of Jean Saint Malo, who in the 1780s had led a group of Africans trying to escape from slavery. Eventually captured by Spanish authorities, Saint Malo was executed in 1784 in front of the Cabildo, in the historic center square of New Orleans—where the hurricane winds had sent pieces of slate flying from the steeple of Saint Louis Cathedral. A foot of water remained in parts of the city for five days.[3] Nonetheless, once the storm passed, many New Orleanians celebrated.

"'Storm proof!' The Record Shows Orleans," the newspaper proclaimed after the hurricane. The mayor quickly rejected outside offers of aid. Surveying the event a month later, the New Orleans Sewerage and Water Board, the agency charged with protecting the city from floods, concluded that its new drainage system had passed a defining test. "It is safe to say," its report asserted, "that no city anywhere in the world could have withstood these conditions with less damage and less inconvenience than has New Orleans." Marshaling statistics from meteorologists like Isaac Cline, the report reasoned that the recent extreme occurrence of wind and rain "renders more remote the probability of a repetition of any of these things in the early future."[4]

It was a curious logic in a city that had seen ninety-two hurricanes or tropical storms since its European colonial founding in 1718.[5] Despite this history, the Sewerage and Water Board believed that even if another big storm came, New Orleans would be safe. The report's authors reflected on the storm's "lessons" this way: "there is no reason why this city and its surrounding country should not continue, even more successfully than heretofore, [its] developments in all directions." The experience of the 1915 hurricane affirmed the consensus among engineers and investors, city planners and politicians, home builders and home buyers, that New Orleans should grow.[6]

The city they created became one of the most celebrated places in the world. "Ain't no city like the one I'm from!" the women in the Original Pinettes Brass Band sang a century later.[7] New Orleans's admirers lauded it as "The Land of Dreams," "The Big Easy," "The City that Care Forgot," "America's Most Interesting City," and "the soul of America."[8] With its jazz, Mardi Gras, and other iconic contributions to world culture, more than any other place in America, New Orleans called to mind creativity, cosmopolitanism, and love of life.

But today, New Orleans also calls to mind catastrophe. The city drowned when its levee system collapsed on August 29, 2005, killing hundreds of people, destroying thousands of homes, and precipitating not only one of the most horrific moments in modern American history, but offering an emblem for the idea of disaster itself: Katrina. The response to the 1915 storm thus cast a century-long shadow, because the new neighborhoods developed after that storm experienced the worst flooding in 2005.[9] More than any other single factor, including the race or class of it inhabitants, the age of a building best predicted how it would fare in 2005. Tracing the outline of the Katrina flood reveals the shape of New Orleans as it stood nine decades earlier: most houses built before 1915 did not flood, but most houses built after the Sewerage and Water Board's 1915 call for further growth did.[10]

Usually, we imagine disasters as exceptions. We describe them as external attacks, ahistorical acts of God, blows from without. That is why most accounts of Katrina begin when the levees broke and conclude not long after. But these stories offer a denuded sense of what happened, why, or what might have prevented the catastrophe. Somebody had to build the levees before they could break.

I begin the story of Katrina in 1915 in order to pursue a different idea: that disasters come from within. Disasters are less discrete events than they are contingent processes.[11] Seemingly acute incidents, like the largely forgotten 1915 hurricane, live on as the lessons they teach, the decisions they prompt, and the accommodations they oblige. Their causes and consequences stretch across much longer periods of time and space than we commonly imagine. Seeing disasters in history, and as history, demonstrates that the places we live, and the disasters that imperil them, are at once artifacts of state policy, cultural imagination, economic order, and environmental possibility.

Katrina's causes and consequences reach across a century. The 1915 Sewerage and Water Board report shaped the rationale for developing the neighborhoods that flooded in 2005. Wrangling over fur trapping rights in the 1920s in St. Bernard Parish shaped the legal struggle for offshore oil in the 1940s, which shaped Louisiana's economy in the 1950s, the state's coastline in the 1970s, and the state's Coastal Master Plan to confront land loss in the 2010s. When the Industrial Canal, dredged for shipping interests in 1918, flooded the homes of veterans during Hurricane Betsy in 1965, the memory of sharecropping shaped how African Americans interpreted the Small Business

Administration loans they were offered as disaster relief. The memory of Hurricane Betsy shaped how New Orleanians responded when the Industrial Canal broke again under the weight of Hurricane Katrina's storm surge in 2005. The promise of the federal Housing Act of 1937 shaped the claims that residents made for a right of return to public housing in 2007. The Louisiana state engineers dynamited a levee in St. Bernard Parish in 1927, which shaped fears in 1965 and 2005 that politicians had lit another fuse. The mutual benefit associations African Americans developed during Reconstruction to provide burial insurance shaped the Social Aid and Pleasure Clubs that offered Louisiana its most popular metaphor for recovery: the jazz funeral. When Jesse Jackson declared in 2005 that, filled with stranded African American Katrina victims, New Orleans's Convention Center looked "like the hull of a slave ship," he was admonishing all who heard him that disasters offer no escape from the past.[12]

And yet, if understanding history usually demands drawing connections between seemingly disparate dots, trying to make sense of what happened in Louisiana after August 29, 2005, also poses the opposite problem, because the hurricane called Katrina did not cause many of the effects commonly attributed to it.

After the storm passed, New Orleans police officers shot and killed unarmed citizens. The Federal Emergency Management Agency gave flood victims trailers laced with formaldehyde. The New Orleans City Council voted to demolish the city's public housing apartments. The Louisiana State Legislature voted to transform the city's public school system into a confederacy of charter schools. Congress voted to fund the largest housing recovery program in United States history; the program appropriated money to homeowners but not to renters. New Orleans police officers arrested musicians for leading jazz funerals without permits, while violent crime plagued the city. Louisiana State University shut down New Orleans's public Charity Hospital, while rates of mental illness surged. The Army Corps of Engineers encircled the city with a new levee system, while the wetlands beyond the walls continued to erode and the city itself continued to sink. A decade after the storm, New Orleans's population had fallen from 484,674 to 390,711. Of the people missing, the vast majority—nearly 92,000 people—were African American.[13] We have come to refer to this sequence of events as "Katrina," but for none of these effects was the hurricane the proximate cause.

The flood line thus tells one important story, but it is not the only story that matters. "Americans have never left our destiny to the whims of nature,"

President George W. Bush declared in September 2005, "and we will not start now."[14] After the flood receded, policymakers reapportioned the challenges the water had posed. Legislators designed recovery programs that favored white people over African American people, wealthy people over poor people, and people who owned homes over people who rented them. These policies reinforced existing inequalities. And they often undermined what the many Louisianians who opposed them argued were essential facts of life: the bonds of family, the solidarity of community, notions of political legitimacy, feelings of cultural belonging, and a sense of moral order.

The etymology of the word *disaster* refers to stars out of alignment; but if the changes in Louisiana after Hurricane Katrina seemed to some to proceed with the force of destiny, it is well to remember, as Shakespeare cautioned, "The fault . . . is not in our stars, But in ourselves, that we are underlings."[15]

KATRINA BRINGS TOGETHER SEVERAL OF THE DEFINING CONCERNS of our time. The climate crisis that seems, at once, to have revealed the power of humans to change the world, and the powerlessness of humans to control those changes; the fossil-fueled growth that made single family homes affordable and vulnerable; the infrastructure that is not up to a warming world; the ongoing state of emergency and the corresponding yearning for sustainability and resilience; the racism that rends our communities; the crushing inequality; the sometimes reckless, sometimes revolutionary, hope that the future might be better than the past—none of these are unique to Louisiana. They define the United States in the twenty-first century. Hurricane Sandy in New York and New Jersey, Hurricane Harvey in Texas, Hurricane Maria in Puerto Rico, and other frighteningly similar events have demonstrated what many Louisianians always understood: that New Orleans's history is America's history and that Katrina is America's possible future.[16]

We often see our problems as unprecedented, but the crises we face challenge the legitimacy of state action, the moral bases of our economy, and the processes of culture that give life its meaning. These are among the most enduring human problems. History can help reveal the range of possible solutions. This book, therefore, means to offer Katrina's history while, at the same time, suggesting new, more capacious ways to make sense of disasters in general.

I grapple with the unsettling truth that disasters have histories. The chapters that follow challenge distinctions between acute catastrophe and enduring trauma, between the natural and the man-made, between cities and their suburban and rural surrounds, and between conservative and liberal politics, while clarifying distinctions among definitions of recovery in the halls of Congress and on the streets of devastated neighborhoods. I engage in a broad search for causes and consequences—asking questions across the fields of urban history, environmental history, Southern history, and African American history, and incorporating insights from sociology, anthropology, geography, and economics—in order to explore the relationship between structural inequality and physical infrastructure. I draw from the archives of congressmen and Communists, the Army Corps and oil companies, and use city plans, geological surveys, oral histories, Census records, and jazz records in order to understand how disasters force people to reckon with the causes of inequality, to debate the proper role of government, and to make sense of change itself.

This book addresses three, overarching questions: Why did people live in such dangerous places? What made these places dangerous? And, how could this happen in the United States? These were the questions that many cried at their televisions as they watched 80 percent of New Orleans and nearly all of neighboring St. Bernard Parish fill with water in the late summer of 2005. Scholars and policy makers have struggled with these questions since, because they are not only about Louisiana, but about how to make sense of twentieth- and twenty-first-century America. And these questions haunt us still, especially as people increasingly understand that Katrina is not receding safely into the past, but looming ever larger as a portent of the future.

I can outline the book's answers to the first two questions quickly. Why did people live in such dangerous places? People lived there because, for over a century, federal programs—including the Swamp Land Acts, the GI Bill, the Disaster Relief Act, the National Flood Insurance Program, and levee building itself—have encouraged building and rebuilding in flood-prone places. What made these places so dangerous? They were not always. Rather, they were made increasingly so over the course of the twentieth century because the benefits of Louisiana's most lucrative industries—shipping and oil—were not first allocated to mitigating their costs, creating a dramatic imbalance of private profits and public liabilities. This arrangement prompted a stunning collapse of land into water, an existential crisis for Louisiana that the new levee system constructed after 2005 did little to address.

The third question, how could this happen in the United States, requires more discussion. Before the 2005 flood, many imagined that somehow, American citizenship promised to prevent such terrible suffering. And still, after the flood, many continued to claim that Katrina would never have happened in a place like New York City. They meant that the promises that American citizenship made to wealthy white people, at least, would protect them from ravages they believed affected only poor African Americans in New Orleans. Most people who made such statements meant them as a critique of racism and economic inequality; they may not have recognized how the critique rested on the idea of American exceptionalism.[17] But carving out an exception for New Orleans, or the poor, or African Americans, insidiously shielded everywhere and everyone else. This was dangerously naïve. Asserting that Katrina's flood only affected people on the margins of society deafens all of us to the siren of its warning.

Racism and poverty are necessary beacons for navigating Katrina's history, because they structure American inequality, often leading to inequities so stark they can be fatal. Yet at times, they can offer insufficient explanations for the suffering cataloged in these pages. This is particularly true when it comes to flood vulnerability. Many observers have assumed or asserted that in New Orleans, as one scholar put it, "topographic gradients doubled as class and race gradients," but the truth is more complicated.[18] When the levees broke, the homes of tens of thousands of suburban, middle-class white people flooded catastrophically, while the homes of New Orleans's poorest African American residents, who lived in public housing, largely did not. There are no straight lines that connect racism or poverty to flood depths.

Instead, I demonstrate that while racism set the stage for whose homes flooded, it took a circuitous route to doing so. The flood was not the result of racist policies or practices in the years directly before the levee breaches in 2005. Rather, racism in federal housing policies from the 1930s through the 1960s—including redlining, segregation, and Veterans Affairs loans that went disproportionately to white people—all enabled the white middle class to move into new homes. Since the only available land was on lower ground in new neighborhoods and suburbs, these homes were located there, while many African Americans continued to live in the inner city. The older parts of the city were on higher ground. Therefore, confining African American families to the older parts of New Orleans ironically spared them from some of the flooding, while the same racist housing policies put white people, and the African American people who managed to access them, at risk.

It is worth lingering on that last point. Racist housing policies moved a predominately white population to new neighborhoods that came with new streets, new schools, more valuable homes and—largely invisible to many of their inhabitants—greater flood risk. African Americans were left to older neighborhoods, deemed less desirable in most ways, although they had the lost-to-view benefit of being at higher elevations. The Lower Ninth Ward offers an exception that proves the rule. The African American neighborhood was low-lying and subject to a devastating wall of water in 2005. But it had not been home to the city's most marginalized citizens. Rather, it had been built by and for middle-class African Americans who had found ways to access the benefits of the local, state, and federal commitments to metropolitan growth and home ownership.

In the long run, the policies and practices that once seemed to enable American progress created catastrophic vulnerability. People who lived in flood-prone parts of metropolitan New Orleans generally did not live there because they were disadvantaged. Rather, they lived there because they had been able to take advantage of the government subsidies required to develop housing in low-lying parts of the region. More broadly, they had benefited from the redistributional policies that created the American middle class and defined the post-World War II American dream. The liberal desire to expand the welfare state combined with a conservative desire to privatize the ensuing growth: this uneasy but expansive détente built America in the twentieth century and imperils it in the twenty-first. It has no better emblem than the federal levee system that surrounded metropolitan New Orleans from the late 1960s until its failure in 2005. The levee system was one of the largest public works projects in United States history—a physical promise of a national commitment to the safety, well-being, and growth of the communities it encircled. But its foundations were not steady enough. And when the system collapsed, those with power tried to prop it back up for themselves on the backs of the already disadvantaged.

The book is divided into two parts. The two halves hinge on the day the levees broke. Dividing the book this way is meant to recognize the importance of that deadly collapse, but also to emphasize that it is what happened before and after the levee failures that gave Katrina its significance. I also look beyond the levee system, because urban history ought more often to be written and understood at the scale of environmental history, without losing sight of how change is experienced at the local level. People in New Orleans and its suburbs have long depended on what happens beyond their modern-day city walls.[19]

Part I of the book describes the construction of Louisiana's vulnerability, starting with an explosion. In April 1927, fifteen miles downriver from French Quarter, the Louisiana state engineers dynamited the Mississippi River levee, flooding the homes of thousands of farmers, fishermen, and fur trappers in St. Bernard and Plaquemines Parishes in an attempt to protect New Orleans from the river's high water. The blast signaled the failure of a century's worth of piecemeal attempts to control the Mississippi. It heralded too a confluence of state power, political ideology, and flood control policy—a regime that enabled politicians and engineers to restructure the earth and how people lived on it in ways that protected and enriched some at the expense of endangering and impoverishing others.

In the 1890s, the wetlands of Plaquemines and St. Bernard Parishes, the counties that frame the hundred-mile stretch of the Mississippi River from New Orleans to the Gulf of Mexico, were granted to local levee boards to manage in the service of flood control. The marshes seemed worthless then, but after the 1927 flood, they were discovered to hold enormous deposits of oil and gas. Flood protection and industrial development thus became intertwined, and often conflicting, processes. The struggle played out over decades in a small-scale war between fur trappers, who used the coastal marshes in common, multinational industrial firms like Standard Oil, which sought to exploit the oil resources, and—as brokers between the two—politicians like Plaquemines and St. Bernard Parish District Attorney Leander Perez. Decisions made during this period caused Louisiana to begin sinking, rapidly, into the Gulf of Mexico. Since the 1930s, more than 2,000 square miles of Louisiana have been lost to the water, and metropolitan New Orleans has become far more vulnerable to floods.

Chapter 2 brings the focus upriver to tell the story of 1965's Hurricane Betsy. Betsy was the defining historical precedent for Katrina and the formative event by which Louisianians made sense of Katrina. During Betsy, a storm surge overwhelmed the Industrial Canal and flooded the city's Lower Ninth Ward, devastating a neighborhood that exemplified both the possibilities and limits for African Americans working to enter the middle class in the decades following World War II. After the flood, debates about disaster relief exploded into a broad struggle over civil rights and urban development, as African American women and white Southern politicians fought to define the disaster and to shape relief programs. Many residents of the Lower Ninth believed that local officials had bombed the levees, as they had in St. Bernard in 1927—that their unequal suffering had been caused by government decisions; it followed, therefore, that the government owed them reparations. When they failed to get the help they believed they were entitled to, many African Americans in the Lower Ninth came to believe that not only had the government caused the flood in the first place, it also had broken a promise to help them recover from it.

In contrast, the white men who controlled Democratic politics, both in Louisiana and in Washington, understood the Betsy disaster to be an act of God that government had no role in causing and no special obligation to fix. They welcomed disaster aid not as reparations but as charity, and as a tonic for federal fractures over civil rights. Put another way, Betsy prompted a debate over the causes of inequality and the promises of citizenship.

Chapter 3 charts the accelerated pace of metropolitan growth and coastal land loss after Hurricane Betsy, focusing on suburban development in St. Bernard Parish. After Betsy, Congress authorized the Lake Pontchartrain and Vicinity Hurricane Protection Project and the National Flood Insurance Program. These major federal investments were meant to forestall the next flood disaster. They ultimately magnified it. The new federal levee system was designed to protect—and the new flood insurance program encouraged—development across a much larger metropolitan region, a geography enabled by oil and gas. For decades following Betsy, federal policies encouraged Americans to move to these new neighborhoods in order to join the middle class. Many people imagine New Orleans to be exotic. But the Katrina flood washed over quintessential twentieth-century American landscapes.

Chapter 3 highlights the growing chorus of critics warning of the threats caused by Louisiana's oil industry, land loss, and an ethos that pitted individual economic progress against community security—including keen predictions of what ultimately occurred when Hurricane Katrina made landfall. But metropolitan growth offered a seductive solution to social problems for much of the twentieth century, and proved difficult to abandon, even in the face of looming catastrophe.

Part II of the book covers Hurricane Katrina and the decade that followed. Chapter 4 focuses on the levee failures and the immediate responses to them in August and September 2005. An inept rescue operation, calls for New Orleans to be abandoned, and a series of racist attacks on African Americans, shaped how people understood what was happening and influenced policy responses. The flood renewed a struggle over the meaning of American citizenship that had endured since Hurricane Betsy, revealing a polity still deeply fractured over conflicting visions of race, nature, government, community, and change itself. Some Louisianians drew from a deep well of anti-statist ideas to argue that the disaster was a problem of too much government, and therefore that the free market offered the best model for recovery. Others understood the catastrophe as a product of market thinking and called for a recommitment to the idea of a commonwealth, often through government action. Katrina was a call to arms for people in New Orleans and across the country—but it called them to opposing sides.

Chapter 5 traces the development and implementation of the policies that remade greater New Orleans after the flood, focusing especially on contests over housing, health care, and education. Although policymakers often couched their recovery proposals in the language of sudden opportunity or local necessity, the policies they proposed usually drew on long-standing and widespread ideas about social reform. Ultimately, political decisions reshaped the region more than the flood itself, dictating who was able to come home and what their lives would be like when they did. The explanation for why more than 90,000 African Americans did not return to New Orleans lies less in a deep and totalizing racist history than in the pointed and contingent work of comparatively recent actors.

The Epilogue explores cultural responses to the flood—and the broader challenges posed by racism, capitalism, and climate change, which, over time, Katrina came to embody. In New Orleans, musicians, Mardi Gras Indians, Social Aid and Pleasure Club members, and neighborhood advocates nurtured a vision of the future that foregrounded justice and community, one that conflicted with the recovery programs pursued by most policy makers. On the coast, especially after BP's Deepwater Horizon oil rig exploded in 2010, roughnecks, shrimpers, and other residents of fast-sinking towns shared the sense that the future imagined by those with power had no place for them. The land around them was disintegrating into the Gulf of Mexico.

In the city, suburbs, and on the coast alike, announcements that the time had come to "retreat" from rising seas often sounded like calls for dispossession, issued by those who would never make such sacrifices themselves. Meanwhile, as people burned the oil being extracted from and shipped through the eroding marshes, the world warmed, and the seas rose higher. To those caught in the crosscurrents of diffuse government bureaucracies and distant corporate structures, the levers of power seemed increasingly inaccessible. And yet, looking back on a century's worth of successes and struggles, Louisianans were becoming more aware of their own contributions—for better and for worse—to the world they had made for themselves and one another.

WHAT IS A DISASTER?

Disasters demand more attention from historians. The day after the 1915 hurricane made landfall, the *New Orleans Item* announced, "City Cut Off From Rest of World."[20] The reference to downed telegraph lines resonates with the way many people have tended to think about New Orleans as an exceptional place, and disasters as exceptional moments, disconnected from the rest of time and space. In 2005, when President Bush called Katrina "a tragedy that seems so blind and random," or when scholars argued that some array of "factors . . . conspired to make the eventual—and inevitable—disaster what it was," they suffered equally from the limiting view of Katrina as sudden break.[21] Katrina was neither random nor inevitable, but both assessments are artifacts of seeing disasters as events without histories.

When people face disaster, they reckon with fundamental questions: what should they try to save, what should they try to leave behind, and who should decide? Who deserves help, why, what kind, and from whom? What caused the disaster in the first place? And what does this disaster mean for the next one? These debates, which ought to fascinate any student, scholar, or citizen, take place in historical context. Sometimes, these debates change the political and cultural commitments that give history its shape. And yet, perhaps because they are so often imagined, almost by definition, to be events that come out of nowhere, for a long time, academic historians largely ignored disasters altogether.[22]

Other social scientists embraced the study of disasters, however, and often explicitly because they seemed to defy history.[23] In a seminal 1961 article, for example, the sociologist Charles Fritz argued that "disasters provide a temporary liberation from the worries, inhibitions, and anxieties associated with the past and future because they force people to concentrate their full attention on immediate moment-to-moment and day to day needs." Disasters, he wrote, cause "the blanking out of the past and future frames of reference," and "provide . . . a clean break from the past."[24] A half-century later, the author Rebecca Solnit argued that because they cause "the suspension of the usual order and the failure of most systems," disasters leave us "free to live and act another way."[25] But Katrina's history undermines hope that, like Noah's flood, our catastrophes might offer a baptism by storm surge.

Studying how a disaster took shape in place and over time, makes clear that the places we live and the disasters that imperil them are produced by the same histories. The land underfoot and the ways people live on it—oil extraction, levee building, states' rights, suburban development, the middle class, coastal erosion, flood insurance, and jazz; the Mississippi River, Standard Oil, the Industrial Canal, the white primary, the Lower Ninth Ward, Chalmette, the GI Bill, Fats Domino, the fried oyster po'boy—and the possibility that all of this will be washed away—this is Louisiana. Trying to disassemble these pieces makes history less comprehensible, not more. Better, instead, to try to figure out the ways they fit together.

One seam in particular that many scholars have been eager to locate is the one that separates the natural from the man-made. Existing studies of disasters often turn on the question, as one investigation puts it, of "where to draw the line between 'natural' and 'unnatural' disasters."[26] To the extent that this approach leads to scrutiny of what, or who, caused harm to others, it remains a vital one. Increasingly, scholars assert that there is no such thing as a natural disaster, because who is in harm's way is the product of political decisions and social arrangements, rather than the inevitable order of things.[27] This essential point lies at the foundation of my analysis. Vulnerability is socially constructed. But to discover that any event is in some way man-made is simply to recognize the fact of human history, not to analyze that history. It is a starting point, not a conclusion.

Rather than asking if a disaster was man-made, therefore, we ought to ask, how was it made? The answer will have to include nature and human nature: water and wind, concrete and clay, politics and culture, conscious choices and unwilled accidents. Our sense of temporal scale, too, must change, because the timelines of human and environmental history are intertwined. Burning fossil fuels has warmed the oceans, amplifying the frequency and intensity of tropical storms.[28] Hurricanes are events in the history of the industrial revolution.

There remains a crucial caveat. During disasters, some people suffer more than others. Disasters, therefore, compel their observers to confront inequality. For people trying to understand inequality, the idea that a certain amount of suffering is inevitable and that some people are bound to be unlucky—in other words, the idea that inequality is natural and that nature can be capricious—has proven to be a durably attractive concept. Sometimes, people wield the idea as a shield, using it to hide their own culpability in causing harm.[29] Other times, people use the natural disaster idea as a way to make sense of their own misfortune.[30] Certainly, in ways this book explores, ideas about natural inequality and nature's caprice structure American law and social policy.[31] Thus, it is necessary to reaffirm that so-called "acts of God" are deeply embedded in the acts of women and men and, at the same time, to recognize that a belief in natural disasters shapes the way that many people respond to them.

Acknowledging that disasters have histories does not mean asserting that those histories amount only to relentless, teleological stories of decline. Many environmentalists and environmental historians describe disasters as nature's response to human efforts to engineer landscapes. They would paint New Orleans's physical expansion in the nine decades following the 1915 hurricane as a defiance of the natural order, and Katrina, as the *New York Times* put it in a headline, as "Nature's Revenge." This dim view leaves little room for the obvious truth that people have sometimes changed the world around them in ways that have made their lives better. To gloss the last century of Louisiana's history as a story of "hubris, stupidity and wishful thinking," may be briefly satisfying in its moral sweep, until one realizes that doing so gathers up Louis Armstrong, Ruby Bridges, Tennessee Williams, my wife Sarah, and over a million other Louisianians with all of their hopes, achievements, and beignets piled high with powdered sugar, and deposits them in the dustbin of history's mistakes.[32]

On the other hand, casting recovery as disaster's inevitable second act is just as misleading. Many have gone so far as to claim that New Orleans improved after the flood, offering heroic tales of resilience, if not redemption. But even if these accounts did not celebrate changes that were, and are, deeply contested, they would remain bewildering to people who know that at the immovable center of Katrina's story are hundreds of needless deaths. Asserting that the city came back better defames those who could not come back at all.

This book looks back on a past in which terrible exploitation sometimes gave rise to extraordinary beauty, and forward to a future in which, we know, some of our most generous plans will give rise to extraordinary suffering. The disaster idea can obscure an ineluctable truth about historical change: things get better and they get worse, often at the same time.

The more I have thought about Katrina, and disaster studies, the more uncomfortable I have become with the idea of "disaster" altogether. A disaster is at best an interpretive fiction, or at worst, an ideological script. After all, there is no objective checklist for differentiating a disaster from other periods of time. You cannot distinguish a disaster from other bad news the way you can distinguish an alligator from a crocodile (when their mouths are closed, you can see more of a crocodile's teeth than an alligator's). Scholars have attempted classification schemes, but they rarely hold up to scrutiny. How many buildings must fall for an event to count as a disaster? How many people must die? Over what space or period of time? Squinting too closely at a problem can blind rather than focus your vision.[33]

Calling something a disaster implies that there is a regular course of things, and that the moment in question was an exception. It suggests that the event was prompted by an exogenous force, that it was extraordinary (rather than ordinary), acute (rather than chronic), local (rather than diffuse), unpredictable (rather than expected), and revolutionary (rather than evolutionary). And so, just as slavery outlines the bounds of freedom, or darkness reveals the extent of light, the idea of disaster limns—and affirms—its inverse: order.

Consider housing. By making a special case out of flooding, the disaster idea normalizes the loss of homes due to economic change. There may be good reasons to distinguish between a person who lost her house in a flood and a person who lost his house because his mortgage went under water, but preemptively deciding that these are categorically different species of events reinforces the political, economic, cultural, environmental, and moral logics that one ought to interrogate. Also, clinging closely to technical definitions is not likely to help us understand the pain of loss, the trauma of displacement, or the wondering why that accompanies any path to homelessness.

Cordoning off moments when things go badly, the disaster idea enables us to perceive the arc of the moral universe as a long, smooth curve toward justice. To name something a disaster is to decry its outcomes as illegitimate, and to call for a restoration of the status quo, instead of suggesting that the status quo may have been illegitimate in the first place. The disaster idea makes enduring suffering appear to be a personal failure. And when people with power seem to recover quickly, the disaster idea allows them to celebrate themselves for beating the odds, without acknowledging the ways that history had loaded the dice in their favor.[34]

"Maybe the mistake we made, right at the beginning," the sociologist Kai Erikson said to me, in a conversation in 2015, "was to call it 'Katrina.'"[35] What

I took him to mean was that it may have been a mistake to use the hurricane's name to refer to how the contingent histories of race, class, community, trauma, inequality, the welfare state, metropolitan development, extractive industry, and environmental change manifested themselves in Louisiana early in this century—a mistake because it risks misleading observers into thinking that the weather had made these histories matter, rather than the other way around.

Furthermore, applying the storm's name in such an encompassing way risks implying that the story of Katrina should be something like the hurricane itself—blustering in, shaking things up, and then quickly dissipating. In reality, I argue, the disaster's causes and consequences extend across a century. "When people talk about 'Katrina' they are not just talking about the storm anymore," one New Orleanian explained in 2008. "It's the insurance crisis, the mental health crisis, the crime, the homeless under the bridge—the whole ball of wax."[36] To continue to isolate the storm as a special moment in time, to name it as a proximate cause for any of these endemic and enduring social circumstances, amounts to a political argument against structural analysis. Removing the frame that the disaster idea imposes frees us to see a much more expansive view of how and why change happens.

Disasters, so-called, are not so different from other moments in time. There often is more to be gained by bringing them down to the *chronos* of history than leaving them in the *kairos* of the sublime. "Unless we are willing to escape into sentimentality or fantasy," Norman Maclean wrote in *Young Men and Fire*, "often the best we can do with catastrophes, even our own, is to find out exactly what happened and restore some of the missing parts."[37] That is what I have attempted to do.

PART I

1 HOW TO SINK NEW ORLEANS

CONTROLLING FLOODS, OIL, AND STATES' RIGHTS, 1927–1965

EMILE RICHE KNEW THE RIVER ACROSS THE ROAD FROM HIS HOUSE in Betrandville, Louisiana, as the Mississippi, but Choctaw people had called it *bulbansha*, "place for foreign languages."[1] In 1927, many of the folks around Betrandville—white, black, and shades between—spoke French; Emile's parents spoke French because they came from Alsace, but Atakapa-Ishak people had lived out on Grand Bayou since before the French arrived in North America, maybe since the muddy river had brought the land itself, and they too spoke French in 1927.[2] Downriver toward Empire, Dalmatians spoke Croatian as they raked oysters.[3] They traded them with "Germans, Italians and Irishmen; Spanish-speaking Filipinos; Chinese, Malays; Portuguese, English, Danes, Greeks, and Swedes."[4] Across the Chandeleur Sound, along the Bayou Terre aux Boeufs and on Delacroix Island, Isleño fur trappers spoke Spanish; they sang *decimas* they had brought with them from the Canary Islands. When the storms came, Isleño old timers summoned the Spanish phrases that cursed the winds, and the motions of the knife that might make the storms change course.[5] It is unclear if the Choctaw word *bulbansha* meant to signal a kind of cosmopolitanism, or something more like Babel.

Nonetheless, on the signboards he posted around his property throughout the 1930s, 1940s, and 1950s, Riche painted his protests in English. English, after all, was the language that Louisiana Governor Oramel Simpson had used in 1927 to announce the plan to protect New Orleans from the Mississippi River flood. How? By dynamiting the levee across from Riche's home, blowing open a crevasse to lower the water level in the city.[6] English was the language, too, that "fifty leading financiers and business men of New Orleans" had used in a front-page resolution "assuring" people like Riche, the truck farmers, fur trappers, and fishermen of Plaquemines and St. Bernard Parishes who were flooded, that they would be given restitution for their losses.[7]

But over time, Emile Riche's experience taught him that the New Orleans businessmen treated their promises just as they treated that levee: as something to break. "IN THE TIME OF THE CREVASSE THE BURGLARS GOT $2200 OF MY MONEY," Riche wrote on one of his signs in 1955, nearly three decades after the flood, when he still had not been compensated. He added a simple appeal: "I WOULD LIKE TO KNOW WHO THE BURGLARS WERE."[8]

The plea was a rhetorical flourish, because Riche already had figured it out. There were many to blame—too many—but he focused on one man: Leander Perez. Perez was the district attorney for Plaquemines and St. Bernard Parishes from 1924 to 1960, and during that long reign in what otherwise might have been an insignificant office, Perez made himself famous as an advocate for "states' rights" in the 1940s and as a segregationist in the 1950s. Riche called Perez the "pocket drainer," because of the way he secreted Plaquemines's oil deposits from the ground and cash from his constituents' pockets.[9] Lording his control over coastal Louisiana's oil rights, the district attorney became a millionaire many times over. Firms large as Standard Oil and Freeport Sulphur supplicated before him. Above all, then, Perez distinguished himself as an autocrat, a man whose despotic control over local affairs made him seem to be a kind of American dictator. The *New York Times* called Perez the "czar of Louisiana's greatest remaining sub-empire," who "rules Plaquemines as a personal fiefdom"; to *Fortune* magazine in 1958, he was the "swampland Caesar" of "the last unconstitutional monarchy in the U.S." At home at Promised Land Plantation, his guests called him "Judge."[10]

The irony, though, is that the political, economic, and environmental order Perez came to represent—one that gave a local politician the power to boss around thousands of well-armed people on their own land, to dictate to the largest industrial corporations in the world, to dare to reshape even the mighty Mississippi River for his own ends—would prove, in the hindsight of history, to be its own undoing. Perez ambitiously attempted to reform the national Democratic Party in Louisiana's image by helping to lead the Dixiecrat revolt; he pursued Louisiana's legal claims to offshore oil royalties all the way to the Supreme Court; and he enacted audacious economic, political, and even military plans to transform Plaquemines into a quasi-independent, self-sufficient parish.

These efforts all backfired. Perez's lifework as "Mr. Dixiecrat," a name he gave himself to demonstrate his commitment to "states' rights," ultimately eroded local power.[11] Similarly, efforts in the name of flood protection ultimately made Louisiana more flood prone. Today, the hundreds of millions of dollars spent on levees and canals are causing the place once known as "The Empire Parish" for its astonishing wealth in natural resources to disintegrate into the Gulf of Mexico.[12] In 2013, the National Oceanic and Atmospheric Administration removed thirty-one Plaquemines place names from the official government map; the places no longer exist.[13] Geologists warn that the majority of Plaquemines Parish may be underwater, lost to the Gulf, by 2050. New Orleans may not be far behind.[14]

In Louisiana, floods, oil, and states' rights are three sides of the same story, because local levee boards owned the oil lands. The struggle to control Louisiana's petrochemical wealth represented a contest between competing political, economic, and social visions, but the fight turned on a geological coincidence: an enormous amount of oil and gas happened to lie under land designated by the government to protect Louisiana from floods. The coincidence of local political power, natural resources, and environmental stewardship could have led to a regime where government agencies managed public lands for the common good. Instead, Emile Riche's nemesis Leander Perez used the coincidence to help create a system in which the public domain could be exploited for private advantage, and the costs and benefits of development would be distributed wildly unevenly.[15]

Masquerading as the natural order of things is a landscape where power and impotence, wealth and poverty, even land and water, have been given shape by identifiable human decisions. Sometimes, the causes are as clear as the sticks of dynamite carefully positioned on the Caernarvon levee in April 1927. In other cases, the causes can be more difficult to see. Nonetheless, a close examination reveals how politicians, policy makers, oil company executives and engineers, flood control experts, real estate developers, and other residents restructured Louisiana's land and the way people live on it. The system that prevailed gave rise to a startling juxtaposition of unfathomable wealth and existential danger.

Most accounts of this period of American history describe the rise of a New Deal order, defined by strengthening federal regulation and narrowing economic inequality. But in Louisiana, Riche witnessed the channelization of the Mississippi River, the dredging of oil exploration canals, and the transformation of public agencies into instruments of private profit—in other words, he saw the privatization of public space, the deregulation of environmental development, the disfranchisement of voters, and the stratification of economic stations. In Perez's efforts to control Louisiana's oil, Riche saw the avant-garde of modern conservatism.[16]

States' rights offered Perez and his renegade flank of white southern Democrats a flexible platform for promoting their vision of the modern South. The pursuit of white supremacy shaped their ideology. So did the pursuit of wealth.[17] The "smell of crude oil mingles with magnolia in that southern revolt," is how one reporter put it at the time.[18] When Perez took lawsuits to the Supreme Court to argue against federal oversight in Louisiana, he was not seeking to maintain racial segregation in the public schools, although he strongly supported that cause, but rather to maintain local control of the state's oil wealth. "States rights include segregation but it includes a lot of other things too," W. H. Talbot, the oil industry attorney and campaign manager for several Louisiana Democratic gubernatorial campaigns reflected, "such as making the federal government keep its nose out of the gas and oil business in Louisiana."[19] Protecting oil interests, the reporter A. J. Liebling wrote, "lies behind much in the South that otherwise seems irrational."[20] "States' rights" heralded a defense of a racial caste system; it also announced an economic platform of limited regulation and unfettered industrial development.

Southern Democrats like Perez, icons for an almost fascist level of government power, used that power in the service of the owners and shareholders of Standard Oil, Freeport Sulphur, and other transnational corporate interests. Working with local government, these firms rewrote Louisiana's Constitution and redistributed its mineral wealth. Even as Governor Huey Long promoted quasi-socialist reforms to make "Every Man a King," and Perez boasted of his parish's "Utopia" with full employment, they were transferring huge amounts of public resources to private markets.[21] Once they yielded influence to the oil interests, local politicians never regained the reins of power.[22]

Riche watched as these decisions combined to sink Plaquemines and St. Bernard Parishes. By the end of his life, they imperiled New Orleans, too.[23] In one of his protest signs, Riche called himself a picture "of depression and starvation at once." He struggled in the ways he could against Leander Perez and the system Perez represented until he died in 1962.[24] That was a long time to spend on what may have seemed a quixotic protest. But four decades after the state engineers directed the Mississippi River to flood his house, the catastrophe was not yet over for him. Disasters can seem acute, his protests remind, but their causes are long in the making and their effects last a very long time.

Riche's warning offers another message, too. It is the most important lesson history can teach: for better and for worse, things might have been different.

SWAMP LAND ACTS

In April 1927, "A Delta official spoke solemnly to all who listened: 'You are witnessing the public execution of a parish.'"[25] An explosion of dynamite heralded the execution. Or rather, a series of explosions, because the levee that convict laborers had constructed in 1915 to protect Emile Riche and the other people of Plaquemines and St. Bernard from the Mississippi River took the determined efforts of the Louisiana state engineers to destroy on April 29, 1927. "Sixty negro laborers, working with pick, shovel and auger practically throughout the day, and 1500 pounds of dynamite, were required to open a breach," the *Times-Picayune* reported.[26] The residents of St. Bernard Parish had resigned themselves to the directives of the National Guard troops who arrived, armed, to order them from their homes. Ten thousand people headed for New Orleans, "a highway of humanity," one reporter observed, "on trucks, in pleasure cars, on wagons, horseback, muleback, afoot, on oxen, goading cattle, leading cattle." "It was Exodus," the reporter wrote, "the evacuation of a people from their homeland."[27]

After a full day of assaults, the levee finally gave way. Two hundred fifty thousand cubic feet of water per second swept across what once might have been called the center of the Western world.[28] Just around the bend of the river, Jean-Baptiste Le Moyne de Bienville had in 1700 kept Louisiana in the hands of its namesake, King Louis XIV, and changed the course of empire.[29] A short walk away was the Chalmette Battlefield, where in 1815 Andy Jackson (his orders translated into French, Spanish, and Choctaw for his polyglot troops) "beat the bloody British in the town of New Orleans," as

Johnny Horton would later sing.[30] The land above and below Caernarvon had offered up vast bounties of timber and sugar. Then there was the river itself, the continent's artery, which for 200 years had allowed New Orleans, the self-anointed "Queen City of the South," to claim much of the hemisphere as her hinterlands.[31] "The position of [New] Orleans certainly destines it to be the greatest city the world has ever seen," Thomas Jefferson had written in 1804.[32]

In 1927, though, the future no longer seemed to beckon along the banks of the lower Mississippi.[33] On the narrow strips of arable land that framed the last hundred miles of the river from New Orleans to the Gulf, the real wealth had been in human chattel, and as the trade in enslaved people passed from living memory, so too did many of the great fortunes that had accrued to the captors.[34] The plantation houses crumbled in the fields, and the quarters behind them emptied.[35] Farther from the river, a terrain of marsh grasses called *prairie tremblante*, "trembling prairie," seemed a murky wasteland. In the hazy, distant view from the nineteenth floor of the new Canal Bank building, in what some still called the American Sector of New Orleans, the downriver parishes looked expendable.[36]

The wetlands downriver from New Orleans had long seemed without value.[37] A federal land surveyor in the 1830s called the region essentially useless, with only "small portions . . . at all fit for cultivation, or any thing else."[38] In 1849, Congress passed the Swamp Land Act, transferring nearly ten million acres of federal wetlands to Louisiana. It was property that the United States had acquired with the Louisiana Purchase, but for which no use had been found. The grant was meant to encourage the state to levee and drain the wetlands—to "reclaim" them, in the language of the bill, as if in some imagined past the marsh had been usurped from its rightful, productive purposes.[39] Louisiana could sell off the timber from the marshes, or try to make it fit for agriculture.

The only stipulation to Louisiana in the Swamp Land Act was that any revenue from the sale of the lands be appropriated first for flood control. "The proceeds of said lands shall be applied exclusively, as far as necessary," the bill stated, "to the construction of the levees and drains aforesaid." Later residents of Plaquemines and St. Bernard would come to imagine themselves as hold-out resisters to federal encroachment, so it is worth noting that the land itself was a gift to them from the national government, appropriated with violence from its original inhabitants and purchased from the French at great expense. It was one of the largest federal grants in the country's history, designated specifically to aid local people.[40]

Beginning in the 1850s, "Louisiana sold huge tracts to individuals for ten and twenty cents an acre." Planters developed sugar and rice plantations on the thin strips of high ground along the river in Plaquemines. But over the ensuing decades, many of the speculators who had purchased large sections of marsh found little value in their holdings. Over time, most neglected to pay their taxes, and ownership reverted to the state.[41]

In the 1890s, the state consolidated the neglected marsh land into levee districts. In 1894, Louisiana Act 18 created the Buras Levee District on the west bank of Plaquemines Parish, and in 1898, the Legislature authorized Act 24 to create the similar Grand Prairie Levee District, covering the east bank of the river. With boards appointed by the governor, the levee districts were meant to oversee the process of managing the state-owned lands, using the proceeds to build levees or construct drainage schemes, as Congress had intended four decades earlier.[42] But aside from developing these legal mechanisms, for the most part the state continued to ignore the marshes.

A few fishermen and trappers, though, began to settle deeper in the swamps. They farmed oysters and hunted muskrats; they caught shrimp and fish to sell at the market in New Orleans. By 1900, there were around 13,000 people living in Plaquemines Parish. Most lived in Belle Chasse and Violet and the other towns down the highway from New Orleans, but some had ventured farther south, down the dirt highway and onto the levee roads, then through the maze of bayous in the marsh.[43]

As Progressives sought to order and regulate life across the United States, the swamps seemed to resist the grasp of state power. People living there called to the writer Lyle Saxon's mind the rogue, unregulated canniness of Jean Lafitte, the freebooting pirate, who operated out of Barataria Bay in the early 1800s. "A boatman must be skilled indeed to find his way," Saxon wrote. "Hundreds of men have lost themselves forever in this reedy marshland." Historically, some lost themselves there on purpose. Before the Civil War, enslaved people escaped to the marshes, organizing maroon communities beyond the reach of slave catchers.[44] Not just men but money, too, was lost in the swamps. "That a great deal of produce has left" St. Bernard Parish "without paying the tax is undoubtedly true," a frustrated assessor noted in 1926.[45] But then, no responsible person would pay taxes on bootlegged rum, which during Prohibition may have been the most lucrative export.

In the early 1920s, officials in New Orleans began to value the marshes for their seeming worthlessness: they could be sacrificed for the sake of the city in times of flood. For decades, the Army Corps of Engineers had embraced a "levees-only" policy for managing the Mississippi, building walls of earth ever higher to try to keep the river on an orderly course. But "[t]he ever present menace of floods," a state official noted in the 1920s, remained Louisiana's "main drawback." Instead of relying on levees alone, he and many others advocated cutting the walls at strategic spots to create spillways. The logic was simple: by restoring some of the distributaries that levees had closed, more water could move down the river faster, safely reducing flood levels. After the 1922 Mississippi River flood, the Orleans Levee Board proposed creating one such spillway—which they sometimes referred to, tellingly, as a "waste weir"—on Plaquemines's east bank, cutting the river levee below the village of Bohemia and its Bethlehem Judea African Baptist Church to try to permanently lower the water level upriver in New Orleans.[46]

The problem was that people inhabited the proposed spillway area. Some lived there, and others used it for hunting, fishing, and trapping. The dead were there too. Narcise Cosse had designated some of his family property in the east bank village of Point Pleasant to create a cemetery for the "burial of White people" in 1921.[47] But in 1924, Louisiana Act 99 authorized the Orleans Levee Board to "acquire by expropriation the necessary property" and then "to remove the levees in the area."[48]

Foreclosing on delinquent taxpayers, purchasing property from owners, and using eminent domain when the owners would not sell, the Orleans Levee Board consolidated ownership of more than 32,000 acres on the east bank of Plaquemines Parish to create what they called "the Bohemia Spillway."[49] The Orleans Levee Board's appraisers were relieved when they finished the job of evaluating the 256 tracts in the proposed spillway, and not just because they had had enough of the mud and mosquitos. The "work had its tragic . . . side," according to the *Times-Picayune*. An appraiser "said that more than once, when he had to go into the home of a couple who had been living there for eighty years and tell them they had to get out, he felt like a murderer." Other times, the appraisers were chased off by "irate farmers with shotguns."[50]

A less direct but still vexing challenge for the Orleans Levee Board was that most spillway residents, even those who claimed legal ownership, lacked clear title to their land. The General Council for the Orleans Levee District Board of Commissioners, Benjamin Waldo, found, "In fully 75% of these transactions there were defects in the titles." When families owned a piece of land, heirs often saw no reason to file formal succession documents to transfer ownership of the title from one generation to the next. Either they and their neighbors knew the land to be theirs, or for whatever reason it did not matter to them if the clerks at the Parish courthouse in Point-a-la-Hache knew. "In a word," Waldo wrote, "every species of title trouble that can occur was present in these conveyances." Waldo did not even attempt a survey of the wetter lands farther from the river.[51]

In some cases, speculators tried to use the creation of the spillway to their advantage. Some landowners had abandoned their properties and lost them to the state because they had not paid their taxes. But by paying off their back taxes, the former owners could "redeem" their properties just in time to be bought out by the Orleans Levee Board. These people galled Waldo because, as he saw it, their "monstrous" profiteering hindered the levee board from pursuing its legislatively mandated purpose of protecting against floods. Once the spillway was complete, he believed, it would be a "great public work, dedicated to the service of the public." Tasked with this noble cause, over the course of nearly two years Waldo managed to secure the Bohemia Spillway for the Board and the people of New Orleans.[52]

Even as the Orleans Levee Board worked to convert a long section of the southern part of Plaquemines into a waste weir, changing fashions were making the marsh look far more desirable. A fur coat became a coveted accouterment during the "Roaring Twenties," and urban tastes made rural trapping lucrative almost overnight. Muskrat pelts that in living memory had only been worth two cents each sold for fifty cents in 1922; the price leapt to $1.75 in 1926.[53] Isleño fur trappers could make as much as $8,000 to $10,000 in a seventy-day trapping season. "The Golden Age had come to the marshes," the *Saturday Evening Post* reported. "Riches and rejoicing flowed over the watery waste."[54]

Those profits prompted an explosion of outside interest and set in motion what would come to be known as the "Trappers' War." Initially, as prices rose in the early 1920s, trappers managed the heightened stakes by marking off their trapping areas with cane poles. The arrangements were unwritten and strict. "It was folk law," an ethnographer observed. "A man's trapping ground was to be honored." The marshes, so long ignored by the outside world, had seemed free for the trappers to use or distribute according to their own logic. But as landowners began to lease formal trapping rights to fur companies and speculators, the unwritten arrangements came under threat.

Trappers called the newcomers "outlaws" because of how they ignored the existing structures of regulation. But then the new leaseholders posted "No Trespassing" signs in the marsh, and what had been accepted practice became, officially, illegal.[55]

The most contentious case involved the Perez family. In 1924, John R. Perez leased nearly 100,000 acres of coastal Louisiana's most lucrative trapping lands. He then leased those same trapping rights to the Louisiana Fur Trapping Company, a company incorporated in Delaware, which in turn tried to rent back to local trappers the right to work the same land they had occupied for years—at dramatically inflated prices. The trappers were incensed. In the fall of 1924, John Perez's cousin Leander Perez, the young district attorney, volunteered to represent the trappers' interests and organized them as the St. Bernard Trappers' Association and Plaquemines Parish Protective Association. Leander represented them himself.[56]

Perez presented himself as an advocate for the people, which had been his habit since he had first entered politics a decade earlier. In 1915, the twenty-four-year-old Perez got his name in the *Times-Picayune* by advocating for federal aid to Plaquemines Parish. The 1915 hurricane had decimated the river levees in Plaquemines, and the cost of repairs overwhelmed the budgets of the local levee boards.[57] So that December, Plaquemines state representative Simon Leopold convened a conference of local leaders and levee board representatives to lobby for a federal appropriation of $700,000 to repair the levees. "Unless the federal government, through Congress, comes to the rescue," the *Times-Picayune* reported, "the people in that territory may be called upon to suffer more disaster, as it will be impossible for the levee authorities to complete the work needed before the next high water." Perez, who had graduated from Tulane Law School the year before and was contemplating a run for the Louisiana House of Representatives in 1916, was one of about two dozen men the paper counted in attendance.[58] His petition for federal aid was a tellingly ironic start for a man who would come to make his reputation by trying to bar the federal government from the same land.

Few saw Perez as a principled politician. He lost his race for the state legislature, but by 1919, he had gotten himself appointed district judge for Louisiana's 29th Judicial District, which covered St. Bernard and Plaquemines Parishes—although not without a legal dispute that stretched on for months and eventually reached the state Supreme Court. Four years later, in 1923, opponents attempted to oust Perez from that judicial appointment, accusing him of carrying a concealed pistol to the bench. While elsewhere in Louisiana politicians staked out positions on a resurgent Ku Klux Klan, in St. Bernard Parish, political alliances formed around more prosaic matters and political spoils.[59] Perez helped organize relief operations during the 1922 Mississippi River flood that broke through the levee at Myrtle Grove. He trumpeted his pursuit of bootleggers during Prohibition, declaring that the parish would not be "an 'easy mark' for their operations." Perez's opponents, though, said he colluded with those same rum runners. By the time Perez rallied the trappers in 1924, he was an increasingly well-established, savvy, and unethical attorney.[60]

The trappers eventually discovered that Perez owned a stake in his cousin's Delaware-Louisiana Fur Company, even as he represented them against it. The fix was in: Perez was a "traitor," a double-agent for his cousin's hated land company.[61] He was profiting two ways from the deal he had structured, without helping the trappers regain the rights to the marshes they thought theirs. In November 1926, the situation boiled over. Perez brought in scab trappers from west Louisiana and Texas. Locals refused to cede their ground. Perez sent a deputy sheriff, Sam Gowland, to remove the trappers. In a violent stand-off at Delacroix Island, Isleños shot and killed Sheriff Gowland.[62]

With its one fatality, the Trappers' War was a small battle in a much larger conflict: the effort by powerful men to consolidate control of land that agricultural people had shared. The English called it the "enclosure of the commons"; Americans, "closing the range."[63] Just as with the Bohemia Spillway, the Trapper's War transformed a vast, inchoate section of marshy swamp with murky ownership, into a legally bounded, quitclaimed and use-designed piece of property. Before, the marshes of coastal Louisiana were unregulated, unmapped, ownership was unclear, and their use was governed by informal arrangements. Few residents paid taxes, and few officials tried to collect them anyway. But by 1928, the Louisiana conservationist Percy Viosca saw that "[p]ublic hunting and trapping grounds are fast becoming a thing of the past."[64] By mapping the marshes and assigning title, the fur interests came to own the swamps, buying and selling space, quieting prairies that once had trembled.

After the Trappers' War, some eulogized what was lost as nothing less than the pastoral American dream. "Trapping means no longer a free and easy roaming life but almost an industrialized existence," *The Nation* mourned, recounting a history in which modern capitalism and rural freedom stood inexorably opposed. "A sturdy group of American citizens . . . has been driven into peonage." The trope of an informal economy in the marshes coming under assault from the forces of capitalist progress was not new, and it would endure for a century. But the story might have had particular poignancy then, as people across small-town America felt their "island communities" disintegrating in an increasingly bureaucratic and centralized national culture.[65]

In most accounts, Perez was said to have lost the Trappers' War, not with the assassination of his agent, but for no reason other than that the fur boom was short lived. In October 1929, the market for muskrat pelts collapsed with the rest of the American economy. But the experience suggested a strategy for what he needed most: a mechanism of control.

LIQUID WEALTH

Perez built on his strategies from the Trappers' War to gain control of land when Louisiana found "the black pearl in the oyster": oil that is, black gold.[66] Oil had first been discovered in Louisiana over a salt dome in Jennings, in southwest Louisiana, in September 1901. Soon, wildcatters were drilling productive wells all over the state. "Magic Ring of Salt Domes Circles City with Liquid Wealth," the *Times-Picayune* marveled in April 1929, referencing the geological formations that were known to contain stores of oil and gas. "Locked deep in the bowels of the earth within a radius of 100 miles of New Orleans, liquid wealth untold is awaiting the magic touch of the drill stem to convert a vast area of swamp, marsh and open water into one of the country's greatest oil fields."[67]

The discovery of oil and the market for it transmuted worthless marsh into liquid wealth. The Louisiana State Legislature enabled public entities to capitalize on the discoveries, authorizing school boards to execute oil, gas, and mineral leases in 1922, and levee boards to do the same in 1928.[68] In May 1928, Humble Oil offered the Orleans Levee Board $16,000 for the rights to explore for oil in the Bohemia Spillway. In St. Bernard, a salt dome was discovered in Lake Lery, near where the governor had blown the levee the year before.[69] In Plaquemines, "nine domes have been reported, all located within the past year, and mostly on state property," the *Times-Picayune* reported in the spring of 1929. "Drilling is already in progress at Spanish Pass, in the desolate marsh country near the mouth of the river, on land leased by the Humble Oil Company and Gulf Refining Company."[70] The same marshes that had been designated as waste weirs, suitable for sacrifice during times of flood, were now among the most coveted pieces of real estate in the South.

The Louisiana oil boom was on. In 1927, Louisiana produced roughly five million barrels of oil. By 1933, the amount more than tripled to more than fifteen and a half million barrels.[71] "Already the big four oil companies have spent hundreds of thousands of dollars each in acquiring mineral leases and in exploring for mineral locations," the Plaquemines *Gazette* reported in 1928, "and their reward, and ours in the parish, has been the location of salt domes, prefacing the bringing in of oil gushers and gas fields the like of which has not been seen anywhere."[72] A decade later, there were over a hundred oil wells in Plaquemines. By 1959, Plaquemines was producing nearly double the amount of oil per year of any other parish in the state.[73] "Oil and gas and sulphur!" an advertisement gushed. "A magic combination of wealth for a Parish and its people!"[74]

Drawing on the lessons of the fur boom, Perez took action to reassign control of much of Plaquemines and St. Bernard's newly discovered mineral wealth. In 1932, as district attorney, he shepherded a proposal through the Louisiana Legislature to amend the state Constitution. His amendment, introduced as Act 143, revised Article XIV of the Louisiana Constitution such that a parish could "assume the debt of a road district, sub-road district, consolidated road district, drainage district, irrigation district, levee district, or school district, wholly within such parish." Another law, Act 164, provided that so long as the debt remained, the police jury would manage the business of the district and collect any revenues.[75]

The changes were obscure and technical. To a casual observer, the Constitutional amendment seemed an act of maybe perverse local beneficence: a parish police jury (Louisiana's county government) would be able to take on the often-perpetual debts of a local bonding district. That may be why it passed in the November 1932 election with little notice. It was also the case that back in 1929, when Standard Oil spearheaded a move to impeach Huey Long after the governor proposed a five cent per barrel tax on oil, Perez had helped to orchestrate Long's successful strategy to stay in office. Long may have offered his help to pass Perez's amendment as a thank you gift. Either way, the *Times-Picayune* described the amendment as "of smaller relative importance," and briefly urged readers to vote for it because it "complies in letter and spirit with the principle of home rule and we see no objection to its adoption."[76]

Perez, however, knew that his amendment would shift the power over Louisiana's most valuable natural resources from the governor to himself. Until now, it was an accident that a public body happened to own the marsh land containing coastal Louisiana's oil and gas deposits, but Perez's bill left nothing to accident. His amendment allowed a police jury to assume management of an indebted levee district. The police jury would remain in charge, collecting all revenues, so long as the debt remained. A savvy accountant would be able to maintain a debt on the levee districts' books. In Plaquemines and St. Bernard Parishes, the Grand Prairie and Buras Levee Districts owned much of the marsh. The governor appointed levee district board members, but local voters chose police jurors. Perez knew from experience that he could manipulate local elections. With an arcane legislative maneuver, Leander Perez had seized the power to control an unimaginable fortune.

Perez then perfected the scheme he had rehearsed during the fur boom. In his role as district attorney, he directed the police jury to assume management of the levee boards and start leasing out the levee districts' mineral rights. Meanwhile, he incorporated the Delta Development Corporation in Delaware (along with several other shell companies) naming friends as officers and himself as counsel. Few in Plaquemines knew Delta Development was Perez's company. Again acting as district attorney, Perez made the police jury sell its mineral leases to Delta Development and his other shell companies for pennies. Through Delta Development, Perez then subleased the same mineral rights to Humble and Gulf and other oil companies for huge sums.[77]

The most important sales came in the mid-1930s. In 1936, the Grand Prairie Levee District leased Delta Development the mineral rights for a stretch of land on Plaquemines's east bank. In 1938, the Buras Levee District leased Delta Development two other tracts on the west bank. Taken together, these leases covered most of levee boards' lands. The Parish retained the right to only a one-eighth royalty on oil revenues from them. It was the minimum royalty allowed by law.[78] Perez got the rest.

Perez amassed a fortune. From 1924 through 1939, as district attorney, Perez earned an annual salary of $6,000. But in 1939 alone, Perez's tax return showed an income of well over $200,000 (adjusting for inflation, that is over $3 million in 2015 dollars). He reported the balance of his income as attorney's fees and dividends from Delta Development Corporation. It was all money skimmed by removing public lands from the public trust. In 1939, while the country suffered the tenth year of the Great Depression, Perez told his friends that he was a millionaire.[79] By then, Perez's wealth was an open secret, prompting accusations from his opponents. When James Morrison campaigned for governor in Port Sulphur in 1939, he told the crowd, "You want to abolish once and for all this little mealy mouthed, double-crossing, professional politician, who goes around saying how much he's done for Plaquemines parish, while at the same time he's getting millions and the people are getting promises." Politics in Plaquemines was a blood sport. "Our attitude is that we'll do anything for our friends," Perez remarked that year, "and to hell with our enemies."[80]

Oil transformed Louisiana. Most noticeably, the oil industry brought new people to the coast. Although Plaquemines's population had declined from over 13,000 people in 1900 to just 9,600 in 1930, with the most substantial drop coming in the wake of the 1915 storm, the population exploded in the 1930s, growing by nearly 30 percent to over 12,000 on the eve of World War II, and to over 22,000 by 1960. Between 1930 and 1960, the population more than doubled.[81] The author Harnett Kane called them "floods of newcomers, rangy, lighthaired men of other Southern states." Older residents called them *les maudits Texiens,* "the damn Texans," even if many of them were not actually from Texas.[82] Oil companies started building their headquarters in New Orleans.

SALTWATER INTRUSION

Along with reshaping Louisiana's demographics, oil companies reshaped the marsh itself. Trappers had danced nimbly on the trembling prairies, but the oil men plowed right through them, dredging "innumerable" canals through the marsh.[83] Two major shipping canals already served New Orleans: the Industrial Canal, which the Port of New Orleans dredged through the Ninth Ward in 1923, and the Gulf Intracoastal Waterway, a federally funded project that spanned the Gulf Coast, and linked up a 9-by-100 foot channel with the Industrial Canal in 1933.[84] A dense network of smaller canals soon crisscrossed the wetlands outside the city as companies developed a massive new infrastructure for exploring, drilling, piping, shipping, and refining oil. The Gulf Oil Company cleared what was probably the first "petroleum related" canal in Venice, at the southern tip of Plaquemines Parish, in 1926. By 1955, there were eight miles of dredged canals in Venice, making "a huge circle 2½ miles in diameter." Freeport Sulphur dredged a massive canal to transport workers and equipment to its Grande Ecaille mine. In the Barataria, companies dredged forty-six miles of canals between 1939 and 1948. By 1962, another 156 miles of canals would be excavated.[85] The network of canals increasingly mirrored the new interstate highway system, cutting speedways through Jean Lafitte's marsh labyrinth as I-10 did the same in New Orleans's Tremé neighborhood.

Canals had consequences. The water in coastal Louisiana's wetlands had been fresh or brackish, but the new canals allowed salt water from the Gulf to intrude deep into the marsh. All that salt killed the "cattails . . . irises, duckweed, cutgrass, bullwhip, and bulltongue" that had thrived in the wetlands. Meanwhile, as tugboats towed drilling barges, and speedboats brought workers back and forth from marsh oil fields, their waves battered the grasses.[86] Narrow canals grew wider. The Gulf crept North.

As early as the 1930s, people across coastal Louisiana started to feel like the land under their boots was sinking. "Men noticed that the ground at the back of their plantations seemed a bit lower," Harnett Kane wrote. "At one spot it was beginning to be wet where surely they had found it dry the previous spring; at another the water stood inches deep, though it had barely covered the soil until a year or two ago." In 1936, the geographer Richard Russell published what was probably the first scientific account of coastal erosion in Louisiana. "Marsh has been invaded by the advance of the sea," he reported to the Louisiana Geological Survey.[87] Later studies would show that from 1932 through 1954, the shoreline retreated an average of nearly nineteen feet per year.[88]

Saltwater intrusion along oil companies' marsh canals was one cause of the erosion, and its effects would accelerate over time; another was that the coast itself was subsiding, sinking into the Gulf under its own weight. Coastal subsidence was an ancient process, part of the gradual, shifting formation of the Mississippi's delta. Previously, subsidence had been measurable only on geological time scales. But in the 1930s, people started to be able to watch subsidence out of their windows. The keeper of the lighthouse on Chandeleur Island, for instance, watched as the northern end of the island "retreated about one-half mile" in just five years, starting in 1931. Sometimes, the whole island vanished under water.[89]

Geologically speaking, floods had built Louisiana. Every spring, snow in the Rockies and Appalachians and everywhere between melted and drained into the Mississippi. The river grew big and muddy, flush with water and sediment. Narrow from Minneapolis to Natchez, the river spread wide toward its mouth, occupying its floodplain. There, the current slackened, the level became shallower, and the Mississippi adorned its delta with a continent's tribute in mud—hundreds of millions of metric tons of sediment a year. The river weighed heavy on the coast, causing the land to subside at a rate of roughly 1.55 mm per year. The existence of Louisiana, though, is evidence that the loss was outbalanced by new deposits. Skimming topsoil from across North America, carrying it to what became Louisiana—this was re-distribution on a geological scale. Year after year, sediment accumulated, the deposits building on each other like compound interest. The river carried nutrients that gave Louisiana some of the most fertile land and water on the planet. For most of history, a Mississippi flood was no disaster, nor anomaly. For tens of thousands of years, the river washing across its delta was a rite of spring.[90]

Then people built houses and farms in the floodplain, and floods—their force magnified as settlers cleared the Mississippi Valley of its trees—became human calamities. There were river floods in Louisiana in 1903, 1912, 1913, 1922, and 1927, each more damaging than the one before. So people constructed levees, first on their own, and then with the help of the federal government, especially after the monumental Flood Control Act of 1936 made flood control, along with navigation, central to the Army Corps' mission. By the late 1930s, the federal levee system largely had secured the river in place, and people in south Louisiana believed they no longer had to fear the Mississippi. The levee system kept the water in place, and also redirected the Big Muddy's mud. Once the levees fixed the Mississippi on a set course, its sediment sailed straight into the Gulf, through the jetties James Eads engineered at South Pass in the 1870s, and out off the continental shelf—falling five thousand feet deep to the bottom of the sea, "disappearing," a geographer wrote, "into the abyss."[91]

Flood control sank Louisiana.

For the most part, the few who were aware of the process saw it as happy side effect, because without sedimentation, the river would be easier for ships to navigate. Indeed, easing the way for ships was the reason the Mississippi River Commission had built levees through Plaquemines Parish in the first place.

The 1920s represented a tipping point in this process. From time immemorial until then, floods deposited sediment, and Louisiana grew. The river finished building the high ground under what became the French Quarter around 1400, more than a half-century after the French in Paris finished building Notre Dame. But as the Army Corps took over and seemed to gain control of the river, Louisiana began to shrink. Southeast Louisiana started losing nearly seven square miles of land per year in 1913. By 1946, the rate had more than doubled to nearly sixteen square miles per year. By 1967, the rate would nearly double again, to more than twenty-eight square miles per year. Solving the problem of flooding from the river had created the problem of flooding from the Gulf.[92] Every year, New Orleans slid nineteen feet closer to the sea.

Percy Viosca, a biologist for the Louisiana Department of Conservation, sounded an alarm as early as 1928. He decried the effects of levees, canals, and land reclamation schemes. "While the building of levees, the clearing of lands, farming, the building of cities and accompanying drainage projects have been justified in order to meet the needs of man," he wrote in the journal *Ecology*, "let us inquire whether it is not possible to overdo this civilization process? I say, emphatically, yes." In Viosca's formulation, too much civilization threatened not only the natural order, but man's fortunes too. He itemized the benefits of the marshes for hunting, fishing, and recreation, and argued that levees imperiled all of those uses. His judgment was unequivocal. "Reclamation and flood control as practiced in Louisiana," he wrote, "have been more or less a failure." He accused those who encouraged developing the wetlands as "killing the goose that laid the golden egg."[93]

UTOPIAS

While a worried few watched the water creep closer, though, most people saw levees and canals as gateways to unbelievable wealth in oil. In 1937, the Louisiana Editors Association, a New Orleans boosters' organization, published out a booklet called "South Louisiana and the Beautiful Gulf Coast." On its cover, an oil derrick spewed a cloud of black smoke. Dollar bills rained down from the cloud.[94]

Canals had other consequences, then, too. Pulling Louisiana's oil into economic reach allowed Huey Long to imagine that every man could be a king. With funds from a severance tax on oil, the state promised textbooks for the young and pensions for the old. With oil money, Louisiana built a state medical school in Baton Rouge, constructed a towering Charity Hospital in New Orleans, and paved the road between the two. Not only did severance taxes on oil pay workers to pave the road, the oil comprised the asphalt itself. Petroleum extracted through canals allowed Gulf and Humble Oil to fuel cars that filled that new highway and, over the ensuing decades, new roads like it across the country. When American airmen dropped bombs on Dresden, the B-17 Flying Fortress may have been burning with oil piped through Louisiana's marsh canals. When immigrants moved from the Lower East Side to Levittown, if they stopped for gas in Queens, there is a good chance that fuel had found its way through a canal in the Louisiana marsh. The American dream was fueled by oil, and a lot of it came from Louisiana.[95]

Oil from the marshes remade politics in Louisiana and around the country. Long's cries to "Share the Wealth" made him a national figure and potential presidential candidate. Some would deride him as the "messiah of the rednecks," others feared his autocratic tendencies, but Long's popularity pushed President Franklin Roosevelt to embrace a stronger social safety net. The welfare system that Huey Long's oil-fueled vision encouraged helped to lift millions of Americans from poverty, redefining the promises of American citizenship.[96]

Meanwhile, even after Perez's raw dealing, Plaquemines remained blessed with "vast mineral wealth," and Perez used it to fund a broad range of public services. Over the course of the 1930s and 1940s, Plaquemines developed what the reporter Lester Velie called, in a *Collier's* profile, "a miniature welfare state." Although Velie was quick to note that the phrase "welfare state" would have been "a phrase repugnant to Perez," it was just what Plaquemines's program of public works and amenities seemed to amount to. The Parish built new schools and new roads, employing local people—Perez supporters, of course—to do the work. "Nearly every loyal family in Plaquemines has at least one relative or in-law on the parish payroll," another reporter observed. Fishermen repaired their boats at the free Parish boatyard. Travelers crossed the Mississippi on the free Parish ferry. Schoolchildren applied for their share of the annual $20,000 Parish college scholarship fund. To pay for it all, the police jury's budget grew from $33,591 in 1936 to $838,805 in 1950. And yet, during those years, the police jury cut local taxes in half.[97] "With the advent of sulphur, oil and gas," Ben Meyer, the tax collector and parish historian recalled later, "we were fast approaching our 'Utopia.'" "Utopias do not just happen," though, Meyer, a Perez-loyalist, cautioned. "There must be a proper setting and a guiding hand to lead us into that state of near perfection."[98]

Perez wielded enormous power. He fixed elections, locally and statewide. There were rumors that he held undated letters of resignation from the members of the levee boards. In the middle of World War II, Perez engaged in his own months-long "Little War" with Governor Sam Jones: Perez erected roadblocks and ordered shots fired in an attempt to have his preferred man installed as the sheriff in Plaquemines. The governor won the dispute, but only after he deployed the National Guard.[99]

Indeed, opponents contested Perez's control at almost every turn. Perez's constituents shot at him or his men during the Little War in 1943, as they had during the Trappers' War in 1926. Nearly every election Perez rigged prompted outrage, if not in the Plaquemines newspaper, then elsewhere in the state. After Perez failed to indict the strikebreakers suspected of killing Angelina Treadaway during a strike at a shrimp picking plant in Violet in 1940, Emile Riche joined over a hundred other citizens of Plaquemines and St. Bernard to sign a petition calling for Perez to be removed from the district attorney's office.[100] Riche signed another impeachment petition the next year, charging Perez with having "diverted to his own private gain, through subterfuge," what ought to have been public oil revenues.[101] But the impeachment efforts failed. Perez dodged the bullets every time.

Perez lorded his control over his parish's mineral rights. "The major petroleum companies themselves handle him like a demijohn of nitroglycerin," the reporter Richard Austin Smith wrote in a Perez profile in *Fortune* magazine. For good reason. When Freeport Sulphur imported workers from Texas in 1936, for instance, Perez had the Legislature levy punitive taxes on sulphur. When Freeport committed to hiring Plaquemines residents, the tax was quickly reduced.[102]

Perez's political opponents made several attempts to remove him from the district attorney's office, but Perez outfoxed them. When, in the early 1940s, Governor Sam Jones's "Crime Commission" investigated Perez's oil dealings, Perez refused to turn over the account books of his corporations; eventually his supporters had the Commission declared unconstitutional on a technicality.[103] A decade later, Congressman Hale Boggs also attempted to expose Perez's double-dealing. After Perez called Boggs a Communist during his 1951 campaign for governor, Boggs had Perez audited by the Internal Revenue Service.[104] The audit revealed that Perez had reported hundreds of thousands of dollars in income from the levee boards. The auditor called these "devious transactions," because of course, the boards could have leased their mineral rights directly and reaped all the profits for the public. But in the end, the audit found "no evidence of fraud in connection with the returns of the corporations or the individual returns of Mr. Perez." His actions had all stayed within the laws he had helped to write.[105]

While Perez embraced a local paternalist patriarchal welfare state in Plaquemines and tolerated the state-level one created by Long and his followers in Baton Rouge, he loathed the federal government. Perez's red-baiting of Boggs was indicative of his increasingly vocal conservatism. Many white southerners long "despised concentrated power." But Perez's belligerent opposition to Washington was outsized to the point of caricature, as when Louisiana Governor Earl Long taunted him, "What are you going to do now, Leander? Da Feds have got da atom bomb."[106]

Perez's anti-statist views helped him find common cause with other white southern conservatives bristling against a Democratic Party that increasingly took its cues from liberal, urban, and African American constituencies. As Perez consolidated wealth and power in Plaquemines, he was able to expand his sights to a larger stage. He ascended to chairmanship of the Louisiana Democratic Central Committee. Then, in 1948, Perez helped to chair South Carolina Governor Strom Thurmond's run for president on the States' Rights Democratic Party ticket. Perez saw himself as the purifying savior of the Democratic Party. Reporter Robert Sherrill would later call Perez "the perfect Dixiecrat" for the way he deployed the ideology of the southern "states' rights" rebellion. Like Thurmond, Perez was a strident racist. But along with race, economic and legal concerns defined Perez's political agenda.[107] For Perez, states' rights meant the freedom to control both African American people and local economic resources without federal oversight or regulation.

After World War II ended, oil development accelerated, and companies increasingly looked offshore for oil. Offshore mineral rights were a nebulous legal area. Perez set out to settle the ownership. Just as Perez had rewritten the Louisiana Constitution to secure his access to mineral rights owned by levee boards, he attempted to redefine the United States Constitution and secure access to offshore mineral rights. He did so while waving the banner of state's rights.

OFFSHORE RIGHTS

In the 1930s, oil companies began applying to the federal Department of the Interior for rights to drill offshore where, geologists were increasingly confident, there were massive oil deposits. But Harold Ickes, the Secretary of the Interior, referred the applications back to the states, suggesting that the "submerged lands" were not in the federal jurisdiction. In 1937, Congress considered a bill "to assert federal jurisdiction over submerged lands." Ickes started holding applications for offshore leases instead of referring them to the various states.[108] In March, Brown & Root, working for Pure Oil and Superior Oil, drilled the first offshore well in the Gulf of Mexico, in what was called the "Creole Field": Gulf of Mexico State Lease No. 1, a mile and a half offshore, in fourteen feet of water. In 1938, North Dakota Senator Gerald P. Nye introduced a resolution declaring lands under the marginal seas of all the coastal states to be a part of the national public domain.[109] The bill did not pass, but it prompted Louisiana to action. In 1938, the State Legislature passed Act 55, "setting the state's southern boundary twenty-seven nautical miles from the coastline."[110] Most likely, it was Perez who developed the argument that Louisiana's claims to this ambitious boundary dated back to French colonial law.

On September 28, 1945, President Harry Truman issued Proclamation Number 2667, asserting federal authority over the continental shelf, and issued Executive Order 9633, placing the resources contained in the continental shelf under the management of the Secretary of the Interior.[111] In other words, Truman announced that the entire expanse of the Gulf Coast accessible by existing drilling technologies were the property of, and would be administered by, the federal government. Although Truman's actions may have had more to do with asserting the United States's authority offshore against other nations, he had nonetheless put the federal government in conflict with Louisiana, Texas, and California—the three states with the largest potential offshore oil deposits.[112]

The conflict took formal shape on October 19, 1945, when the federal government accused California of trespassing on federal offshore lands. The ensuing legal case, *United States v. California*, would test which jurisdiction would control a fortune. In 1947, as the case moved through the courts, Kerr-McGee drilled the first productive well "out-of-sight-of-land," ten and a half miles off the Louisiana coast from Morgan City. Congress meanwhile considered dozens of bills on the question of the so-called "tidelands," the name given to offshore regions. Tensions rose. In June 1947, the Supreme Court ruled against California and ordered the mineral rights assigned to federal control on October 27, 1947.[113]

The decision terrified Louisiana officials. "To put it mildly, we were in one hell of a fiscal mess," Earl Long's Lieutenant Governor Bill Dodd wrote later. "Since over one-third of our state's operating budget was being financed from revenues accruing from our Tidelands, overnight we literally went from riches to rags."[114] The federal government began to pursue a similar suit against Louisiana, and the facts seemed fundamentally similar to the California case.

But Truman hoped for an amicable solution that would not further alienate southern Democrats who were already threatening to bolt the party because of his support for civil rights (which included implementing the Fair Employment Practices Committee, opposing the poll tax, and supporting anti-lynching legislation).[115] With Texas's powerful congressman Sam Rayburn—whom Truman often called on to corral southern Democrats—acting as an intermediary, Truman attempted to strike a deal over the tide-lands with Earl Long.

At a meeting in the fall of 1948, with Rayburn working on Truman's be-half, and Dodd and Louisiana Attorney General Bolivar Kemp negotiating for Long, the president offered Louisiana "two-thirds of revenue within the three-miles boundary offshore . . . and 37.5 percent of revenue beyond it." The Truman administration also offered to allow Louisiana to keep offshore roy-alties the state had already collected, to manage future offshore leases, and to levy state taxes on oil extracted from them. And the federal government would drop its suit against Louisiana.[116]

The proposal took the state's delegation by surprise. "[We] were in hog heaven," Dodd recalled later. "It sounded too good to be true," he wrote. "The president was offering us far more than we hoped to get, for we had never asked for more than nine miles of Tidelands." California's attorney general told Dodd he hoped that his state would get "half as good a deal as Loui-siana was getting."[117]

The only person in the room who balked was Leander Perez. He had con-vinced the governor to appoint him to an unpaid position as special assis-tant attorney general in order to help lead the state's response. Perez told Rayburn that he would tell Long to reject the "compromise." "At that," Dodd recalled, "Rayburn blew his stack." The meeting broke up without a resolution.[118]

The Louisiana delegation left Washington and returned to Baton Rouge to meet with the governor. According to Dodd, with the exception of Perez, Long's advisors all urged him to accept Truman's offer. After all, it was more generous than the state had expected, and the California precedent all but guaranteed that the state stood to lose all of its claims in court. Dodd left the meeting convinced that Long would sign on.

Then Perez used his power in Democratic and Dixiecrat politics to black-mail Earl Long. In the lead-up to the 1948 election, as chair of the Loui-siana Democratic State Central Committee, Perez had already removed the Democratic Party name and emblem—a rooster—from beside Harry

Truman's name on the ballot and given them instead to Strom Thurmond. Perez made a similar threat to Long. The governor's nephew Russell Long was running for Senate. Earl wanted Russell's name listed on both the Democratic and States' Rights party lines. Perez threatened to remove Russell from the Thurmond/rooster line, leave him listed only as "Democrat," and put the Republican candidate Clem Clarke as the States' Rights candidate for Senate. If Russell Long was listed only next to Truman, and not next to Thurmond, and with no rooster alongside his name, he was sure to lose the election. Earl Long capitulated and rejected Truman's offer.[119]

Although the oil industry did not take a public stance in the fight between the states and the federal government, privately they supported local control because it was easier to influence; Perez's gambit, in turn, resonated with accusations that the Dixiecrats kowtowed to big business. Observers noted the curious hold that the tidelands issue seemed to have on the Dixiecrats. Calling themselves "true white Jeffersonian Democrats," for instance, 5,000 people gathered at a conference at the Jackson, Mississippi, municipal auditorium in February 1948 to disclaim the efforts of non-southern Democrats in Washington, DC. The conference adopted a ten-point resolution. The first plank criticized Truman's civil rights efforts, including the Fair Employment Practices Committee, and his "anti-lynching, anti-poll tax, anti-segregation and similar bills." The second plank encouraged the "preservation of American ideals." The third plank committed the party to "condemning efforts of the federal government 'to confiscate the tidelands as manifesting a strong tendency towards the destruction of state rights.'"[120]

To critics of the Dixiecrats, Perez's oil holdings offered a revealing example of the party's pecuniary agenda. Perez's "business interests," the newspaper columnist Thomas Stokes wrote in the fall of 1948, "explain the economic influences behind the Dixiecrat campaign." Stokes decried the movement as a conspiracy. "It is based upon exploitation of so-called 'states' rights' and the racial issue to serve selfish private interests," he argued, "including oil, utilities, textile and finance, among others, to end once and for all any threat from new dealism that Harry S. Truman took over from Franklin D. Roosevelt."[121] Thomas Sancton, a liberal reporter based in New Orleans, made similar observations. "The financial stake in the issue of federal control," he wrote in *The Nation,* "is staggering." Like Stokes, Sancton argued that the Dixiecrats were using racism to shield their economic interests from scrutiny. The Dixiecrat claims for political autonomy seemed to have less to do with freedom than with a consolidating economic elite.[122]

After Louisiana rejected Truman's offer, the federal government asserted its legal claim by filing *United States v. Louisiana* in December 1948. Perez argued Louisiana's case before the Supreme Court, but his reasoning found little traction among the justices. In June 1950, the Court decided the case in favor of the federal government, against Louisiana. "Protection and control of the area are indeed functions of national external sovereignty," Justice William O. Douglas wrote. "The marginal sea is a national, not a state concern." On the same day, Texas lost a related case for its own claims to offshore mineral rights. Texas Attorney General Price Daniel had litigated both the tidelands suit and Texas's side in *Sweatt v. Painter*, defending the University of Texas Law School's "separate but equal" stance. Combining opposition to federal control of the tidelands and federal civil rights legislation, Daniel called his trip a "two-pronged 'march on Washington.'"[123]

The decision was a devastating blow to Louisiana. The state continued to try to get a better deal for decades. In 1953, Congress passed both the Submerged Lands Act and the Outer Continental Shelf Lands Act, which together fixed the states' boundaries at three nautical miles from the coast. Louisiana Attorney General Jack Gremillion filed a new suit in response, claiming a somewhat more expansive boundary, but he was finagling over the margins. The state had lost mineral rights worth billions of dollars—and the ability to control what happened on its coast. "Tidelands in Louisiana," Bill Dodd wrote, "should be a synonym for *disaster*."[124]

The courts affirmed Louisiana's state boundary at the three-mile limit from the coast, but even that modest boundary threatened to retreat along with the eroding coastline. In 1957, as the tidelands dispute dragged on, Gremillion requested the first "comprehensive study of coastal erosion in Louisiana." The purpose of the study was to determine where Louisiana's coastline had stood in 1812. Louisiana desperately wanted to at least claim a fixed water boundary because by 1957, it was clear that the Gulf of Mexico was rapidly encroaching on the state.[125]

With the loss of the "tidelands" mineral rights, Louisiana lost its main source of revenue. The old age pensions and public works programs became increasingly difficult to maintain. The private interests that came to control the coast had little regard for the public good. The oil industry's canals and the federal government's levees were sinking the state. The utopia people had viewed on the horizon in the 1930s retreated out of sight.

2 HELP!

HURRICANE BETSY AND THE POLITICS OF DISASTER IN THE LOWER NINTH WARD, 1965–1967

LUCILLE DUMINY MADE IT TO THE RED CROSS OFFICE. WHEN SHE finally reached the front of the line, the woman at the desk asked her if she needed help. Duminy straightened her back and stared the woman in the eye, incredulous. "Could you repeat the question, please?" So the agent asked again, "Do you need assistance?" Duminy believed the government had risked killing her and her family because they were black. She had barely slept in days. Her husband was in the hospital. She and her two children had nearly drowned. Her need was dire. If it hadn't been, she said, "Do you think I would waste my time coming over here to ask to get whatever you're going to give me?" Duminy had been through hell, and "was getting, what they say, 'pissed off.'" So she continued: "You know the Gulf of Mexico . . . do you see the water they have in there?" "Yes," the agent said. "Well that's how much water we had!" Duminy shouted. "I could see just the roof of my house. That's all I could see. And you're asking me what I need? I need everything! I need a house and everything that goes in a house! I lost things that I can never replace."[1]

Lucille Duminy was desperate, and she was not alone. When Hurricane Betsy came down on Louisiana "like a sledgehammer" on September 9, 1965, the floodwalls along Industrial Canal collapsed—or, Duminy suspected, were bombed—allowing an ocean of water to surge through New Orleans's Lower Ninth Ward.[2] The flood stretched from Gentilly into St. Bernard Parish, but the worst of it was in the Lower Ninth, where more than 6,000 houses flooded. Most of those houses belonged to African Americans.[3] The water stood for more than a week, washing the smiles from photographs, disintegrating furniture, floors, and walls. The flood drowned at least fifty people, some in the attics of their own homes, houses that represented, for them, a hard-earned piece of the American dream.[4] For Lucille Duminy and thousands of others like her, yes, they needed help. This chapter is about the help that Lucille Duminy did, and did not, receive in the course of what was called, at the time, "the most terrible natural disaster to hit our country."[5]

While Duminy and her neighbors in the Lower Ninth Ward experienced Betsy as a disaster, they never thought of it as "natural." They believed that their suffering had been caused by human decisions; it followed, therefore, that they were owed reparations. They lobbied for direct cash aid that would offer them the autonomy to recover as they believed best. The Civil Rights Act, the Voting Rights Act, and the promise of the Great Society had led the people of the Lower Ninth Ward to see themselves, tentatively but increasingly, as partners with the federal government. After Betsy, they tried to call on that partnership.

When they failed to get the help they believed they were entitled to, African Americans in the Lower Ninth Ward came to believe that not only had the government caused the flood in the first place, it had also broken a promise to help them recover from it. The welfare state, they learned, was like a levee: politicians could make cuts for some to give security to others.

In contrast, the men who controlled Democratic politics, both in Louisiana and in Washington, understood the disaster to be, in President Lyndon Johnson's words, an "injury that has been done by nature"—an act of God that government had no role in causing and no obligation to fix.[6] Although some legislators initially advocated for grants, temporarily finding common cause with their devastated constituents, the logic of their disaster politics started from this different premise. They did not envision relief as restitution for damages wrought by human action; they saw it as charity for an unlucky few in the wake of a blameless accident. Thus, when confronted by conservatives who argued that providing grants to individuals was an illegitimate role for the federal government, they were willing to retreat.

The relief program these men created after Betsy hinged on loans, rather than grants, from the federal Small Business Administration (SBA). The amount of aid was unprecedented, but in the Lower Ninth Ward, the policy seemed perverse. The loans forced people into debt to the same government they believed responsible for their losses in the first place. "FORTY YEARS

OF DEBT IS NOT FREEDOM!" posters cried out from telephone poles across the ravaged Lower Ninth.[7] Some residents were too poor to qualify for the loans in the first place, and for those that did qualify, the loans often amounted to a second mortgage against a house that no longer existed. The debt bound them to a neighborhood that had proven unsafe.

In Washington, however, politicians celebrated the relief funds that flowed to Louisiana as a tonic for the nation. After decades of railing against federal intervention, proponents of states' rights suddenly welcomed federal involvement. "Americanism in our State has perhaps been reawakened and revitalized," Louisiana Governor John McKeithen told Congress, because "when we got in trouble, no fault or no suggestion was made, 'Well, you people have been talking down there about States rights: you can take care of your own problems.'"[8] These politicians believed they had not only pioneered a program of compassionate disaster assistance, but also had helped to repair a country fractured by struggles over civil rights.

After Betsy, some Louisianians recognized that in an age of growing federal welfare programs, disasters presented a complex problem, one that would reoccur in the future. The *Louisiana Weekly* published an editorial arguing for a careful examination of the flood. "We are fully aware that [an] inquiry cannot return a single hurricane dead or a single penny of the hundreds of millions of dollars in property losses," the editors wrote in 1965. "But we are also aware that Hurricane Betsy will not be the last or necessarily the worst such catastrophe. Therefore, unless we learn some vital lessons from it, we may be courting the greatest disaster yet."[9] More than a half century later, Hurricane Betsy still has several "vital lessons" to offer.

The first lesson is that human decisions create vulnerability. People do not tend to find themselves living in risky places because of cosmic bad luck. Structures of power push them there. "Natural disasters," so called, are never as acute, nor as inevitable, as that term implies.

Second, Betsy shows how different understandings of nature, race, and federalism influenced disaster policy. The way people interpreted the disaster shaped the claims they made for relief. Betsy made landfall in Louisiana just after the passage of the Voting Rights Act and the urban rebellion in Watts, California, in the midst of fierce national debates over poverty, civil rights, and states' rights. The specific questions Betsy prompted, about what caused the disaster and who was responsible for recovery, resonated with broader disputes over the proper role for government in addressing racial and economic inequalities.[10] Many understood the debates about Betsy's causes and consequences as a struggle over what American citizenship was, or ought to be, worth.

Betsy's third lesson is to demonstrate the power of the histories that people tell themselves. In the accounts that circulated among residents of the Lower Ninth, people described themselves less as victims of the storm than as victims of the state. This understanding informed how they made sense of Katrina four decades later, when their neighborhood served observers from around the world as "a diorama for all aspects of the city's tragedy," as one city planner put it.[11] And yet, many who made claims about the neighborhood's significance did not know much about it.[12] Examining Betsy brings the Lower Ninth Ward into focus. As its residents long insisted, its history encompasses not just the desperate hours when floodwater washed across the neighborhood, but also the policies that transformed the area from a marginal swamp into a place of possibility, the arrangements that put people in harm's way, and the practices that compounded the catastrophe afterward.

THE CITY'S BUSTLING SECTION BEYOND THE INDUSTRIAL CANAL

The floodwalls that collapsed during Hurricane Betsy lined New Orleans's Industrial Canal, and the canal was a century in the making. Starting in the 1820s, city boosters longed to create a shortcut that would allow ships to bypass the final circuitous stretch of the Mississippi River between New Orleans and the Gulf of Mexico.[13] In 1896, the Louisiana State Legislature authorized the Board of Commissioners of the Port of New Orleans to construct a waterway between the river and Lake Pontchartrain. The canal would run through the swampy southeastern section of New Orleans, an area that had been settled, slowly, in the first half of the nineteenth century, mostly by people unable to afford to live in drier parts of town. When construction finally began in 1918, the commission pronounced the Industrial Canal "a monument to the power of Man over the forces of Nature, and to the progress of a community that will not say die."[14] The canal cut the city's Ninth Ward in half, defining a 300-block area from the canal downriver to the St. Bernard Parish line: the Lower Ninth Ward.

Prone to flooding, the Lower Ninth had long been a difficult place to develop. When French colonists founded *La Nouvelle-Orléans* in 1718, the town occupied the high ground at a big bend in the Mississippi River—the crescent that would give the "Crescent City" its nickname. Over the next two centuries, plantations up the river ("uptown") from the old quarter, or farther from it ("back of town") grew into *faubourgs,* those suburbs in turn were incorporated into the city, and New Orleans became the most populous place in the South by 1820, a status it maintained until 1950. But surrounded by Lake Pontchartrain to the north, Lake Borgne to the east, and the Mississippi to the south and west, New Orleans is practically an island, which is why its early European residents called it *Ile d'Orléans.* Water and swamps had long constrained the physical size of the city.[15]

In the early twentieth century, the city embarked on an ambitious project to drain the swamps with a municipal pump system. As part of that effort, and to encourage industrial development, the city installed pumps along the Industrial Canal.[16] The pumps encouraged development but did not fully resolve the drainage problem. During a hurricane in 1947, for instance, a storm surge overtopped the levees on the Industrial Canal and other drainage canals, flooding large portions of the city's newer neighborhoods. The Lower Ninth saw ten feet of water.[17] Yet development continued.

Following World War II, there was a building boom in the Lower Ninth Ward, financed in large part by subsidized loans available to returning veterans through the federal GI Bill. The neighborhood's population tripled between 1940 and 1960 and became increasingly African American. In 1940, the population had been 11,556 and about 69 percent white. In general, most houses were on the higher ground near the Mississippi, although the majority of African Americans lived on comparatively lower ground, farther from the river, where the land sank toward the wetland around Bayou Bienvenue. By 1960, the population was 33,002, and about 68 percent African American. Over the previous two decades, the white population had increased by 2,722; the African American population by 18,699. The large majority of white people continued to live in houses built before the war, in the riverside part of the Lower Ninth called Holy Cross. The African American newcomers lived in new homes built in the lower, more recently drained and developed areas.[18]

As African Americans moved to the Lower Ninth, white people settled in the suburbs. Just east of the parish line in St. Bernard, where the land often was just as low-lying as it was in the Lower Ninth, the population more than quadrupled between 1940 and 1960, from 7,280 to more than 32,186 residents. The new residents there were almost exclusively white: in 1960, white people comprised 93 percent of the St. Bernard population. The population of Jefferson Parish more than quadrupled too, and in 1960, was 85 percent white.[19] In the nineteenth century, neighborhoods in New Orleans had tended to be relatively integrated, with black workers living on smaller streets between white-occupied boulevards.[20] But by 1960, living arrangements in metropolitan New Orleans were increasingly defined by racial segregation.

The new residential subdivisions in St. Bernard Parish offered white families a place to move into the middle class, and the Lower Ninth was, similarly, a neighborhood for African American families on the ascent. African Americans in the Lower Ninth had higher incomes, on average, than African Americans elsewhere in the city. The Lower Ninth also was, disproportionately, a neighborhood of African American homeowners. Across the city, 44 percent of white families lived in homes they owned, compared to 25 percent of African American families. In the Lower Ninth, however, 54 percent of African American families owned their own homes.[21] Lucille Duminy and her husband Walter, a nurse assistant at the Public Health Service Hospital, were excited when they bought their place on Charbonnet Street in 1949 for just under $10,000. Their circle of friends in the neighborhood included a preacher, a deliveryman, a bank clerk, a secretary, and two people who worked at the post office. Some of the women—like Dolores Parker, who dreamed of going to Howard University but settled for a degree in education from Dillard, in New Orleans—taught at the local segregated public schools.[22]

Most new residents arrived from older parts of the city.[23] The Joshuas left the Central City neighborhood, for instance, after the Housing Authority announced plans to expand the Magnolia Projects, a public housing development, onto the block where they were renting a home. When Ida Belle and Ike finally saved enough money to pay for all the building materials— since the days of sharecropping, debt had been a scourge on African American families, and Ida Belle was "afraid of debt"—she was thrilled to come to what she called the "thriving" Ninth Ward. "You had that group of people who had come down here with a dream," she said of her neighbors, "with a hope of improving their life for themselves and their children." "Our goal was to be property owners," Ida Belle asserted, and indeed for many African Americans, a house in the Lower Ninth likely represented the first time anybody in their families had ever owned a home in America.[24]

The world came to know one Lower Ninth resident, Antoine Dominque, Jr., through his string of hit songs on the radio. He was the eighth child of Calice and Donatile Dominique, Creole-speaking sugarcane farmers who had moved to New Orleans from Vacherie, Louisiana, after the 1927 flood. Antoine was born the next year. He grew up across from the Industrial Canal on Jourdan Avenue, in a house and community full of music: *banco* or *la la* parties on Saturday nights, dancing after leaving Mass on Sundays, and starting in 1938, an upright piano in the family living room that Antoine took to with such intensity that he would often forgo afternoons with friends to work over the worn ivory keys. In 1950, Antoine started making records. He used the name "Fats" Domino. A decade later, when he had become one of the wealthiest African American men in the country, *Ebony* reported that he was "unwilling to leave his old neighborhood in the city's bustling section beyond the Industrial Canal." Fats Domino built himself a $200,000 house on Caffin Avenue.[25]

Although Domino's outsized success was an exception, with hard work, his neighbors in the Lower Ninth were earning a measure of economic security. A suite of local, state, and federal policies shaped how and where upward mobility was possible. The Sewerage and Water Board had drained the swamp and made the Lower Ninth habitable. The Housing Authority had displaced families like the Joshuas from their old neighborhoods. Racist housing covenants, drafted by private developers, kept African American families out of many new neighborhoods. The federal GI Bill helped veterans to secure mortgages and created incentives for new construction. Jobs in the public schools, the public hospital, and the post office paid the bills. Since Emancipation, the federal government's help had been essential to African American progress. To be sure, more often than not, the Lower Ninth's unpaved streets carried tax dollars out of, but not back into, the neighborhood.[26] But even in a southern city where the law usually worked against them, some public policies reached African Americans and offered them a crucial hand up.

The stakes over who had access to public resources were particularly high for the Prevosts. When, in 1960, a federal court order compelled New Orleans to comply, finally, with the Supreme Court's 1954 school desegregation decision in *Brown vs. Board of Education*, Dorothy's daughter Tessie was one of three African American girls to integrate McDonough 19, the white elementary school in the Ninth Ward.[27] That struggle put the Prevosts and other African American families in direct conflict with a coalition of resistant racists led by Leander Perez. Perez, a leader in the "states' rights" movement for decades, used the occasion to draft legislation creating a State Sovereignty Commission, with subpoena powers, to fight the federal government, his long-time antagonist in his effort to limit regulation of Louisiana's oil. Meanwhile, he helped white students circumvent the desegregation order by arranging for some to transfer to schools in St. Bernard Parish, and for others to attend a new, segregated Ninth Ward Private School. "Don't wait for your daughter to be raped by these Congolese," Perez told an audience of 5,000 at a Citizens' Council meeting in New Orleans's Municipal Auditorium, a few days after Tessie started at McDonough 19. "Don't wait until the burrheads are forced into your schools. Do something now."[28]

Perez's words were stronger than some might venture in public, but many white voters and the politicians they elected to office shared his views. Since the 1948 "Dixiecrat Revolt," Democrats in Louisiana had carried the banner of the "states' rights" cause. In 1956, the state's entire Congressional delegation had signed the "Southern Manifesto" opposing racial integration.[29] The white consensus in Louisiana had long been that African Americans were unequal to white people and did not deserve access to the full benefits of citizenship.

PRO BONO PUBLICO

The fight over the public schools epitomized New Orleans's stark stratification. From where Victor Schiro sat in the Mayor's Office in City Hall, for instance, in the Central Business District where all the roads had been paved for decades, New Orleans looked fine. When the Democrat announced his platform for reelection in 1965, he declared that under his administration, New Orleans had "entered its Age of Fulfillment! Every economic index points towards even more spectacular growth."[30] But from the point of view of most African Americans, Schiro's boast was simple boosterism. Seventy-five percent of black people in New Orleans lived close to poverty.[31] Twenty percent of the population earned more than 44 percent of the city's income, a ratio more lopsided than most other southern cities; the poorest 20 percent earned only 4 percent of the city's income.[32] A study in 1969 would show that more than 38 percent of New Orleans's black families lived in poverty, compared with only 8 percent of nonblack families.[33]

The city's white elites put their power on ostentatious display. During Mardi Gras, the Carnival krewe Rex paraded through the streets on a float emblazoned with the motto *pro bono publico*—"for the public good." The slogan might have heralded an expansive understanding of social welfare, but the club's vision was, like the membership, whites only and paternalistic. They reveled in the practice of tossing trinkets down to throngs who gathered to beg them, "throw me something mister!" During the 1927 Mississippi River flood, the club and a few others like it had been home to the men who convinced the governor to dynamite the river levee below New Orleans, devastating people in St. Bernard and Plaquemines Parishes to reassure investors that they would protect their urban properties at any cost. In the 1930s, they had been the most strident opponents of Governor Huey Long's efforts to "Share Our Wealth" and aid the state's poor.[34] In the 1960s they remained a privileged cabal, stubbornly hoarding their wealth and power. When the mayor of New Orleans ceremonially gave King Rex the key to the city on Mardi Gras day, it was a funny sleight, because these same men owned the streets all year round.

African Americans were left on their own to stitch together holes in the social safety net. They organized Social Aid and Pleasure Clubs, mutual aid societies that offered their own annual parades and pursued more egalitarian ideas of communal obligation. These groups and their parade traditions had roots in the gatherings of Africans in Congo Square, maroon communities of escaped slaves, and the associations of free people of color before Emancipation. Like their more democratic ethos of economic welfare, the Social Aid and Pleasure Clubs' parades performed a vision of community that contrasted sharply with the white Mardi Gras. While Rex cordoned off its onlookers onto crowded sidewalks to beg for trinkets from above, the Afro-Creole second lines invited everybody to participate, dancing together and sharing the street. When a member died, his club would help pay for his funeral, and also provided him with a funeral procession to celebrate his memory: these were New Orleans's famous "jazz funerals."[35]

By 1965, some New Orleanians were considering how to make the national social welfare system more closely resemble their own informal practice of taking care of each other—part of a national program that President Lyndon Johnson called the "Great Society." Johnson ambitiously reimagined how the federal government might help citizens. "I want us to wipe poverty off the face of the South," Johnson declared in New Orleans in October 1964, "and off the conscience of the nation."[36] The federal government would be much more active in local communities, particularly poor communities. In 1964 and 1965, the federal Civil Rights Act and federal court orders compelled New Orleans to combine its racially segregated school districts, public housing developments, and patient wards at its public Charity Hospital.[37] The 1965

Voting Rights Act started a process of securing African American influence in electoral politics in the South. After the Voting Rights Act passed, the number of African American voters in New Orleans nearly doubled.[38] "America is at the beginning of a bright, new era," the *Louisiana Weekly* declared. Long overwhelmed by a racist structure that kept them from assuming their place as full citizens, in 1965, African Americans had good reasons to view the future as full of possibility.[39]

The federal programs empowered people white Louisiana elites never would have, enabling African Americans to circumvent local racists. Dorothy Prevost, for instance, became secretary for the Committee for Progressive Action for the Lower Ninth Ward, an organization supported by federal War on Poverty funds. Her husband Charles also served on the committee.[40] Ida Belle Joshua got involved with the Total Community Action Program in the Ninth Ward, another early organizing effort of the War on Poverty. She served as chairperson of the Ninth Ward's Area Beautification Committee, and she and her husband helped to develop a neighborhood council. Ike soon became president.[41] Increasingly, African Americans felt they had the imprimatur of the federal government on them when they advocated for local changes.[42]

White Democratic politicians understood that the new federal programs, which called for the "maximum feasible participation" of grassroots leaders, were designed to eliminate them as power brokers.[43] They knew that federal aid would translate into federal power. After decades of fighting against federal support for civil rights, they had refined a politics that portrayed the federal government as a distant enemy from whom they protected their constituents. But floods challenged this politics.

THE FLOOD

On Friday, September 3, the *Times-Picayune* ran a short article about an "intense and dangerous storm" forming in the Atlantic.[44] Three days later, the paper reported "big" Hurricane Betsy "posed no immediate threat to any land areas."[45] At a press briefing at the capitol in Baton Rouge the following Wednesday, Governor McKeithen said the state Civil Defense chief had briefed him on a "complete operational chart and plan," but he concluded that the storm seemed "completely unpredictable" and that any threat still seemed to be "some time off."[46] The Thursday morning paper reported that

Hurricane Betsy was coming, but asserted that the storm "posed no immediate threat" to New Orleans.[47] The reports were wrong. The next day, the *Times-Picayune* headline blared, "HURRICANE SLAMS INTO N.O."[48]

In the Lower Ninth, Lucille Duminy had heard on the radio that a storm might be coming. She stocked up on some extra food and water, just in case. She watched the forecasters on television, and they never mentioned evacuating. "It's just a storm," she thought. "Why worry?" Still, Lucille's parents drove up from their home downriver in Plaquemines Parish, believing they would be safer in the city.[49] At Ida Belle Joshua's house, four blocks from the Industrial Canal, things were worrisome enough without the weather. She had breast cancer and was scheduled for a mastectomy on Friday. Her baby son had a fever. But like families across south Louisiana, the Duminys and the Joshuas "buckle[d] down for a hard storm."[50] Thursday brought rain and punishing wind.

Late Thursday night, in the midst of the storm, Ida Belle heard a huge boom, a thunderclap that seemed to come from right under the house. Outside, she "saw all this water gushing—coming to us from the levee." In what seemed like an instant, water covered the porch and was in the house. Luckily, Ike had his fishing boat right by the porch. There was no time to get dressed. "Just bring your ass out of here and get in this boat!" Ike yelled. Throwing a raincoat over her nightgown, Ida Belle grabbed her children and jumped into the boat, in a river that once was Forstall Street.[51]

Between 10:00 and 10:30 p.m., in at least four places, the floodwalls lining the Industrial Canal had collapsed. An emergency crew tried to fill the breaches with sandbags, but around midnight, with winds gusting at over 125 miles per hour, they had to seek refuge. The circulating winds pushed the Gulf's water toward the coast. In previous generations, thousands of acres of marsh might have helped to dampen the surge, but now the Industrial Canal, designed as a shortcut from the Gulf, funneled tides sixteen feet above normal directly into New Orleans. The water overwhelmed the infrastructure. The neighborhood's major pump station lost power. An ocean of water flooded into the Ninth Ward.[52]

Up and down the Joshuas's block, people fled to their porches and roofs and screamed for help. The family overloaded Ike's boat with as many neighbors as they could fit. The boat could barely move against the current. Debris kept overwhelming the motor, so all night, the family rowed with makeshift oars, going back as much as forward, just trying to reach Ike's aunt's two-story house around the corner.[53]

When the Joshuas finally got there, the water was so high they jumped out of the boat right into the second floor. That one tall house was like an island in the middle of a surging river. Four rooms were packed with people who had swum or floated over on couches. At around ten on Friday morning, the Joshuas and a few others set off in Ike's boat for the Claiborne Avenue Bridge over the Industrial Canal, the closest route out of the Lower Ninth.[54]

The Duminys lived farther from the Canal than the Joshuas, so the water did not come with the same ferocity, but the car Lucille had recently paid to repair was quickly too flooded to drive. They would have to walk to safety. Lucille wrapped a blanket around her grandmother, and the family waded into the water. Gripping fences, they pulled themselves toward the McCarty School on Caffin Avenue, where they hoped they would find refuge. Lucille's oldest son, Steve, steadied his grandmother on one arm and his mother on the other. He carried his little nephew around his neck.[55]

Together, they made it to the school. They waded up the stairs to join a group of people already huddling on the second floor. Lucille and her mother sat down and started saying the rosary. Steve looked at the two women praying and asked if they were all going to die. Around midnight, two Red Cross agents came to the school. It was the first official help the Duminys had seen. The agents asked if anybody was sick or elderly or needed medication. People said they needed food. The officials left and never came back.[56]

Without help from the National Guard or the Red Cross, the flood victims rescued themselves. A "ragtag armada" of citizens in fishing boats started showing up at the McCarty School.[57] A white man offered to take the Duminys to the St. Claude Bridge. His boat was not big enough to hold the whole family, so Lucille sent her ailing husband, mother, and grandmother. She begged the man to come back for her and her children as soon as he could. An hour and a half later, the man returned. Unlike the Red Cross, he kept his promise to Lucille.[58]

The Duminys reunited amidst a crowd of survivors on the St. Claude Bridge early Friday morning, but in many ways their trouble was only beginning. Walter was vomiting because of his kidney stones. Lucille's grandmother could barely walk. They all were soaked and exhausted. After a while, a city bus drove by, but the driver refused to let the Duminys board. First, he said it was because electric wires were down across the city and it was too dangerous to drive. Then he said there was no place to take them. Lucille assumed the real reason was because her family was black. But when she yelled out to the driver, "We're not cattle! . . . [it's] like slavery in here!"

Lucille's uncle told her to shut up. "Wherever they bring us," he warned her, "they're going to find out what you said."[59]

African Americans saw racist decisions shaping what was happening to them. Lucille saw it in the Red Cross agents who never returned, in the dirty cattle car that finally picked her up, and in the eyes of the bus driver who would not. Worst of all, Lucille and others saw racism in the flood itself.

Many people in the Lower Ninth believed that city officials had bombed the Industrial Canal floodwall, sacrificing African Americans in the Lower Ninth for the sake of the rest of New Orleans's residents. Dorothy Prevost said she heard on the radio that the levee breach was Mayor Schiro's doing.[60] Ida Bella Joshua realized later that the boom she heard just before the flood started rising must have been the explosion that burst the levee.[61] One Ninth Ward woman said she believed Schiro "had the canal blown up so the water could come on [the Lower Ninth] side." When an interviewer asked how she knew that, she said simply, "everybody knew."[62] That local knowledge traveled. An NAACP lawyer wrote the New Orleans branch from Washington to find out if the rumors were true and, if so, whether they needed assistance with a legal case.[63]

Although historians have dismissed this accusation as "a groundless urban myth," there is evidence that official actions may have exacerbated the flood in the Lower Ninth.[64] In October 1965, the Sewerage and Water Board issued a report on its activities during and after the hurricane. The report does not suggest anything akin to a levee bombing; quite the opposite, it describes city employees' intrepid attempts to manage a terrible situation. Still, read alongside a sociologist's unpublished 1970 "selective analysis of organizational response" to Betsy, an hour-by-hour account based on interviews with Army Corps personnel, suggestive contours of the decision-making process about where to put the floodwater emerge.

Both accounts describe a 4:00 a.m. meeting on Friday, September 10, during which engineers focused on a siphon running under the Industrial Canal—and readied a plan to trap as much of the flood as possible in the Lower Ninth. The siphon normally carried rainwater from the neighborhoods west of the Industrial Canal to the pump station in the Lower Ninth, which then pumped the water into Bayou Bienvenue. But at the early morning meeting, officials raised concerns that the siphon could funnel water the other way, from the Lower Ninth into the rest of the city. Around 9:00 a.m., city engineers proceeded through the flood in an Army "duck" vehicle to a vantage point on the Claiborne Avenue Bridge, and at 11:00 a.m., the Sewerage and Water Board, working with the Orleans Levee Board and the Army Corps, decided to close the floodgates.[65]

At the height of the flood, in other words, officials directed water to gather higher in the Lower Ninth. Neither report ventures an analysis of how much harm was prevented or caused as a result of this quiet decision, but the strategy was just as many in the Lower Ninth suspected: the official response involved action that sacrificed them in order to protect the rest of the city.

New Orleanians with power had a history of deciding who would be flooded. Although a later scholar called the idea that a government official would bomb a levee "crazy," that is precisely what happened thirty-eight years earlier. African Americans in the Lower Ninth knew that a few wealthy New Orleanians had pressured the governor into dynamiting the Mississippi River levee during the 1927 flood, destroying thousands of people's homes.[66] It is not crazy to presume that what has happened before might happen again.

Broader precedent, too, helped to make the story sound plausible. One man called the mayor's office during the flood to report that African Americans believed Schiro had bombed the Industrial Canal to keep citizens of the Ninth Ward from voting; only six months had passed since Louisiana's Senator Allen Ellender had vowed to filibuster against the Voting Rights Act "as long as God gives me breath."[67] African Americans had reasons to believe a claim about efforts to suppress their franchise.

The shape of the Lower Ninth itself was evidence for victims trying to interpret what had happened to them during the harrowing evening of September 9. The way the Industrial Canal cut through the neighborhood seemed proof that people with power would put the Lower Ninth at risk to serve their own economic interests. Even as Betsy demonstrated the danger of dredging canals through the city, the Army Corps continued working to connect the Industrial Canal to a new, larger canal called the Mississippi River–Gulf Outlet—a complex that many believed would exacerbate flood risk across eastern New Orleans and St. Bernard Parish. Indeed, residents of St. Bernard who flooded during Betsy soon sued the federal government, claiming that the Mississippi River–Gulf Outlet had increased their vulnerability.[68] African Americans knew they lived in greater peril because of decisions being made beyond their control.[69] They understood that structural inequalities could take the form of physical infrastructure.[70]

In sum, much of what African Americans knew about the world made credible the idea that their government would allow them to perish in a time of crisis, or even work to put them in greater danger.[71] They knew the people in power in New Orleans to be the kinds of people who would, and had, done so. In the Lower Ninth, residents carried that understanding forward as they tried to recover: it made Betsy a disaster for which people could be held responsible. "They wanted us to die right here" in the Lower Ninth, is what Lucille Duminy thought. Thirty-one people did die right there in the flood, the large majority of them African American.[72]

THANK YOU, MR. PRESIDENT

The collapse of the Industrial Canal's floodwalls had put African Americans in the Lower Ninth Ward in particular danger, but Hurricane Betsy's damage extended across the state and the color line. Congress would soon describe the storm's miserable tally, "both in terms of numbers of people affected and in terms of monetary losses," as "greater than any previous natural disaster."[73] Schiro called Betsy "the most serious thing that has ever happened to us."[74] The Red Cross estimated that more than 13,000 houses in New Orleans had suffered major damage, and nearly 80,000 endured some form of damage.[75] Across the state, 1,568 homes were destroyed, and 21,188 had suffered major damage. The storm had prompted 260,000 people to flee their homes. Friday night, the city's shelters housed more than 96,000 of these "refugees," as some called them, many of whom came to the city from across flooded rural areas of coastal Louisiana. Across the affected areas in several states, seventy-six people had died, 21,000 had been injured, and a billion dollars in property had been destroyed.[76]

Overwhelmed by the scale of the damage, Louisiana politicians called the White House. Senator Russell Long and Congressman Ed Willis called President Johnson early Friday afternoon and told him the people of Louisiana "need your help." "Aside from the Great Lakes, the biggest lake in America is Lake Pontchartrain," Long said. "It is now drained dry. That Hurricane Betsy picked the lake up and put it inside New Orleans and Jefferson Parish and the Third District." A tree had fallen on Long's own house. "I don't need no federal aid," he insisted. "But, Mr. President, my people—Oh, they're in tough shape."[77]

The members of Congress emphasized the political benefits Johnson could reap by visiting a state he had lost to conservative Republican Barry Goldwater in the 1964 presidential election. "You could pick it up just like looking at it right now by going down there as the President just to see what happened," Long told Johnson. Willis added, "you could elect [New Orleans congressman] Hale Boggs and every guy you'd want to elect in the path of this hurricane by just handling yourself right." Long, Willis, and Boggs had all supported Johnson; their opponents were eager to link them to the unpopular civil rights programs that had cost Johnson the election in Louisiana. The hurricane offered a chance for these Democrats to do something white Louisianians would welcome. "You go to Louisiana right now," Long advised the president. The president agreed.[78]

Air Force One arrived in New Orleans just hours after Hurricane Betsy left. The plane carried the president, both of the state's senators, three congressmen, the secretary of agriculture, the surgeon general, the federal highway administrator, and the director of the Office of Emergency Planning. At the airport, Johnson announced he had come "to pledge to you the full resources of the federal government to Louisiana."[79]

Johnson, Schiro, and McKeithen toured the city as a show of concern. Their motorcade traveled as far east as the flooded end of the St. Claude Bridge, where the Duminys had been a few hours earlier. Other evacuees were still gathered there when Johnson arrived. McKeithen, encountering the Ninth Ward flood for the first time, called the devastation "the worst he had seen in his lifetime."[80] Then they drove a few blocks back up St. Claude Avenue to an emergency shelter at the George Washington School. There was no electric power. Johnson walked through the dark building holding a lantern to his face. "This is your president," he called out to the exhausted people there. "I'm here to help you." Emerging from the school, the president issued orders "to get them some water in there as soon as we can."[81]

Evacuees huddled in desperation across the city. Dorothy Prevost and Ida Belle Joshua spent three nights at a makeshift shelter at the New Orleans Army Terminal, just west of the Industrial Canal. The building had been closed for years and was dirty and overcrowded. The toilets backed up immediately. There was little medical assistance. Dorothy tried to help a woman with two small children by tending to one of her babies; he nearly died in her arms from dehydration. "If we stay in this place," Dorothy's husband told her on their third day in the shelter, "I'm going to lose my mind." Those who could left the shelters as soon as possible and stayed with family members.[82]

People not lucky enough to have family able to take them in went to the Eighth Naval District Station in Algiers. There were over 8,000 people there by a week after the storm; later in the month, estimates went as high as

14,000. "They are refugees, without a home to go to," a reporter described. Ninety-eight percent of the people there, he estimated, were black.[83]

Before the president left New Orleans, he announced what the federal government would do to help. Following the governor's request, the president formally declared Louisiana a "disaster area," invoking the Federal Disaster Relief Act, the 1950 law that had created federal authority in emergencies. The disaster declaration allowed federal money to flow to the city for emergency repairs to public facilities like streets and schools.[84] The Army Corps was already removing debris and trying to drain the flooded parts of the city, and the Department of Agriculture was already providing emergency food to the Red Cross shelters; within days, Red Cross volunteers from thirty states would feed more than 200,000 people. The Red Cross would receive federal disaster aid too. The president had dispatched 600 Army personnel from Fort Polk to assist the National Guard in staffing the shelters and patrolling the city, because officials were worried about looting.[85] The Small Business Administration would start Saturday processing loans for rebuilding: 30 year loans at 3 percent interest.[86] "The Federal Government will continue to do everything possible," Johnson concluded in a fourteen-page telegram to Victor Schiro, "to help bring your stricken areas back to a state of normally [sic] in the shortest amount of time.[87]

Two days later, the *Times-Picayune* praised Johnson for his visit in an editorial entitled "Thank You, Mr. President." Edwin Willis called Johnson's actions in New Orleans "the stuff that leadership is made of."[88] The politics of the president's visit had worked just as the congressmen suggested.

City boosters eagerly broadcasted news of an easy recovery. Two days after the hurricane, the *Times-Picayune* declared "Betsy a Big One But Wound Not Deep." Once debris was cleared from the streets, the paper declared, "one will see little evidence that Betsy was here." Three days after Betsy, the Chamber of Commerce announced that all major department stores in the city had reopened. Less than a week after the storm, the Tourist and Convention Commission advertised that all major tourist facilities were "nearly normal."[89] Schiro directed his staff to mount a public relations campaign declaring the city open for business.[90]

The happy vision of recovery was true only if one excluded the Ninth Ward and its thousands of homeless, many of whom remained in emergency shelters. As the department stores were reopening, police rescued an "elderly Negro woman" in the Ninth Ward who "was standing on a chair on top of her stove, up to her neck in water. She told rescuers she had been in that position since Tuesday night."[91] Ten days after the city was declared open for tourists, the Army Corps reported to Schiro that a "considerable pocket of water remain[ed]" east of the Industrial Canal.[92]

Residents had trouble simply returning to their homes to see what sort of damage might await them. Schiro had declared "emergency conditions" and posted National Guardsmen at the limits of the Lower Ninth.[93] Nobody could get in without being fingerprinted and producing a deed to their house, or similar identification—documents most people had left behind and had been destroyed by the flood. A city council member suggested that looters be "shot on sight." Lucille Duminy called the approach fascist—"just like, how they say, 'Heil Hitler,'" she said.[94] The victims were being treated like criminals.[95]

Many survivors struggled to access aid programs. A social service worker in the Ninth Ward found "a great deal of uncertainty about what the Red Cross can provide, what SBA can provide, what to expect from insurance adjusters, and many stories about consumer fraud." He believed that "underlying all of this is a basic feeling of being deserted, 'why weren't we told' or 'why did we have to wait two days to be rescued.'"[96] By the time Duminy found herself waiting in the long line to speak to a Red Cross agent at City Hall, she had very low expectations for any kind of help. When she asked a Red Cross agent for food, the man told her to come back the next day for a ration voucher. Duminy explained to another agent that she was carrying her elderly grandmother, and that her husband was vomiting blood. "Well, I don't have no way of taking care of that," the agent responded. Connections through Walter's job at the Public Health Service Hospital finally helped him get admitted to Charity Hospital. Duminy, her children, her mother, and her grandmother took refuge with a succession of family members.[97]

BETSY ISN'T OVER FOR US!

Frustration mounted, and the debate over the disaster's causes and consequences grew increasingly heated. In a speech in New Orleans to the Mid-Continent Oil and Gas Association two weeks after the storm, the prominent nuclear physicist Edward Teller argued Betsy showed that Louisiana's Civil Defense was "not prepared to cope with the hurricane, let alone the nuclear disaster it is supposed to plan for." "Your city had hours of warning,"

Teller asserted. "Why wasn't it anticipated that the levees of the industrial canal might break?" The major African American papers locally and nationally, the *Louisiana Weekly* and the *Chicago Defender,* reported Teller's speech on their front pages.[98] His comments reaffirmed the widespread understanding among African Americans that Betsy was not a natural disaster, but one for which humans bore responsibility.

Teller's criticism bought swift indictments from Louisiana's elected officials. Governor McKeithen called Teller's comments "little short of criminal."[99] Mayor Schiro accused Teller of "making unauthorized and irresponsible statements." "Teller's observations have no basis," New Orleans congressman Edward Hébert announced. He asserted that a storm surge like the one that had flooded New Orleans was "completely unpredictable."[100]

Declaring the flood unpredictable offered a way to deny human responsibility for its damage. The New Orleans *States-Item* attributed the devastation to the "water-spawned evil spirits of the weather world."[101] McKeithen was more direct. He "stressed that nobody in authority could be blamed for the disaster."[102] While in the Lower Ninth people talked about Betsy in terms of bombed levees, in Washington President Johnson talked about Betsy as an "injury that has been done by nature."[103] When the President's Office of Emergency Planning issued its official report on the federal response to the disaster some months later, its first sentence was a steadfast declaration of innocence: "Hurricane Betsy was a natural phenomenon."[104]

Hébert, in particular, understood that if accusations of human culpability were allowed to stand, demands for government relief would follow. He condemned both in the same breath. At the same meeting where he asserted that a storm surge was impossible to predict, the *Louisiana Weekly* reported that Hébert also "address[ed] himself almost exclusively to the Negroes present" and announced, "this was not the time for charges of any kind." The congressman knew that African Americans believed white politicians were responsible for putting them in danger and tried to foreclose claims on the government for help. "This time is not one to lean on others," Hébert told them, disparaging solidarity as dependency, an enduring conservative trope, "but rather a time to show our responsibility as individuals."[105]

Hébert's admonition did not staunch the discontent with the government response, and at the Algiers Naval Base, Elizabeth Rogers began to organize in protest. All sorts of things about how the Army and the Red Cross administered the shelter bothered the white, 77-year-old Ninth Ward Communist—from the better treatment whites received to the fact that an "officious" Catholic priest, claiming he was "looking for dope," confiscated some onions from her husband Walter. What upset Rogers most, though, was what she considered to be a twisted structure for aiding people harmed by the flood.[106]

The Rogerses had experience with disaster relief. In 1957, Walter had earned a Red Cross citation for his service as a construction worker, assisting with rebuilding efforts in Cameron Parish, in southwest Louisiana, after Hurricane Audrey. The Small Business Administration had made relief loans then similar to the ones it was now offering New Orleanians. Walter and Elizabeth both knew that despite low interest rates, the SBA loans had left people in Cameron struggling under mountains of debt.[107]

On September 20, in the Algiers shelter, the Rogerses founded the Betsy Flood Victims (BFV). The BFV had two primary demands. First, the BFV called for a "moratorium on collections for ruined time-payment purchases"—in other words, a permanent freeze on mortgage payments and other debts. "Let real estate . . . companies (and Governments) pay for damages they did nothing to prevent," Elizabeth Rogers asserted on a handbill. The BFV's second demand was for $10,000 grants, not loans, per family to allow people in the Lower Ninth to rebuild. "We are builders of this area against heavy odds (swamp land, poor schooling, unemployment, prejudice). We'll be builders wherever we are," the leaflet said, adding that, "$10,000 is chicken feed compared to all our suffering."[108] Soon after, Rogers added four more demands: "Free food stamps to needy," "Rent control (as in World War II)," "End Vietnam war—apply that wasted money to home needs," and "Safe levees for all New Orleans."[109]

Elizabeth Rogers did not know that while she was imagining what recovery might mean, some politicians were considering the same question.[110] "Sorrow and sympathy are not enough," McKeithen admonished. He called on Louisianans to open their homes to victims. "The disaster and human misery that all of us saw," the governor said, "must make us answer the question Cain asked of Abel, 'Am I my brother's keeper?' and the answer must be, 'Yes,' and the time is now."[111]

McKeithen looked to the scripture and foresaw the end of days for a certain strain of southern resistance to the federal government. On September 25, a special subcommittee of the House Committee on Public Works met in New Orleans to investigate Hurricane Betsy and the government response. Most of the Louisiana delegation affirmed their newfound gratitude for the federal government. McKeithen described Louisiana as "greatly appreciative of the spontaneous and enthusiastic manner in which the Federal Government has come in here to help us." Gauging the scope of the damage in the state, McKeithen recognized that "the only people we can look to for the tremendous amount of money" required to rebuild from this storm, and build a hurricane protection system to prevent against another was "the Federal Government in Washington, D.C." McKeithen acknowledged that it had not been long ago that he and other white Louisianians had been clamoring for secession in the face of federal civil rights legislation. But now, he said, "We are proud of our great Nation's coming to our aid and our help in this time of trouble and distress."[112]

Praise for the federal government abounded. Schiro added that, as mayor of New Orleans, he had "not been denied one request, whether it be a hundred trucks additional or whether it be any function that the Federal Government could participate in and help us." The Louisiana Director of Public Works heralded the president's order to "cut the red tape." "It is unbelievable what can be done when you have the proper legislation" and "the State and Federal know-how," he said.[113]

On October 1, Senator Russell Long made an ambitious proposal to the Senate. He introduced a bill that effectively offered disaster relief grants to individuals. The plan would cancel $5,000 of any SBA loan debt incurred for uninsurable flood damage.[114] At the Congressional hearing, McKeithen had asserted the need for the largely unprecedented policy: homeowners "who have lost all" already had mortgage debt. Their homeowners' insurance would not cover flood damage.[115] Now, "they are faced with not only having to pay off installments on the personal things that are completely destroyed," but also—with SBA loans as their only option—"faced with a situation of buying some more."[116] On these points, McKeithen sounded more or less exactly like Elizabeth Rogers.

Edward Hébert, in contrast, continued to caution against direct aid to individuals. He argued that Americans were illegitimately "inclined to think that when the Government agencies go into operation, they go into operation to help [them] individually." Hébert opposed redistribution. He asserted that the federal government should not be in the business of helping alleviate a man's worries about the "empty stomach he has got," "those little naked children who lost all their clothes," or "the future of his family." The congressman said he feared raising false expectations among needy people.[117] Later, Hébert explained to a reporter, "even in the time of disaster . . . the main effort and responsibility rests on the individual and not on the federal government."[118] Hébert's position reflected the Dixiecrat's conservative view of the role of government, and represented the effort of an unreconstructed signatory to the Southern Manifesto to try to limit federal reach into his district.

Without an endorsement from Hébert, whose constituents likely stood to benefit the most from the proposal, other members of Congress would not support the cost of Long's aid plan. Despite advocacy from Schiro and petitions from New Orleanians, the bill died in the Senate.[119]

In place of the Senate bill, Boggs introduced the Southeast Hurricane Disaster Relief Act in the House of Representatives, which canceled up to $1,800 of SBA loans, after a borrower had paid off the first $500. There was no provision for renters, even if they had lost all their possessions. This kind of loan forgiveness still represented an unprecedented expansion of federal disaster aid to individuals, but it was much less ambitious than the initial proposal. Congress quickly passed Boggs's bill, and Johnson signed it on November 8.[120] Nobody in Congress seemed to consider how the law encouraged people to rebuild their homes in flood-prone places. Nor, once the program began, did any representative object to the SBA's practice of drawing the disaster loans from funds that previously had been designated to support African American–owned businesses.[121]

The so-called Betsy "Forgiveness Bill" infuriated the BFV. Elizabeth Rogers sent a petition signed by more than 3,000 Ninth Ward residents to Senator Long in June 1966 stating, "When you and Rep. Boggs got Congress to legislate 'partly forgivable' SBA loans to repair Betsy flood victim's homes (all uninsurable for flood), the majority of 9th Ward homeowners got no loans; we're too poor." Nearly a year after the hurricane, the letter asserted, "Betsy isn't over for us!"[122] Long ignored the petition.[123]

In the Lower Ninth, people were especially frustrated to learn that they were treated differently from people in neighboring parishes. When Lucille Duminy helped her mother return to her home downriver in Empire, Louisiana, she was amazed to see that Plaquemines Parish "did better than New Orleans did." Leander Perez made it easy for residents of his parish—white and black, Duminy said—to get mobile homes. They could at least be able to sit under their own roofs for Thanksgiving dinner. People in Plaquemines also received $5,000 grants directly from the parish. "Judge Perez, as bad as he was, that's what he gave to the people," Duminy observed. It was the cruelest irony: Louisiana's most notorious elected racist seemed to be doing right by his constituents.[124] Perez seized the moment to revive his argument that Louisiana deserved a larger share of offshore oil revenues. "This would minimize a further drain on the Federal Treasury," Perez testified at a Congressional hearing, "and enable the State to do its fair share of such protective work to save many hundreds of lives in the future and billions of dollars of further damage from more hurricanes and tidal waves which are bound to come almost annually."[125]

When Ida Belle Joshua grew suspicious that white people outside of the city might be getting a better deal, she started attending meetings in St. Bernard Parish, "to see if the terminology was the same." Like Duminy discovered in Plaquemines, Joshua found that in St. Bernard, the parish government was distributing aid in grants, rather than loans. "The logic for that was that they were at the ceiling of their indebtedness. They couldn't borrow any more money, so they gave them full grants to build back," Joshua explained. People in the Lower Ninth were in the same straits, but the reliance on federal funds rather than local oil revenues meant that "there [was] no such thing as a grant for anybody who's suffering from the Ninth Ward. People will go borrow money, buy rugs, and put it over the old floors."[126] Perez could distribute local revenues without threatening his power, because offering disaster relief affirmed his paternalistic role. Hébert, however, saw in federal disaster relief the potential to unsettle his position. Taken to its logical end, as Hébert and members of the Betsy Flood Victims alike well knew, a federal commitment to compensating people for structural inequalities would be revolutionary.

The disaster called Betsy continued to take its toll long after the hurricane passed. For the next two years, to any official whose address they could find, the BFV continued to voice their protest.[127] But if they ever were satisfied, the prolific Elizabeth Rogers did not note it. The group officially dissolved on March 30, 1967, its efforts to address Betsy subsumed by what Rogers and others saw as the need to reform urban policy more broadly. "BFV wound up," Rogers wrote on the outside of her folder of handbills and protests letters, "after which the struggle shifted to urban renewal as shown herein."[128]

Urban renewal indeed proved to be a struggle in the Ninth Ward. Some New Orleanians saw in the federal program an opportunity to secure funding from Washington to repair lingering flood damage and to make other long-needed civic improvements. But with the immediate crisis past and anxious to stem the federal reach into the state, the Louisiana State Legislature refused for years to pass the enabling legislation necessary for the state to apply

for urban renewal grants. In the Ninth Ward, the legislature's objection delayed rebuilding and made more ambitious infrastructure improvements
impossible. In January 1967, the *Chicago Defender* described the Ninth Ward
as "neglected by the city," with "insufficient lights, insufficient police protection, inadequate schools, segregated public housing of a low quality, [and]
lack of sufficient water and gas mains." Many homes remained empty. "If
urban renewal is not forthcoming," the *Defender* reported, "the community's middle-class members plan to move into all-white areas of the city, where
they can get the facilities to which they consider themselves entitled."[129]

A group led by the Ninth Ward activist Leontine Luke circulated petitions in favor of urban renewal, and their efforts revealed a tenuous new coalition being forged in the wake of civil rights, voting rights, and the War
on Poverty. Ida Belle Joshua recalled that after Betsy, the neighborhood
"didn't return financially, but there was an upsurge of community activists.
That's when we went into our stance in terms of trying to organize the community."[130] In February 1967, McKeithen and Schiro joined Luke and other
African Americans from the Ninth Ward in Washington, DC, to lobby the
Department of Housing and Urban Development for federal aid.[131] But the
state legislature's continued intransigence made the requests moot. Louisiana
remained the last state in the country to hold out against urban renewal.[132]
The federal funds would have helped Louisianians black and white, but
as when Perez considered shutting down the public schools rather than de-
segregating them, or when Hébert opposed a bill that would have sent millions of dollars to his suffering constituents, a strong bloc of white people
believed that it was better to forgo public funding and public services altogether than to have to share them with African Americans. Racism could
undermine white people's support for government to help any American,
regardless of race.

After the flood, a man from the Ninth Ward wrote to Hale Boggs to say
that he was under water on his SBA loan. "I have more bills now then I got
money coming in," he wrote. "I am a voter now," he asserted, probably in
reference to the Voting Rights Act, "and I would like to do all the things
that should be done. So if you can help us please do." Boggs wrote some letters on the man's behalf to the SBA, but the records do not show the case
ever having been resolved. His newfound empowerment did not seem to add
up to much.[133] Another African American man from the Lower Ninth wrote
to Lyndon Johnson, Russell Long, and Victor Schiro to say that despite losing
everything, his father had only received $15 from the Red Cross. Because he

was over 65, his father was only eligible to borrow $2,500 from the SBA, a quarter of what it would cost to repair his house. For all the politicians' talk of "Americanism," he told his elected officials, "I'm losing faith in this wonderful country of ours—losing faith fast."[134] It took the Joshuas a year to rebuild their home on Forstall Street; in the meantime, they moved in with Ida Belle's mother in the Magnolia Projects, the same public housing development they had fled twenty years earlier for the Lower Ninth. Lucille Duminy spent a decade in debt to the SBA. The stress, she said, caused "ulcers and nervousness."[135]

After Betsy, the white politicians congratulated themselves for their role in what seemed to them a complete and speedy recovery. Boggs asserted "this cooperative effort by the federal, state and local governments has revealed man's humanity to man."[136] McKeithen found faith in the federal government. Johnson strengthened allies for—and in a way, pioneered the possibilities for—the Great Society and his War on Poverty. Schiro got reelected. And in the Lower Ninth Ward, where as Elizabeth Rogers observed in 1967, "all the flood-slum-debt-health problems remain," people relied on cousins, brothers-in-law, and across-the-street neighbors to help.[137] "When I saw all my people," Duminy recalled upon going home after the flood, "I said, 'If they could survive, I can, too.'"[138]

A big storm hit Louisiana on September 9, 1965. What flooded Duminy and thousands of others in the Lower Ninth, though, was a broken flood-wall running alongside a canal that served distant interests. In the hours that followed the levee failure, there was little help to be found amid the flood-waters, except what the terrified people could muster for themselves. And in the months and years after Betsy, even though these New Orleanians harbored a bold vision for what American citizenship might mean, a vision that aligned in important ways with one gaining currency in Congress and the White House, and they advocated for that vision, sending up their best people for service in local and national activism, their letters went largely unanswered. The system that did emerge put them in debt to the federal government, an indebtedness forged when the government failed to give them useful tools to help themselves.[139] "It's been depressing if you just sit and think about the deterioration, the hurt, and the harm that has been done," Ida Belle Joshua recalled in 2003, "to a thriving community of people who had a dream."[140]

For African Americans in New Orleans's Lower Ninth Ward, the high tide of American liberalism arrived in the form of a flood.

3 THE NEW NEW ORLEANS

LOUISIANA GROWS AND SHRINKS, 1967–2005

O N APRIL 8, 1942, AS JAPANESE SOLDIERS ROUTED THE ALLIES IN Bataan, the members of the New Orleans Association of Commerce gathered at Antoine's Restaurant, in the French Quarter, for a banquet.[1] The Association's guests of honor that evening were members of a special House of Representatives subcommittee in town to investigate the problem of defense worker housing. Winning the war, the congressmen believed, required increasing military production, and for Louisiana factories to effectively aid that effort, officials estimated that the region would need to accommodate 100,000 new workers and their families, maybe more, as soon as possible. At Antoine's, the businessmen and the politicians discussed that deceptively difficult question: Where would all these people live?

To the private developers and local officials lobbying the visiting congressmen, one piece of the answer was obvious: the federal government would need to help foot the bill for the new homes. Without federal help, they asserted, New Orleans would not grow.[2]

New Orleans needed federal funds because by the 1940s, the only places the city could expand were difficult to build on, making private developers reluctant to invest in them. At Antoine's, local officials specifically promoted the possibility of constructing 26,000 new housing units along the Industrial Canal, north of the Ninth Ward, in present-day Gentilly and New Orleans East, near the shores of Lake Pontchartrain. Low-lying and prone to flooding, the existing wetlands in these areas would need to be drained; only then could the City run sewer and water lines, which local officials also asked the federal government to sponsor. "This is an area that New Orleans would not have developed for many years" because of the environmental challenges, one visiting Congressman noted.[3]

Boosters in neighboring St. Bernard Parish disparaged New Orleans's proposal. They were lobbying for federal housing subsidies, too. "We would be recreant in our duty if we refrained from claiming superiority in home-building sites," Edwin Roy wrote in a *St. Bernard Voice* editorial, arguing that the city's sites were "of the marsh variety."[4] Roy's point, more bluntly stated, was that New Orleans was asking for federal money to build houses in the swamp. But then, so too, more or less, was St. Bernard. It was not the first time the federal government had considered subsidizing New Orleans's metropolitan expansion into low-lying land, and it would not be the last.

Beginning during the 1930s and continuing for the rest of the century, federal policies—and millions of dollars in federal funds—directed Louisianians away from the high ground near the Mississippi River, and into drained swamps near Lake Pontchartrain. Even as the goals of federal housing policies changed over the decades, their geographical effect in metropolitan New Orleans remained remarkably consistent. When the Home Owners' Loan Corporation bailed out homeowners during the Great Depression in the 1930s, the federal government downgraded old neighborhoods by the river and favored new neighborhoods by the lake. When the GI Bill of Rights subsidized mortgages for veterans of World War II in the 1940s and 1950s, the federal government discouraged rehabilitating older buildings at the city's core and urged new construction in lower-lying areas on the metropolitan periphery. When the National Flood Insurance Program began offering homeowners economic protection from flood damage beginning in the late 1960s, the federal government wrote the rules in ways that effectively subsidized development in flood-prone areas. When the Army Corps of Engineers constructed the Lake Pontchartrain and Vicinity Hurricane Protection Project in the 1970s and 1980s, the federal government justified the cost of the enormous levee system with the prospect of hundreds of thousands of people moving to previously uninhabitable parts of the region.

Why, over the course of the twentieth century, did people increasingly move to more flood-prone parts of Louisiana? The federal government paid them to.

New Orleans's twentieth-century history mirrors metropolitan history across the country. The city's development was propelled by the same federal programs, and with similar geographical outcomes. The commitment to growth this history reflects represented an attempt to expand the middle class and extend the benefits of homeownership to a widening number of Americans. It represented, too, a vast détente between the liberal desire to expand the welfare state, and the conservative demand to privatize the ensuing wealth. It seemed to promise abundance for all without the need for redistribution from anyone. But the imbalance of private profits and public liabilities made the social and environmental order increasingly unsteady.

The same policies that created these new neighborhoods also contributed to their vulnerability. The powerful pumps that lowered the water table and made the ground dry enough to build on also caused the land to sink. Parts of Gentilly subsided by nearly a foot during the half century following its development, which was significant for a neighborhood where early developers had boasted, perhaps too generously, of home sites "fifteen inches above the street grade."[5] Sections of Lakeview sank more than four feet. Few New Orleanians lived in homes below sea level at the beginning of the twentieth century; by the end of the century, the majority did.[6] While the pumps drained fresh water from within the city, the Mississippi River–Gulf Outlet—a shipping canal dredged by the Army Corps of Engineers—along with hundreds of miles of smaller canals dredged by oil and gas companies, drew salt water closer, eroding the coastal wetlands. And as people in New Orleans and across America used oil to warm their houses and gas to fuel their cars, burning up fossil fuels as they traversed the new roads and highways that made metropolitan expansion possible, the carbon gathered in the atmosphere; the world warmed, causing the seas to rise. By 2005, New Orleans was effectively on the coast, its residents falling ever deeper in their hydrological hole, separated from the increasingly strong hurricanes in the Gulf of Mexico by only by the Army Corps's levee system, which remained unfinished, and itself was sinking.

The history of how federal subsidies shaped metropolitan New Orleans, and the vulnerabilities they created, is crucial to making sense of the fundamental question of Katrina's impact: who flooded. The facts have been widely misreported and misunderstood. In 2005, many observers assumed that the water coursing through Louisiana's broken levees only flooded the homes of poor African Americans who lived in the city, while sparing those of middle-class whites who lived in the suburbs.[7] They could base that assumption not only on news reports that emphasized African Americans' suffering, but also on a solid understanding of what is often termed environmental racism.[8] In New Orleans and across twentieth-century America, inequality often took geographic form, with "tragic walls . . . separat[ing] the outer city of wealth and comfort from the inner city of poverty and despair," as Martin Luther King Jr. put it in 1967.[9] The historic city centers (and rural towns) where most African Americans lived suffered from inadequate infrastructure, sickening pollution, and a toxic barrage of other vulnerabilities. Their plight was no accident. Coalitions of conservative businessmen and white racists effectively used the American welfare state to create and maintain racial, economic, and spatial inequalities, making white suburban wealth and African American urban poverty two sides of the same fence line. Suburbanization often amounted to a process of plundering cities and their African American residents, and removing the spoils to the metropolitan fringe.[10] To Americans watching Katrina unfold on television, therefore, it simply seemed logical that black people in New Orleans would be at much greater risk from the flood than white people in the suburbs. Many reasoned, with good cause, that was just how American inequality operated. The conventional wisdom about Katrina's impact, however, was wrong.[11] When the levees broke in 2005, nearly every single home in St. Bernard Parish experienced some degree of flooding.[12]

According to a straight-line theory of environmental racism, St. Bernard should have been safe. It was, in many ways, a quintessential segregated, middle-class, suburban county. The parish's population was over 90 percent white when Leander Perez opened his segregation academies there in the 1960s, and it remained nearly 90 percent white when Hurricane Katrina made landfall a half century later. Of Louisiana's sixty-four counties, in 2000, St. Bernard had the third highest concentration of white people. The median household income was more than 30 percent higher in St. Bernard than it was in New Orleans.[13] Full of respectable ranch houses on tidy lots, St. Bernard was something like a Louisiana Levittown. And yet, a higher percentage of people living in St. Bernard flooded than in New Orleans. How could this be so?

Racism helped to determine flood vulnerability, but in a confounding way. By the 1930s, the only places available for new residential development were in lower-lying parts of New Orleans and its suburbs. The federal benefits that enabled people to move to these desirable new neighborhoods went primarily to white people. Poorer African Americans, in contrast, often could not access those benefits, so they remained primarily in older parts of the city, on higher ground.[14] Upward mobility is a misnomer: for most of the twentieth century, moving to a more valuable house often meant moving to lower-lying land. Residents of St. Bernard Parish were vulnerable to flooding precisely because they were the people who had enjoyed many of the most generous benefits of twentieth-century American citizenship.

If subsequent events later confirmed the extent to which America's most disadvantaged citizens could not rely on the state, Katrina's flood lines first traced the extent to which middle-class white Americans did. Racism thus contributed to more systemic vulnerabilities, too. The desire among many white people to limit African Americans' access to the social safety net often led them to an ideological opposition to government action of any kind. Opposition to government action, particularly federal action, not only led to racial inequalities in wealth and well-being, but also to a weaker state in general, one that ultimately lacked the capabilities to adequately protect anyone who relied on it, regardless of race.[15]

All catastrophic infrastructure failures are unintended; that is what defines them as failures. But often, they are a specific species of unintended event, the kind the sociologist Robert Merton once termed an "unanticipated consequence." Decisions focused on immediate rather than long-term outcomes, he observed, can set in motion "processes which so react as to change the very scale of values which precipitated them."[16] These disasters, in other words, are products of the same histories they upend.

The flood that washed over metropolitan New Orleans in 2005 was the unanticipated consequence of trying to build a world that could accommodate both racial equality and racial segregation, both a safety net and ceaseless expansion.

THE HOME OWNERS' LOAN CORPORATION IN NEW ORLEANS

The desire to build and subsidize a growing middle class, leavened with more concern about race than topography, defined federal housing efforts since at least the 1930s. The first major federal foray into residential housing policy was the Home Owners' Loan Corporation (HOLC), a New Deal effort to "provide emergency relief with respect to mortgage indebtedness" for the millions of Americans who faced the prospect of defaulting on their mortgages and becoming homeless during the Depression.[17] HOLC's significance was vast: it announced a federal commitment to supporting homeownership and contributed to the rise of the now ubiquitous long-term, self-amortizing home mortgage. Between 1933 and 1936, HOLC enabled more than one million citizens in default to refinance their mortgages with these more affordable and predictable loans. In doing so, because federal agents needed metrics for evaluating the financial risk of home mortgages across the country, HOLC also promulgated a national set of standards for real estate appraisal.[18]

When appraisers working for HOLC embarked on a major effort to assess metropolitan New Orleans's real estate market in 1939, they believed that the presence of African Americans represented a bigger threat than floods to the city's property values. HOLC instructed its appraisers to assess New Orleans's neighborhoods according to criteria including the age and quality of the housing stock, the distance from heavy industry, and the race and class of the neighborhood's residents. Based on their evaluations, assessors assigned one of four grades to an areas—A, B, C, or D. Class "A" neighborhoods were, in the words of the federal appraisers, "hot spots . . . the new well-planned sections of the city," the most secure areas for mortgage lenders. Class A areas were "homogenous." Class "B" neighborhoods were "completely developed." "They are like a 1937 automobile," an appraiser wrote in 1939, "still good, but not what people are buying today who can afford a new one." Class "C" neighborhoods were considered declining, "characterized by age, obsolescence, and change of style; expiring restrictions or lack of them; infiltration of a lower grade population," and "'jerry' built areas." A C classification meant that the area included "neighborhoods lacking homogeneity," where "good mortgage lenders are more conservative." Class "D" areas were considered hazardous, places where the decline predicted in class C neighborhoods "ha[s] already happened." They were defined by "detrimental influences . . . undesirable population or an infiltration of it. Low percentage of home ownership, very poor maintenance . . . vandalism . . . [and] unstable incomes."[19] If African Americans lived in a neighborhood, appraisers downgraded it. "As a rule," the appraisers noted, "Negroes" in New Orleans "are concentrated in the 'D' areas."[20] But African Americans—who comprised nearly 30 percent of New Orleans's 1930 population—lived in neighborhoods throughout the city, which may be why HOLC's survey rated most of New Orleans as class C or D.[21]

HOLC's appraisers seem to have understood racial segregation to be both a cause and inevitable consequence of real estate market values. African Americans were pushed out of neighborhoods deemed to be desirable, making those places became even more desirable according to HOLC's classifications; and vice versa, African Americans were pushed into neighborhoods deemed to be in decline, and their presence in them led appraisers to believe they were even more undesirable. For example, HOLC's assessors noted several African Americans living on Calhoun Street, Uptown, "right in the center of an area of beautiful homes, in the expensive class and occupied by white people." Appraisers gave the area a B rating, but only because they believed that, "within the next 12 months steps will be taken to eliminate this undesirable section."[22]

The appraisers knew that New Orleans was prone to floods and attributed the city's comparatively high housing costs to the "tremendous expenditures" necessary for drainage. They estimated that it cost $3,275 to make an acre of New Orleans land habitable, with $1,475 of that amount going toward drainage alone.[23] The appraisers observed new neighborhoods where, because of poor soil conditions, "foundations in many houses have either slipped or sunk and it has been necessary . . . to put in new foundations." They noted, too, that the Works Progress Administration was funding new streets in parts of the city where subsidence had buckled the pavement.[24]

And yet, the federal assessors believed that "the danger of floods has been eliminated."[25] An 1895 plan developed by the city's Drainage Advisory Board had prompted decades of concerted public works to create a municipal drainage system that could remove rainwater and groundwater alike. A system of canals and pipes, and a series of extraordinarily powerful pumps designed by the engineer A. Baldwin Wood, seemed to have proven successful. Because of these civic improvements, between 1900 and 1914, the assessed taxable value of property in New Orleans increased by nearly 80 percent. Removing standing water in the city, which bred mosquitoes—along with the corresponding extension of the sewer system and provision of drinking water—also decreased the incidence of disease that had been a scourge on nineteenth-century New Orleans. Yellow fever deaths decreased from 70 per 100,000, in 1899, to virtually zero by 1913. The overall death rate fell by 25 percent during that same period, and by 75 percent between 1900 and 1925—by which time the drainage system covered 30,000 acres of the city, and comprised 560 miles of canals and pipes.[26]

In 1939, the drainage system allowed assessors for the Federal Home Loan Bank Board to declare, in a confidential field report, that the city's "tremendous drainage problem . . . has been solved at great cost by the installation of the largest pumps in the world."[27] The appraisers understood New Orleans's floods as remnants of the city's past, not part of its future. "With the development of the drainage system . . . the swamps disappeared and this land became as well drained as the ridges," a geographer asserted in 1944. "For all practical purposes," he wrote, "topography as an ecological factor has disappeared."[28] This, despite the fact that as the drainage system lowered the water table, 30 percent of the city had sunk below sea level by 1935.[29]

Rather than permit African Americans to move into new developments on recently drained land, since the 1920s, racist housing covenants, as well as local and state segregationist statues, had sought to restrict them to older, higher parts of the city.[30] By 1939, when HOLC published its "Residential Security Map" for metropolitan New Orleans, the agency rated all neighborhoods bordering the Mississippi River—the city's highest ground—class "D."[31] Nowhere in the city meaningfully above sea level received an A or a B rating. In contrast, the few small sections of the city that appraisers assigned A ratings all were either at or below sea level. "The wealthy . . . must build new houses on vacant land," an influential economist with the Federal Housing Administration asserted in 1939. "High rent or high grade residential neighborhoods must almost necessarily move outward toward the periphery of the city."[32] As far as the federal government and its real estate experts were concerned, most of the highest ground in New Orleans was economically hazardous and financially risky, while the safer investments were the newly drained parts of the city, in the former back swamp. New Orleans became increasingly segregated as white people moved from the city's comparatively integrated historic core, into new whites-only neighborhoods on the periphery.

SPRAWLING INTO ST. BERNARD PARISH

By the early 1940s, in the midst of World War II, city and federal officials alike argued that draining New Orleans's wetlands and subsidizing new housing there represented a national priority. At the 1942 Congressional hearing, for example, when Congressman Boykin encouraged his fellow committee members to appropriate the city's full request for housing subsidies, he based his recommendation on the importance of expanding the Higgins shipyards in New Orleans. Workers at the Higgins plants on the Industrial Canal, in far eastern New Orleans, and elsewhere across the city constructed so-called "Higgins boats," the amphibious landing craft that the Allies would rely on for the invasion at Normandy in 1944. In 1942, New

Orleans shipyards held over $1 billion in government contracts. One historian later wrote that shipyard founder Andrew Higgins "seemed to incarnate the self-made, self-confident swashbuckling industrialist of American folklore," even though, tellingly, his success was premised nearly entirely on orders from the federal government. He embodied the practice embraced by most members of Congress at Antoine's that evening: the federal government would subsidize private growth, so that local firms could contribute to the national effort to make the world safe for democracy. Local businessmen like those assembled by the Association of Commerce would profit over the long term. Everybody would win.[33]

The war and the industrial production the war necessitated raised the expectation of widespread development not just in New Orleans, but in St. Bernard Parish, too. "There should be a record-breaking building boom in St. Bernard, and fresh population of considerable proportions," the *Voice* reported in April 1942, citing the Higgins plant and other new factories rumored to be coming near the Orleans–St. Bernard parish line. The "wave of development," the paper predicted, "will make the house-shortage in St. Bernard, long existent, still more acute, and further create opportunities for the development of subdivisions, both old and new."[34]

New subdivisions like Green Acres, in Arabi, just over the Orleans Parish line from the Lower Ninth Ward, promised a benign, pastoral suburban modernity. During the war, they were designed with workers at nearby defense plants in mind. The federal government encouraged their developers by providing waivers on wartime material restrictions and encouraged potential buyers with subsidies from the Federal Housing Administration (FHA); local funding paid for drainage and levees. Advertisements boasted of Green Acres homes' "modern single, two bed-rooms, living room, dinette, kitchen, hardwood floors, floor furnace, insulated ceilings, tile bath, tile drain boards in kitchen, kitchen cabinets, large clothes closet, laundry room and slat awnings." After the 1944 passage of the GI Bill of Rights, the advertisements also noted, "If you are a veteran, and employed, you can purchase . . . [the] houses without any down payment."[35]

Government spending was central to the St. Bernard boom, because populating the parish required what the secretary of the Police Jury had described, in a 1941 announcement, as a "broad civic program." It was not just that the federal government's wartime procurement needs lead to widespread factory employment. On the local level, the parish passed bond issues to finance sewerage and drainage, to build a sewerage disposal plant, to pave and blacktop roads, to provide for street lights, to fund the fire department, to build new schools and fund a new parish-wide school district, and to provide other basic civil necessities and broader civic amenities.[36] The state government paved the state highways and built bridges. The federal government also was involved in ways ranging from the US Public Health Service's "campaign of extermination" against the parish's mosquitoes, to the FHA's innovative program, introduced in St. Bernard in 1941, of long-term mortgages for farm families, the beginning of the FHA's sustained effort to make home ownership more accessible.[37]

The public investments were designed to entice and support, not supplant, private enterprise. In St. Bernard, this pattern worked well in the 1940s. Once the state and the parish paved the roads, for example, St. Bernard Bus Line, Inc., a private company, began carrying passengers from Arabi and Violet to New Orleans.[38] Similarly, throughout the war years, the St. Bernard Chamber of Commerce, the parish newspaper, and local boosters all lobbied the Army Corps of Engineers to dredge Bayou la Loutre and Bayou Yscloskey, in order to make them navigable, to aid the seafood industry. The efforts, largely coordinated in Washington, DC, by Congressman Edward Hébert, seemed successful. By 1947, the *Voice* was able to report that "the seafood industry of St. Bernard is on the ascendancy." In short, these government subsidies remade the land and water, at significant expense, to create common spaces that might increase the commonwealth. Call it the construction of natural advantage.[39]

These investments drew more people to St. Bernard, as the end of the war increased the demand for new housing. The population grew by more than 50 percent during the 1940s, from 7,280 in 1940 to 11,087 in 1950. In the late 1940s, a visitor driving down the state highway, through Arabi, Chalmette, Meraux, Violet, and Delacroix, would see "villages which are rising to the dignity of towns."[40] During the 1950s, the population nearly tripled. Many of those newcomers, who were almost exclusively white, may have been fleeing the threat of school integration in New Orleans. By 1960, the parish's population was over 32,000.[41]

The new suburban homeowners—factory workers, fishermen, and other working people, who subdivided the outsized plantations of the old aristocracy into modest but respectable tracts of homes and yards—represented a novel type on the American scene: the middle class. They were supported by an alliance of corporate firms and a growing federal government. It was the great compromise forged during the New Deal.[42] Capital moved back and forth among public and private interests. Between 1944 and 1954, for example, the US Department of Veterans Affairs guaranteed 27,925 home loans in metropolitan New Orleans, representing over $187 million in real estate investments.[43] Those loan guarantees enabled and encouraged veterans to buy new homes from private developers in suburban subdivisions like Chalmette Vista, which opened in 1950. Then in 1952, Chalmette Vista, Inc. donated land it owned for a new high school in St. Bernard—on the condition that the Parish purchase additional land from the corporation nearby for a new stadium.[44] Similarly, in 1951, the Kaiser Aluminum company opened a $145 million plant on 280 acres in Chalmette, with a 500-foot-tall smokestack towering over the parish. The plant offered hundreds of jobs and boasted of its important role as one of St. Bernard's largest taxpayers. In 1959, Kaiser Aluminum went so far as to make a small ceremony out of paying its tax bill; a photograph of a plant manager handing a $314,909.66 check to the deputy tax collector appeared on the front page of the local newspaper.[45] A year later, though, the public-private alliance showed signs of fraying: citing lower energy costs at its plants in other states, Kaiser announced it would lay off 900 employees. The newspaper responded with an editorial calling on St. Bernard to "work towards establishing a good business climate" by cutting taxes.[46] The pie seemed to shrink nearly as soon as it left the oven.

Like the New Deal broadly, suburbanization could take the form of a radical experiment in leveling racial and economic inequality, or serve as a mechanism for amplifying those same inequalities.[47] While the policies and practices that supported the growth of the white suburban middle class sometimes reached African Americans—as in the case of the veterans who populated the Lower Ninth Ward—they could just as easily preclude African Americans from enjoying the benefits of development. In June 1954, for example, O. C. W. Taylor, cofounder of the *Louisiana Weekly*, helped to broker a quarter-million dollar deal for the African American Crescent City Country Club to buy a 137-acre estate on the river in Violet, with plans for another $150,000 investment in a new golf course, tennis courts, a place for Sunday school classes, and other new facilities. The plans were heralded nationally in *Jet* magazine. But although it was the sort of development the police jury usually worked to accommodate, in this case, officials quickly passed an ordinance thwarting the project. The ordinance, which prohibited the operation of a club within 8,500 feet of a school, was ostensibly race neutral. But coming immediately on the heels of the Crescent City Country Club's announcement, and affecting no other organization, most likely, it was crafted specifically to keep the club's African American membership out of the parish.[48]

Five years later, in 1960, as white Louisianians continued to seethe in the wake of the *Brown* decision, Leander Perez used St. Bernard as his staging ground for resistance to school integration. Perez arranged to bus white students from Orleans Parish's Ninth Ward to Arabi, where he financed an annex on the public elementary school to accommodate them.[49] Voters in St. Bernard embraced these politics. In the 1960 presidential election, the segregationist States' Rights candidate Orval Faubus defeated both John Kennedy and Richard Nixon in St. Bernard, winning with 44 percent of the vote in the parish, compared to 21 percent statewide.[50]

The combined effects of government policy and racist custom transformed St. Bernard into a segregated white suburb. During the parish's twenty years of extraordinary growth from 1940 to 1960, while the white population increased by nearly 24,000, the African American population increased by fewer than one thousand. The differential growth meant that from 1940 to 1960, the African American population of St. Bernard fell from roughly 20 percent to just 7 percent. By 1960, St. Bernard had the second highest percentage of white people of any parish in Louisiana.[51] African Americans, meanwhile, often moved into the homes that white people left behind in the older parts of the city. The percentage of African Americans in the New Orleans population grew from 30 percent, in 1940, to 37 percent, by 1960, representing an increase of nearly 85,000 people. "Private housing for Negroes . . . is essentially not new housing," one observer noted in 1957. "It is essentially replacing whites in the Crescent."[52]

Meanwhile, just as the parish border separating St. Bernard from the Lower Ninth did not truly create a fully segregated world, the placid, pastoral modernism of the new subdivisions could never really be separated from the heavy industry that made them possible.[53] Noxious smoke from the Kaiser plant wafted across Chalmette Vista. The wages the factories paid were not sufficient to pay for even the subsidized mortgages, leading workers at St. Bernard's American Sugar Refinery to stage a three-month strike in the spring and summer of 1953. The stagnant Violet Canal stank. The drinking water tasted of oil.[54]

Fur trappers, who continued to operate in eastern parts of the parish, near the coast, were among the first to seek redress for the perils of suburban and industrial development. At a 1953 Police Jury meeting, thirty trappers—carrying a petition signed by over 400 others—decried how levees and canals starved the marsh of fresh water, making it uninhabitable for muskrats. Knowing their audience, the trappers stressed the economic benefits that would accrue if the Police Jury invested in diverting freshwater from the Mississippi River into the marsh. The trappers also presented their work on the land as sustainable, in contrast to industries that might boom then bust. "The time will come when something will occur that will cut down the pace of industry," one man asserted, "and . . . residents of the parish will have to again depend upon the rats to help them earn a living."[55] The Police Jury proposed a study, infuriating the trappers who saw the situation as an emergency.[56]

The environmental concern that united people was flood control. In September 1956, Hurricane Flossy caused over a million dollars in damage in St. Bernard. The fishing village of Shell Beach, on the shore of Lake Borgne, was "wiped off the map" in the storm. Although Shell Beach and other eastern parts of the parish were the hardest hit, the St. Bernard Grove subdivision and other new developments near Violet and Chalmette also saw floodwater when the storm surge overtopped levees along Bayou Bienvenue.[57] The extent of the Hurricane Flossy flood especially alarmed many of the parish's new families, who had arrived to their new suburban homes with the understanding that they were safe.[58] A proposal for the Army Corps of Engineers to dredge a shipping channel across the length of the parish aggravated their fears.

THE MISSISSIPPI RIVER–GULF OUTLET

Ever since it constructed the Industrial Canal in the 1920s, the Port of New Orleans Commission had wanted to expand the network of interior shipping canals. The ambitious centerpiece of their plan came to be known as the Mississippi River–Gulf Outlet, or MRGO: a seventy-six-mile, deep draft channel connecting the Industrial Canal to the Gulf Intracoastal Waterway, which would enable ships to enter New Orleans without venturing into the Mississippi River or Lake Pontchartrain at all, but rather by cutting across the wetlands on the southwestern side of Lake Borgne, connecting with the Gulf Intracoastal Waterway, and from there, heading straight into the Industrial Canal.[59]

The Army Corps of Engineers had investigated the idea in 1930, in response to lobbying by the port, but determined that there was "no necessity for another deep-water outlet, either for emergencies or to provide for increasing commerce."[60] During and immediately after World War II, however, the Corps started to change its position in the face of more local lobbying, including a supportive resolution from the Louisiana State Legislature, and a 1944 campaign visit to New Orleans by vice presidential candidate Harry Truman, who praised the MRGO as resonant with the Roosevelt administration's belief that "power—navigation—irrigation—should be developed and utilized for the common good."[61] The Corps also embraced a cost-benefit calculation that predicted a modest economic return on the federal investment, because of savings to shippers—although the numbers only worked in favor of the project after the Corps reduced its assessment of annual maintenance costs by more than 25 percent. The Corps formally endorsed the plan for a channel in 1948 and Congress authorized construction of the MRGO on March 29, 1956.[62]

The MRGO was met by immediate resistance in St. Bernard Parish. People were concerned, first of all, that they had been left out of the planning process. They complained that the canal would cannibalize developable land to serve interests in New Orleans, rather than in St. Bernard. They worried, too, that the MRGO would contribute to traffic problems: residents of St. Bernard already loathed the Industrial Canal for causing interminable waits to cross its bridge, which frequently opened to let ships pass. A new shipping channel stood to make traffic even worse.[63]

But most of all, people in St. Bernard worried that the MRGO would make the parish more vulnerable to floods. "The question uppermost in everyone's mind," the *Voice* reported in December 1956, was "how will the property-owners and residents of this parish be protected from tidal-overflow? Will there be levees to hold the waters of a 600 foot canal from overflowing the entire parish when the next hurricane strikes?"[64]

St. Bernard lobbied the federal government for flood protection. In May 1957, the president of the Police Jury, Henry Schindler, wrote to Congressman Hébert that Hurricane Flossy had "demonstrated our continued susceptibility to such dangers depending upon the whims of nature." Schindler asked that the fill dredged for the MRGO be used to build new, stronger, and higher levees around the parish. "Without proper protection," he asserted, "our natural advantages will be for naught."[65]

In September 1957, as concern mounted, the Police Jury appointed a Tidewater Channel Advisory Committee, chaired by Joseph Meraux, to formally investigate the proposal. Thirty-five years old, Meraux was the son of

Louis "Doc" Meraux, a mentor and coconspirator of Leander Perez's, and the former parish sheriff who had help lead the charge against the Isleños at Delacroix during the Trappers' War. When the elder Meraux died in 1938, Joe inherited his father's fortune, which included vast, often secret, land holdings. In 1957, Joe Meraux likely owned more land than anyone else in St. Bernard.[66] Joining Meraux on the commission were nearly twenty other powerful citizens, including his uncle Claude Meraux, a district judge, Louis Folse, a state senator, August Campagna, a state representative, and Edwin Roy, the editor of the *Voice*.[67] These were the sort of men who normally endorsed development; their appointment to a committee that ostensibly would criticize the MRGO suggests how little support the project had in St. Bernard.

Roy, the newspaper editor, did not wait for the Tidewater Committee to issue its report. Beginning in November 1957, he attacked the channel idea in a series of eight front-page editorials, all running under the ominous headline "IS ST. BERNARD PARISH DOOMED." The lack of a question mark implied that the answer was obvious. He unleashed a barrage of concerns, ranging from traffic to depreciating land values to potentially harmful effects on commercial oyster beds. But Roy saved his most dire warnings for the threat of floods. The channel, he argued, would "cause the marshlands to disappear due to subsidence." He accused the city of "sacrificing the entire Parish of St. Bernard as it did in 1927 when the levee at Caernarvon was destroyed to save the city from destruction by the Mississippi River." The 1927 flood was never far from mind in coastal Louisiana: it offered the archetypal example of government helping the rich and hurting the powerless, transforming what might have been equitable structures of protection into deadly weapons of discrimination.[68]

The local objections went unheeded in the face of the much more powerful forces working in favor of the channel. Construction began on December 10, 1957. At a site near where the Industrial Canal met the Intracoastal Canal, speakers including Congressmen Hébert and Hale Boggs, and Senators Russell Long and Allen Ellender, lined up to praise the project and to vow to secure the $96 million in federal appropriations necessary to complete the work of dredging the 650 foot-wide path seventy-six miles through the wetlands that buffered the eastern reaches of the parish.[69] When the politicians had pushed a ceremonial plunger, announcing the start of construction with a "huge dynamite blast," the *Times-Picayune* called it a "helpful explosion for world trade."[70]

Four months later, on April 1, 1958, the Police Jury's Tidewater Channel Committee issued its report. It was a harrowing document, confirming the dire consequences that Roy had previewed in his editorials the year before. The committee predicted that once the massive channel was cut through the marsh that presently protected St. Bernard from the Gulf, "the full fluctuation of the tide will be felt throughout the Parish." The tides would hurt the wetlands, enabling "the intrusion of high saline content water into areas normally fresh or only slightly brackish." Presumably those effects would take some time to unfold, but the report also warned of immediate perils. During hurricanes, the committee cautioned, "the existence of the channel will be an enormous danger to the heavily populated areas of the Parish due to the rapidity of the rising waters reaching the protected areas in full force through the avenue of this proposed channel."

The Tidewater Committee's assessment of the MRGO was damning. The cost of compensatory flood protection would be "astronomical." Communities on the far side of the channel "will become ghost settlements," with current residents "forced to abandon their homes . . . without . . . compensation for such losses." Worst of all, the committee concluded, there was "a distinct possibility that the existence of the proposed channel to the rear of this vast, and valuable, marsh area will within the foreseeable future cause the marsh lands to disappear due to subsidence." St. Bernard Parish would not benefit in any way from the MRGO, the committee asserted, and was "about to be placed in the inevitable position of again being sacrificed for the benefit of the City of New Orleans as occurred in the breaking of the levees at Caernarvon and the digging of the Industrial Canal."[71]

The economic boon the MRGO's boosters promised never came, but the environmental collapse predicted by its opponents did. People started noticing changes in the land even before the channel opened to ships in 1968. We "could see it," Junior Rodriguez recalled. "It was obvious, and it was dramatic."[72] The MRGO allowed the Gulf to flow into St. Bernard's wetlands, and salinity levels quickly increased in some places from two to three parts per thousand of salt content to twenty parts per thousand—a shift that would kill the marsh.[73] "All of a sudden," Pete Savoye, an avid fisherman who lived nearby, noticed, "there's no more crawfish." The grass along the channel died. As the years went on, the changes became even more alarming. Savoye would take his boat out to fish near an island, then a week or two later, when he returned, the island would be "gone. Disappeared." The cypress trees died.

The tides changed, too. Before, the tide "would take a day or two to raise two feet" in Bayou Bienvenue; after the Corps dredged the channel, Savoye said, the tide "would raise maybe six or eight feet in a day. It would just come right on in. Nothing to stop it."[74] When parts of St. Bernard flooded during Hurricane Betsy, many blamed the MRGO for funneling the storm surge into the parish.[75] The channel grew an average of forty-seven feet wider each year.[76]

The collapse of the marsh drove people to action. "When I saw everything dying, I knew that something had to be done," Savoye said. At an August 30, 1973, meeting, Sherwood Gagliano, the environmental scientist who first studied the rising salinity levels, presented a petition to the Corps, signed by 1,200 people, calling for the MRGO to be closed. "Coastal zones can no longer be considered the wastelands of the nation," he asserted.[77] A parish official there called the MRGO "one of the most ill-conceived public works projects" and a "rank disaster."[78] In 1976, Junior Rodriguez won a seat on the Police Jury, and in the early 1980s, he and Savoye both joined a new St. Bernard Parish Coastal Zone Advisory Committee. They went to meeting after meeting to press the Corps to close the channel. "Here they come to bitch about the MRGO again," Corps officials would grumble. But "that was the most important thing that I could think of," Savoye said. "And they were the people that was supposed to help us."[79]

As recently as the early 1950s, residents of St. Bernard had eagerly lobbied for federal subsidies for development. But over time, many came to the shocking realization that, as Savoye put it, "The Corps of Engineers was our enemies."[80]

THE LAKE PONTCHARTRAIN AND VICINITY HURRICANE PROTECTION PROJECT

In 1955, Congress had directed the Army Corps to consider the problem of hurricane protection in metropolitan New Orleans. The Corps had completed a study for what it called the Lake Pontchartrain and Vicinity Hurricane Protection Project (LPVHPP) in 1962. Three years later, after various bureaucratic reviews and approvals, the Corps sent the plan to Congress. It arrived at the Committee on Public Works in July 1965, less than two months before Hurricane Betsy made landfall.[81] Looking back after Betsy, the authors of the Committee on Public Works' report asserted that the levee system the Corps had proposed, "would have eliminated the flooding of developed areas in the city of New Orleans [and] the Chalmette area of St. Bernard," decreasing the cost of damages by $85 million and "greatly reduc[ing]" the number of deaths.[82] Congress quickly approved construction. President Lyndon Johnson signed the bill authorizing the LPVHPP on October 27, 1965.[83] The vast sweep of the project's embrace linked the fate of Americans across lines of race, class, and neighborhood. Designed to safeguard more than 150 square miles of metropolitan New Orleans, the scale of the LPVHPP made it one of the most ambitious public works projects in American history.[84]

The LPVHPP was meant to protect greater New Orleans from what the Army Corps referred to as a Standard Project Hurricane, or "one that may be expected from the most severe combination of meteorological conditions that are considered reasonably characteristic of the region." Working with the US Weather Bureau, the Corps determined that a Standard Project Hurricane for New Orleans would have a one in 200 chance of happening in any given year. The Corps described such a storm as being "similar in intensity to the September 1915 hurricane." The Committee on Public Works understood that the LPVHPP was not designed to withstand all storm surges—the Standard Project Hurricane was the lower of two standards that the Weather Bureau developed; the other was called the Probable Maximum Hurricane. Nonetheless, the Corps was confident in the LPVHPP's design. The agency asserted that for the area of New Orleans between the Industrial Canal and the Jefferson Parish line, the "combination of structures" it proposed, "will provide essentially complete protection from all hurricanes."[85]

The LPVHPP amounted to a concrete wall around the metropolis. The Corps had come to that design after rejecting what it had referred to as a "high level plan," which would have involved raising existing levees around New Orleans, including along the three drainage canals that cut into the city. Instead, the Corps adopted what it called the "barrier plan," because it hinged on a massive barrier—nine feet tall and nearly six miles wide—that would cross the east side of Lake Pontchartrain, from eastern New Orleans to Slidell, in order to prevent storm surges from entering the lake (which is, in reality, a brackish bay) in the first place. Gated openings would allow for navigation channels at Chef Menteur Pass and the Rigolets. New and enlarged levees would "front . . . developed or potentially developable areas" across St. Charles, Jefferson, Orleans, and St. Bernard Parishes. The Corps would build higher floodwalls along the Industrial Canal and new levees along the MRGO. At the lakefront in New Orleans, the Corps would raise levees to eleven and a half feet. The Corps estimated that the LPVHPP would cost $79.8 million. The federal government would pay 70 percent, and state and local governments would contribute the balance. The Corps also mentioned other methods that might protect Louisianians, including "the establishment of building codes and zoning regulations, provision of adequate havens of refuge, and organization of hurricane preparedness committee to formulate plans for effective preventive measures, evacuation and rescue work." These measures, the Corps noted, could be achieved "at no cost to the United States."[86]

Even as the Army Corps noted that "intangible benefits" of the project included "the protection of human life," it justified the system primarily with an analysis of economic costs and benefits. The Corps based its evaluation on the premise that the population of metropolitan New Orleans—including Orleans, Jefferson, and St. Bernard Parishes—would more than double over the coming half century, from 868,480 in 1960 to more than 2 million by 2010. The Corps believed that most of the growth would occur beyond the city's historic core: in Jefferson Parish to the west, and beyond the Industrial Canal to the east. Given this anticipated population boom, the Corps predicted that with new protections against flooding, over the next fifteen years, land in the region it called Chalmette (which reached from the Industrial Canal to Paris Road, including the Lower Ninth Ward) would more than triple in value, from $3.7 million to over $13 million. With development as it stood in that area in 1961, the Corps estimated that the new levee system would prevent an average of $1.2 million in flood damages annually. But with the future development the Corps projected—which it anticipated in part based on the completion of the MRGO—the economic benefits of protection would quadruple, preventing, the Corps estimated, an average of $4.8 million in flood damage per year. The Corps's projections were even more ambitious for the areas it called Citrus and New Orleans East, which included the sections of New Orleans east of the Industrial Canal and north of the MRGO. The Corps estimated that the new levee system would decrease the cost of flood damage in the area, as it was currently developed, by an average of $7.2 million per year. But considering the development that the levee system would support over the next twenty years, according to the Corps's projections, the system would decrease the cost of flood damage by an average of $36.7 million per year.[87] The scale tipped in favor of the project based on the growth it would support.

Although Congress had hurried to authorize the LPVHPP after Betsy, it made appropriations in a piecemeal fashion—and the Corps undertook a series of new studies to update its designs—so the Corps did not show meaningful progress on the new system for several years. By 1973, the Corps had constructed new concrete floodwalls along the Industrial Canal. In 1974, the Corps reported that it had completed the first phase of more than seventeen miles of new levees in New Orleans East and more than twenty-seven miles of new levees in Chalmette. But by 1975, a decade after Betsy, the Corps had still not begun construction on the Lake Pontchartrain barrier, which was the linchpin of the whole system. In 1971, the Corps had projected that the system would be complete by 1978; in 1976, it revised its projection to 1991. The estimated cost had increased to over $350 million. In the meantime, the LPVHPP became subject to the new regulatory regime heralded by the National Environmental Policy Act of 1969 and the Clean Water Act of 1972.[88]

The Clean Water Act prompted the Army Corps to hold public hearings on the LPVHPP. On February 22, 1975, Louisianians filled the University Center Ballroom at the University of New Orleans, a short walk from Lake Pontchartrain, to consider the plan. The meeting revealed an enormous amount of local concern. Many of the people present, including the mayor of Slidell and the president of the town's Chamber of Commerce, testified to their worry that the barrier plan would increase flood risk for communities along Lake Pontchartrain's north shore. Others argued against the basic assumptions in the Corps's cost-benefit analysis. The Corps had asserted that the LPVHPP's cost-benefit ratio be would 1 to 12.6—but only after writing off the potential costs of the loss of wetlands. A representative of the Orleans Audubon Society observed that "assigning even very modest economic value to the marshes" would make the cost-benefit ratio "barely favorable." He accused the Corps of "favor[ing] enrichment of a few landowners at the expense of us taxpayers" and noted the important role that wetlands played in dissipating storm surges. Similarly, a representative from the Sierra Club, William A. Fontenot, criticized the Corps for "basing many of the benefits of the project on land reclamation and future developments in wetlands areas," which, "once drained . . . will have the greatest potential for flooding of anywhere in [the] New Orleans Metropolitan Area."[89]

The most dramatic testimony at the hearing came from a scientist who not only argued against the LPVHPP but called for giving up on the idea of trying to protect New Orleans altogether. "In the long haul," Michael Tritico asserted, "New Orleans, as we know it, will have to be abandoned.

Such a thing may sound unacceptable but it will happen whether or [not] anyone wants to admit it. Not because the Army didn't give it their best, but because common sense and natural powers will eventually exert themselves." New Orleanians needed to "relocate to higher grounds," he concluded. "I would, personally, rather experience the hassle of moving than the nightmare of being in this city when a levee does not function properly."[90]

Despite the concerns raised at the public hearing, the Army Corps announced in August 1975 that it would proceed with the project as designed. In December, a group of activists organized as "Save Our Wetlands" sued to prevent construction of the Lake Pontchartrain barrier and in December 1977, a judge issued an injunction against the barrier plan.[91] In response, the Corps began reevaluating the LPVHPP's design, including studying again the feasibility of what it had called the "high level" plan. The new study took more than six years to complete, but in July 1984, the Corps announced that it now considered the high level plan to be "the most feasible plan for providing hurricane protection." Rather than trying to prevent storm surges from entering Lake Pontchartrain, the hurricane protection system would rely on higher and stronger levees and floodwalls encircling the region. In part owing to these changes, in 1990, the Corps estimated that 23 percent of the system remained incomplete.[92]

A metropolitan region home to an expanding middle class, living in affordable, single-family homes: this was the vision the LPVHPP promised, and it had wide appeal. The LPVHPP seemed to resolve a conundrum at the heart of twentieth-century American politics. On the one hand, it embodied the liberal desire—forged during the New Deal and emboldened during the Great Society—to use the federal government as a bulwark for all citizens. Few projects offer a better emblem of the welfare state than the protective embrace of the levee system, which encircled Americans without regard to race, class, or neighborhood. On the other hand, the project accommodated, too, the conservative demand that government action spur private growth. The cost-benefit analyses that served as the LPVHPP's justification only favored the project when the Army Corps factored in how the levee system would encourage new development across the region.

The sprawling metropolis limned by the LPVHPP represented, too, a geography and political economy of oil. In 1972, the oil company Shell erected New Orleans's tallest building—a corporate office tower 250 feet taller than the capitol building Huey Long had constructed in Baton Rouge in the 1930s—symbolizing the soaring importance of the state's oil industry. Oil made it affordable for individuals to commute in cars, for the state to pay for the roads, and for the federal government to build the levee system around them. But oil and the commitment to growth it helped to inspire also undermined those same possibilities, as the Mississippi River–Gulf Outlet and other shipping channels and oil canals increased the city's vulnerability to the very storm surges that the levee system was meant to protect against.[93]

On January 1, 2005, the Army Corps reported that the LPVHPP remained only 80 percent complete. Of the more than $716 million cost now projected, the Corps had spent approximately $452 million. In a February 2005 report, the Army Corps noted, "Continuing land loss and settlement of the land in the project area may have impacted the ability of the project to withstand the design storm. Refinement of existing computer models to assist in determining the impact of these environmental changes on the project will continue."[94]

THE NATIONAL FLOOD INSURANCE PROGRAM

The LPVHPP was supposed to prevent New Orleans from flooding again, but it did not do anything for people who lived beyond its walls. Congressional representatives, watching the debates that Hurricane Betsy had given rise to, understood that flooding would remain an enduring, national problem. The growing precedent of providing federal funds to disaster victims threatened to make disaster relief an ever more expensive proposition. Flood insurance—financed by premium payments from potential recipients— offered an attractive solution.

Private insurers had offered flood insurance from the late nineteenth century until 1927, when the losses from the Mississippi River flood drove private companies from the market. In 1956, Congress had passed a federal flood insurance act, but never funded or implemented the program.[95] After Betsy, the same report that had prompted Congress to authorize the levee system called for Congress to "review and reconsider an overall disaster insurance program."[96] In response, in the Southeast Hurricane Disaster Relief Act, Congress directed the Department of Housing and Urban Development (HUD) to study the possibility of the federal government providing flood insurance.[97]

Officials at HUD grappled with two problems that had long confounded proponents of the idea. The first was a challenge for insurers. Unlike the risk of fire, for example, flood risk was not distributed evenly among homeowners. Because people living outside of a floodplain were unlikely to purchase flood insurance, it was difficult for insurers to assemble a risk pool that could make flood insurance viable, let alone profitable. The second problem challenged policymakers. Like the broader project of flood control, flood insurance threatened to enable people to move to areas of greater risk. "If misapplied," the geographer Gilbert White warned in a 1966 report for the Committee on Public Works, "an insurance program could aggravate rather than ameliorate the flood problem."[98] Just as the construction of levees encouraged people to move into floodplains, providing flood insurance encouraged people to accept the economic risk of living in flood-prone areas.

HUD officials attempted to resolve these challenges by presenting flood insurance as part of a broader effort to limit Americans' exposure to floods in the first place, rather than a way of paying for disaster relief after the fact. The architects of the program saw the opportunity to forestall disasters. "Floods are an act of God," White asserted, but "flood damages result from the acts of men." The centerpiece of a rational flood program, White argued, should be a national effort to map flood hazards, to inform local regulations on development.[99] HUD Secretary Robert Weaver similarly advocated, in the preface of the study the agency submitted to Congress, that flood insurance be "part of a program of land use adjustment" that served as "a means of discouraging unwise occupancy of flood-prone areas."[100]

In August 1968, Congress passed the National Flood Insurance Act, which created the National Flood Insurance Program (NFIP), and established the Federal Insurance Administration, based within HUD, to administer it.[101] The law codified many of HUD's recommendations meant to discourage building in flood-prone areas. First, Congress charged the NFIP with mapping flood hazards across the country within five years. The resulting risk map, which came to be known as a Flood Insurance Rate Map (FIRM), was a prerequisite for a community's eligibility for the program. Second, the law required local jurisdictions to institute land use regulations to prevent development in places the FIRMs indicated were hazardous. (In 1969, HUD defined these "Special Flood Hazard Areas" as places with a 1 percent chance of flooding each year; HUD called for the first floor of new construction to be built above the anticipated level of a so-called 100-year flood.) Third, although the federal government would provide subsidies for homeowners already living in flood-prone areas, no subsidies would be available for new construction. Rather, homeowners would be charged a more expensive, actuarial rate, which was meant to discourage development in floodplains and ultimately make the NFIP economically self-sustaining.[102] Finally, Congress authorized HUD to purchase homes that had been insured by the NFIP and subsequently damaged beyond repair, with the ultimate goal of moving existing residents out of flood-prone areas entirely. (Congress did not provide funding for HUD to purchase or otherwise expropriate flood-prone properties until 1979, and then only modestly.[103]) Private insurers would sell the policies, but the NFIP would determine the flood risk, the actuarial rates, and provide the subsidies at no risk to the private companies.[104]

In June 1969, Metairie, Louisiana—the suburb on the western side of the 17th Street Canal that separates New Orleans from Jefferson Parish—became one of the first communities to formally enter the NFIP. In 1970, sections of St. Bernard Parish became eligible too.[105] In New Orleans, however, the NFIP initially alarmed homebuilders, who understood that strict floodplain regulations would hinder new development and unsettle confidence in existing neighborhoods. "It is the expressed intent of the act . . . to discourage any further development in areas designated as a flood path or an area which has repeatedly been flooded in the past," the president of the New Orleans Home Builders Association told a reporter in August 1970. "That just about takes in all of New Orleans."[106] Thus, like many communities across the country, New Orleans was slow to embrace the NFIP. By 1972, when Hurricane Agnes caused extensive damage across the East Coast, only $5 million of $400 million in losses were covered by the NFIP, and there were fewer than 100,000 insurance policies in force nationwide.[107]

To encourage more homeowners to purchase coverage, Congress increased the premium subsidy and, in December 1973, passed the Flood Disaster Protection Act, which required home buyers in Special Flood Hazard Areas to purchase flood insurance in order to secure a mortgage from any federally regulated lender. The Act also repealed an earlier provision that would have denied federal disaster relief to people who had not purchased flood insurance within a year of becoming eligible.[108] By 1980, a year after the NFIP was transferred from HUD to the new Federal Emergency Management Agency, approximately 2 million homeowners held coverage through the National Flood Insurance Program. In 1994, the National Flood Insurance Reform Act pushed lenders to enforce the mandatory purchase requirement; by the end of that decade, there were 4 million policies in force across the country.[109]

Over that time, the NFIP became a system for authorizing development rather than preventing it. Lax attention to flood risk and inadequate enforcement of building codes made vulnerable properties eligible for the premium subsidies.[110] In 1989, a committee chaired by Gilbert White observed that people were continuing to move into flood-prone areas, putting "increased property at risk," and that "losses to the nation from occupance of . . . areas subject to inundation are continuing to escalate."[111] Five years later, in 1994, a House of Representatives task force on disasters asserted that because of federal disaster policy, "people are encouraged to take risks they think they will not have to pay for."[112] The NFIP was supposed to impute the costs of building in hazardous places into the cost of insurance, but in reality, by distributing the costs of subsidizing the program across the country, the NFIP became the trap that White had warned of in 1966: rather than preventing development in flood-prone areas, flood insurance had encouraged it.[113]

When Norman Robinson bought his house in New Orleans East in 1992, for example, he was the sort of person who had choices about where to live. After serving as a White House correspondent for CBS News, and completing a prestigious journalism fellowship at Harvard, Robinson—a native of Toomsuba, Mississippi, and a Marine Corps veteran—moved to New Orleans to work as a television news anchor for the local NBC affiliate.[114] When he first arrived, Robinson moved to Algiers, settling in a neighborhood the NFIP rated Flood Zone B—meaning it was outside of the 100-year floodplain. But after a year on the West Bank, Robinson joined a rising southern African American middle class who were gathering in New Orleans East.[115] He bought his new home—a 3,300 square foot, two-story brick house on a wide, oak-lined street in a subdivision called Spring Lake—for $154,000. Robinson thought of it as a "typical middle American neighborhood." He spent nearly every Saturday working in his garden or sitting by his pool. He called the backyard his "weekend refuge," and married his wife Monica there. Over the years, Monica said, she "knew everybody everywhere" in the neighborhood.[116] That their house sat more than seven feet below sea level, in a neighborhood classified Flood Zone A, a Special Flood Hazard Area, and came with a federal requirement to purchase flood insurance, did not give the Robinsons pause.[117] The same seemed to be true of most of their neighbors. Despite the fact that New Orleans East averaged nearly six feet below sea level, and the FIRMs developed over the course of the 1970s classified most of the area as a Special Flood Hazard Area, the population more than doubled in the three decades following the passage of the NFIP.[118] By 2000, roughly one of every four African American New Orleanians lived in New Orleans East.[119]

The increase was not as dramatic, but the trend was the same on the other side of the Intracoastal Canal in St. Bernard Parish: the population grew by more than 30 percent from 1970 to 2000, even though the NFIP had classified many of the places where new development occurred as Special Flood Hazard Areas.[120] When Tanya Franz bought a house in Chalmette in 1997, for example, she moved into a neighborhood that was built after the NFIP mapped it as vulnerable to a 100-year flood.[121] Franz had grown up in Arabi in the 1980s, and her desire to stay in the parish was common among her middle-class white professional neighbors. Once she earned a degree from Louisiana State University's Health Sciences Center in New Orleans, and started a career as a registered nurse, Franz decided she was ready to be a homeowner. Her parents helped her to finance the $115,000 purchase price, and Franz worked with a developer to build a new house on Despaux Drive. The lot was down the street from Saint Mark's Catholic School, where she hoped to send her son to kindergarten. Franz chose many of the home's features herself, including the color of the bricks: pink. After her second son was born in 1999, Franz added a pool and a hot tub. "Trust me, it wasn't a mansion," she recalled later, "but for me it was my little dollhouse." She lived one house down from the 40 Arpent Canal, a drainage ditch that separated her neighborhood from the fast-eroding wetlands on the south side of the MRGO, but she never worried about flooding.[122]

The NFIP underwrote a sense of economic and physical security in vulnerable places. When Hurricane Katrina made landfall, 62 percent of New Orleanians lived below sea level, and 67 percent of New Orleanians carried flood insurance—the tenth highest rate for any community in the country, compared to a national rate of 5.4 percent. In St. Bernard Parish, more than 68 percent of single-family homes were covered; in Jefferson Parish, the rate was 84 percent, the highest in the country. Across the state of Louisiana, of the 113,053 single-family homes that sustained flood damage during Katrina, nearly 73,000, or greater than 64 percent, were covered by flood insurance, nearly thirteen times the national average.[123]

In many ways, Chalmette and New Orleans East represented the new political economy of the Ronald Reagan era. Their sprawling geographies relied on affordable gasoline. Their segregated populations accommodated both rising African American affluence and enduring white power. The federal programs that enabled their development demonstrate, too, how the ambitions of the New Deal order came to rest on an ideological commitment to growth. The massive public works of the Lake Pontchartrain and Vicinity Hurricane Protection Project aspired to protect New Orleanians without regard to race or class; it necessitated new growth in order to meet Congress's desired ratios of costs to benefits. With the National Flood Insurance Program, the federal government attempted to provide economic security in a field that private industry had fled, but Washington demanded that the program meet the profit-and-loss standards of a capitalist marketplace nonetheless. In order to make the program "self-sustaining," lawmakers weakened its coverage and loosened its regulations. Over time, the ideological compromises that supported the LPVHPP and the NFIP proved to be just as unstable as the ground under the new homes they subsidized.

STORM WARNING

In 1990, Congress passed the Coastal Wetlands Planning, Protection and Restoration Act, commonly called the Breaux Act, after the bill's author and sponsor, Louisiana Senator John Breaux. It was the first major federal attempt to address the gathering crisis of land loss. The Breaux Act committed the federal government to paying for 85 percent of the cost of coastal restoration projects that would be identified by a new task force, which Congress directed to pursue "a goal of no net loss of wetlands as a result of development activities." The Act also tried to push beyond traditional economic metrics for determining the benefits of wetlands, asserting that whenever federal law required cost-benefit analyses, "the net ecological, aesthetic, and cultural benefits, together with the economic benefits, shall be" considered.[124] In the meantime, though, the Army Corps continued to operate with a narrower view of value. In 1991, for example, the Corps rebuffed Louisiana's request that the agency use sediment dredged from the MRGO to replenish eroding wetlands, asserting the process was too expensive. Instead, the Corps dumped the sediment into open water.[125] And the Corps would later argue that constructing the flood protection measures along the MRGO for which St. Bernard Parish long lobbied, "would have invalidated the cost-benefit calculations that were an essential underpinning" of the project's authorization.[126]

In 1998, after eight years of study, the task force created by the Breaux Act—formally, the Federal Louisiana Coastal Wetlands Conservation and

Restoration Task Force, composed of representatives from the Corps, the EPA, and several other federal agencies, working with the Governor's office and Louisiana's Wetlands Conservation and Restoration Authority—published *Coast 2050: Toward a Sustainable Coastal Louisiana*. Sherwood Gagliano was a member of the planning management team, which drafted the report. "The rate of coastal land loss in Louisiana," the report began, "has reached catastrophic proportions." Over the previous century, the report asserted, more than 1,500 square miles of Louisiana's wetlands had sunk into the Gulf of Mexico; the state was continuing to lose twenty-five to thirty-five square miles of land per year. In response, the plan sought "to sustain a coastal ecosystem that supports and protects the environment, economy and culture of southern Louisiana, and that contributes greatly to the economy and well-being of the nation."[127]

Sustainability evoked ideas of a stable, natural order, but the plan was premised on massive feats of engineering, including diverting sections of the Mississippi River. *Coast 2050* called for closing the MRGO to deep draft navigation within six to fifteen years, too, noting that it served "only 2–3 large ships per day."[128] The St. Bernard Parish Council also passed a resolution in 1998 calling for the Corps to close the MRGO.[129] The Corps acknowledged that the Parish "has long requested the closure of the channel because, in addition to the environmental damage, they believe that the channel serves as a funnel for hurricane surges."[130]

The threat the MRGO posed became increasingly common knowledge. In 2002, the *Times-Picayune* reported that those advocating for the MRGO's closure saw it as "a shotgun pointed straight at New Orleans, should a major hurricane approach from that angle."[131] Pete Savoye spread the word by means of a three-foot square model of St. Bernard Parish that he built with fellow members of the St. Bernard Sportsman's League. The men constructed miniature plywood replicas of the Kaiser plant and the sugar refinery, the little houses, and other points of interest that defined their home place. The MRGO cut through the center. Savoye brought the model to schools, senior centers, and anywhere else that would have him. "I would pour blue water in the Gulf of Mexico," Savoye recalled. "And when I would put a break in the levee, then it would flood all of St. Bernard Parish and Orleans Parish."[132] Originally 650 feet wide, by the early 2000s, the MRGO's eroding banks had spread to an average of nearly 2,000 feet. It was directly responsible for destroying at least thirty square miles—and maybe more than seventy square miles—of marsh in St. Bernard Parish.[133]

"I don't mean to be an alarmist, but the doomsday scenario is going to eventually happen," said Gregory W. Stone, director of the Coastal Studies Institute at Louisiana State University in September 2004, as Hurricane Ivan loomed in the Gulf of Mexico—prompting a massive voluntary evacuation from New Orleans, although the storm weakened just before landfall, sparing the city. Earlier that year, a Federal Emergency Management Agency exercise called Hurricane Pam had anticipated that a slow Category Three hurricane would precipitate the deaths of over 9,000 people in St. Bernard, and 24,000 more in New Orleans. Mark Davis, the executive director of the Coalition to Restore Coastal Louisiana, which had lobbied for the Breaux Act, told a reporter, "We're running out of tomorrows."[134]

On August 27, 2005, as Hurricane Katrina strengthened in the Gulf of Mexico, Junior Rodriguez, then the St. Bernard Parish President, recovering from a heart attack, sat in the passenger seat as his wife Jesse drove their car down to the end of the road. They reached the levee and peered over. The gathering winds had already driven water to nearly the top of the levee. The couple sat there for a moment, before turning around to head toward the St. Bernard government complex where they would ride out the storm. Junior asked Jesse to take the old road back, rather than the highway. "Why?" she asked. "Because," he answered, "I want you to look at it real good." "Because if this thing keeps coming, all you going to have, kid, is memories," Junior said. "You'll never see this place again, not the way it was."[135]

Three years later, after the flood, Sherwood Gagliano, the scientist who had spent the last four decades working with people like Rodriguez and Savoye to warn about the MRGO's dangers, sat in a New Orleans courtroom, testifying in a trial brought against the Army Corps of Engineers by Norman Robinson, Tanya Franz, her parents, and other flood victims in St. Bernard and the eastern parts of Orleans Parish. "From your own study, observations, reports, meetings with the Corps," a lawyer asked him, "how would you describe the MRGO?" "As one of the greatest catastrophes in the history of the United States," Gagliano answered. Their exchange continued this way:

LAWYER: "Was it predicted by you?"
GAGLIANO: "By me and others."
LAWYER: "Was it preventable?"
GAGLIANO: "Yes."[136]

Sewerage and Water Board map of New Orleans. The shaded neighborhoods are described as an "unbuilt area for future construction" (July 1902). New Orleans Sewerage and Water Board.

Cartoon after the 1915 hurricane. The text reads, in part, "New Orleans . . . can wedder a storm like no udder city ever done before" (September 30, 1915). *New Orleans Item.*

Dedicating the Industrial Canal lock (May 5, 1923). US Army Corps of Engineers, New Orleans District.

Dynamiting the Mississippi River levee to create an "artificial crevasse" in St. Bernard Parish (April 29, 1927). US Army Corps of Engineers, New Orleans District.

South Louisiana and the Beautiful Gulf Coast (ca. 1936). Louisiana Editors Association.

Leander Perez
considers Louisiana's
claim to offshore oil
rights (May 24, 1955).
Robert W. Kelley/The
LIFE Picture Collection
via Getty Images.

Emile Riche with his protest sign, which reads, in part "Leander Perez keep out"
(June 2, 1955). Robert W. Kelley/The LIFE Picture Collection via Getty Images.

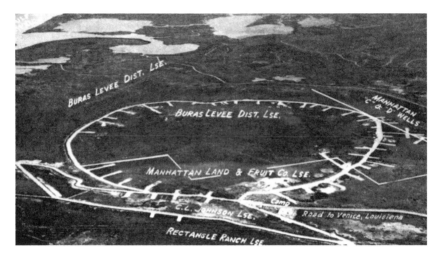

Oil canals in the marshes of Plaquemines Parish (July 11, 1955). *Oil & Gas Journal.*

Groundbreaking for the Mississippi River–Gulf Outlet (December 10, 1957). US Army Corps of Engineers, New Orleans District.

Dredging the Mississippi River–Gulf Outlet (December 9, 1959). US Army Corps of Engineers, New Orleans District.

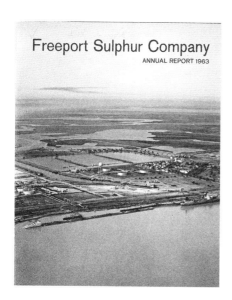

Freeport Sulphur Company operations in Plaquemines Parish (1963). Freeport McMoRan.

Fats Domino at home in the Lower Ninth Ward (1960). *Ebony* Magazine / Smithsonian National Museum of African American History & Culture.

Flood in the Lower Ninth Ward after Hurricane Betsy (September 11, 1965). US Army Corps of Engineers, New Orleans District.

President Lyndon B. Johnson surveys New Orleans from Air Force One after Hurricane Betsy (September 10, 1965). LBJ Library photo by Yoichi Okamoto.

Betsy Flood Victims (September 1965). Wisconsin Historical Society, WHS-68872.

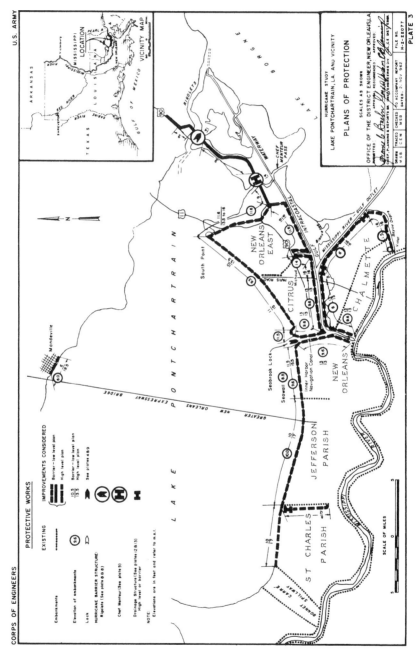

Lake Pontchartrain and Vicinity Hurricane Protection Project "Plan of Protection" (1962). US Army Corps of Engineers.

Breach in the Industrial Canal (August 30, 2005). Vincent Laforet/Associated Press.

Angela Perkins cries, "Help us, please!" (September 2, 2005). Brett Duke/The *Times-Picayune*, via the *New Orleans Advocate*.

Louisiana State Police officers patrol in New Orleans (September 2, 2005). Brett Coomer/Associated Press.

President George W. Bush surveys New Orleans from Air Force One after Hurricane Katrina (August 31, 2005). White House photo by Paul Morse.

Sign on St. Charles Avenue, which reads, in part, "looters will be shot" (September 1, 2005). Bill Haber/Associated Press.

House in Chalmette, painted with message that reads, in part, "use this to fill MRGO!" (November 2005). Infrogmation/Wikimedia, GNU Free Documentation.

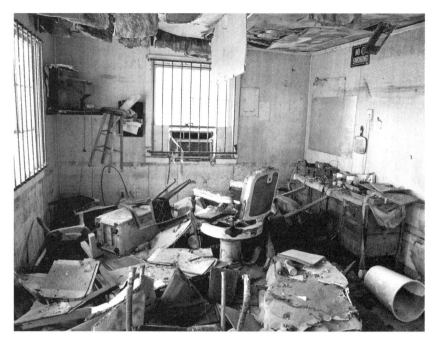

Looking Glass Beauty Salon in the Lower Ninth Ward (May 2006). Maura Fitzgerald.

ACORN members at City Council meeting (May 2006). Maura Fitzgerald.

Pamela Mahogany protests in front of the St. Bernard housing project (June 2006).
Maura Fitzgerald.

Mardi Gras Indians parade in front of the B. W. Cooper housing project
(March 2008). © Andy Horowitz.

Empty lot near the Industrial Canal floodwall (March 2009). © Andy Horowitz.

The Greater New Orleans Hurricane and Storm Damage Risk Reduction System (2014). William Widmer/Redux.

PART II

ON SEPTEMBER 1, 2005, ANGELA PERKINS MADE IT TO THE CON-vention Center. When she finally reached what was supposedly a shelter of last resort, nobody was there to offer help. Perkins dropped to her knees, closed her eyes, and cried, "Help us, please!" She summoned the attention of the people around her, each as desperate as the next, and led them in a chant: "Help us! Help us! Help us!" Three days after Hurricane Katrina made landfall and the levee system collapsed, most of New Orleans was underwater. Hundreds of people had drowned. The survivors remained in terrible danger, after days without food or water, their strength fading in the blistering heat. Perkins had floated to the shelter on a mattress with only the clothes she was wearing and a pair of slippers. In the days since, she had soiled her pants and lost her slippers. She had not slept. "We was dirty, we was stinky, we was sick, we was dehydrated," she recalled. "We was—what do they say?—traumatized."[1]

The next day, Perkins's picture was on the front page of the *Times-Picayune*, under a huge headline drawn from her plea: "HELP US, PLEASE."[2] The image of her despair shot around the world, one in a barrage of emblems from the ongoing catastrophe: People stranded on roofs, some waving American flags, others white towels. People wading through floodwater. People marooned on highway overpasses. Babies wilting in the relentless sun. Bodies floating face down. Roofs arrayed like tombstones in the dark water. Pitiful images of a failed state.[3]

A year later, in August 2006, Perkins was 500 miles away, living in San Antonio, Texas. She was happy to have a job as a cashier at a parking lot, making nine dollars per hour, "something I never earned in New Orleans," she said. Although her thoughts often turned to Louisiana, she did not consider returning home. It was impossible. The Department of Housing and Urban Development had boarded up the Magnolia Street Housing Project, where Perkins had lived her entire life. Before the storm, her neighbors in the Magnolia had called Perkins "Big Seven" because she had raised seven children there. In June, the federal agency had announced it was going to tear the Magnolia Projects down.[4]

By one way of thinking, Perkins's displacement had little to do with Hurricane Katrina. Her apartment had not washed away.[5] The federal policy of demolishing large public housing developments, called HOPE VI, was not a response to the storm, but rather dated to 1992. Another New Orleans development, the Saint Thomas Projects, had already seen the wrecking ball before the storm. On the other hand, the decision to demolish the Magnolia Projects, along with New Orleans's three other remaining large public housing developments, was difficult for many to imagine absent the circulating mass of wind and rain that passed over Louisiana on August 29, 2005. "We finally cleaned up public housing in New Orleans," Louisiana Congressman Richard Baker announced a few days after the hurricane, referring to how people like Perkins, her children, and her neighbors had been exiled from their homes. "We couldn't do it, but God did," Baker added.[6]

Whether or not he believed, literally, in divine intervention, by subsuming canal building, coastal erosion, climate change, metropolitan subsidence, failed levees, mandatory evacuation, and decades of local, state, and federal housing policy into the mystifying proclamation that "God did it," Baker's statement was one of many from policy makers who claimed that Katrina's consequences were propelled by forces beyond human control, rather than by their own self-fulfilling prophecies.[7]

It is true that when the levees broke, water flowed from the Gulf of Mexico into metropolitan New Orleans according to the force of gravity. But nothing else occurred with the same disinterested logic. Racial and economic inequalities, endemic in Louisiana before the flood, widened after—but not because of some inexorable implications of where the water settled. Rather, social arrangements before the flood and policy decisions after created possibilities for some and foreclosed them for others.

4 DO YOU KNOW WHAT IT MEANS TO MISS NEW ORLEANS?

HURRICANE KATRINA, AUGUST–SEPTEMBER 2005

A SERIES OF SPECTACULAR GOVERNMENT FAILURES DEFINED THE catastrophe in Louisiana. The local, state, and, most of all, the federal government proved unable to provide the basic protections that most people believed to be their right as citizens of the United States and their due as members of the human family. The Army Corps of Engineers proved unable to engineer a hurricane protection system that protected against hurricanes. The Regional Transit Authority proved unable to transport people across the region. The Federal Emergency Management Agency proved unable to manage emergencies. The New Orleans Police Department proved unable to police themselves, let alone New Orleans. The National Guard proved unable to guard the nation. The Commander in Chief proved unable to command.

Nobody wished for these failures, but many had worked hard to produce the circumstances that brought them about. By the early twenty-first century, the ideology that Leander Perez had advocated and financed had become, in many ways, the reigning philosophy of American conservatives. The Dixiecrats had been obsessed with extracting oil, combating Communism, hamstringing the federal government, cutting taxes, and securing white supremacy. Now these pursuits suffused the American state. The crusade for oil led to the war in Iraq, which stretched the military thin. Anti-Communism, recast as anti-terrorism, led to the Department of Homeland Security, which had little concern with New Orleans's well-known vulnerabilities, but commanded much of the federal apparatus that was meant to protect against them. Withering attacks on federal action led to a crisis of federal legitimacy. Tax cuts led to weak social programs and a depleted commonwealth. The pursuit of white supremacy led many white people to see African Americans as foolish, undeserving, violent, and criminal. Refracted through a blinding faith in the morality of the so-called free market, a belief in white supremacy also led many to blame victims for their own misfortune.

The hurricane called Katrina began, as the National Hurricane Center described it, as "the interaction of a tropical wave, the middle tropospheric remnants of Tropical Depression Ten, and an upper tropospheric trough."[1] The causes and consequences of the disaster that took the storm's name, however, had begun decades earlier. They endured long after the storm clouds cleared.

THE STORM, THE FLOOD, AND THE RESPONSE

Somewhere off the coast of the Bahamas, the wind began to spin in the direction of a clock running backward. On August 24, the World Meteorological Organization consulted a predetermined list and named the tropical storm "Katrina." On August 25, Katrina's sustained winds surpassed seventy-four miles per hour, making it the fifth Atlantic hurricane of 2005. On August 26, Hurricane Katrina entered the Gulf of Mexico. By early Saturday morning, August 27, its winds had increased to 115 miles per hour. On the Stafford-Simpson Hurricane Wind Scale, Katrina was a Category 3 hurricane, and the winds continued to strengthen.[2]

Governor Kathleen Blanco declared a State of Emergency in Louisiana. She wrote a letter to George W. Bush requesting that the president declare a State of Emergency as well, which pursuant to the Robert T. Stafford Disaster Relief and Emergency Assistance Act, would enable the White House to offer "direct federal assistance for work and services to save lives and protect property."[3] Officials in St. Bernard and Plaquemines Parishes issued mandatory evacuation orders.[4] At five o'clock Saturday night, New Orleans Mayor Ray Nagin also declared a State of Emergency and urged people to evacuate, as he had before Hurricane Ivan the previous summer. Nagin may have been reluctant to issue a mandatory evacuation order because of how many New Orleanians lacked the means to comply: evacuating is expensive, and more than a quarter of the city's population, approximately

131,000 people, lived in poverty. Evacuating also challenged elderly people and people with disabilities.[5]

Saturday evening, the National Weather Service issued a hurricane warning for New Orleans and reported that the storm could reach Category 4 status the next day.[6] Max Mayfield, the director of the National Hurricane Center, called Nagin and Blanco, "to make absolutely sure that they understood how serious the situation was."[7] By six o'clock Sunday, August 28, Katrina reached Category 5 status, meaning its winds were gusting at 160 miles per hour.[8]

At ten o'clock Sunday morning, the National Weather Service issued a dire bulletin, warning that Hurricane Katrina was likely to cause "human suffering incredible by modern standards." Writing from the National Weather Service office in Slidell, Louisiana, meteorologist Robert Ricks predicted "devastating damage." Ricks, who had lived through Hurricane Betsy in the Lower Ninth Ward, wrote, "Most of the area will be uninhabitable for weeks . . . perhaps longer." He forecast an apocalypse. "At least one half of well constructed homes will have roof and wall failure," and "all wood framed low rising apartment buildings will be destroyed," he wrote. "High rise office and apartment buildings will sway dangerously . . . a few to the point of total collapse. . . . All windows will blow out. . . . Airborne debris will be widespread. . . . Persons . . . exposed to the winds will face certain death if struck. Power outages will last for weeks."[9]

An hour later, at eleven o'clock Sunday morning, Nagin announced that the storm surge was likely to "topple" the levee system, and called for a mandatory evacuation, the first in the city's history.[10] Louisiana's "contraflow" plan was in effect, making most interstate highway lanes one way away from New Orleans and the coast. Approximately 1 to 1.2 million Louisianians fled the metropolitan area in 430,000 cars, filling the one-way interstates. Ninety-two percent of the 67,000 people living in St. Bernard Parish, and 97 to 98 percent of the 27,000 people living in Plaquemines Parish evacuated.[11] Probably 75 percent of New Orleanians evacuated in advance of the storm, while some 130,000 people remained in the city. For people unable to leave, Nagin opened the Superdome as a "refuge of last resort." By Sunday night, approximately 10,000 people, many using city buses, had taken shelter there.[12]

Hurricane Katrina made landfall at 6:10 a.m. Monday, August 29, just outside of Empire, Louisiana, at the town of Buras, in Plaquemines Parish. The storm was weaker than predicted. It landed in Louisiana as a Category 3, with maximum sustained winds of 126 miles per hour. As the storm moved north, it veered to the east. Hurricane Katrina's eye missed New Orleans by approximately twenty miles. The National Weather Service concluded that in the city, Hurricane Katrina was a Category 1 or Category 2 storm. The sustained winds probably never rose above eighty miles per hour.[13] The storm surge retained the power of a larger hurricane, and caused horrific damage across the Mississippi Gulf coast, but in New Orleans, the winds did not topple high-rise apartment buildings or hurl cars through the air. In Washington, DC, the Director of Homeland Security Michael Chertoff, whose purview included the Federal Emergency Management Agency, believed that New Orleans had "dodged the bullet."[14]

But the levee system crumbled.

Over the course of Monday morning, August 29, the Mississippi River–Gulf Outlet and the Intracoastal Canal funneled Hurricane Katrina's storm surge toward the eastern side of the city, and water flooded into St. Bernard Parish and New Orleans East. Floodwalls failed on the east side of the Industrial Canal and water flooded into the Lower Ninth Ward. Floodwalls failed on the west side of the Industrial Canal and water flooded into the Upper Ninth Ward. Floodwalls failed on the London Avenue Canal and water flooded into Gentilly. Floodwalls failed on the 17th Street Canal and water flooded into Lakeview. Over the next two days, water continued to flow through as many as fifty levee breaches, spreading out across the city, "filling the bowl," until gravity's work was done, and the water level in New Orleans and St. Bernard matched the water level in Lake Pontchartrain. Many flooded areas were above sea level.[15]

The failure of the Lake Pontchartrain and Vicinity Hurricane Protection Project put nearly 77 percent of New Orleans and essentially all of St. Bernard under water. In New Orleans, approximately 372,000 people's homes saw some amount of water, out of a total population of 485,000; 23,672 homeowners would later describe their houses as "more than 51 percent destroyed." In St. Bernard Parish, 65,000 people's homes—nearly 97 percent of the parish's residents—were directly affected by flooding. Storm surge flooded vast stretches in neighboring parishes too. In Plaquemines Parish, 11,000 people's homes flooded, nearly half of that county's population. In Jefferson Parish, another 181,000 people's homes saw water. All told, in Louisiana alone, nearly 634,000 people were "acutely impacted by flooding."[16] At least 800,000 people had been displaced.[17]

The homes that flooded constituted the city built after New Orleans began its expansion beyond the highest ground near the Mississippi River in ear-

nest during the first decades of the twentieth century. Some of the neighborhoods that flooded had long been home to privileged citizens, while other
neighborhoods were sites of enduring disadvantage. In some cases, the demographics of the flooded neighborhoods had changed dramatically over
time. To be sure, the homes of New Orleans's wealthiest residents, in the
French Quarter and the Garden District, stayed dry. But upper middle class
whites in Lakeview, middle class African Americans in Gentilly and New
Orleans East, working class African Americans in the Lower Ninth, working
class whites across the St. Bernard Parish line in Chalmette, and the rich
white people living across the Jefferson Parish line on the exclusive streets
of Old Metairie, all relied on the same interconnected system of levees, floodwalls, drainage canals, and pumps.[18] When the infrastructure failed, they
were all imperiled. The New Orleans that flooded was the metropolis financed by the Federal Housing Administration and the GI Bill; it was the
city fueled by oil and gas and built for cars and commuting; it was the city
of single-family homes. It was not primarily poor New Orleans or rich New
Orleans, nor was it white New Orleans or black New Orleans, that flooded
during Katrina. It was twentieth-century New Orleans.[19]

For the people who did not evacuate, the flood was hell.[20] Likely well more
than a thousand people died in Louisiana as water rose across the state.
Scholars with the Centers for Disease Control and Prevention (CDC) and
the Louisiana Office of Public Health estimated 971 "Katrina-related deaths"
in Louisiana and 15 deaths among Katrina evacuees in other states. Of these,
682 died in New Orleans, 157 in St. Bernard Parish, and 42 in Jefferson Parish.
Half of Louisiana's victims were 75 years old or older; 51 percent were black.
Seven people died at the Superdome, 14 at the airport, 10 at the Convention
Center, 103 at nursing facilities, 192 in hospitals. The largest number—317
people, according to CDC estimates—died in their homes. Three hundred
and eighty-seven people drowned. Two deaths were reported as homicides,
and 4 as suicides. The authors described their study as "conservative," and
suggested an "upper bound estimate of 1,440" Katrina deaths. Because of the
scale of catastrophe, there will never be a definitive accounting.[21]

The majority of the dead were African American. Of the 682 New Orlea-
nians in the state's official casualty count, 459 were classified as African
American, and 196 as white. These disproportionate impacts reflected the
city's racial composition: African Americans represented 67 percent of
New Orleans's population, and 67 percent of New Orleans's flood victims.
In St. Bernard Parish, African Americans represented 7.3 percent of the

population and, with twelve African Americans counted among the casualties, 7.6 percent of the parish's flood victims. A similar equivalence held in Jefferson Parish.[22]

Angela Perkins survived. She rode out the storm in her daughter's third-floor apartment in the B. W. Cooper public housing development in Central City, along with thirteen members of her family. At first, it was fun to have everybody together. "We were just laughing," she remembered. Then the wind picked up, and things got scary, but after several hours, the storm passed, and the wind calmed down. The trouble started once Perkins left her daughter's home.

After braving flooded streets to get to the Superdome, Perkins and her family were turned away and sent to walk another two miles to the Ernest K. Morial Convention Center, where she joined thousands of others. It was hot. There was no electricity. The plumbing did not work, and the bathrooms quickly became unbearable. There was no food. There was no water. There were no police officers or relief workers in sight. Some people huddled together. Others fought. "There was the stench, the boredom, the anxiety, the discomfort, and the crushing feeling of helplessness," a reporter wrote. A man stuck at the Convention Center with Perkins thought, "It was as if all of us were already pronounced dead."[23]

Like tens of thousands of other Americans, Perkins did not see meaningful help from any level of government for four days after the storm. "We need everything you've got," Governor Blanco told President Bush on Monday, August 29, the day the hurricane made landfall. Michael Brown, the former commissioner of the International Arabian Horse Association whom Bush had appointed FEMA director, assured Blanco that FEMA would send 500 buses to New Orleans the next day to enable an evacuation.[24] But no buses came Tuesday. Bush wrestled Blanco for control of the National Guard, a political dispute between a Republican president and a Democratic governor over the mechanics of federalism that delayed the response of a federal government already hollowed by anti-statist divestment and stretched by wars in Afghanistan and Iraq, in a presidential administration that had subsumed emergency management into a broader anti-terrorism focus and appointed an unqualified crony as director of FEMA. No buses came Wednesday, either. The White House released a photograph of Bush peering out of the window of Air Force One as it flew over Louisiana, carrying the president back to Washington, DC, from his vacation in Texas. The image was meant to suggest the president's concern; instead, it became a symbol of his distance from the emergency. It was not until Thursday morning, September 1, that buses finally arrived to evacuate people from the Superdome. But Perkins and thousands of other people remained stranded at the Convention Center and elsewhere across the city. At Memorial Hospital, on Claiborne Avenue, fifty-two patients lay waiting in a hot and dark intensive care unit.[25]

In a televised interview on Friday morning, September 2, Michael Brown told a reporter that he had only learned about the thousands of people at the Convention Center the day before. "How is it possible," the reporter, Soledad O'Brien, demanded, "that we're getting better intel than you're getting?" Later that day, in a radio interview, Mayor Nagin begged the White House to, "get off your asses and do something, and let's fix the biggest goddamn crisis in the history of this country."[26] Buses finally arrived to evacuate the Convention Center on Saturday morning, September 3.[27] Forty-five of the intensive care patients at Memorial Hospital died before help arrived there, some of their deaths possibly hastened, or caused, by their doctors' efforts to ease suffering with palliative drugs.[28]

At a press conference in Mobile, Alabama, on Friday, September 2, Bush praised Brown—"Brownie, you're doing a heck of a job," he said—even as people remained in New Orleans, waiting for help a full week after the hurricane made landfall. The anger was palpable. Homeland Security Secretary Michael Chertoff replaced Brown with Coast Guard Vice Admiral Thad Allen as director of hurricane relief operations, and Brown resigned on September 12.[29]

A shocked national audience watched what appeared to be not only the failure of government to safeguard citizens, but a collapse of the social order. Media outlets summoned stereotypes with deep cultural histories to imply that while white people faced the emergency as self-reliant, rugged individualists, black people were devolving into criminal, savage freeloaders. A pair of photographs that circulated on the internet, for example, showed New Orleanians wading through chest-deep floodwaters, carrying bags. The first, distributed through the Associated Press, depicted a black man. The caption said he had been "looting a grocery store." The second photograph, taken for Getty Images, depicted a white man and a white woman; its caption said they were photographed, "after finding bread and soda from a local grocery story."[30] White people "find," the comparison suggested, but black people "loot." Blinded by racial assumptions about vulnerability, many media reports elided the presence of white people altogether. "Almost all of them that we see," said CNN anchor Wolf Blitzer on September 1, "are so poor, and they are so black"—even though many of the abandoned flood victims were white.[31]

Soon, reports of atrocities began to stream from the flooded city. "The situation in New Orleans, which had seemed as bad as it could get, became considerably worse yesterday," the *New York Times* reported on September 2, "with reports of what seemed like a total breakdown of organized society." "On the dark streets, rampaging gangs take full advantage of the unguarded city," CNN reported. "It is a state of siege." Reports of people looting stores swelled into stories of snipers shooting at police, which festered to accounts of outright savagery. A Fox News anchor reported, "looting, fires and violence. Thugs shooting at rescue crews." An MSNBC reporter asserted, "People are being raped. People are being murdered. People are being shot. Police officers being shot." On September 3, a *New York Times* columnist wrote, "America is once more plunged into a snake pit of anarchy, death, looting, raping, [and] marauding thugs." On September 6, on Oprah Winfrey's national television program, New Orleans Police Chief Eddie Compass said "We had little babies in [the Superdome] . . . some of the little babies getting raped." Nagin told Winfrey that in the Superdome, people were "in an almost animalistic state . . . watching hooligans killing people, raping people." The *Huffington Post* ran an article asserting that, "black hurricane victims in New Orleans have begun eating corpses to survive."[32]

The stories were not true. "Ninety-nine percent bullshit," is how a National Guardsman who was in the Superdome later described them. Instead, the rumors reflected a belief, evidently widely shared, that the social order was a thin veneer, and that impoverished African Americans could quickly descend into a Hobbesian state of nature.[33] Yet the opposite was true. "Ninety-nine percent of the people in the Dome," the Guardsman who was there asserted, "were very well behaved." Other National Guard members who were at the Superdome and the Convention Center echoed that assessment. What they actually saw, they said, challenged their racial prejudices. "Some of these guys look[ed] like thugs, with pants hanging down around their asses," a Guardsman recalled, "But they were working their asses off, grabbing litters and running people" to the medical triage area at the Superdome, once one was finally established. The Orleans Parish District Attorney later reported that there were four confirmed murders during the week following the storm, including one in Perkins's place of refuge, the Convention Center, and none at the Superdome. For comparison, in 2004, New Orleans averaged more than five murders per week.[34]

Nonetheless, authorities responded to the false rumors of atrocities as if they were true. It was a deadly misappraisal. On August 31, Governor Blanco ordered the police and National Guard to suspend their search and rescue mission and instead focus on restoring order in the city. At a televised press conference, Blanco stood with members of the National Guard and announced, "They have M-16s, and they're locked and loaded." The governor declared, "I have one message for these hoodlums: These troops know how to shoot and kill, and they are more than willing to do so if necessary, and I expect they will." The threat was echoed at the local level. Warren Riley, the New Orleans Police Department's second-in-command, instructed officers to "take the city back."[35]

Licensed to kill, and believing that savage gangs had besieged the city, New Orleans police officers shot at least nine people during the week after the storm. On September 1, a police officer shot Keenon McCann as he helped to distribute water to flood victims from a Kentwood Springs bottled water truck on the Claiborne Avenue overpass. Police say McCann brandished a pistol; no pistol was recovered from the scene. On September 2, a police officer shot and killed Henry Glover, a thirty-one-year-old father of four, then another officer set fire to Glover's body and dumped it over a levee. On September 3, a police officer shot Danny Brumfield in the back, outside of the Convention Center, where the forty-five-year-old man had taken refuge with his family after their home in the Ninth Ward flooded. The officer who shot him said Brumfield was attempting to stab him with a pair of scissors; members of Brumfield's family, who witnessed the shooting, said he was trying to flag down the officer for help. No scissors were recovered from the scene. On September 4, police responded to reports of an officer shot near the Danziger Bridge over the Industrial Canal. When they arrived, the police officers shot six unarmed people, and two of them died: James Brissette, a seventeen-year-old boy, and Ronald Madison, a forty-year-old man who was mentally disabled. Madison was shot five times in the back. No weapons were recovered from the scene. All of these people were African American. When some people nearby got in a scuffle, Perkins said a police officer at the Convention Center forced her to her knees and pointed a gun at her, too. "Made us look like animals," she said. "Like we deserved whatever was happening to us."[36]

Police outside the city treated New Orleanians as a contagion to be quarantined. They hardened the racial geography of the metropolitan region, using their power to focus the effects of the flood on African Americans in the city. Police officers stopped people from walking across the Mississippi River on the Crescent City Connection bridge into the unflooded Jefferson Parish suburb of Gretna. Some reports suggested that police fired warning shots over the heads of the would-be evacuees. A week later, the Gretna City Council passed a resolution supporting the police. "This wasn't just one man's decision," Gretna's mayor announced of the move to prevent flood victims from taking refuge there. "The whole community backs it." Officials in St. Bernard Parish similarly were reported to have tried to keep New Orleanians out, by piling cars across roads from Orleans Parish. There were two roads between the Lower Ninth and St. Bernard, and one was named for Leander Perez, who had led the fight for segregation in the parish. It was fitting that on the street that bore his name, people built physical roadblocks that reaffirmed the boundaries between city and suburb.[37]

Where officials saw a threatening underclass, many African Americans trapped in the city perceived a different kind of disorder: they saw government officials abusing their power and abdicating their responsibility. "This is criminal," Malik Rahim, a former Black Panther, wrote in a September 2 dispatch from Algiers, his New Orleans neighborhood on the West Bank, that was shared widely. African Americans were the victims of incompetence, he argued, not perpetrators of violence. "People are dying for no other reason than the lack of organization." Trains or buses could have evacuated everyone from New Orleans before the storm, he asserted, but now guards were keeping volunteers from helping. Even worse were the "gangs of white vigilantes" Rahim saw roaming the streets of Algiers. "Any young Black they see who they figure doesn't belong in their community, they shoot him."[38]

At once abandoned and attacked, African American New Orleanians came to seem, to many observers, not just victims of a horrific accident, but the newest casualties in an enduring racist assault. "George Bush," the rapper Kanye West asserted during a televised fundraiser for Katrina victims on September 2, "doesn't care about black people." The New Orleans poet Kalamu ya Salaam soon wrote "a superdome system of thought," a piece that began: "They are trying to kill us!"[39]

After four days at the Convention Center, Angela Perkins was finally rescued, carried out of New Orleans by helicopter and into a diaspora of flood survivors. The largest groups of people went to Houston and Baton Rouge, but Louisianians soon spread across all fifty states. Meanwhile, thousands of members of the National Guard began working their way through the city on a door-by-door recovery mission. After searching a house, they marked the front with an "X." In the bottom quadrant of the X, the National Guard survey teams noted, in spray paint, the number of dead Americans they had discovered inside. "It was the worst thing I've ever seen in my life," Perkins said later.[40]

The desperate days took their toll. A study of people like Perkins, New Orleans mothers with low incomes, found that nearly half exhibited "probable" post-traumatic stress disorder after the flood, and that "the prevalence of probable serious mental illness doubled." More than one in four people said they had a close friend or family member who had died.[41]

Viewed from a distance, Katrina's causes can seem so tangled that it is hard to imagine unraveling the knot—so it is important to remember that the threads always could have been braided into a safety net rather than set as a snare, thrown as a lifeline instead of tied as a noose. As the storm approached the coast, the Regional Transit Authority might have evacuated people in its fleet of public buses. FEMA might have made enough food and water ready for people who could not leave. Once the levees broke, the governor might have tasked the National Guard to protect people instead of property. The New Orleans Police Department might have focused their efforts on rescues rather than playing out a fantasy of racial Armageddon. But because of racist disregard, a failure of empathy, and basic ineptitude on the part of a government bureaucracy once imagined by many to be among the most powerful in human history, these things did not happen. That is why so many people died—among them Melvin Alexie Jr., who died of an ear infection, for want of antibiotics; Edward Starks, who died of diabetic shock, for want of insulin; and Onelia Cherrie, who died of dehydration, for want of water. For those who survived—among them Alexie's father, Starks's aunt, and Cherrie's son, who tried their best to care for their kin until the end—the trauma endured.[42]

WHAT WAS THE DISASTER?

From the beginning, what constituted the disaster named Katrina was in the eye of the beholder. The debate over the disaster's causes and consequences consumed the nation, becoming a proxy battle in the ongoing ideological war about how to account for inequality, what ought to be the proper role of government, and how to make sense of change itself.

Political ideas framed what people saw in New Orleans. Liberals perceived the flood and the anemic response that followed as manifestations of structural inequality and systemic racism; they believed that divestment had impoverished African Americans and left them especially vulnerable. For liberals, the crisis revealed the need for a robust federal commitment to rebuilding New Orleans and to developing stronger social protections across the country. For conservatives, however, New Orleans's situation suggested the opposite. The catastrophe revealed to them how dependent some people, African Americans in particular, had become on government. Conservatives understood this dependency to be, at best, a result of perverse policy incentives created by a bloated bureaucracy or, at worst, a moral failing of the lower class. Either way, the prescription was less government intervention, not more. The flood, in this view, represented a kind of market correction.

Race, especially, split how Americans understood what was happening in New Orleans. The majority of white people saw a natural disaster, a product of bad luck, perhaps aggravated by the illegitimate actions of criminal African Americans. The majority of African Americans, on the other hand, saw a racist country that had put people in harm's way, refused to help them, and then criminalized their efforts to help themselves. A national poll conducted in early September demonstrated the extent to which black and white people looked at New Orleans and saw two different pictures. Two-thirds of African Americans believed that "the government's response to the crisis would have been faster if most of the storm's victims had been white," but only 17 percent of white people agreed. About so-called looting, 57 percent of African Americans thought "people who took things from homes and business in New Orleans were mostly ordinary people trying to survive during an emergency," while only 38 percent of whites agreed. The same percentage of whites believed that "most who took things were criminals taking advantage to the situation." Seventy percent of African Americans said they had "felt angry" because of what was happening, compared with 46 percent of whites. Seventy-one percent of African Americans believed "the disaster shows that racial inequality remains a major problem in the country," while only 44 percent of whites agreed.[43]

The sharpest claims of culpability came from the African Americans, often from the Lower Ninth Ward, who called upon theories of causation that had circulated after Hurricane Betsy to assert that an unspecified government agent had bombed the floodwalls along the Industrial Canal. At a Congressional hearing in December 2005, for example, New Orleans activist Dyan French Cole told a House Select Committee investigating Katrina, "I have witnesses that they bombed the walls of the levee."[44] Conservative pundits ridiculed the idea, but historian John Barry's account of the 1927 flood—which described Louisiana Governor O. H. Simpson's order to dynamite the river levee downriver from New Orleans—became a best-seller, offering readers a historical precedent for these New Orleanians' suspicions. The charge of a levee bombing remained an idea on the fringe, but it resonated with the understanding, shared by many liberal observers, that racism had inured government officials to the needs of New Orleans's citizens, both before and after the flood. The feeble rescue effort seemed to confirm their belief that government officials, particularly in a conservative Republican administration, would treat African Americans as disposable citizens.[45]

The theory that someone had bombed the levee also offered a tangible rebuttal to the Bush Administration officials who insisted on calling Katrina a "natural disaster," implying that the catastrophe was inevitable and outside of their control. "The tragedy showed the helplessness of man against the fury of nature," President Bush argued later, thereby excusing his administration for its failure to respond adequately. After all, the logic went, how could FEMA stand up to God? Other conservatives embraced the tautological argument that the weak federal response—which was, in part, the product of decades of their work to divest the federal government of its resources—confirmed their belief that so-called big government could never do any good in the first place.[46]

Some Bush Administration officials took the exculpatory rhetoric even further, blaming flood victims for their own suffering. The Secretary of the Department of Homeland Security, Michael Chertoff, told a reporter, "Local and state officials called for a mandatory evacuation. Some people chose not to obey that order. That was a mistake on their part." Like Chertoff, FEMA director Michael Brown used the word "choice" to suggest that many New Orleanians might have evacuated but opted not to. "Unfortunately," he told CNN, the anticipated high death toll was "going to be attributable a lot to people who did not heed the advance warnings."[47]

The assertion that many people "chose" not to evacuate before the hurricane represented an argument against the concept of structural inequality. Government at all levels had invested millions of dollars to build a system of roads and bridges that enabled people with their own cars to evacuate, but it was of little utility to the approximately 132,000 New Orleanians who did not have access to a vehicle, including more than a third of African American households.[48] They would have needed a functioning regional bus or train system to evacuate. When they tried to walk out, neighboring towns blocked the roads. But language invoking choice obscured those realities, and in their place affirmed the idea that in the American system, natural forces and the "invisible hand" of the free market worked in concert to enforce a moral code that rewarded initiative and punished lassitude.[49]

On September 24, as evacuees took stock of their new surroundings across the country, trying to sort out what was possible with the $2,000 debit cards FEMA had issued to every evacuated household, Hurricane Rita made landfall in Louisiana.[50] Rita's storm surge passed through the broken levees and flooded the Lower Ninth Ward and sections of St. Bernard Parish again with as much as twelve feet of water. New levee breaches occurred in Plaquemines Parish. Because the drainage pumps remained damaged, one to two feet of floodwater sat in Lakeview and Gentilly, unable to be pumped out. The hurricane caused extensive damage across the state and delayed the ability of Katrina evacuees to return to even nonflooded parts of the region. "There is only so much we can do against the forces of Mother Nature," Lt. Col. Richard Wagenaar, the New Orleans district commander for the Army Corps of Engineers, said, premising his comments on gendered assumptions about an unruly nature. "At some point it just exceeds the capabilities of man."[51] It is not clear if the commander's statement was meant more as a defense of his agency, or a recognition of its defeat. Meanwhile, New Orleans flooded again.

BROKEN LEVEES

Why did the levee system fail?

New Orleans was supposed to be protected against a storm like Hurricane Katrina. When Congress authorized the Lake Pontchartrain and Vicinity Hurricane Protection Project in 1965, it directed the Army Corps of Engineers to build a levee system for the metropolitan region that would withstand what it called a Standard Project Hurricane, meaning, "one that may be expected from the most severe combination of meteorological conditions that are reasonably characteristic of the region." The Army Corps envisioned such a storm as "similar in intensity to the September 1915 hurricane"—which in New Orleans, roughly speaking, Hurricane Katrina was.[52] The risk had been long foreseen, and a plan was in place to address it.

But in 2005, forty years later, a plodding bureaucracy and piecemeal federal appropriations process had left the hurricane protection system unfinished. What had been completed had been undermined by the failure of the Army Corps to provide adequate oversight of contractors who did not always meet design standards, to properly maintain what had been built, or to incorporate new knowledge about the region's hazards or the system's vulnerabilities. It was shot through with one knowledgeable engineer called "signs that indicate lethal arrogance," and what one federal judge described as "gross incompetence."[53] The Army Corps itself later acknowledged that, as it stood in 2005, the hurricane protection system, "was a system in name only."[54]

In proximate, measurable ways, the flood was the Army Corps's fault.[55] As Hurricane Katrina pushed water into Lake Borgne, for example, the storm surge encountered an eleven-mile stretch of levees essential to the protection of St. Bernard Parish. The section remained incomplete, standing several feet shorter than plans stipulated. Moreover, a team of engineers working under the auspices of the National Science Foundation—called the Independent Levee Investigation Team (ILIT)—later discovered, as part of a searing forensic audit, that "an unfortunate decision had been made" to construct them largely out of "highly erodible sand and lightweight shell sand fill" dredged from the Mississippi River–Gulf Outlet, likely to save the cost of importing stronger material. The storm surge then encountered another stretch of levees abutting Lake Borgne, which were meant to protect New Orleans East. These levees too, the ILIT found, had been constructed out of "highly erodeable sands and lightweight shell sands" dredged from the nearby Gulf Intracoastal Waterway. The levees "could instead have been constructed using well compacted clay fill with good resistance to erosion," the engineers noted, which was what the Army Corps's own guidelines had called for since at least 1978. But in both cases, the levees washed away, causing neighborhoods to fill with as much as twelve feet of water.[56]

Then the Gulf Intracoastal Waterway and the MRGO funneled the storm surge into the Industrial Canal. Had the Canal's floodwalls been anchored correctly, a limited amount of water would have washed over the top of the Canal into the Ninth Ward. But the steel sheet piles that supported the floodwalls had not been set deep enough, so water seeped underneath, undermining their integrity from below. Before the water reached the top of the Canal, the concrete walls collapsed in two places. Catastrophic waves washed across the Lower Ninth and St. Bernard Parish from the west, soon merging with the flood pouring through the failed levees along Lake Borgne to the east.[57]

When the storm surge entered Lake Pontchartrain, Hurricane Katrina's winds pushed the water into the London Avenue Canal, the Orleans Avenue Canal, and the 17th Street Canal. Local and federal officials alike had long known that these three drainage canals amounted to "'daggers' pointed at the heart of . . . New Orleans," as the ILIT put it; as early as 1878, the New Orleans City Surveyor had warned that, "heavy storms would result in water backup within the canals, culminating in overflow into the city," and in the 1980s, the Army Corps had recommended building floodgates where the canals connected to the lake.[58] But the Sewerage and Water Board (the agency responsible for draining water from within the city, which controlled the canals) and the Orleans Levee Board (the agency charged with keeping water out of the city, which would control the gates) objected. They imagined scenarios where one agency wanted to the gates open and the other closed, which could prove cumbersome and potentially dangerous.[59] Instead, the Orleans Levee Board pushed for a solution that the Corps suggested was more expensive, but equally safe: lining the canals with floodwalls. In the early 1990s, the Orleans Levee Board convinced Congress to authorize the floodwalls approach and to make the necessary appropriations. The Corps began installing floodwalls on the three canals in 1993, completing them by 1999. But possibly misunderstanding their own internal technical analyses, the Corps did not adequately anchor the new floodwalls, leaving them unstable.[60] The storm surge in the London Avenue and 17th Street Canals likely never got within four feet of the tops of the floodwalls. Nonetheless, the floodwalls collapsed.[61] Water coursed through the drainage canal breaches for three days, causing the vast majority of the flooding in the city's core. (The Corps estimated 70 percent, while the ILIT estimated 80 percent.[62]) Floodwater remained in parts of New Orleans until October 11, forty-three days after the hurricane passed.[63]

On the eve of the storm, New Orleans did not have the hurricane protection Congress had authorized in 1965.[64] Nonetheless, had the Army Corps followed its own guidelines and employed the standard, contemporary best practices for what it had constructed, the most devastating levee breaches most likely would not have occurred. The flood in New Orleans and St. Bernard would have been limited to rainfall and water that washed over the tops of the levees. The Army Corps argued that without the levee and flood-wall breaches, the flood in metropolitan New Orleans would have been reduced by two-thirds, and the economic damage by half. But an analysis by the State of Louisiana Forensic Data Gathering Team—informally called "Team Louisiana"—showed that the flood would have been reduced by as much as 90 percent and that, across the metropolitan area, the average flood depth would have stayed under 2.3 feet. The ILIT reached a similar conclusion.[65]

Another problem was that for forty years, the Army Corps, and its sponsors in Congress, did not update the Lake Pontchartrain and Vicinity Hurricane Protection Project to accommodate the realities of coastal erosion, sea level rise, and metropolitan subsidence. Between 1965, when Congress authorized the Army Corps to begin construction of the hurricane protection system, and 2005, when Hurricane Katrina made landfall, the coastal wetlands surrounding New Orleans collapsed into the Gulf of Mexico at a rate of twenty to twenty-eight square miles per year, for a total of well more than 725 square miles lost to the sea (an area more than twice as large as the city of New Orleans itself, and more than thirty times the size of Manhattan). That marsh had acted as a barrier between the city and the Gulf; according to one Army Corps estimate, every two miles of marsh absorbs a half a foot of storm surge. But the marsh and the protection it had offered when the levee system was designed were gone.[66] The Army Corps's own Mississippi River–Gulf Outlet was responsible for the loss of at least thirty square miles of protective wetlands—it created a channel 2,000 feet wide for storm surges to approach the city. Nonetheless, despite widespread national awareness of the issue, the Army Corps did not adjust its plans to the new reality.[67]

In 1989, Congress had directed FEMA to consider the impact that sea level rise might have on the nation's flood vulnerability, focusing in particular on the viability of the National Flood Insurance Program. FEMA concluded that "there [was] no need for the NFIP to develop and enact measures now in response to the potential risks that would accompany increasing sea levels." FEMA did note that in Louisiana, "shoreline erosion and land loss rates are presently the highest in the country." The agency called for "special attention to the situation in Louisiana . . . in the near term," but did not describe the necessary actions. Nothing was done.[68]

Since the 1960s, metropolitan New Orleans had sunk nearly two feet relative to the water around it. In that time, global climate change had caused sea levels in Louisiana to rise nearly half a foot, while the settling of decomposing soils—and the drainage system's lowering of the water table—had caused land across the metropolitan area to subside more than one and a half feet.[69] Since it was developed in the early twentieth century, much of the city had settled two feet—and parts as much as ten feet.[70] Across Louisiana, from the 1960s through the 1980s, the relative sea level had risen at an average of nearly a half an inch per year. Locally, conditions often were even more dire. At the banks of Lake Pontchartrain, for example, New Orleans East had subsided at the rate of approximately one inch per year.[71] Subsidence meant that the Army Corps's levees effectively would be lower than plans called for. Nonetheless, the Army Corps did not factor subsidence into its construction. Instead, as Ivor van Heerden, the outspoken Louisiana State University (LSU) scientist who led the Team Louisiana investigation, put it, the hurricane protection system was "managed like a circa 1965 flood control museum."[72]

Louisiana State University fired van Heerden. He was dismissed in 2009 because, van Heerden claimed, university administrators feared his criticism of the Army Corps might imperil the lucrative grants LSU received from the agency. Van Heerden sued for wrongful termination, alleging that he had been "subjected to a multi-year campaign of retaliatory harassment after he made critical comments" about the Army Corps. LSU settled the case in 2013, after spending almost one million dollars on litigation, when van Heerden released emails showing the university indeed had pressured him to stay silent about the evidence he had uncovered of the Army Corps's malfeasance. The American Association of University Professors censured LSU for its actions against the scientist; other independent experts, and the Army Corps itself, confirmed van Heerden's analyses. Nonetheless, he did not regain his position in Louisiana.[73] No member of the Army Corps of Engineers was disciplined for the failure of the hurricane protection system.

In 2006, thousands of Louisianians filed lawsuits against the Army Corps, seeking compensation for the losses caused by the levee failures. The cases were consolidated under umbrella proceedings called *In re: Katrina Canal Breaches Consolidated Litigation*. In 2008, a district court ruled that the Flood Control Act of 1928 made the Army Corps immune to most of the suits.[74] "While the United States government is immune for legal liability for the defalcations alleged herein," the judge, Stanwood Duval, noted, using a term that refers to a kind of debt, incurred by means of a breach of trust, that cannot be discharged, even in bankruptcy, "it is not free, nor should it be, from posterity's judgment concerning its failure to accomplish what was its task."[75] The Fifth Circuit Court of Appeals upheld the dismissal in 2012, although some flood victims continued to pursue their claims until 2019, when the Supreme Court refused to hear a further appeal.[76]

Junior Rodriguez, the St. Bernard Parish President, offered a blunt assessment in the course of a long deposition. "Son," he said, "let me tell you something. . . . After what I see with Katrina, if I had my way, I'd have filed murder charges against the Corps of Engineers." Rodriguez had spent decades watching the wetlands fall away, the MRGO widen, and the Army Corps drag its heels. "Those people," he said, "murdered 127 people in my parish."[77]

IMAGINING THE FUTURE

On September 28, 2005, Mayor Ray Nagin announced that he was lifting New Orleans's mandatory evacuation order. Beginning September 30, residents could return to parts of the city that had not flooded severely, and on October 5, New Orleanians would be allowed to return everywhere—except the Lower Ninth Ward, which remained flooded. Across the city, the tap water was not safe to drink, the power remained out in some areas, and schools and hospitals were closed. The same day he lifted the order, citing the absence of any sales tax revenue, Nagin laid off 3,000 city employees, half the city's workforce. The governor had indefinitely postponed local elections, which had been scheduled for November 12. Nonetheless, Nagin declared, "New Orleans is back open."[78]

Many people lacked the means to return, but those who could find a way encountered a city in shambles. In flooded neighborhoods, houses that had floated off their foundations sat wilting in yards or on the roads—covered, along with their contents, with a putrid and often toxic mix of sludge and mold that some called a "Katrina patina." "The only description I could give you," Lee Boe told an interviewer of his house in Chalmette, "is it looked like everything melted, like a candle melts." Considering the work that lay ahead, Boe thought, "there must be something pretty powerful to want to keep you here." Like tens of thousands of others across metropolitan New Orleans, his first task upon returning was to gut his home: disembowel it of its contents and strip it down to the studs.[79]

Congress had passed several bills in the midst of the flood to finance draining the city and assist with restoring its basic infrastructure. On

September 2, 2005, Congress appropriated $10.5 billion for "immediate needs." Congress also authorized the Small Business Administration to offer low-interest disaster relief loans, as it had after Hurricane Betsy.[80] On September 8, Congress approved another $52 billion, which was apportioned across the Katrina-damaged areas of Louisiana, Mississippi, and Alabama; the bulk of the funds went to FEMA, which had been spending an average of $2 billion per day on its rescue efforts providing "shelter, food and medical care."[81] Approximately twenty-two million tons of debris had to be cleared from Louisiana alone. Much of the wreckage from across New Orleans was trucked to a new landfill in the New Orleans East neighborhood of Versailles, which Nagin opened by emergency order, infuriating the predominately Vietnamese-American community who lived nearby. Across the city, refrigerators—once full of food and now noxious albatrosses—were dragged to the street in the hopes that a garbage truck might one day appear to haul them away. Bound closed with duct tape, some of them had been transformed into mordant, curbside billboards: "SMELLS LIKE FEMA," "KATRINA YOU BITCH," "LEVEE BOARD VICTIM," "TO GEORGE W. BUSH: FUCK YOU."[82]

As the mayor lifted the evacuation order, New Orleans faced questions that stood to aggravate both the personal traumas and ideological debates that shrouded the city: What should be rebuilt? Who ought to decide? The flood's devastation—the necessity of doing *something*—gave rise to competing visions of the future. These visions, in turn, drew on competing understandings of history, and competing ideas about how change happened.

Some argued that New Orleans should not be rebuilt. Others believed that New Orleanians, victimized by failed federal infrastructure and a botched rescue effort, had a so-called "right of return." Some framed the debate over the future of New Orleans as a struggle of rational science against irrational emotion, or economics versus culture. Still others perceived a racial conflict of white against black. Many agreed with President Bush who, on September 15, in a televised speech from an empty Jackson Square, had asserted, "there is no way to imagine America without New Orleans, and this great city will rise again." But even those who agreed that New Orleans must rise again held wildly divergent ideas about what kind of city ought to rise. As the *Times-Picayune* columnist Lolis Eric Elie told an interviewer, "The stuff you want to change ain't the stuff I want to change."[83]

The first prominent visions of New Orleans's future imagined the city's obliteration. On September 2, before the city had been evacuated, Dennis

Hastert, the Republican House Speaker, had called for New Orleans to be demolished. "It looks like a lot of that place could be bulldozed," he told a reporter. On September 6, the *Washington Post* published a geophysicist's editorial asserting that a "quantitative, science-based risk assessment" revealed the city's ultimate failure to be inevitable. "Should we rebuild New Orleans, 10 feet below sea level, just so it can be wiped out again?" the professor, Klaus Jacob, asked. "It is time," he concluded, "to constructively deconstruct, not destructively reconstruct."[84]

Deeply encoded in the disaster idea is the belief that physical destruction creates the possibility of social transformation. Malik Rahim, for example, told an interviewer that, "no other city in America [has] been given this opportunity." The former Black Panther's "this is criminal" email had helped to inspire the Common Ground Collective, a grassroots effort of volunteers in the Ninth Ward to provide health care for flood victims and, later, to help gut flooded houses. When Rahim imagined New Orleans's future, he perceived the prospect of a progressive utopia: a city with a high minimum wage and universal health care, encircled by restored wetlands, and freed from fossil fuels.[85]

While the disaster-as-opportunity idea prompted visions of solidarity and social responsibility for some, it inspired fantasies of elite control for others. "The first rule of the rebuilding effort should be: Nothing Like Before," the *New York Times* columnist David Brooks wrote in a September 8 essay. Brooks shared Rahim's sense of opportunity, but not his idea of what to make of it. "Most of the ambitious and organized people abandoned the inner-city areas of New Orleans long ago," Brooks continued, drawing on discredited theories about an African American culture of poverty. "If we just put up new buildings and allow the same people to move back into their own neighborhoods, then urban New Orleans will become just as rundown and dysfunctional as before." When Barbara Bush, the president's mother and the former first lady, visited evacuees at the Houston Astrodome, she remarked, "So many of the people in the arena here were underprivileged anyway, so this is working very well for them."[86]

Other writers were even blunter about their desire to create a new New Orleans devoid of many of its former residents. "The hurricane drove poor people and criminals out of the city, and we hope they don't come back," a New Orleans realtor told a reporter in early September. "The party's finally over for these people . . . and now they're going to have to find someplace else to live." A wealthy white resident of unflooded Uptown told the *Wall*

Street Journal, "Those who want to see this city rebuilt want to see it done in a completely different way: demographically, geographically and politically."[87]

Embracing a capitalist ethos that lionized so-called free market solutions to social problems, influential policy makers proposed plans to fracture communities, asserting that New Orleanians would be better off as putative free agents. "Shouldn't we be insuring the people, not the place?" Harvard University economist Edward Glaeser asked, for example. He proposed giving flooded New Orleanians lump sum payouts or vouchers to encourage them to move elsewhere. "Perhaps, if significant funds are given to New Orleans residents to help them start life anew in some more vibrant city, then there will be a silver lining to Katrina after all."[88]

The notion that clouds have silver linings—that catastrophes of death and loss may be redeemed by the changes they set in course—was, for many Americans, an article of faith. This faith resonated with a Christian theology of sacrifice, but in its modern American incarnation, it represented, most of all, a capitalist belief that progress comes through a process of "creative destruction." It was a belief that change is natural, inevitable, and synonymous with progress; it was the conviction that a better future will emerge from the rubble of the past. And it seemed to fit the present moment particularly well, perhaps because when the economist Joseph Schumpeter coined the phrase "creative destruction" in 1942, he had embedded it within a hurricane metaphor. "The perennial gale of creative destruction," he wrote, "incessantly revolutionizes the economic structure from within, incessantly destroying the old, incessantly creating a new one." Creative destruction, Schumpeter asserted, "is the essential fact about capitalism."[89] The idea of creative destruction encouraged people to embrace disasters as necessary, if painful, cosmic acts of discipline: as acts of God's invisible hand.

The promise of creative destruction resonated, too, with the hopeful insistence that the disaster had created a blank slate. New Orleans "reverted almost to a state of nature—or at least as close to one as we are ever likely to see," a pair of scholars wrote, for example, and "the opportunity to start over provides a chance to do better." It was a common frame, and one that required a highly articulated ideological apparatus. It took some work, after all, to perceive a blank slate when 113,000 New Orleanians' homes had not flooded at all; and even in flooded areas, the water had done nothing to wash away the property rights, legal obligations, institutional affiliations, community connections, family bonds, cultural traditions, and other affective ties that linked people to place. Rather than wipe the slate clean, the flood had deposited another layer of memories onto the stratigraphy that defined home.[90]

"The question facing all of us," Lance Hill, a New Orleans activist wrote, "will be, 'In whose image will New Orleans be reconstituted?'" Suncere Shakur, who hurried to New Orleans from Washington, DC, to join Malik Rahim at the Common Ground Collective—one of thousands of volunteers who began traveling to Louisiana to gut houses, provide health care, and aid flood victims in other ways—feared Katrina was likely to incite "gentrification on steroids," with developers profiting on the displacement of African Americans. On October 9, members of the Hot 8 Brass Band came home from Baton Rouge, Atlanta, and elsewhere in the diaspora to lead the city's first second line since the storm—a jazz funeral for Austen Leslie, a chef who had died after evacuating to Georgia. Behind the band, someone carried a sign that read, "We won't bow down. Save our soul."[91]

While activists warned that private actors might plot to prevent African Americans from returning to New Orleans, key federal officials described it as a *fait accompli.* As Secretary of the Department of Housing and Urban Development, Alphonso Jackson had as much power as any other single person to shape the city's future. "Whether we like it or not," he told a reporter on September 25, "New Orleans is not going to be as black as it was for a long time, if ever."[92]

5 REBUILDING THE LAND OF DREAMS

2005–2015

THE FLOODED CITY HAD PRESENTED A COMPARATIVELY SIMPLE problem: how to get people out of the water. But once the water was drained, the moldy city with a flood line snaking its way about the eaves posed a murkier set of political, economic, and moral challenges: how to reconstitute a place long distinguished, at once, by its poverty, violence, vulnerability, neighborliness, creativity, and love. "Every day we are faced with difficult choices," the writer Kalamu ya Salaam observed. "Everyday, we ask ourselves what is this New Orleans we want to save."[1]

A decade after the flood, it was clear that African Americans, the poor, and others with less access to power had lost many of the battles over the future of the city, debates which had often seemed to pit progress against history, economics against justice, the people who claimed to represent the city's best interests against the people who claimed to represent its soul.[2] They had not lost for lack of struggle. When the Bring New Orleans Back Commission presented a plan that would have prevented people from some of the city's lowest-lying and largely African American neighborhoods from rebuilding, for example, a widespread revolt helped to ensure the shape of the city would stay as it had been. But when the Housing Authority of New Orleans announced its intention to tear down the city's public housing developments, as when Louisiana State University closed Charity Hospital, the Board of Elementary and Secondary Education dissolved the Orleans Parish public school system, or Congress lowered the standard of flood protection it authorized for the region, an uncoordinated but powerful set of actors overwhelmed the New Orleanians who took to the streets, and the courts, to advocate for stronger social protections.

The contests over the future of housing, health care, education, and flood protection each turned on the same fundamental question: whether to restore or reorder metropolitan New Orleans. In doing so, they grappled with the logic of US disaster policy. Most welfare programs are redistributive, funneling tax dollars down the income curve in order to reduce inequalities. Disaster relief is different. Most disaster relief programs seek to restore inequalities, not mitigate them. The goal is to reestablish the status quo ante and uphold the preexisting order. Welfare policy may provide housing to the homeless, for example, but a person who was homeless before a flood is not eligible for a disaster relief grant to build herself a house afterward. If she applied, her application would be discarded as illegitimate. She might even be arrested.[3] Conceiving of disasters as extraordinary accidents, recovery policy usually is designed to return things as they were before.

The suite of post-Katrina policies did not just restore existing inequalities, however; these policies often magnified them. Consider a comparison between two neighborhoods on opposite margins of the city: Lakeview and the Lower Ninth Ward. Lakeview is on the city's west side, bordering Jefferson Parish and the 17th Street Canal. The Lower Ninth is on the city's east side, bordering St. Bernard Parish and the Industrial Canal. Before the storm, both low-lying neighborhoods were home to nearly precisely 19,500 people each, although Lakeview's population was 95.6 percent white, and the Lower Ninth's population was 95.6 percent black. The median household income in Lakeview, $49,500, was roughly 50 percent above the Louisiana average; the median household income in the Lower Ninth, $20,000, was roughly 40 percent below it.

On August 30, the day after the levee failures, Lakeview and the Lower Ninth were both under water. Looking down from above, there would have been little to distinguish one archipelago of roofs from the other.

A decade later, however, there was no mistaking which place was which. The racial demographics of the neighborhood had not changed much since before the storm: in 2015, Lakeview remained 90 percent white, and the Lower Ninth remained 90 percent black. But economically, the wealthy were wealthier, and the poor were poorer. The median household income in Lakeview had increased to $77,000, or more than 70 percent above the state average, while the median household income in the Lower Ninth had fallen compared to inflation, to just under $23,000, or 50 percent below the state average. Even more dramatic was the basic fact of who had returned. Before the flood, the neighborhoods had been the same size. But in 2015, Lakeview's population was around 17,000, while the Lower Ninth's population was around 6,300.[4]

The reason that nearly 90 percent of Lakeview's pre-storm population had returned, compared to less than a third of the Lower Ninth's, is that recovery policies reapportioned the challenges the water posed, making Katrina's burden comparatively heavier for African Americans and the poor. After the flood, state appraisers found that that the average cost of home repairs was $78,000 higher in Lakeview than it was in the Lower Ninth. But in ways this chapter examines, the state's formula for calculating recovery grants benefited white people in Lakeview more than it benefited African Americans in the Lower Ninth. Thus, once the insurance companies and government recovery programs had cut their checks, people in the Lower Ninth found themselves economically worse off than people in Lakeview: the average gap between insurance settlements and recovery grants, on the one hand, and the cost of repairs, on the other, became nearly $31,000 larger in the Lower Ninth than in Lakeview.[5] In other words, even though people in the Lower Ninth started off needing less money to restore their homes, recovery programs ultimately put them in a deeper financial hole than people in Lakeview.

Looking backward, some observers thought it was natural that African Americans would be worse off. But in this case, as in others, Katrina provided an occasion for racial and economic inequalities to be sharpened and ordained by policy and practice, and only then observed—variously with sorrow or satisfaction—as if they were timeless features of the social landscape. Consider again the case of Lakeview and the Lower Ninth: the two neighborhoods saw the same water, but in one neighborhood, nine out of ten residents returned, and were celebrated as symbols of American resilience, while in the other, only three out of ten returned, while the empty homes of their former neighbors lay in ruins, festering in the national imagination. There was nothing natural about it.

SHRINK THE CITY

On September 30, 2005, the same day he lifted the evacuation order, New Orleans mayor Ray Nagin announced the Bring New Orleans Back Commission (BNOBC), which would guide the city's planning for the future. The seventeen-person advisory panel—composed of two women and fifteen men, seven of whom were CEOs and three of whom were bank presidents—was chaired by Maurice "Mel" Lagarde, a white executive with the Hospital Corporation of America, a for-profit hospital operator, whose home on St. Charles Avenue had not flooded, and Barbara Major, the African American executive director of the St. Thomas Health Services, a not-for-profit community health clinic, whose house in New Orleans East had flooded.[6] The Commission's Urban Planning Committee, chaired by local developer Joe Canizaro, a wealthy, white, Republican resident of suburban Metairie, hired the Urban Land Institute (ULI), a not-for-profit land use and real estate research organization composed largely of real estate developers—Canizaro himself, a key Nagin supporter and friend of President George W. Bush's, was a former chairman—as its consultant. "I think we have a clean sheet to start again," Canizaro told a reporter as the BNOBC got to work. "And with that clean sheet we have some very big opportunities."[7]

For many urban planners, the way forward seemed obvious: shrink the city. Katrina's lesson, in their view, was that the sprawling metropolitan region was not sustainable or safe. With the hurricane protection system in shambles, prudence dictated that Katrina's flood line ought to define the limits of development. The planners assumed a technocratic posture, but underlying it often was the fear that it would be inhumane to encourage people to return to places that were, demonstrably, unsafe to live. Underlying their answers, too, was the sense that New Orleans's twentieth-century metropolitan expansion represented capitalist growth run amok, that Katrina was, as the *New York Times* put it in an editorial, "Nature's Revenge," and that planners' strong hands were necessary to bring the city back into balance.[8]

The planners believed the shape of the new New Orleans ought to look much like the shape of the city a century earlier. This was ULI's key determination, and it seemed to be the consensus view of the first people to return, full time, to the city. At a November 14 town hall meeting with ULI, which more than 200 people attended, the "resounding refrain," according to the *Times-Picayune*, was "learn from our history." In other words, "use the original footprint of the city—along the Mississippi River and its high ridges—as a guide for land use." This may have seemed a particularly attractive idea to the people present because, as one observer noted, they "resided on those same 'high ridges' they recommended for prioritization." Canizaro, whose position empowered him to ambitiously reimagine what was possible in New Orleans, nonetheless told a reporter that it was inevitable that "poor folks don't have the resources to go back to our city. . . . So we won't get all those folks back. That's just a fact."[9]

Two weeks later, on November 28, when ULI presented its preliminary recommendations to the BNOBC, it proposed that the city privilege neighborhoods that had not flooded. The team of consultants divided New Orleans into three "investment zones," according to the extent of flood damage. Zone C comprised the riverfront areas that had not flooded. ULI urged (in the words of a written report subsequently released in January) that, "Whether for initial economic recovery, historic preservation, temporary housing, or other short-term benefits, activity in this zone should move forward . . . with all haste." Zone B included sections of the city that had suffered varied amounts of damage, and ULI encouraged a block-by-block approach; the consultants imagined that residents from the most devastated areas might relocate here. Investment Zone A, amounting to roughly a quarter of the city, included the neighborhoods that had suffered the greatest damage: the entire lakefront from Lakeview through Gentilly and New Orleans East, and much of the Lower Ninth Ward. In these areas, the ULI cautioned, "great care must be taken to work closely with residents to determine the exact patterns of reinvestment necessary to restore and create a functional and aesthetically pleasing neighborhood." The ULI suggested that this zone should explore "open-space allocations for wetlands, recreational parks, or open-water retention systems."[10] The language was circumspect, but the implication was clear: ULI was suggesting not rebuilding parts of the city's hardest-hit areas soon, if ever.

African American political leaders rejected the idea of depopulating black neighborhoods so they could serve as flood control infrastructure for rebuilt white neighborhoods. Representatives of the places shaded into Zone A lashed out at the concept of shrinking the city. We are "not going to be shoved to the back of the bus," asserted Councilwoman Cynthia Willard-Lewis, who represented much of eastern New Orleans and the Lower Ninth. By alluding to the civil rights movement, Willard-Lewis signaled that she saw the plan as a racist affront to her constituents. Councilwoman Cynthia Hedge-Morrell, who represented Gentilly, viewed the plan as a "proposal to eliminate our neighborhoods from New Orleans."[11] "Take out of the report that the east [New Orleans East] isn't coming back," former state representative Sherman Copelin, a resident of the upscale Eastover subdivision, told the ULI consultants at the November 28 meeting. "We don't need permission to come back!" he asserted. "We are back!" Prioritizing areas that had not flooded seemed to them a perverse approach. Responding to the criticism, Nagin promptly announced his intention to "rebuild all of New Orleans," raising questions about his commitment to the planning process he had initiated.[12]

Opposition to the ULI plan grew as word of it spread, and a growing chorus of New Orleanians insisted on rebuilding the entire city. On December 15, the New Orleans City Council passed a resolution, sponsored by Willard-Lewis and Hedge-Morrell, asserting, "it is the intent of this Council to ensure that all neighborhoods be included in the timely and simultaneous rebuilding of all New Orleans neighborhoods," and initiated its own redevelopment planning process focused specifically on flooded areas. At a Council meeting on January 6, 2006, Council President Oliver Thomas asserted, "To say you're not going to fix this community or that community, you're not honoring the dead." The next day, former New Orleans Mayor Marc Morial insisted the solution was a stronger hurricane protection system. "With Category 5 protection, every neighborhood can be rebuilt," he said at a speech in New Orleans East. Morial, then the president of the National Urban League, rejected "the false premise" of a "reduced footprint" and called for "equity planning in the redevelopment of all neighborhoods." Flood protection in New Orleans, Morial claimed, was an all-or-nothing proposition: there was no way to protect some, but not all, neighborhoods.[13]

Calling for so-called Category 5 protection resolved a conflict at the heart of the most widely shared liberal assessment of New Orleans. Assuming that Katrina's flood line encircled mostly poor, African American citizens, many liberals blamed systemic inequality (variously described as racism, capitalism, or environmental injustice) for herding America's most vulnerable people into its most hazardous places. From this perspective, justice demanded public policies that would help disadvantaged people move to higher ground. But the nascent rebuilding plans seemed to sacrifice African Americans for the safety of whites. And from that perspective, justice demanded public policies that would help African Americans return home. Critics did not always acknowledge that returning home would mean returning to those very same, still dangerous places. Nevertheless, a restoration of the promise of 1965's Lake Pontchartrain and Vicinity Hurricane Protection Project—public works big and strong enough to protect everyone—could resolve the ethical paradox, if there was any way such a system could be built. And this was a problem that neither Congress, with its appropriating power, nor the Army

Corps of Engineers, at work trying to construct temporary repairs, had yet begun to tackle. The insistence that the challenges heralded by rising seas and sinking land would not be balanced on African American backs thus represented a revolutionary position, but one that could easily become a deferral to the blithe hope that engineering might solve the problems that politics could not.

Regardless, the BNOBC adopted the ULI's proposals to shrink the city. The Commission's Urban Planning Committee released what it called an "Action Plan for New Orleans: A New American City," on January 11, 2006. The BNOBC's plan imagined spending $4.8 billion on a new light rail line connecting the airport to the Central Business District. It also proposed a new medical complex with a neuroscience facility, new school buildings that doubled as community centers, homes raised on pilings in some flooded neighborhoods, and other homes cleared and given over to green space—transforming neighborhoods into parks and wetlands that could contain floodwater in the future. The BNOBC called for every neighborhood in the city to engage in a citizen-driven planning process to gauge former residents' desire to return, and to complete their plans by May 20, 2006. In the meantime, the BNOBC advised the city "not to issue any permits to build or rebuild in heavily flooded and damaged areas": in other words, to declare a moratorium on work in flooded neighborhoods. The BNOBC proposed a budget of approximately $18.5 billion, with $12 billion dedicated for a "Crescent City Recovery Corporation." Resonant with a bill then under consideration in Congress, the agency would be empowered to buy damaged homes from flooded neighborhoods. "As a last resort," the BNOBC proposed, the Corporation should also have the power of eminent domain. In other words, despite Nagin's earlier assurances, the BNOBC seemed to be advocating the abandonment of much of the city. If residents wanted to return, they had four months to find a way to reclaim their neighborhoods. If they failed, a new, quasi-public agency would have the power to seize their homes.[14]

The BNOBC plan included a map of proposed new parks and urban wetlands, which the *Times-Picayune* edited and published on the front page of the next day's paper. Six shaded green dots covered large sections of Broadmoor, Gentilly, the Lower Ninth, and New Orleans East, representing "approximate areas . . . expected to become parks and greenspace." Predominantly white and wealthier Lakeview, some noted, was not slated for green space, even though it had flooded catastrophically. "Mama," Elaine Tobias yelled to her seventy-five-year-old mother Doris, when she saw the plan on the internet while staying in Baytown, Texas, far from their flooded home in New Orleans East, "they plan on putting a greenway on your house."[15]

The *Times-Picayune* quickly endorsed the "responsible" plan, even as it acknowledged that it would lead to the "death of [some] neighborhoods." The BNOBC's proposal, in this view, represented an implicit acknowledgment that the pre-Katrina city had been unsafe and unsustainable.[16] New Orleanians who saw their neighborhoods disappear behind the green dots on the *Times-Picayune*'s map, however, were "furious." At the meeting unveiling the BNOBC's proposal, they called the plan "'audacious,' 'an academic exercise,' 'garbage,'" and "a no-good, rotten scheme."[17]

Some understood the plan as a racist plot—the return of urban renewal, as it was sometimes criticized, in the 1960s, as "negro removal." "If this plan goes forward as it is, many people's worst fears about our African American heritage and population will come true," asserted an official from the New Orleans Preservation Resource Center. Suncere Shakur believed that white elites were "using Katrina as an excuse to move their agenda . . . pushing black people of out their homes and their communities so they can sell their land off to the corporations." He had a point: in a study reported in the *New York Times,* a sociologist suggested that if the city adopted the BNOBC plan, New Orleans stood to lose half of its white—and more than 80 percent of its African American—residents.[18] Race, again, moderated how people understood the problem. In a survey of 2,500 Louisianians conducted later that spring, 63 percent of African Americans said it was "extremely important" that New Orleans "return to its pre-hurricane racial mix," compared to 25 percent of white people. Fifty percent of white people said it was "not at all important."[19]

The threat of what came to be known as the "green dot plan" galvanized New Orleanians, black and white—those who had managed to return, and those who remained in the diaspora—to respond with an explosion of neighborhood-level organizing and activism. "All hell broke loose," as one Broadmoor resident put it. Neighbors organized associations and advocacy groups, sometimes with crucial support from the Association of Community Organizations for Reform Now (ACORN), the national working-class coalition that had 9,000 members in New Orleans. They put up signs in front of their flooded houses: "Broadmoor Lives!" "I am coming home! I will rebuild! I am New Orleans!" The city population swelled on weekends, with people driving in, from wherever they were exiled, to work on their houses.[20] Bertha Irons, living temporarily in Lafayette, Louisiana, came back to

Gentilly to plant flowers in front of her flood-ravaged house. She wanted her neighbors to know she was coming home. She told her husband, "we're going to give some hope and inspiration to this block." Father Vien Nguyen, pastor at Mary Queen of Vietnam Church in eastern New Orleans, began organizing his parishioners because, "our right to return [has] been impinged upon by people who have no right do so. In fact, no one has the right to do so." "There is no 'they,'" Jerrelyn Madere realized. "You know, 'When are "they" going to fix my house? When are "they" going to give me permission to come home? When are "they"'—there's no 'they.' It's us."[21]

The surge of activism pushed Nagin to abandon the BNOBC's recommendations and to commit to rebuilding the whole city as it stood before the flood. "I don't care what people are saying Uptown," he asserted in a speech on Martin Luther King Day. "This city will be chocolate at the end of the day." In his 2002 mayoral campaign, Nagin had appealed largely to white voters. But he would go on to win the 2006 election—which had originally been scheduled for March 4, until the governor postponed it, by emergency order, to May 20—with the support of approximately 80 percent of African American voters.[22]

City Hall began issuing building permits across the city without regard to flood vulnerability or proposed future plans. Once committed to this approach, Nagin's administration worked to circumvent floodplain building codes, making it easy for homeowners to appeal the damage estimates FEMA had assigned to their homes in a regionwide survey. A damage estimate of more than 50 percent came with a National Flood Insurance Program (NFIP) requirement that homeowners raise their houses, which promised to lessen the chance of future flood damage, but also could be prohibitively expensive. Arguing that the estimates had been assigned too arbitrarily, Nagin instructed City Hall staffers to try to acquiesce to homeowners who appealed, so that they would not have to do the work. Within two weeks of his "Chocolate City" speech, Nagin's City Hall began issuing up to 500 building permits per day. One City official called the process "a plan by default."[23]

Lost with the BNOBC's vision were planners' ambitions for a strong hand in redesigning the city according to what they imagined to be principles of safety and sustainability. Instead, New Orleanians embraced the hope that a stronger levee system could protect them from future storms and insisted that it was the only equitable way forward. This approach had the appeal of distilling the disaster's causes to broken levees, clarifying the culprit as the Army Corps of Engineers, and identifying the solution as Category 5 hurricane protection for the entire region. It identified the city's flood vulnerability as an infrastructure problem to be solved by levee engineers, rather than as a structural problem for urban planners. It bracketed the moral tension inherent in the struggle between a right to return home and a right to safe housing. In this view, consolidating housing onto higher ground—or enforcing a new building code that would require houses to be lifted up out of the floodplain—represented, at best, a callous affront to traumatized flood victims desperate to return home. At worst, it seemed an illegitimate extension of government power, a shadowy land grab, or a racist attempt to purge African Americans from the city.

On the surface, it appeared that New Orleans's approach to the fundamental problem of where to rebuild was basically *laissez-faire,* but the defeat of the BNOBC plan unsettles the common argument that New Orleans's post-Katrina redevelopment policies were primarily "free-market-oriented," "neoliberal," or a case study in so-called "disaster capitalism."[24] Emphasizing the influence of profit-seeking firms, or the market writ large, accounts of disaster capitalism can too readily discount the enduring power of government. In reality, local, state, and federal policies shaped New Orleans after the flood, and not in ways that are reducible to market capture on the part of some industry, or to an ideological attack on the idea of community itself. The market did not dictate that New Orleanians would resettle the full expanse of the city's twentieth-century footprint. Nor did the city's wealthy elite; indeed, this class—previously the mayor's most influential allies—lobbied for just the opposite approach, calling for limits to growth (perhaps now that such limits would not affect them personally). But they failed, because citizens seized the democratic process to oppose them. Advocating their commitment to home and to self-determination, an African American- and labor-led coalition of neighborhood-based groups forced City Hall to authorize and enable their vision of rebuilding the whole city. This was less disaster capitalism than democracy.

Disaster capitalism, as a theory of patterned change, also struggles to account for the continuities between pre- and post-flood political economic arrangements. Just as the idea of disaster can reify the idea of a stable status quo ante, the concept of disaster capitalism—a sudden turn toward capitalist practice, yoked to state power—can imply an antediluvian before, when government operated as a benevolent social welfare apparatus beyond the reach of the market. No such situation ever existed in the United States, let alone in New Orleans. Capitalism did not blow into the city with the storm. Ever since European colonists dispossessed indigenous people of their homeland, financed their exploits with a currency speculation scheme known as the "Mississippi Bubble," and brought enslaved Africans by ship and coffle to labor in their fields, factories, and bedrooms, capitalism—in its historically contingent, racialized, and gendered formations—has influenced who lived in Louisiana, and where. It is therefore difficult to identify a sudden shift in the behavior of the city clerks who went busily about lowering damage estimates in order to restore the sprawling shape of the city as it had stood in 2005. They were engaged in a venerable process when they worked to speed some people's way home. There were continuities, too, in how government action ultimately slowed, or stopped, the way home for others.[25]

THE FEDERAL GOVERNMENT'S ROAD HOME

The federal government's defining role in the rebuilding process came, first and foremost, by what it elected not to do. In September 2005, Louisiana Senators Mary Landrieu and David Vitter introduced the Louisiana Katrina Reconstruction Act, a $250 billion bill that would have committed the federal government to transformative action on a scale comparable to Franklin Roosevelt's Works Progress Administration. But critics dismissed the proposal as "brazen," and the bill never came up for a vote.[26]

Then, in November 2005, the Congressional Black Caucus introduced the Hurricane Katrina Recovery, Reclamation, Restoration, Reconstruction and Reunion Act of 2005, which would have authorized an "unprecedented response" to the challenges in Louisiana as the beginning of a "renewed and sustained effort to eradicate poverty in the United States" by 2015. Observing "how poverty can make it impossible for people to respond in ways necessary to protect their own interests," the Congressional Black Caucus proposed to repay flood victims for all of their economic losses, and also to increase, by billions of dollars, federal appropriations to programs in health, welfare, and education. The bill attracted ninety-four cosponsors, but never came up for a vote.[27]

Similarly, in November 2005, the House Committee on Financial Services marked up the Hurricane Katrina Recovery Corporation Act of 2005, which would have created a $30 billion recovery corporation, authorized to buy out entire neighborhoods it deemed unsafe or nonviable. The bill had been introduced by Baton Rouge Republican Richard Baker in October, and was subsequently endorsed by Nagin, Louisiana governor Kathleen Blanco, and Louisiana's Congressional delegation. By the early winter, members of the Bring New Orleans Back Commission had assumed that Baker's bill would pass; indeed, it was the policy mechanism they had in mind when they imagined putting a recovery corporation with the resources to reshape the city at the center of their redevelopment plan. In the words of New Orleans City Council member Jay Blatt, the so-called Baker Bill seemed to offer New Orleans's only chance to avoid "becoming a Wild West of opportunistic house-flippers and fly-by night developers who will create an incoherent hodge-podge of a city." Nonetheless, on January 25, 2006, the White House's liaison for the Gulf Coast recovery effort, Donald Powell, argued that the bill "put government in the real estate business" and needlessly "add[s] another layer of bureaucracy." Without support from the White House, the bill never came up for a vote.[28]

Although the appropriations Congress did make were unprecedented in size, they represented only a fraction of what Louisiana's Congressional delegation believed the state needed. In response to Hurricane Katrina (and Hurricane Rita, with which it was combined in most bills), Congress would ultimately appropriate $120.5 billion. Of that total, approximately $75 billion was dedicated to emergency relief, rather than rebuilding. And this amount was split among Texas, Louisiana, Mississippi, Alabama, and Florida.[29]

Then a dense screen of subcontractors filtered away much of the federal money before it reached New Orleans. Major corporations, including Shaw and Bechtel, secured large government contracts for crucial emergency tasks such as removing debris, securing tarps to roofs, or supplying temporary housing. These companies then hired second tier subcontractors, which hired their own third tier subcontractors, which then subcontracted yet again. Sometimes five or six corporate layers took a cut of the federal money, putatively for administration, oversight, or other bureaucratic management. The primary contractors refused to disclose how much they paid their subcontractors, but reports suggested that the rivers of federal money leaving Washington often barely trickled into New Orleans. One debris removal contractor testified at a Congressional hearing, for example, that while the federal government paid the primary contractor $23 per cubic yard hauled, the local firms doing the work only received $6 a yard. An auditor from the Army Corps—to which FEMA itself subcontracted the contracting process—confirmed that prime contractors regularly "showed markups for management, overhead, and profit ranging from about 17 to 47 percent of the subcontractor's costs." "Obviously," even the conservative Republican State Representative Steve Scalise acknowledged at the hearing, "the taxpayer is not getting the best deal."[30] Public efficiency and private profits were difficult goals to reconcile, because a totally efficient system of delivering public funds to individuals would have yielded no private profits at all.[31]

That tension was pronounced in what became the state's central intervention in the recovery: the housing assistance program called the Louisiana Road Home. Congress allocated $13.4 billion for longer-term rebuilding in Louisiana. The money came in the form of Community Development Block Grants (CDBG), emergency appropriations that Congress approved on December 30, 2005, and June 15, 2006.[32] Louisiana directed $7.5 billion of its CDBG funds to aid citizens whose homes had been damaged or destroyed. (In November 2007, after Democrats became the majority party, Congress appropriated an additional $3 billion to Louisiana for this purpose.[33]) Governor Blanco issued an executive order to create a new state agency, called the Louisiana Recovery Authority (LRA), to administer the funds.[34] She named the board's twenty-six members, whom the *Times-Picayune* classified as her "close allies, wealthy business executives, Washington power brokers, and university officials," and appointed Norman Francis, the president of Xavier University, as chair.[35] Andy Kopplin, Blanco's former chief of staff who became the LRA's executive director, described the state's effort as "the single largest housing assistance program ever done anywhere."[36]

The Road Home plan promised homeowners grants of up to $150,000 to cover their uninsured losses. As it was crafted under the auspices of the LRA over the winter and spring of 2006, and endorsed by the Louisiana State Legislature and then the federal Department of Housing and Urban Development (HUD) in May 2006, grant recipients either could choose to rebuild, or to have the state buy their damaged house.[37] One premise of the program was to compensate homeowners for the failure of the federal levee system: many homeowners lived in places where flood insurance had not been required, and standard homeowner's insurance would not cover flood damage. Whatever other insurance payouts a person might receive, though, would be subtracted from his or her Road Home grant.[38]

The Road Home's policy prescriptions shaped the future of metropolitan New Orleans in three key ways. First, the Road Home authorized and subsidized rebuilding the whole region. The shape of the city and its suburbs would be determined by how individual homeowners chose to use their grants, rather than by strict city or regional plans that directed or prevented development.[39] Second, the Road Home encouraged homeowners to stay in Louisiana. People who left the state would sacrifice 40 percent of the maximum grant. Third, the Road Home offered no direct incentives or subsidies for renters, who before the flood had represented 51 percent of New Orleans's population. The entire program was structured to support homeowners. At Louisiana's request, HUD waived the normal requirement that 70 percent of CDBG funds go to people with low and moderate incomes and instead lowered the threshold to 50 percent.[40]

The State of Louisiana subcontracted the Road Home's administration. In June 2006, Louisiana awarded the $756 million contract to a Virginia company called ICF International, which had also helped to draft the recovery plan. "The No. 1 criteria" for hiring ICF, LRA director Andy Kopplin said, "is the speed that they can get underway." "Once we get the green light," an ICF vice president asserted, "we will have boots on the ground within hours." In July 2006, within a month of announcing ICF's contract, approximately 90,000 people had registered with Road Home, out of 123,000 people whose homes the state initially estimated to be eligible. State officials predicted that homeowners would start seeing checks by late August.[41]

A year after the flood, the help many New Orleanians had been waiting for seemed to finally be on the way. It was desperately needed, because while life had returned to normal in a few parts of the city, many neighborhoods remained in dire straits. The state's official estimate was that 191,000 people—39 percent of the city's pre-flood population—had returned, but the count was sketchy, and included 52,000 residents of the West Bank; likely well under a third of flooded residents had returned.[42] Fewer than half of the city's schools were open. Entergy, the region's gas and electric utility, had declared bankruptcy. The Sewerage and Water Board's pipelines were "literally a sieve." Few city buses were running. Murder rates were surging. Hospitals were closed. The trailers provided by FEMA were laced with formaldehyde. The people who lived in them wrestled with what one man called "the horrible unending of not knowing."[43]

Despite confident announcements from the Road Home, the wait continued. By the beginning of 2007—six months after the state contracted with ICF, a year after Congress began appropriating billions for housing, and eighteen months after the flood—only 101 Road Home applicants had received grants. More than 91,500 homeowners had applied.[44] The delay prompted enormous public criticism; outspoken members of the Citizens' Road Home Action Team advocated for changes to the program, and the

Louisiana House of Representatives unanimously passed a resolution calling on the State's Office of Community Development to fire ICF.[45] Yet the company's process remained lethargic.[46]

For two years, little federal aid for permanent housing reached New Orleans. By the second anniversary of the hurricane, 78 percent of applicants across the city still had not received their Road Home grants. An estimated 68 percent of the population had returned, including residents who had not flooded, but only about 30 percent of the 100,000 former residents of New Orleans East had come home. Fewer than half of the city's schools were open. Few rental units had been repaired, and rental costs continued to climb.[47] As did the murder rate, which was already among the highest in the country. In January 2007, 5,000 New Orleanians paraded in solidarity behind the Hot 8 Brass Band—whose snare drummer, Dinerral Shavers, had been murdered—to City Hall. Some referred to it as a "March For Survival."[48]

Yet another year and a half passed before ICF could announce meaningful progress. In January 2009, the contractor reported having distributed 121,461 grants valued at $7.63 billion. The average grant was approximately $63,000.[49] Before those checks arrived, most people were able to rebuild, or they were not, because of resources they already had, or lacked, before the flood. The National Flood Insurance Program, in contrast—a federal benefit that also was administered by private companies—settled nearly all of its claims, amounting to $16 billion in payments across the Gulf Coast, by the first anniversary of the flood in August 2006; indeed, most of the 162,000 claims had been settled months earlier.[50] But for more than three years, the most significant fact about the signature housing recovery program was its effective absence.[51]

In part, the Road Home's delay was the product of a bureaucratic morass that many flood victims found nearly impossible to navigate. LRA and Road Home officials gave conflicting and incorrect instructions. Strict reporting rules, ostensibly designed to prevent fraud, were vexing. Between interviews, forms, and other requirements, one RAND Corporation study counted twelve major stages to the Road Home application. The program was so slow that some suspected ICF of purposely delaying grants. Doing so would have served the company's interests. After all, as the anthropologist Vincanne Adams observed, ICF had to "orchestrate a type of *bureaucratic failure* in order to allow profits to stay within the company long enough to raise quarterly and year-end fiscal calculations rather than being distributed downward to recipients who bring essentially no profit to the company."[52] In other words, ICF profited to the extent that it was slow to disburse grants.

One of the many Road Home requirements was that homeowners had to show clear title to their properties. This proved confounding because many people had lost that paperwork in the flood. And the rule was especially challenging for poor and African American homeowners. Mainstream banking was less accessible to them, so they were more likely to have obtained credit through lease-to-buy or other nontraditional mechanisms, or to have inherited their homes without filing for succession, and thus may never have possessed the required documents in the first place.[53]

The Road Home further discriminated against African Americans by aligning grants with a real estate market that had devalued African Americans' homes and neighborhoods since at least the Home Owners' Loan Corporation surveys of the 1930s. Up to the $150,000 maximum, the LRA capped awards at the lower of two values: the cost to repair the house, or the house's pre-storm market value. But the cost to repair many homes exceeded their market value. And because of past practices of underdevelopment and racism, the market value of property in African American neighborhoods tended to be significantly lower than that in white neighborhoods. Ninety-three percent of African American homeowners in New Orleans owned homes with a market value of less than $150,000, for example, compared to only 55 percent of white homeowners. Therefore, only 7 percent of African American homeowners were even potentially eligible for a full Road Home grant, compared to 45 percent of white homeowners.[54] In effect, even when they faced identical damage to their homes, the market value cap entitled white New Orleanians to larger Road Home grants than African Americans.

Few people got enough from the Road Home to replace the homes they lost, and the wait was excruciating for nearly everyone, but the racial disparity in resources available to rebuild was vast. Across the state, according to a comprehensive study of grants closed as of late June 2008, the average gap between the cost to repair and the amount of insurance and Road Home coverage was under $31,000 for white people, but over $39,000 for African Americans. In white, upper middle class Lakeview, the average gap was $44,000. In the mostly African American New Orleans East, the average gap was $69,000. In the Lower Ninth, the average gap was greater than $75,000. More than 90 percent of homeowners in the Lower Ninth received less in insurance payouts from all sources than the cost to repair the damage from the levee failures. More than 66 percent of homeowners in the Lower Ninth and New Orleans East came up more than $40,000 short. The average Road Home grant in the Lower Ninth was $93,401, compared to $109,777 in Lakeview.[55]

Edward and Angela Randolph faced a $190,500 gap between grants and insurance settlements, on the one hand, and what it would actually take to repair their house in New Orleans East, on the other. If the Road Home formula had been based on objective need, rather than subjective markets, the Randolphs would have been eligible for the maximum $150,000 grant. But their grant was capped at the pre-storm market value of their house, which a state appraiser estimated to be $135,000. Therefore, after deducting the amount they had already received, the Road Home offered the Randolphs only $16,650. They remained more than $173,000 short of what they needed.[56]

The Randolphs sued the Louisiana Recovery Authority. As one of five named plaintiffs in a suit brought by the Greater New Orleans Fair Housing Action Center (GNOFHAC) in November 2008, Edward claimed the LRA's formula had violated the Federal Housing Act of 1968, which outlawed racial discrimination in housing. The GNOFHAC's complaint estimated that more than 20,000 African American New Orleanians had been adversely affected by the Road Home's formula, and that the reliance on pre-storm market values had shortchanged these homeowners by over half a billion dollars. During the years the state fought the lawsuit, the bank nearly foreclosed on the Randolphs' house twice. Angela dropped out of school a few courses short of a degree in accounting. Edward had a heart attack. After a judge found that the LRA had "offered no legitimate reason for taking pre-storm home values into account," the LRA settled the case in July 2011. The Road Home made $62 million more available to homeowners still trying to rebuild six years after the flood. The Randolphs, though, got nothing.[57]

In its final accounting, the Road Home reported that it distributed 130,052 total grants across Louisiana, amounting to $9.02 billion in funds, for damage from Hurricanes Katrina and Rita. Homeowners in New Orleans received 46,920 grants, totaling of $4.32 billion, meaning the average award was approximately $92,000. In New Orleans, the vast majority of Road Home recipients opted to rebuild: little more than 1 percent, 5,264 grantees, sold their houses, and of these, only 1,570 elected to move immediately out of the state. Homeowners in St. Bernard Parish received 12,365 grants, totaling $1.06 billion, meaning the average award was approximately $85,000. In contrast to what happened in New Orleans, more than a third of Road Home recipients in St. Bernard—4,504 total—chose to sell their old homes rather than to rebuild. Across the state, 54 percent of grant funds were awarded to households with low and moderate incomes—which was approximately $1.5 billion less than the state would have been required to give such households, had Congress not lowered the standard requirement that 70 percent of CDBG funds go to people with lower incomes.[58]

The Road Home program represented a commitment to disaster relief on an unprecedented scale and enabled many thousands of people to rebuild their homes who likely would not otherwise have been able to afford to do so. But it did so in a way that encouraged people to remain in flood-prone neighborhoods, and that affirmed and widened existing inequalities. Market values offered no escape from the history of racism, but rather trapped flooded homeowners within it.

RENTAL HOUSING

The less wealth a Louisianian had accumulated before the flood, the less disaster relief programs tended to offer him afterwards—and vice versa, because Katrina relief policies were designed in ways that often required wealth to benefit. Small Business Administration loans required collateral. Tax incentives required the ability to spend in order to receive the benefit. The Road Home program made homeownership a prerequisite for the most substantial post-Katrina subsidy, and then awarded grants according to a logic that reaffirmed preexisting economic disparities in real estate values. Even Road Home subsidies nominally meant to aid renters provided aid to landlords, rather than tenants, again privileging ownership.

Indeed, the practice of restoring wealth to those who already had it, as a hallmark of Katrina policy making, was particularly apparent in the tentative steps that HUD and the LRA made to aid tenants. FEMA estimated that 48,000 units of rental housing in New Orleans had been severely damaged or destroyed in the flood, amounting to 40 percent of all rental units in the city. The LRA made no resources directly available to renters. But, as part of the Road Home, the LRA did announce plans to allocate $859 million in CDBG funds for tax incentives and interest-free loans for landlords to repair or replace 40,000 apartments. From its inception, the LRA acknowledged that "the replacement of rental housing will fall far short of the rental housing lost due to insufficient funds."[59]

The initial policy of the LRA's "Small Rental Property Program," a rebuilding subsidy for owners of one- to four-unit apartment buildings, was to reimburse owners for repairs only after their restored units were inhabited. Thus, access to the benefit required not just ownership, but substantial cash on hand, or a construction loan. In New Orleans—where many rental units were halves of so-called "doubles," in which owners lived on one side and rented the other—landlords often did not have access to such resources. This was a key reason the Small Rental Property Program failed to have a significant impact, except by its effective absence. Over the course of nearly four years following the storm, the program disbursed only 761 grants across the entire state, totaling $55.5 million. For that work, the LRA paid ICF International $41.8 million. Meanwhile, during the first year after the flood alone, rents in New Orleans increased an average of 39 percent, putting the cost of what rental housing that did exist out of reach for many former tenants.[60]

The antipathy toward renters was even more pronounced at the local level, in St. Bernard Parish, where the Parish Council executed a series of legal maneuvers to prevent former tenants from coming back or new ones from moving in. First, in November 2005, the Council passed an ordinance prohibiting the construction of new multifamily housing in the parish. Then, in September 2006, the Council prohibited homeowners from renting a single-family house to anyone, without a special permit, who was not a family member "related by blood." The ordinance not only limited rental opportunities, but effectively fixed the racial demographics of the parish, in which 93 percent of homes were owned by white people. When the Greater New Orleans Fair Housing Action Center threatened a lawsuit, the Parish rescinded the exemption for blood relatives, but it continued to limit rental housing. In September 2008, for example, the Parish Council put a moratorium on the construction of housing developments with more than five units. "You know what it's going to bring," a white St. Bernard woman told a reporter. "I'm not going to say it, but you know."[61] The GNOFHAC sued again—as, later, did the Department of Justice—accusing St. Bernard of violating the Fair Housing Act.[62] After years of appeals, the Council settled the cases in May 2013, finally relenting on its efforts to limit the construction of rental housing seven years after the flood.[63]

It is difficult to gauge the effect of St. Bernard's protracted battle to repel rental housing and, some alleged, African Americans, but data suggests that the residents who feared these changes accurately perceived what was happening around them. The share of owner-occupied housing units in the parish did fall from 75 percent, in 2000, to 54 percent, in 2010. During the same period, the parish's African American population increased, both in absolute numbers and as a percentage of the population. In 2000, 5,122 African Americans lived in St. Bernard, representing 7.6 percent of the population; in 2010, there were 6,350 African Americans, representing 17.7 percent of the population. Most likely, these new residents were drawn from the 119,076 African Americans who had been counted in New Orleans in 2000 but were absent in 2010.[64]

The African Americans who may have moved from New Orleans to St. Bernard defied not just five years, but many decades of efforts meant to divide city from suburb. Nonetheless, looking across the parish line shows how the privileges that had disproportionately accrued to St. Bernard before the flood continued to do their work, joining the suite of policies that created and magnified those differences afterward. The boundary between St. Bernard's Arabi neighborhood and New Orleans's Lower Ninth Ward lies just east of Jackson Barracks, where the name of Louisiana Highway 39 changes from Claiborne Avenue to Judge Perez Drive. The "Welcome to St. Bernard Parish" sign there is an important marker of political jurisdiction, but not topography or flood risk. After Hurricane Katrina's storm surge breached the Army Corps's levees, the sign was buried under water and impossible to see. But as time passed, the boundary grew increasingly visible. Five years after the flood, in the Census tracts abutting the parish border, the population on the St. Bernard side had fallen from 2,258 to 1,356, while the population on the New Orleans side had fallen from 5,713 to 1,919. In other words, in 2010, the St. Bernard side of the line had regained 60 percent of its pre-flood population, while the New Orleans side had regained only 34 percent. The view from the place where Claiborne met Judge Perez thus affirmed the extent to which, over time, political and economic policy, rather than topography, came to define people's circumstances.[65]

PUBLIC HOUSING

Residents of public housing may have been the most revealing casualties of post-storm policy making. Their homes survived the flood, but the social vision that supported them did not.

Public housing had long been important—and divisive—in New Orleans. The city had been among the first to take advantage of the Housing Act of 1937, an ambitious public response to the trauma of the Great Depression. New Orleans began opening segregated public housing apartments to residents in 1940, and built ten large housing projects by 1964, along with several smaller developments. By the mid-1980s, public housing was home to approximately 50,000 New Orleanians, or nearly one in ten city residents, a rate that put it ahead of many cities of similar size. When New Orleans's public housing opened, it was celebrated as an innovative and humane social support and lauded as architecture. Nonetheless, because of federal divestment and local mismanagement, and despite robust histories of community organizing and tenant activism, New Orleans's public housing developments were, by the 1970s, increasingly defined by high rates of violent crime and drug addiction, even as they continued to provide more stable housing than might otherwise have been available to their residents.[66]

By the 1990s, the Housing Authority of New Orleans's (HANO) primary goal, reflecting national policy, was the destruction of public housing. In 1996, Congress waived a long-standing requirement that any demolished public housing be replaced, unit-for-unit.[67] That same year, HANO received a federal HOPE VI grant to tear down the 1,510 apartments in the St. Thomas public housing development. After evicting some 3,000 residents, HANO began the demolition of St. Thomas in 2000, replacing it with a Walmart and 660 new housing units, 182 of which were reserved for "public housing eligible families," and the rest of which were meant to be for families with more money. Only one hundred families who had lived in the old development were able to return to the new one, which was renamed River Garden. HANO pursued similar processes of eviction and demolition at other developments across the city in the 1990s and early 2000s.[68] Of the more than 14,000 units of public housing that once stood in New Orleans, 7,379 remained standing in 2005, and only 5,146 were occupied.[69] All but a very few of the residents were African American.

After the flood, political ideology, not flood damage, imperiled what public housing remained. Compared to much of the city's housing, New Orleans's largest public housing complexes weathered the hurricane and the flood relatively well. HANO's initial inspections found only limited damage to three of the so-called "Big Four" developments, C. J. Peete, B. W. Cooper, Lafitte, and somewhat more moderate damage at the fourth, St. Bernard, which together accounted for 3,077 of the apartments that had been occupied before the storm.[70] Gloria Williams, for example, must have been relieved when she returned to her home of twenty-four years at C. J. Peete and found it had not flooded. In four hours, she and her sister cleaned up the apartment and prepared to move back in. Then HUD turned off the water and the electricity and she had to leave. Months after Mayor Nagin lifted the evacuation order for the city's other residents, the buildings remained closed. Williams and her sister were sent to a FEMA trailer park one hundred miles away, in rural Baker, Louisiana. At a later Congressional hearing, Williams referred to it as a "concentration camp."[71]

Adrift in Katrina's diaspora, former residents of public housing grew increasingly concerned. Knowing that the reigning policy consensus was to dismantle public housing—and recalling statements from Congressman Richard Baker, who had announced just after the hurricane that, "We finally cleaned up public housing in New Orleans," and HUD Secretary Alphonso Jackson, who had asserted that "New Orleans is not going to be as black as it was for a long time, if ever"—many came to believe that a plot was in place to keep them from returning home. The sense that they were under attack increased in February 2006, when City Council President Oliver Thomas invoked stereotypes of public housing residents as lazy and undeserving to argue in favor of new work requirements for residency. "We don't need soap opera watchers right now," he asserted. Gloria Williams came to believe that "HUD's plan is about keeping us from home for a long time, probably until we die." In April 2006, HANO began constructing barbed wire fences around the vacant apartment buildings. And although HANO and HUD had not yet completed an assessment of storm and flood damage, officials began to argue that the apartments were uninhabitable.[72]

In June, former residents began protesting in front of their shuttered buildings, camping in a tent city they called "Survivors Village." Armed with brooms, they threatened to break down the fence and clean up their own apartments. "You don't take a Hurricane Katrina, where people have . . . lost everything," Pamela Mahogany, a former resident, argued, "and say, 'Y'all can't come back to your home,' but everybody else, Lakeview and everybody else, they coming back." "They're trying to steal New Orleans from us," is how another former resident saw it. But many New Orleanians, white and black, wanted the projects gone. "If I could bomb it," a retired African American teacher living down the street from the St. Bernard development asserted, "I would."[73]

Public housing represented a central front in the battle for New Orleans, which continued to seem, to many in the city and afar, a referendum on America itself. The United Nations criticized the rumored plans to tear down New Orleans's projects, arguing—in a joint statement from the Special Rapporteur on Housing and the Independent Expert on Minority Issues—that their demolition "could effectively deny thousands of African-American residents their right to return to housing from which they were displaced by the hurricanes." The National Trust for Historic Preservation, too, registered its objection to demolition. Then, in June 2006, a civil rights organization called the Advancement Project partnered with Loyola Law School professor Bill Quigley, local NAACP attorney Tracie Washington, and other lawyers to file a federal class action lawsuit against HUD, on behalf of former residents, "to secure their right of return."[74]

New evidence confirmed what residents and their advocates had been arguing for nearly a year: it would be faster and less expensive to renovate the projects than to rebuild them. A licensed inspector hired by the Advancement Project surveyed 133 apartments at each of the Big Four complexes. He found that in nearly all cases, they were habitable as is, or could be made so with basic housecleaning. Indeed, HUD's "Preliminary Recovery Plan" from early June 2006 suggested that even at St. Bernard, the most damaged of the Big Four developments, repairing all units—including those closed before the storm—would cost approximately $41 million, and an "extensive modernization" would cost $131 million, compared to $197 million for demolition and new construction.[75]

Nonetheless, on June 14, 2006, HUD Secretary Alphonso Jackson announced that HUD planned to tear down B. W. Cooper, C. J. Peete, Lafitte, and St. Bernard, and to redevelop the sites as "mixed-income" housing.[76] Agency officials sought not just to make the case for demolition, but to diminish the opportunities for public debate. "It would be nice if we could by pass the public portion of the [Public Housing Agency] plan process," William Thorson, HUD's HANO administrative receiver, wrote in an email. "If there was a way to do that," the federal agent wrote of circumventing the participation of the people whom he was meant to serve, and who would be most affected, "it would be swell."[77]

In contrast, in March 2007, Maxine Waters, a Democratic congresswoman from California, introduced the Gulf Coast Hurricane Housing Recovery Act, which sought to bring former residents home, in part so that they could fully participate in the debate over their future. The bill did not foreclose redevelopment, but it did guarantee former residents a "right of return" by August 1, 2007. It also required local housing authorities to locate former residents and whenever possible, to enable them to return to the same public housing project they had lived in before they evacuated, or at least to the same neighborhood. "All we ever asked the Housing Authority for, or HUD, or anybody," Donna Johnigan, a thirty-year resident of B. W. Cooper, told Representative Waters' subcommittee, "was to give us the resources, the tools, and the funding, and let us take care of ourselves, because we have always done that." Waters's bill passed the House 302-125, with the unanimous support of Louisiana's bipartisan Congressional delegation. But Louisiana senator David Vitter—arguing that public housing was "no less deadly" than the flood itself—opposed the plan. The Senate never voted on the bill.[78]

After months of local and national debate, one procedural step remained to formally close the projects: even though HUD ultimately controlled their fate, the City Council had to issue demolition permits. On December 20, 2007, the day of the City Council vote on the permits, hundreds of people came to protest against demolition. Few were allowed in the Council's chamber. Outside, protestors chanted and yelled, "Let those people in! Let them in! This is not Germany!" Some pounded on the locked gates surrounding City Hall. New Orleans police officers sprayed people outside with tear gas and, inside the Council chamber, Tased a person who was protesting. City Councilwoman Shelley Midura called the protestors "demagogues and terrorists." "Katrina has come in and washed it away," one housing official argued, even though the projects were still standing. The Council voted unanimously in favor of demolition.[79]

That winter, nearly 12,000 people in New Orleans were homeless. Double the pre-storm number, and possibly amounting to one in every twenty-five city residents, it might have been the highest homelessness rate recorded in modern American history.[80]

Two months after the Council vote, on Mardi Gras, Jerod "Big Chief Rody" Lewis gathered the Black Eagle Mardi Gras Indians outside the boarded up B. W. Cooper housing projects, where he had grown up, and which he and his tribe still knew by its old name, Calliope. For decades, the Calliope had been the Black Eagles' "coming out spot" on Mardi Gras morning. Since 1981, when his father Percy "Big Chief Pete" Lewis passed, Rody had been the man to lead them out the door. This year, in their handmade suits of beads and feathers, the Black Eagles assembled beyond the fence, and Rody began the day with a prayer. He knew the Calliope would soon be gone. But for now, the empty buildings stood as hollow monuments to the vision of a right to housing for all, a vision from the New Deal that had endured in New Orleans, if fitfully, for much of the twentieth century. In the streets, Big Chief Rody's signature song went, "Noooo, no, no, no, no no, Joe don't want to go." Perhaps those were among the words he chanted that Carnival morning, as the Black Eagles ritually ushered their old homes, and the claim on the city they once embodied, into the mythic realm of memory.[81] The federal government's primary post-storm intervention in the lives of New Orleans's public housing residents was to finance the destruction of their homes.[82]

In August 2011, six years after the hurricane, only around 200 families who had evacuated from the Big Four housing projects had moved into the new apartments built on the old sites. Of the 3,077 families who had lived in the Big Four before HUD closed the projects, only about half, 1,512 families, had made it back to New Orleans altogether. HUD had never been able to locate more than 600 families whom it evicted from the Big Four. Gloria Williams, who had cleaned up her own apartment in C. J. Peete in four hours, finally resettled in the new development on the same site, renamed Harmony Oaks, in 2011. It was her sixth home in as many years. Compared to many of her old neighbors, she was fortunate. When Rody Lewis died, at 49, in November 2013, only thirteen families had moved into the new buildings at the place he had called Calliope, but which had been renamed Marrero Commons. The Big Chief of the Black Eagle tribe was not among them.[83]

CHARITY HOSPITAL

The fate of New Orleans's public hospital was similar to that of its public housing: the building survived the flood, but not the political contests that followed.

Charity Hospital had long been the centerpiece of Louisiana's system for caring for indigent citizens. Louisiana law made any state resident who was "medically indigent or medically needy . . . eligible to be admitted for any form of treatment," at one of the state's eight public hospitals, of which New Orleans's was the largest.[84] In the early 2000s, more than one in five people in metropolitan New Orleans lacked health insurance, and Charity—part of a Mid-City complex with University Hospital known, formally, as the Medical Center of New Orleans—was where they were most likely to receive care. In 2003, for example, Charity was responsible for nearly 90 percent of outpatient services, and more than 80 percent of inpatient services, for those unable to pay. It was also the region's only Level 1 trauma center, and the teaching site for medical students at LSU and Tulane. In a song he composed for the 250th anniversary of the institution's founding, Allen Toussaint had written, "With opened doors that never close / Where you're never turned away / 24 hours a day / Charity's always there." Founded in 1736, nearly as old as the city itself, the place seemed an enduring part of New Orleans's social fabric.[85]

But like public housing and other pieces of social infrastructure dating from the New Deal era, Charity Hospital also had long served as a fraught proving ground for debates over what the state owed citizens. For years, there had been calls for New Orleans to build a new indigent care facility to replace the twenty-story limestone tower that had housed the hospital since 1939, and to replace the centralized, state-funded vision of health care it represented.[86] Most recently, in May 2005, Adams Management, a consultant hired by LSU—which had managed Charity since 1997—had described the existing hospital as "hopelessly outmoded" because of "years of deferred maintenance, lack of reinvestment . . . and changes in privacy regulation." Adams encouraged LSU to "seriously consider" building a new facility on the other side of Tulane Avenue. The consulting firm projected that a new hospital could be complete by 2013. In the meantime, Charity remained the place where all New Orleanians could count on receiving decent health care.[87]

The hospital weathered the hurricane without significant incident, but the levee breaches caused the building's basement and first floors to flood. Because much of the facility's mechanical infrastructure, including its backup electrical generators, was located in the basement, the hospital lost electricity and running water. Evacuation was delayed, in part, because of rumors that snipers were shooting at rescue workers. Approximately 1,200 people, half of whom were patients, and half of whom were family members and staff, remained in the building without lights or air conditioning for six days. Nurses and doctors ventilated patients by hand, in shifts. The food service staff rationed food and water. When members of the Louisiana Department of Fish and Wildlife arrived on September 2 to evacuate the hospital, custodians helped to carry patients to the agency's boats. It was a searing experience, but when she left, Kiersta Kurtz-Burke, a Charity physician, expected that "we would be back in that hospital treating patients within a matter of weeks." But Don Smithburg, the chief executive of LSU's Health Care Services Division, which operated Charity, had a different idea.[88]

Federal disaster policy created a strong financial incentive for LSU to keep the building closed. The Stafford Act dictated that when the cost of repairing a damaged public building "to its predisaster condition" was less than 50 percent of the cost of replacing it, FEMA's Public Assistance Program— effectively a federal insurance program for public buildings—would pay for repair. But when the cost of repairs exceeded 50 percent of the replacement cost, FEMA would pay for a full replacement.[89] Thus, while nearby homeowners lobbied to have their damage estimates revised beneath the 50 percent threshold so they could avoid the expensive National Flood Insurance Program regulation that they raise their homes out of the floodplain, the Stafford Act thrust LSU onto the opposite side of a similar calculus: a higher damage estimate would ensure a federal windfall.[90]

The Stafford Act presented Louisiana with the possibility of securing federal funding for a new hospital. But rather than opening up a debate about the merits in terms of public health, the law narrowed it into a technical question of damage estimates. FEMA's initial assessment was that repairs would cost $23 million. LSU's initial assessment was nearly $258 million. Because LSU's figure was more than 50 percent of what Adams (which again served as LSU's consultant) calculated to be the full cost of replacing the hospital, the university was arguing, in effect, that it was due $395 million in FEMA funds.[91] Activists and others calling for Charity to reopen joined FEMA in asserting that most of the repairs LSU described as necessary predated the flood, and were a result of deferred maintenance.[92] Some Charity physicians also claimed that LSU or its agents physically sabotaged the building. They circulated photographs from late September 2005 showing the emergency room gleaming after it had been restored by the members of the Army's Joint Task Force Katrina, paired with photographs taken several months later, when the rooms were trashed. Smithburg, the LSU official in charge of Charity, rejected the charges of sabotage, and continued to assert that concerns about mold and contaminated water pipes made the building unusable.[93]

LSU's refusal to consider reopening even parts of Charity left a hole gaping in New Orleans's safety net. By early November, LSU had either laid off or furloughed 3,500 of 3,800 former employees of Charity and University Hospitals. The remaining staff worked in a tent hospital in the Convention Center, seeing approximately 500 patients per day, until February 2006, when executives there said they needed the space back to prepare for conventions that had been scheduled for June. LSU then opened a Level 1 trauma center at the Elmwood Medical Center in Jefferson Parish, and a new, temporary clinic in a former Lord & Taylor department store near the Superdome.[94] Mental health care was especially compromised. The rate of serious mental illness doubled in New Orleans during the year after the flood, while the resources available for people with mental illness fell even more precipitously. A year after the flood, one in twelve adults in metropolitan New Orleans described their mental health as "fair or poor." Nearly a quarter of people who previously had relied on Charity Hospital described their mental health as worse than the year before. The New Orleans coroner reported that the city's suicide rate had tripled.[95]

And yet, sick people had far fewer places to seek treatment. On the first anniversary of the hurricane, the American College of Emergency Physicians announced that the "number one cause for the mental health crisis" in New Orleans was the loss of Charity's psychiatric services. Before the flood, Charity Hospital had housed a forty-bed Crisis Intervention Unit, and ninety-seven beds for psychiatric patients; these did not reopen. Before the flood, 208 psychiatrists were licensed in metropolitan New Orleans; a year later, only forty-two had returned. Of those forty-two, only seventeen of those accepted Medicaid patients, and most only worked part time. "We had a large mentally ill population before Katrina," the New Orleans Police Department's crisis coordinator told a reporter in September 2006. "There wasn't much for them before, and now there is nothing."[96]

Katrina's death toll continued to rise in ways the coroner did not formally record. Rates of stillbirth increased. There were nearly 50 percent more death notices in the *Times-Picayune* during the first six months of 2006 than there had been during the same six-month stretch in 2002 or 2003. "I thought I could weather the storm, and I did," one woman told a reporter. "It's the aftermath that's killing me."[97]

As the squabble with FEMA dragged on, LSU pursued plans for a new medical center—a process that involved assembling a seventy-acre plot of land in lower Mid-City. The proposed site included a number of parking lots and uninhabited buildings, but also was home to 618 people, living in 265 housing units. The area was part of the Mid-City National Register Historic District.[98] On February 23, 2006, LSU and the Department of Veterans Affairs (VA) announced a "memorandum of understanding" that they would construct two new hospitals—a replacement for Charity, and one for the VA

Hospital, which the Department had sought to construct since 2004—as the centerpieces of a new biomedical district. Smithburg announced, "This is not intended to be your mother's Charity Hospital."[99]

Many criticized the plan. In March 2006, 150 people, organized by the activist groups Doctors Without Hospitals and the People's Hurricane Relief Fund, protested outside of Charity's shuttered doors, calling on LSU to reopen Charity. "Our patients," Kurtz-Burke asserted, "cannot wait five to seven years for a new facility to be built."[100] In April 2006, the New Orleans City Council and the Louisiana State Legislature both passed resolutions calling on LSU to reopen Charity. The State Legislature also ordered an independent assessment of the building; when it was finally completed in August 2008, it substantiated earlier claims that even a complete modernization of the existing structure would save more than $100 million, and be two years faster, compared to constructing a new building. But LSU continued to press its case, maintaining that the flood had rendered the hospital uninhabitable, and insisting that FEMA pay for the full cost of constructing a new one. In May 2006, LSU announced a preliminary plan for a thirty-seven acre, $1 billion Charity replacement.[101]

At the same time, the city and state considered replacing the Charity model altogether. In April 2006, the consulting firm PricewaterhouseCoopers—which the Louisiana Recovery Authority had hired to evaluate the state's health care system—issued a report echoing LSU's call for a new building and pressing the state to dismantle the Charity system. The consultants urged Louisiana to redistribute funding from its Charity system to private institutions, which would absorb the former patients. PricewaterhouseCoopers proposed a revolution in health care based on the claim that the private market was stable and government inherently unreliable: the Medicaid Disproportionate Share funding on which Charity depended, the consultants asserted, was "vulnerable to general economic conditions," because it relied on state tax revenues.[102] Some, including Senator David Vitter, embraced the recommendation, arguing that directing government funding for uninsured patients to private hospitals would ensure that poor people received care equal to those with insurance. The argument resonated with calls for "mixed-income" housing to replace traditional public housing. But just as critics saw calls for mixed income as veiled efforts to funnel federal funds to private developers, they similarly saw the new model imagined for serving Louisiana's poor as a way to siphon off government funding to private hospitals.[103]

LSU and the VA together formally announced the plan for a new medical complex on November 25, 2008. By that time, the Road Home had paid forty-one property owners a total of $3.2 million to restore their homes in the space the new hospitals would occupy. Wallace Thurman, for example, had already spent $50,000 to repair his flooded home on Palmyra Street. Now the city was going to bulldoze it.[104]

The debate over Charity at once focused and fractured a vast universe of concerns about New Orleans after the flood. Viewed from different angles, the constellation of agendas variously aligned with or obscured each other. LSU wanted a new hospital building, but sometimes seemed to prefer maintaining the old system of public funding for indigent care. Some conservatives wanted to rehabilitate the old Charity Hospital building, too, because it was less expensive than constructing a new building, but they wanted to replace the funding model with privatized care. Those who wanted to replace the Charity funding model split among people who believed the funds ought to be redirected as a direct subsidy to private hospitals, and those who believed the funds ought to contribute to the expansion of Medicaid insurance coverage for individual citizens. Some liberals lionized Charity Hospital as providing accessible health care for all, while other liberals saw it as an institutionalized, segregated, second tier. Some historic preservationists wanted to save the building, regardless of what might happen inside. Other advocates, including the New Orleanians who sued LSU for closing Charity without the State Legislature's approval, wanted better access to health care, regardless of where. And many New Orleanians, like those who paraded in a "second line to save Charity Hospital" in August 2009, continued to want, most of all, to see Charity Hospital restored to what it had been before.[105]

It took nearly four and a half years to resolve LSU's claim. In the meantime, Barack Obama had won the 2008 election for president, in part based on his critique of the Bush administration's inept response to the Katrina flood. In 2009, after financial markets had collapsed around the globe, Obama signed a roughly $800 billion stimulus bill, to which Senator Mary Landrieu attached a provision meant to finally resolve the Charity dispute. Her legislation created an arbitration process for FEMA Public Assistance appeals.[106] Bobby Jindal, the former Republican Congressman who won the 2008 race for governor after Kathleen Blanco retired, railed against what he called "the historic spending and expansion of government" caused by the stimulus bill. At the same time, Jindal's administration continued to lobby Congress and FEMA for hundreds of millions of dollars for the new hospital and many other projects. From FEMA's Public Assistance Program alone, Louisiana had averaged $25 million in disbursements per week from late 2007 into 2009. Those federal funds insulated Louisiana from the economic free fall experienced by many other states, suggesting the benefits of government spending. Jindal's appointee to direct the Louisiana Recovery Authority, Paul Rainwater, acknowledged in Congressional testimony, "No other state in the nation has been blessed with such generosity from Congress and the American people."[107]

On January 27, 2010, by means of Landrieu's arbitration process, the Civilian Board of Contract Appeals held FEMA responsible for what had grown to the estimated $474.8 million cost of replacing Charity Hospital. The State Legislature appropriated another $300 million.[108]

The blank slate that many prophesied Katrina would bring arrived, in Mid-City, five years after the storm, when heavy equipment cleared houses and business from the twenty-seven city blocks the new medical complex would one day occupy. "They bulldozed everything down on me when I was 80," Wallace Thurman said, after the State knocked down the house he had rebuilt. The flat expanse lay just northwest of the Charity Hospital building Huey Long had imagined during the Great Depression, which stood tall and empty.[109]

By then, in 2010, anguish and expectation juxtaposed on the streets of New Orleans as if the city itself were a hospital that had combined the waiting rooms for its cancer and maternity wards. By some measures, New Orleans had finally turned a corner. "We are no longer recovering," Mitch Landrieu announced in his inaugural address as mayor that May. "Now, we are creating. Let's stop thinking about rebuilding the city we were and start dreaming about the city we want to become." According to the 2010 Census, New Orleans's population was 343,829, or 71 percent of what it had been in 2000; it continued to grow at a rate faster than almost any other city in the country. A 2010 study suggested that of the people then in the city, 10 percent had moved since the flood—and these people were "substantially younger, more educated, more likely to be white and more likely to be renting." New Orleanians new and old rejoiced when, in February 2010, the New Orleans Saints won the Super Bowl. Tax breaks expanded after Katrina encouraged the growth of the local film industry, and some started referring to New Orleans as "Hollywood South." One booster described New Orleans as "something of a 'Cinderella' in economic development terms."[110]

But it was a "tale of two recoveries," in the words of James Perry, the director of the Greater New Orleans Fair Housing Action Center, who had run a losing campaign against Landrieu for mayor. Two in ten New Orleanians that summer said their lives were better since the storm, but three in ten described their lives as worse. Nearly 30 percent of New Orleanians lived in poverty, the same rate as before the storm.[111] New Orleans was one of America's most blighted cities, with nearly 48,000 vacant homes. Three to six thousand people lived in those abandoned buildings, and the majority them had been stably housed in New Orleans before the flood. Among the New Orleans neighborhoods with the biggest population losses were those that had once had public housing developments. In St. Bernard Parish, the population was 53 percent of what it had been in 2000, reflecting the loss of more than 31,000 former residents.[112]

There was a profound racial disparity in the city's changing demographics. The 2010 Census revealed that the African American population had decreased 119,076 since the previous Census, while the white population had decreased 22,528. Put another way, the African American population had fallen 36.5 percent since 2000, while the white population had fallen by less than half that amount, 16.6 percent. In 2000, African Americans had made up 67.3 percent of New Orleans's population; in 2010, they represented 60.2 percent.[113]

Race, too, defined how New Orleanians understood the state of the city five years after the hurricane. Forty-two percent of African Americans surveyed during summer of 2010 described their individual lives as "still disrupted by Katrina," compared to 16 percent of whites. Sixty-six percent of African Americans believed that New Orleans, as a city, had not yet recovered, compared to 49 percent of whites. Forty-two percent of African Americans said the city was a worse place to live than it had been before the storm, in contrast to 28 percent of white people. Compared to white people, African Americans were far more likely to describe themselves as "very worried" that their children would not be able to get a good education, that the levees would not protect their neighborhoods, that they would not be able to find a good job, that they could not afford a decent place to live, or that they would be a victim of a violent crime.[114]

African Americans were also much more likely to report being very worried that they would not have access to health care if they needed it—and for the years it took LSU to resolve its Charity dispute with FEMA, a wide-ranging contest over who deserved medical care, what kind, where, and who should pay for it, took place on the narrow ground of storm damage estimates. The Stafford Act transformed an encompassing debate about the promises of citizenship into a dispute about the damage wrought, ostensibly, by nature. "We didn't close the hospital," an attorney for LSU asserted, as he contended with a lawsuit filed by historic preservationists, seeking to save Charity. "It was closed by the hurricane." As was often the case, those advocating the most profound changes often disclaimed any responsibility for what they had worked so hard to achieve.[115]

Although some analysts later classified Charity's closure as another case of disaster capitalism, that ill fits a story that involves the federal and state government drawing on plans that predated the storm, in order to commit over $2 billion to the construction of two, new public hospitals.[116] Rather, the situation has hallmarks of a long-standing, if uneasy, compromise between contrasting visions: a liberal commitment to significant government spending in the public interest, and a conservative insistence that private profit and growth serve as the measures of success.

In August 2015, a decade after Charity closed, the new hospital opened with a new name: University Medical Center. The new VA Hospital opened more than a year later, in November 2016. "Is it worth the price our patients had to pay?" Peter DeBlieux, University Medical Center's interim chief medical officer, wondered aloud to a reporter, weighing the state-of-the-art building against the decade many New Orleanians had gone without a hospital at all. "That's far too complex a question for me to answer." Kiersta Kurtz-Burke was more definitive. "I'm very confident saying that people died as a result of Charity Hospital being closed," the doctor said. "They didn't die on a rooftop, they didn't die in an attic, they didn't die from drowning," she explained. "But these are people who are really victims of disaster—and of the response to the disaster, of choices that were made in the rebuilding of the city."[117]

THE RECOVERY SCHOOL DISTRICT

When George W. Bush considered Katrina from the vantage of a half decade remove from the flood, in a memoir called *Decision Points*, he filled his account with rumors and metaphors that excused his administration's failures. Katrina was a "natural disaster," a "tragedy that showed the helplessness of man against the fury of nature," wrote a man who wielded more power than almost any other in history. "No one predicted that the levees would break," he claimed in the face of many prominent examples to the contrary. After the levees broke, "chaos and violence in New Orleans" prevented rescues, because "the police force was powerless to restore order," he asserted, referencing media reports long since retracted. The former president did not describe feeling haunted by the memory of the hundreds of people who had drowned. "The worst moment of my presidency," he wrote, was when the rapper Kanye West said on television that Bush did not "care about black people." Then, after the regrets and obfuscations, the former president identified a reason for pride: the transformation of New Orleans's schools.

In his memoir, Bush described the dismantling of New Orleans's public education system, and its replacement with a confederacy of charter schools, as "the most uplifting change of all" to come from Katrina. "Public schools that were decaying before the storm have reopened as modern facilities," he wrote, and "dozens of charter schools have sprouted up across the city, offering parents more choices." Bush's organic metaphors of growth and decay implied that the changes were not the result of policy decisions, but part of a natural cycle of death and rebirth, of which the storm was the crucial agent.[118]

In reality, though, the flood and the new school regime that followed it were connected only by the rhetoric of activists who capitalized on the moment to pursue their vision of radical reform. Here is a case that the "disaster capitalism" frame might better fit. The storm did not blow away the possibility of a single, locally elected school board managing the city's schools, nor did it topple the union contracts of the thousands of people who worked in them. No feature of federal disaster policy created incentives for state officials to abandon the concept of the neighborhood school, the way the Stafford Act had prodded LSU to insist that the flood had destroyed Charity Hospital. Rather, Louisiana's post-storm experiment in school governance was thoroughly political, the product of ambitious reformers who sought to reinvent New Orleans's school system.[119]

Before the storm, the Orleans Parish school system often was classified as among the worst in the country. In the early 2000s, a majority of New Orleans's 65,000 public school students failed the state's standardized test, called the Louisiana Educational Assessment Program. "That means they are nonfunctional in today's society," declared a Republican state senator whose district included part of New Orleans. "Our children are being committed to intellectual slavery." The 2004–2005 graduation rate was 56 percent.

A federal investigation of corruption, which began in 2002, ultimately led to more than two dozen indictments for various kinds of graft and fraud within the Orleans Parish school system.[120] These high-profile problems came with caveats. For example, New Orleans's poor children disproportionately attended public schools, and standardized test scores generally are more highly correlated with their socioeconomic circumstances than they are with school quality. Similarly, no strong evidence suggested that the Orleans Parish School Board's bureaucratic mismanagement seriously affected what teachers did in classrooms. Regardless, few viewed New Orleans's schools with anything other than grave concern. The system's fiercest critics argued that the traditional district of neighborhood schools itself was a broken relic.[121]

Inspired by a national movement, these reformers gathered under the banners of school "choice" and "accountability," and called for charter schools. In 2003, school reform advocates secured the passage of a state constitutional amendment, and accompanying legislation, that authorized the state to take over so-called failing schools. The new law established a "Recovery School District," overseen by the Louisiana State Board of Elementary and Secondary Education (BESE), which could assume responsibility for schools that did not meet certain threshold "School Performance Scores," a nominally objective metric largely based on students' test scores. The bill had been hotly contested. Proponents lauded it as a tool for circumventing corrupt bureaucracies and enabling necessary structural changes, while critics saw it as a pretext for undercutting local control, attacking unions, and privatizing education. Although the law theoretically applied throughout Louisiana, it was designed and understood to apply specifically to New Orleans. As of the summer of 2005, the Recovery School District had taken over five schools from the Orleans Parish School Board and reopened them as charter schools with independent operators.[122]

After the storm, local and state officials moved quickly to transform more New Orleans schools into charters. On October 7, 2005, Governor Blanco signed an executive order announcing "emergency suspensions" of several laws regulating the creation of charter schools, including the requirement that teachers and parents vote on the transfer of an existing school to a charter operator. The same day, the Orleans Parish School Board voted to reopen thirteen unflooded schools on the West Bank, all as charter schools.[123]

Then, at the November special session, the State Legislature passed Act 35, which dramatically expanded the state's reach in New Orleans. While the existing law had set a threshold for takeover that only a few schools met, the new law classified the entire Orleans Parish school district as "Academically in Crisis," labeled any school in the district with a School Performance Score below the state average as failing, and authorized the state to take over their operations. The state quickly shifted control of 107 more New Orleans schools to the Recovery School District. "This is a silver lining and a once-in-a-lifetime opportunity," the Louisiana state superintendent asserted. Only fifteen schools remained under the purview of the Orleans Parish School Board, and eleven of them were charters.[124] The bill passed despite the objections of most of the New Orleans delegation, who argued it was inappropriate to make such drastic changes at a time when public participation was nearly impossible. Only one of the BESE's eleven members was elected by New Orleans voters, so the new law effectively silenced the local voice on the future of the city's schools.[125]

Act 35 changed the education regime in New Orleans dramatically. Before, the locally elected Orleans Parish School Board oversaw a coherent district of New Orleans schools; now, the statewide Board of Elementary and Secondary Education would have responsibility for schools that would remain largely independent of each other. Before, the superintendent set general policies that applied to all schools in the district; now, especially as the Recovery School District authorized charter operators to manage its schools, individual school principals would create policies unique to each school. Before, the school a student attended usually was defined by neighborhood; now, students would attend schools in any part of the city, so long as they were accepted by application or lottery. Before, closing schools was rare, and embedded in a political process; now, the idea of closing a school believed to be failing would be considered normal and triggered by test scores. Before, teachers had to be certified, and their employment was covered by a collective bargaining agreement with the United Teachers of New Orleans; now, teachers did not have to be certified, and would not be unionized. Reformers were exhilarated. "I say 'Thank you, Katrina' all the time," the Orleans Parish School Board president told a reporter.[126]

The new school regime dissolved the contracts of the approximately 7,500 employees of the Orleans Parish School Board, which had been one of the city's largest employers, particularly of African American professionals. In September, the school board's employees had been placed on what was referred to, with nebulous legal significance, as "disaster leave without pay." Then, after the passage of Act 35, they were fired, although a lawsuit the teachers filed in protest delayed the effective date until March 24, 2006. The layoff notice directed those seeking to appeal their dismissal to visit the school board's building, which had been destroyed in the flood.[127]

Many saw their dismissal as yet another example of the city's dispossessing African Americans after the storm. Of the approximately 4,300 employees who were teachers, 71 percent were African American.[128] The former employees sued, claiming that their union contract had been violated, but the case dragged on without resolution. Meanwhile, as the schools began to reopen and hire new staff, former teachers were passed over: by the 2007–2008 school year, only a third of New Orleans's former teachers had been rehired within the city (another 18 percent had taken jobs in neighboring parishes.) By the fall of 2013, fewer than one of every four former New Orleans teachers were still in New Orleans classrooms. The racial impact of the turnover was significant: the percentage of black teachers fell from 71 percent in 2005 to 49 percent in 2013—and the rate continued to fall, because that year, only approximately one of every three new teachers hired was African American.[129]

In their place, absent the constraints of a union agreement or the requirement that teachers be certified, the Recovery School District and the independent operators it chartered recruited a new kind of teacher: white, inexperienced, from outside the city, and often affiliated with Teach for America. Joining a broader influx of thousands of new residents who came to work in not-for-profit organizations or otherwise to be in a place widely understood as ground zero for social reform in the United States, these new teachers had far less experience that the people they replaced.[130] During the 2004–2005 school year, 83 percent of New Orleans teachers had at least four years of teaching experience. In the 2007–2008 school year, only 46 percent of teachers did. In schools operated by the Recovery School District, 60 percent of teachers had taught for less than one year. The new teachers were also much less likely to be from New Orleans. In 2005, 60 percent of New Orleans teachers had undergraduate degrees from local colleges. In 2014, only 34 percent of New Orleans teachers had gone to college in the city.[131]

The school reform advocates lauded choice, competition, and data in ways that equated a functioning democracy with a free market. Paul Vallas, the Recovery School District superintendent, called New Orleans "the greatest opportunity for educational entrepreneurs, charter schools, competition and parental choice in America." Celebrating the perceived virtues of private enterprise cast public bureaucracy as the central challenge that children needed to overcome in order to succeed. The ideology of school reform thus reinforced a broader conservative critique of government itself.[132]

In 2014, the former teachers and staff lost their case against the school board when the Louisiana Supreme Court reversed a string of earlier rulings that had been more sympathetic to their cause. By that time, Gwendolyn Ridgley, one of the lead plaintiffs in the lawsuit, had died. After thirty-two years of teaching in the city, she had never returned to New Orleans. Ridgley's lawyer said that once she lost her job, she was unable to secure health insurance, and did not receive adequate medical care. She succumbed to cancer, at the age of 61, in 2012. Katrina's lesson, Ridgley told an interviewer before she died, was that "when you respond, make sure your responses are to everybody, not just a select group of people."[133]

Meanwhile, after several years of inconclusive standardized test results—and disputes over special education, expulsion policies, and transportation—the reformed school regime showed evidence of meaningful academic improvement. A careful study released in 2015 suggested that, along with increasing rates of high school graduation and college matriculation, the reforms had increased average student achievement on standardized tests by 8 to 15 percent (or 0.2 to 0.4 standard deviations). The study's authors reported that improvements on this scale may have been unprecedented for any school district "in such a short time."[134]

And yet, other measures of children's well-being told different stories. According to the Census Bureau, in 2015, nearly four of every ten children in New Orleans lived in poverty, which was almost twice the national average, and which represented no change from a decade before. In a survey of more than 1,000 ten to sixteen year olds in the city, conducted from 2013 to 2015, 16 percent of the children worried about having enough food to eat or a place to live. Two in every ten had met the criteria for post-traumatic stress disorder, compared to a national average of 5 percent. More than 12 percent of the children were clinically depressed. Four in ten New Orleans children had witnessed a shooting, stabbing, or beating. Eighteen percent had witnessed a murder. More than half of the children in the survey had experienced the murder of someone close to them. One in three New Orleans kids said they worried about not being loved.[135]

None of these measures was a consequence of school reform. Nor would schools necessarily be the first or best place to try to tackle the consequences of racism, poverty, violence, and the anguish that accompanies them. But by stripping the locally elected school board of its authority, jettisoning a unionized teacher corps, abandoning the idea of the neighborhood school, fetishizing "choice" and "accountability" and, in doing so, affirming the cruel optimism that most children's individual intellectual acuity could possibly empower them to surmount structural obstacles, reformers made it more difficult for citizens to perceive systemic wrongs, let alone to take collective action to right them. "With the lack of one central authority, the obstructionists cannot gain a foothold," the president of the Louisiana Board of Elementary and Secondary Education had boasted to a Congressional subcommittee in 2006, "There are too many meetings to monitor." In her written testimony, she listed firing employees, breaking the union, and making it more difficult for citizens to participate in school governance beneath the headline, "Unintended Consequences (Positive)."[136] Reform left New Orleanians with more data but less democracy.

Moreover, the rhetoric of reform valorized competition, conditioning New Orleanians, young and old, to think of themselves and their most significant institutions as engaged in a ruthless struggle, where stability was stagnation, success a numbers game, and failure an inevitable feature of progress. At the 2006 hearing, the BESE's president bragged to Congress that New Orleans now had "the most free market public education system in the country." She did not pause to consider the many ways that the desperate social circumstances of New Orleans's children were produced by the same market and market values that the new school regime aspired to emulate.[137]

THE NEW LEVEE SYSTEM

In a city rent by divisions of personal experience and political vision, this was the one principle that seemed to unite everyone: New Orleans needed a levee system that would protect it from another hurricane like Katrina. A 2006 survey found that 98 percent of New Orleanians wanted levees "rebuilt stronger to withstand a category 5 hurricane, even if that will cost substantially more." That fall, a group of women activists organized as Citizens for 1 Greater New Orleans gathered over 50,000 signatures on a petition calling for the State Legislature to reform the levee board system. The legislature endorsed their plan, and a subsequent constitutional amendment passed with 94 percent of the vote in New Orleans, again reflecting the consensus that the city needed credible flood protection.[138] The state created the Coastal

Protection and Restoration Authority to serve as a unified agency for coastal restoration and hurricane protection. "Make levees, not war," read the slogan on t-shirts and bumper stickers.[139] Without the ability to prevent another flood, all the other debates seemed moot.

At first, Washington seemed to agree. "The Army Corps of Engineers will work . . . to make the flood protection system stronger than it has ever been," President Bush announced in September 2005. Then, in December, Congress directed the Army Corps to "consider providing protection for a storm surge equivalent to a Category 5 hurricane," and to produce a plan for "Category 5 protection" within two years. But the Corps missed Congress's deadline by a year and a half. When it finally did issue its final report in August 2009, four years after the hurricane, the Corps estimated that building "Category 5 risk reduction" for metropolitan New Orleans—a string of defenses that would defend against storms that had a 1 in 400 chance of happening each year—might cost anywhere from $59 billion to $139 billion. The National Academy of Sciences, charged with peer review, criticized the Corps for not offering a plan at all, but rather a vast list of options, thousands of pages of alternatives, without a path for action.[140]

In the meantime, New Orleans faced an immediate problem: the need for flood insurance. Without flood insurance, New Orleanians would be unable to secure mortgages, no homes would be rebuilt, and any possible recovery would stop dead in its tracks. But in order to remain covered by the National Flood Insurance Program, FEMA, which administered the NFIP, would have to certify that the region was protected against a so-called "100-year storm." (Statistically, an event that has a one in one hundred chance of occurring each year has a 26 percent chance of occurring over the course of a thirty-year mortgage, and a 63 percent chance of occurring over the course of a century.) In March 2006, the White House announced that the Army Corps's initial repairs, completed in advance of the 2006 hurricane season, would not meet the NFIP standard.[141] FEMA agreed to maintain New Orleans's NFIP coverage temporarily, in anticipation of improved levees, but Bush administration officials began to hedge on their initial commitment to Category 5 protection. Instead, they offered support only for the 100-year protection necessary for the city to remain in the NFIP. The administration thus put Louisiana in a bind. The state could not afford to risk antagonizing Washington with calls for stronger levees, because it needed to maintain the federal commitment to flood insurance. In the end, the predicament forced Louisiana to accept what Mark Schleifstein, a *Times-Picayune* reporter, called a "devil's bargain": flood insurance, at the expense of meaningful flood protection. The promise of Category 5 protection drifted away.[142]

In November 2007, Congress lowered the standard of protection for metropolitan New Orleans from the 200- to 250-year level it had authorized after Hurricane Betsy, to the 100-year level.[143] The Corps had called its post-Betsy public works a "hurricane protection system," but it described its post-Katrina project as a "risk reduction system." That same month, California Representative Zoe Lofgren had introduced the Gulf Coast Civic Works Act, which would have provided federal funding for 100,000 jobs constructing public works, including creating a Conservation Corps to "focus on wetland restoration" among other flood protection projects. The bill was referred to committee, and never came up for a vote.[144] Washington had abandoned the goal of protecting New Orleans from the next Hurricane Katrina.[145]

The Greater New Orleans Hurricane and Storm Damage Risk Reduction System did attempt to address the most dangerous failings of the system it replaced. A $1.1 billion, 1.8-mile long, 25-foot tall concrete wall stretched across the Mississippi River–Gulf Outlet and the Gulf Intracoastal Waterway, designed to prevent storm surges from funneling into the city from the east. A sixteen-foot tall floodgate was designed to prevent storm surges from entering the Industrial Canal from Lake Pontchartrain. Similar floodgates crossed the 17th Street Canal, the Orleans Avenue Canal, and the London Avenue Canal, designed to prevent storm surges from entering the drainage canals; large pumps at Lake Pontchartrain were designed to enable the city to continue to drain rainwater from within the city, even when the gates were closed. The Army Corps "armored" levees across the region, covering them with grass, concrete, and other materials designed to keep them from being scoured away and collapsing, even if they were overtopped.[146] From 2005 to 2009, Congress appropriated $14.43 billion to pay for the new system.[147]

Despite these important improvements, few observers believed that the 100-year standard was an acceptable level of protection for a major city.[148] The Association of State Floodplain Managers, for example, recommended a 500-year standard as a minimum for urban areas. Similarly, the Independent Performance Evaluation Task Force—the Army Corps team that audited the 2005 levee failures—called the 100-year standard "far too risky." "We too often optimize based on immediate cost and accept short-term gains instead of long-term solutions," the engineers asserted. "This is a national cultural malady that can only be reversed if the public demands a change in policy."[149] A 2011 Army Corps study estimated that if a storm surge over-topped the levees, nearly 1,000 Louisianians would die. Looking back, in 2018, Garret Graves, the Republican Louisiana Congressman and former chair of the state's Coastal Protection and Restoration Authority, admitted to a reporter, "All along we knew that 100-year was somewhat voodoo math."[150]

FEMA formally certified the Hurricane and Storm Damage Risk Reduc-tion System as meeting the 100-year National Flood Insurance Program standard on February 20, 2014, but noted how vulnerable much of the city remained. FEMA's preliminary Flood Insurance Rate Maps, which the agency released in 2009, continued to classify many neighborhoods as Spe-cial Flood Hazard Areas, meaning they were likely to flood during a 100-year storm, and homeowners would be required to carry flood insurance to secure a mortgage.[151] Knowing that these maps could shape the city's future—dictating property values, insurance premiums, and perceptions of the city's viability—the city appealed FEMA's determination, and prevailed. In 2016, FEMA announced that flood insurance would not be required in most of New Orleans. The next year, more than 3,000 policy holders in New Orleans dropped their flood insurance coverage.[152]

All the while, the Gulf of Mexico continued to advance toward the new levees, as Louisiana's coast sank into the water. The Coastal Master Plans drafted by the Coastal Protection and Restoration Authority, the state agency charged with leading Louisiana's efforts at flood protection, reflected a crisis accelerating because of a lack of meaningful action at any level: local, state, national, or global. What the agency had characterized as a worst-case sce-nario for land loss in its 2012 plan, came to seem the state's best-case sce-nario by 2017. According to the Coastal Protection and Restoration Author-ity's analysis, even if its plan were fully funded, at a cost of over $50 billion, and succeeded in creating 800 square miles of wetlands over the next half century, Louisiana still would lose at least 400—and perhaps as much as 3,300—square miles of land in the coming fifty years.[153] Meanwhile, in St. Bernard Parish, voters twice rejected a tax increase necessary to pay for maintaining the parish's levees and drainage pumps. The increase would have cost each homeowner an average of $38.25 per year. The second time the ques-tion was on the ballot, in May 2015, the measure to protect more than 45,000 residents in St. Bernard Parish failed by 513 votes. Only 12 percent of eligible voters had gone to the polls.[154]

Back during the summer of 2007, Donald Powell, the former chair of the Federal Deposit Insurance Corporation, whom President Bush had appointed to coordinate federal recovery efforts, had talked with a reporter about the then-nascent plans for the region's new hurricane protections. "In my view, you should be able to trust the United States," Powell said. "People thought they were protected, and the levees breached. We need to bridge that trust gap. That's what these levees are about." He told the reporter that the two questions Louisianians asked him most often were, "When are we going to get Category 5 protection?" and "If another Katrina hits, are we safe?"[155] A decade later, the questions could be answered: never, and no.

THE NEXT TIME NEW ORLEANS FLOODS, MANY ARE LIKELY TO OB-serve the situation with an abundance of pity and a measure of scorn. Looking backward, they will call the city's fate inevitable. Some might think it deserved, even welcome. "Those poor people," they will say, "deciding to live where they ought not. They will be better off elsewhere."

May Katrina's history chasten such critics. What came to be known as New Orleans's "recovery" involved a decision not to even aspire for a hurricane protection system that could truly protect the city. That joined a decision to evict people from their homes in the face of a homelessness crisis, a decision to close the hospital in the midst of an epidemic of suicide, and a decision to help children by firing their parents. It extended decades of decisions that had encouraged citizens to depend on promises that their government often proved unwilling, or unable, to keep, and decades of decisions that had apportioned the state's wealth and its liabilities in perversely unequal measure. These actions made Louisiana into a place very different from the one many other New Orleanians wanted, and might have created, had they the means to do so.

The people with the most power to decide such things are rarely the ones most affected by the decisions. In the end, it seems to me that the pain our collective actions impose upon some people, followed often by the blinding insistence that their suffering was somehow fair, or natural, or inevitable, is not the cause or consequence of some external disaster. It is the disaster itself.[156]

EPILOGUE

THE END OF EMPIRE, LOUISIANA

T HE ENVIRONMENTAL PRECARITY, ECONOMIC INEQUALITY, RACIAL
enmity, political division, bureaucratic ineptitude, social trauma, and resistance to all of these things that defined much of the Katrina disaster
might have happened anywhere in the United States. Their causes were
national, and their consequences were manifested many places across the
country. But it mattered that the broken levees had been meant to protect
Louisiana. As the world peered down on the region through the hazy understanding that enveloped a place known widely but not well; as the exi-
gencies of the flood gave way to the existential crisis of land loss, and the
BP oil spill underscored the insidious dilemmas wrought by an economy
built around oil extraction, the struggle over the region's future came to
represent not only a debate over a set of public policies, but a referendum on
a way of life.

The summer of 2010, five years after Hurricane Katrina, Philip Simmons
was rebuilding his house. He knew what he was doing. At sixty-eight years
old, this was the third time he had rebuilt after a hurricane. He had started
by laying mudsills in the ground the way his great uncle Sid had taught him,
salvaging the remains of a storm-tossed church for lumber. The mudsills
braced pilings that lifted Simmons's house up into the air, higher than ever
before. The house now stood twenty-one feet above the ground. Sooner or
later, Simmons knew, this house too would be flooded or blown down in a
storm. For the time being, though, the new windows framed long views of
the strip of land and marsh in Plaquemines Parish, twenty miles from the

mouth of the Mississippi River, where his family had lived and worked since the late eighteenth century. They had come to that place when it was claimed by Spain, and remained as it was traded to France, bought by the United States, and taken, briefly, by the Confederacy. Mostly, though, Philip and his wife Gloria liked to think of the place as their own. They hoped to stay there as long as they could.

Simmons lived on the west bank of the Mississippi River, but most of his ancestors going back two centuries were born on the east bank. The family moved west after the 1915 hurricane. In the mid-1920s, the Orleans Levee Board expropriated a vast section of the east bank to create a "waste weir" flood outlet and blocked off the road south of Pointe-a-la-Hache. Then, in order to lower the threat to New Orleans during the 1927 Mississippi River flood, the governor ordered the state engineers to dynamite the levee in Caernarvon, flooding Plaquemines's east bank. Hurricanes Betsy, Camille, Katrina, and Isaac each took their turn washing away what remained of the old towns. By 2010, there was little left to recall that the Simmonses or anybody once lived on the lower east bank. But if you knew where to go, down a narrow bayou toward a few remaining oak trees, amidst the patches of solid ground where Simmons grazed cattle, you could still find the half-acre his great uncle Narcise Cosse had set aside in 1921 for Point Pleasant Cemetery. There, Simmons's uncle Sid, his brother Joe, his mother Anna Marie, and several dozen other relatives lay in an increasingly agitated rest.[1]

As he worked on his raised house, Simmons's thoughts kept turning to Point Pleasant. Like many of the people buried there, Simmons had spent his life working closely with the land and water around him. "We lived off the land, pretty much," he explained. Simmons had grown up raising farm animals, raking oysters, shrimping, crabbing, and trapping mink, otter, raccoons, and nutria rats. His uncles had taught him well. In 1959, when Simmons was sixteen, he won the state 4-H muskrat pelt grading contest. Simmons's uncles had run a shipyard and a sawmill in Plaquemines, processing ancient cypress tress they harvested with a two-man crosscut saw called a *passé-partout*. His father had worked for the Freeport Sulphur Company. At some point in their lives, all the men in his family took a stint in the oil field.[2]

Scholars have a phrase for how economies built around extracting natural resources tend to work out for local people: they call it "the resource curse." By the early twenty-first century, Louisiana had the highest concentration of petrochemical plants in the United States, and the highest rates of several forms of cancer. In 2009, the oil company BP reported $14 billion in profits, while Louisiana, where a significant portion of those profits originated, ranked seventh in the nation for the percentage of citizens living below the poverty line. Sea levels were rising faster on the Louisiana coast than nearly anywhere else on the planet.[3]

As was the case for many Louisianians, storms and rebuilding had long defined the Simmonses' lives. "Hey, I can survive, I'm a survivor," he asserted. "You see that *Survivor* on TV? That ain't nothing." But by the time Hurricane Katrina came, nature felt more unsettling than it had in the past. That summer of 2010, Simmons's yard was a jumble of tractors, bush hogs, augurs, and other heavy equipment. He was rebuilding his house out of the wreckage—or the salvage—of a church whose congregation did not return after the hurricane. He had intervened to save lumber that otherwise would have been sent to the dump. "I said, 'man, look. That wood's too good to just destroy.'" And he pointed out, "We don't have any trees left now."[4] It would be wrong to call him a scavenger, living off of the demise of others. Rather, his adaption showed what it took to survive in the context of a community that was disappearing around him.

Simmons's uncles had raised him to aspire to a kind of balance. He remembered learning that principle as a boy, going fishing. In his memory, the fish were so plentiful that he could catch speckled trout without any bait, all he needed was a white rag on a hook. "Of course, we didn't waste it. We caught what we needed," he recalled. "If we caught more, we threw them back." It was a simple precept that seemed to have been abandoned over the years. People got "greedy." "Now, some people, they want to go out there and kill them all," he rued. Growing up, Simmons's family had lived off the land. But in 2010, as he sat in a house that hovered on pilings twenty-one feet above the advancing sea, the land no longer supported him. Nearly 2,000 square miles of coastal Louisiana had disappeared over the course of his life.[5]

On April 20, 2010, in the Gulf of Mexico, eighty-five miles southwest of Simmons's house, BP's Deepwater Horizon oil rig exploded. BP had been drilling nearly 5,000 feet deep in a section of the Mississippi Canyon. As the oil began to spew, the Army Corps of Engineers opened the locks near the mouth of the Mississippi, hoping the river's current would push the oil away from shore. The oil would have poisoned Simmons's oysters and killed the pastures where he grazed his cattle, a herd he was slowly rebuilding after most of his 600 animals drowned during Katrina. Instead, the river's fresh water killed his oysters and flooded Point Pleasant Cemetery. When Simmons ferried a guest across the river to visit the cemetery that summer, he opted to stay in his boat, and gave instructions to take care when walking around in the mud. The flooding was unearthing bones. One day soon, Simmons assumed, his family's remains would be washed away.[6]

When Simmons considered Point Pleasant Cemetery and the region around it, he perceived a place caught between two great, distant powers. The first was a government that was too big to worry about local problems, harming while trying to help. The other was a corporation—the community's economic lifeblood—guilty of terrible negligence. To neither did he have any recourse.[7]

The house that Simmons was rebuilding in Plaquemines Parish, sixty-five miles downriver from New Orleans, was about halfway between the towns of Triumph and Port Sulphur, in a community called Empire. Philip Simmons was living through the end of Empire, Louisiana.

NO PLACE LIKE HOME

Before Katrina, Louisiana had the most stable population of any state in the country. Eight out of ten people in Louisiana, in 2000, had been born there. Nearly nine out of ten African Americans who lived in New Orleans before the flood had been born in the city (in Atlanta, by comparison, the rate was fewer than six out of ten.) "We all lived right here, within a mile of one another," explained a person from St. Bernard Parish, where before the flood, the nativity rate for all residents had been nearly 90 percent. "And for the first time in our life, everybody's gone. Everybody's scattered."[8] Even those who were able to return felt the places they once knew changing around them, sometimes beyond recognition.

In part because of their long family connections, people often understood themselves in terms of place, and many considered Louisiana to be a place apart from the rest of the United States. This was especially true of New Orleans. In both the local and national imagination, New Orleans was the country's well-spring of creativity, the internal rebuke to the tyranny of the Protestant work ethic. It was the putative "Big Easy" and the "birthplace of jazz," the country's libido and its id, the place *Time* magazine called "America's Soul Kitchen."[9] To be sure, these clichés had been distilled in a cauldron of racism and sexism, and served up by a corporate tourist industry that often functioned in precisely the opposite manner from the image its agents worked so hard to promote. But the stories people hear and tell about themselves become their own kind of truth. Watching the city drown made many New Orleanians feel even more attached. "We know what it means to miss New Orleans," as one man put it.[10]

When critics called for the city to be abandoned—or given over to creative destruction and remade according to the profit motive—some New Orleanians called on the city's reputation for cultural distinctiveness as a defense. After all, nobody who had chosen to live in New Orleans before the storm had done so because of the city's infrastructure or economy, Nick Spitzer asserted. The folklorist and radio producer argued that what made the "chronically broken infrastructure, often retrograde policing, weak and illicit governance, and subpar public schools . . . worth enduring . . . was the creative . . . lifestyle associated with enduring creolized cultural vernaculars of the cityscape." In a September 2005 interview with Spitzer, Allen Toussaint, the New Orleans songwriter, extended that point. He considered how he had lost his recordings, his sheet music, his Steinway piano, and everything else in his Gentilly home, but concluded that he could persist because "the spirit didn't drown."[11] Levees could save lives, but they could not make life worth living.

"Fuck you you fucking fucks," was Ashley Morris's response to those who wanted New Orleans to change. In a November 2005 blog post, Morris, a New Orleanian who worked as a computer science professor at DePaul University—commuting, weekly, to and from his job in Chicago—lashed out at those proffering visions of a new New Orleans thoroughly transformed. "I'm so glad all you Chicagoans have figured out exactly how to fix New Orleans. Look at your own nasty city and explain why you can't deal with snow other than to throw tons of salt on the road, and why you can't buy a beer for under $5." Morris had a fleur-de-lis, New Orleans's unofficial symbol, tattooed on his arm. "Fuck you, you fucking fucks," he wrote again. If New Orleans should not be rebuilt because of its vulnerability to floods, he continued, then similar logic ought to have applied to "that cesspool Chicago after the fire, that Sodom San Francisco after the earthquakes, Miami after endless hurricanes, or New York because it's a magnet for terrorists. And," he added, "fuck Kansas, Iowa, and your fucking tornadoes." He considered the diaspora of New Orleanians in Texas and Georgia. "Fuck you Houston and Atlanta. No matter how many of our residents you steal . . . you still ain't got no culture," he wrote. "One of our neighborhoods has more character than all of your pathetic cookie-cutter suburbs laid end to end." He concluded his essay, characteristically, "Fuck you, fuck you all."[12]

"All these other places are nice and stuff, but ain't nothing like New Orleans," Philip Frazier, the tuba player who founded the Rebirth Brass Band, argued in 2005. "Without New Orleans," he said, "there is no America." There was a radical potential to the way some New Orleanians theorized why they and their city mattered, because many came to see themselves as defending a vision of quality of life that could not be reduced to economic terms. Second lines, jazz funerals, Mardi Gras, and a litany of lesser holidays with their own rites of observance that transformed the civic calendar into a perennial ritual of social aid and pleasure—these offered ways for New Orleanians to make sense of the challenges they faced. Asserting the importance of New Orleans's culture was thus a way of asserting the importance of humane culture, anywhere. "What's happening in New Orleans right now is a test for the soul of America," said Donald Harrison, the trumpeter and Mardi Gras Indian. "If we say the cultural roots of this city are unimportant," he asserted, "then America is unimportant."[13]

The struggle over intangible culture could be starkly material. Like the poorly paid musicians at the front of the parades, the Social Aid and Pleasure Clubs that organized the city's second lines every Sunday found themselves celebrated from afar but seemingly under attack from the moment they returned home.[14] On January 15, 2006, approximately 300 people, some back in the city for the first time, began strutting through Tremé for the first major second line after the flood. As they moved through the streets, neighbors heard the call—the syncopated drums and propulsive horns—and thousands more people came out of their houses to join the parade, reclaiming St. Claude, Orleans, and Claiborne Avenues, presenting themselves to each other as a vision of community, restored. It was likely the biggest gathering in the city since the flood. "We exorcized Katrina," one man declared. Tamara Jackson, a founding member of the VIP Ladies and Kids Social Aid and Pleasure Club, who had helped to organize the second line, said that dancing behind the Rebirth Brass Band in her "renew orleans" shirt was "the greatest moment of my life." Then, near the end of the four-hour parade, gunshots silenced the music and left three people wounded in the street. When she heard the shots, Jackson ran toward the gunfire and found a man lying on the ground. She used her belt as a tourniquet to slow his bleeding until the paramedics arrived.[15]

Two weeks later, on January 31, 2006, the New Orleans Police Department announced that it would raise the cost of parade permits. Before the storm, clubs had paid $1,200 per parade. Now, the Police Department announced, clubs would have to pay $4,445 and post a $10,000 bond in order to cover the costs of police protection as they danced through their neighborhoods. Unaffordable to working-class club members, the new fees amounted to a punishing tax on African American creativity and public culture. Indeed, coming close on the heels of the Bring New Orleans Back Commission's proposal to turn many of the city's predominately African American neighborhoods over to green space, the new fees seemed part of a plot to deprive African Americans of their right to the city altogether.[16]

In November 2006, an alliance of clubs Tamara Jackson founded, called the Social Aid and Pleasure Club Task Force, worked with the Louisiana ACLU to sue the city and the police department, claiming the fees violated their Constitutional rights to speech and assembly. "Many members of the Clubs . . . are persons struggling to return" to New Orleans, their complaint asserted, "dealing with the loss of family unity, the loss of homes, and the loss of normalcy." "Rather than encouraging their return," the city "has instead created barriers to the resumption of an important means of expression for these returning New Orleanians." The fees, they asserted, threatened to end the second line. "What the criminals could not destroy the City is," Jackson's lawsuit argued. "Rather than protecting, it is punishing the victims."[17]

Although Jackson's lawsuit compelled the New Orleans Police Department to lower parade fees four months later, an important victory, musicians, Mardi Gras Indians, and those that followed them through the neighborhoods continued to find themselves under assault.[18] After Kerwin James died in September 2007, for example, his family and friends did what people in the Tremé neighborhood had done, famously, for generations: they took to the streets. Tremé was known around the world for its jazz funerals. James had played and sang in Tremé's streets many times himself, as the tuba player in the New Birth Brass Band, as had members of his family. James's mother Barbara Frazier played organ in the neighborhood's Christian Mission Baptist Church. His brother Philip Frazier played the tuba, and his brother Keith Frazier played the bass drum, both in the Rebirth Brass Band, the renowned group they had founded together in 1983. Even though he had died two years after the hurricane, Kerwin "was definitely a Katrina victim," as far as Philip was concerned. "He was really worried about mama during and after the storm," Philip explained. "He was worried about his band, about us, he took it really hard and then he got sick." Kerwin suffered a stroke in 2006 and died the next year. He was thirty-four years old. Five days after he passed, Philip, Keith, and another hundred friends and family gathered in the early evening to march through the neighborhood and sing hymns; a traditional preamble to a jazz funeral called "bringing him down," it was a way of connecting with the dead. The mourners were singing the spiritual "I'll Fly Away" when police officers arrived and started grabbing at musicians' instruments. They were accused of parading without a permit and disturbing the peace. Police soon arrested the snare drummer Derrick Tabb, of the Rebirth Brass Band, and the trombonist Glen David Andrews, who had recently been awarded a prestigious National Heritage Fellowship with the Treme Brass Band.[19]

After public outcry, the charges were dismissed. The animosity between the police and the people they were meant to protect endured, however. So did friction between white newcomers and the African American bearers of the culture that ostensibly drew them to the city. Housing costs in Tremé tripled in the years after the flood—consistent with a dramatic increase in housing costs across the city, particularly in unflooded neighborhoods—and by 2013, the percentage of white residents doubled, to 36 percent. Some 80 percent of them had been born outside of the state. Most people assumed that one of these new wealthy white residents had called the police.[20]

Some dismissed paeans to local culture as essentializing, or as blithely obscuring structural problems, but for many Louisianians, the stakes could not have been higher. The city's music, cuisine, parades, funerals, and civic calendar affirmed who they were in a world that often seemed to refuse to recognize them.[21] Phrased in terms of "New Orleans exceptionalism," the argument risked making Katrina appear a parochial problem, narrowing the scope of its causes and consequences by suggesting that they obtained only in this one unique place, which was unlike any other. But claims of cultural distinctiveness—and the public practice of the city's iconic traditions— offered a way for marginalized people to assert that they mattered. Citizens celebrating themselves and each other in the streets of the city, collecting the brilliance of the individual dancers into a coherent whole, always in forward motion, led by artists from the neighborhood: this was the vision offered by the second line, in contrast to the dominant mode of recovery as a legal thicket of policy proposals, premised on cost-benefit analyses, and processed by distant subcontractors. The signal moment of a Mardi Gras Indian chief's appearance came when he spread his arms wide and his feathered suit expanded around him, filling the street with virtuosic, working-class, African American beauty, performing a vision of a people who, as the Indian chant goes, "won't bow down / don't know how," even if it was only for a spot of time, before the police arrived, sirens blaring, to push him back onto the sidewalk.[22] New Orleanians wanted good jobs, schools, health care, levees, policing, and government as much as anybody—indeed, they knew better than most the toll taken by their absence. But they knew, too, how much other forms of social aid and pleasure could matter.

A study of New Orleanians living in Texas three years after the flood found that more than half would have preferred to be in New Orleans. Asked why, 69 percent said simply, "New Orleans is home." "I miss Mardi Gras," one woman explained. "That was part of the fabric of being a citizen."[23]

Lumar LeBlanc moved to Texas, too. But even after he surrendered his house in New Orleans East to the Road Home program and spent what he called five "comfortable" years in Houston, he still thought of himself as a New Orleanian. Nearly every Thursday, LeBlanc drove 350 miles back to play the snare drum with the Soul Rebels Brass Band at Le Bon Temps, an Uptown bar. It was important to LeBlanc to keep playing there even after he moved. "We don't want it to die down," he said. "That's why we make the drive." With the Soul Rebels, LeBlanc took the skills he had learned performing traditional New Orleans jazz with the Young Olympia Brass Band and applied them to contemporary hip hop songs, connecting the old and the new. "What New Orleans still has on the rest of the world," he explained to an interviewer, was "the authentic mystery of music."[24] In 2009, the Soul Rebels recorded an original song called "No Place Like Home." After shout outs to the Saints, St. Louis Cathedral, hot sausage, Zulu, and a litany of other local icons, vocalist Winston Turner sings: "I refuse to die if I don't have a brass band at my funeral." To imagine a funeral devoid of the familiar communal rites was to envision not just one's own death, but the loss of the city itself. "It's not New Orleans. It's not home," he sings. "You know what I'm saying?" The love song for home betrayed the pervasive fear that the new New Orleans was at risk of becoming unrecognizable.[25]

Tradition is not stasis; it is change that feels "collectively self-authored," stable, and recognizable. As a process of change, tradition is the opposite of disaster, in which the present seems to arrive out of nowhere. Artists like LeBlanc and the Frazier brothers, whose genius lay in using tradition to create the future out of the past, knew that New Orleans could continue to exist as a place name on the map, but if it was not authentically connected to what it had been before, as far as they were concerned, it might as well have been lost. Many other New Orleanians, like the ones Tamara Jackson led through the streets, knew this too, or at least felt the weight of its challenge.[26]

A study of patients at the Tulane Medical Center showed that admissions for myocardial infarctions at the downtown hospital more than tripled during the six years following the storm. The researchers attributed the increase to higher rates of chronic stress. But the doctors also noted another change. Usually, admissions for heart attacks spike on Monday mornings, when people endure the stress of starting a new week at work. After the flood, however, the timing shifted: more New Orleanians had heart attacks on evenings and weekends. "We feel like that may be the result [of] . . . being exposed to the rebuilding efforts," one of the study's authors explained. In New Orleans after Katrina, going home could break your heart.[27]

Ashley Morris, the vituperative blogger, once described New Orleans as "the only city that ever loved me back." He died of a heart attack in April 2008. He was forty-five years old. The Hot 8 Brass Band led his funeral procession, and the Big Easy Roller Girls paraded behind his casket on skates.[28]

OIL AND WATER

For most observers, the event President Barack Obama soon described as "the worst environmental disaster America has ever faced" unfolded as an efficient drama. For eighty-seven days, BP's Macondo well spewed more than 134 million gallons of oil into the Gulf of Mexico—the largest spill in United States history. A live video feed broadcast the billowing brown spectacle from 5,000 feet underwater. Images of oiled pelicans, the tarnished state bird, flocked on the front pages of national newspapers.[29] CNN anchor Anderson Cooper took up residence in Louisiana. Then, on July 10, BP plugged the leak. The coverage, like the oil, seemed to dissipate.[30]

Few people on the coast experienced that tight narrative arc. Calling the incident the "BP oil spill" conditioned inquirers to blame BP, and to measure its duration by the length of time that oil was allowed to spill. But none of that reflected how the spill was experienced in Louisiana. For people on the coast, what could appear on the surface to be an acute, chemical event, became absorbed into a chronic and diffuse cultural trauma.[31] When the president responded to the spill by announcing a moratorium on new deep water drilling—which many believed imperiled Louisiana's economy more than the oil spill itself—it confirmed many Louisianians' gathering sense that the benefits of change accrued elsewhere, while the costs were carried by them.

The experience of Katrina, compounded with the oil spill, increasingly served Louisianians as a metonym for federal illegitimacy. It all felt like a plot to Cherri Foytlin, who had moved to Louisiana from Oklahoma when her husband got a job working on an offshore rig in 2005. "I feel like right now we're a big political ploy to get something else done, to get green energy in, which I'm all for," she explained in July 2010, "but I'm just saying maybe it's not the focus right now. Maybe the focus might be capping the well and taking care of the people and the wildlife, but that's just me. I'm nobody." She said many of her neighbors had been disillusioned by the federal response to Katrina, which had made landfall several months before she arrived in the state. Now, she joined them in their discontent. "Definitely," she said, "I lost all faith in the government."[32] Native Americans like Foytlin could look back on more than two centuries of violent conflict with the federal government. White people seethed that the federal government upset the proper order of things since emancipation. African Americans had known the federal government, at best, as an unreliable partner since the retreat from Reconstruction. But now, as fractured as the experience of Katrina had been across the lines of race and class, it came to serve as a common shorthand for the inept use of state power, or the callous abdication of state responsibility. Floods and oil spills seemed like problems America ought to be able to solve. When a solution was not forthcoming, the country came to seem a place beyond repair.

In September 2014, a federal court found that the spill had been "the result of" BP's "gross negligence" and "willful misconduct." But aside from misdemeanor charges for two BP employees—one rig supervisor pled guilty to a pollution charge, the other to a charge relating to having deleted text messages about the cleanup from his phone—no criminal penalties were assessed against anyone working for BP.[33] In April 2016, the court formally approved a $20.8 billion settlement.[34] BP negotiated the deal such that the majority of its payments were tax deductible. Of the $61.6 billion total that BP spent on the spill, it reported its actual after tax costs to be $44 billion, which meant that the federal government effectively subsidized $17.6 billion in BP's costs.[35] When the agreement was announced, BP's chief financial officer told shareholders, "the impact of the settlement on our balance sheet and cashflow will be manageable and enables BP to continue to invest in and grow its business."[36]

Oil had always been bitter medicine for Louisiana. Oil and other petro-chemicals kept the state's economy alive, even as they sank the state itself. By 2015, there were approximately 50,000 wells across the Louisiana coast, serviced by more than 9,000 miles of canals. The oil industry was responsible for approximately $1 billion per year in tax revenue to the state, and some 65,000 Louisiana jobs. Oil canals also were responsible for between 30 and 59 percent of all land loss. Roughly a quarter of the state's coastal wetlands—nearly 1,900 square miles of Louisiana—had had fallen into the Gulf since the 1930s. The state's 2017 Coastal Master Plan predicted that without action on a dramatic scale, at least another 1,200 square miles, and perhaps more than 4,100 square miles of land, would be lost in the coming fifty years.[37]

In a perverse twist, BP's settlement represented the first meaningful funding for the Coastal Master Plan, which outlined and modeled the state's efforts to forestall land loss and protect against floods and was projected to cost over $90 billion. Taken together, Louisiana expected to receive $8.7 billion from the BP settlements over fifteen years. The majority of the money would be dedicated to the Coastal Restoration and Protection Authority.[38]

The BP settlement complemented a broader attempt to lift the hex of the "resource curse," by means of a strategy that left the state even more reliant on oil extraction. In December 2006, Congress had passed Mary Landrieu's Gulf of Mexico Energy Security Act, increasing the state's share of offshore oil revenues. According to one estimate, Louisiana's failure to accept President Harry Truman's 1948 offer—37.5 percent of federal revenue from oil and gas extracted more than three miles from the state's coast—had cost Louisiana well more than $30 billion (a number not adjusted for inflation).[39] The new law provided that, beginning in 2017, Louisiana could expect to receive $175 million per year in oil revenues. It would be the largest consistent source of funding for the coastal protection plan.[40] But by the time the more generous apportionment took effect in 2017, falling oil prices meant that Louisiana received only 40 percent of what it had anticipated. The vagaries of finance capitalism took material form: the state announced it would have to postpone flood control and land building projects.[41]

"I ain't proud to be American no more," Dean Blanchard said in 2015, sitting in his office in Jefferson Parish, reflecting on how the oil spill had changed his life. His shrimp processing business was down 85 percent since 2010. The previous five years had taught him that the "government is being run by oil companies." He did not have a kind word for either. In 2013, the

Southeast Louisiana Flood Protection Authority had sued ninety-seven oil companies for the damage they had done to the wetlands, asserting that the companies were responsible for the increased costs of flood control caused by its canals. Many understood it as a last-ditch effort to fund meaningful efforts to slow land loss. Louisiana Governor Bobby Jindal quickly opposed the suit, accusing the levee board of having "been hijacked by a group of trial lawyers," and signed a bill passed by the state legislature to stop it. The bill was later found to have violated the state's constitution, but regardless, a federal court ultimately dismissed the Authority's suit. Blanchard felt at a loss. "I mean, who are you going to call over here? You going to call your senator? Or your representative? They've been on BP's payroll since they've been in politics." His conclusion: "The system's messed up."[42]

Increasingly, policy makers talked about the coming necessity of what was often called a "managed retreat" from the coast, a kind of green dot plan writ large, for the whole state. Louisiana's 2012 Coastal Master Plan alluded vaguely to this future, referring to "voluntary relocation and acquisition measures."[43] The plan's glossy pages were full of maps, but offered no guide to why the places on them mattered to people, or what abandoning them might mean. The plan did not ask with any rigor about why people lived there, or how, for how long, what made them want to stay, or to leave, or how the answers to these questions may have changed over time. Like many other policy documents, it purported to offer solutions, although it seemed divorced from what many believed to be the problems that most needed to be solved. And besides, solutions that do not feel fair are not solutions at all.

Outside the concrete embrace of the federal levee system, on land that was drowning before his eyes, Reverend Tyrone Edwards considered the growing calls for him, his neighbors, and the congregants at his Zion Travelers Baptist Church to move inland. Like four generations of his family before him, Edwards lived on Plaquemines Parish's east bank, in a small African American community called Phoenix. Phoenix stood between Caernarvon, where Louisiana's state engineers dynamited the levees in 1927, and Bohemia, where, since 1926, the east bank levee ended altogether, and the Orleans Levee Board's Bohemia Spillway began. Just across the river from Phoenix was Ironton, another little African American settlement, where Edwards had helped to lead the fight against Plaquemines Parish president Chalin Perez, Leander Perez's son, to secure running water, in 1980.[44]

After Hurricane Katrina, which had pushed nine feet of water across Phoenix, Edwards had founded the Zion Travelers Cooperative Center, taking his inspiration from the book of Nehemiah: "Let us arise and rebuild." The Center secured donations to buy hammers, saws, and other tools it loaned out to community members, who also could receive vouchers to buy lumber. "FEMA wasn't giving people hope; the insurance companies weren't giving people hope; so we had to give people hope," Edwards said. By 2015, the population of Phoenix was higher than it had been before the storm.[45]

Louisiana's Coastal Master Plan hinged largely on a strategy of diverting the Mississippi River—sending portions of it through the levees, in highly engineered pipes—so that the river's sediment could build new land to partially replenish what was sinking. Proponents described the river diversions as a restoration of the same process by which the Big Muddy had built Louisiana and asserted that they represented the state's only hope. There was a plan to build one such diversion, the Mid-Breton Sediment Diversion, near Phoenix. Edwards knew it might help slow the process of coastal erosion. He also knew that it would change the salinity levels in the marsh, killing oysters, causing fish to flee, and thereby destroying his neighbors' livelihoods.[46]

Proponents argued that because diversions could help the larger numbers of people farther from the coast, and in New Orleans, they were necessary sacrifices—trade-offs that served the greater good. Edwards rejected the concept. "Because we have been sacrificing all of our lives," he said, "we don't have anything left to trade."[47] Edwards advocated the more inclusive vision once embodied by the ambitions of the old levee system: a commitment to public works that might embrace everyone in their circle of protection. He knew that most Americans were more comfortable viewing his trouble as occurring on the periphery, down there, to those people. But in the meantime, he watched as people supposedly much closer to the center than the margins than he was—in New York during Hurricane Sandy in 2012, for example—flooded too. Seas were rising everywhere. Katrina's history did not seem to be receding into the past so much as echoing into the future.

Phoenix was once home to Edwards's enslaved ancestors, and he thought sometimes about the wounds wrought by the overseer's lash. "Their blood is in this soil," he said of his forebearers. His great-grandfather had served as a representative to the 1868 Louisiana Constitutional Convention. The document adopted there had outlawed slavery and had affirmed, for the first time in Louisiana's history, that "all men are created free and equal." Edwards woke up each morning as a free man on the same spot where his ancestors had bled, and fought, and secured their freedom, and his. "Tell me again what you think you are asking me to sacrifice," Edwards said, "and why you think it is mine to give."[48]

WHAT IS POSSIBLE

On August 27, 2015, President Barack Obama visited New Orleans to mark the tenth anniversary of Hurricane Katrina. He spoke at a gleaming new community center in the Lower Ninth Ward, which he praised as a "symbol of the extraordinary resilience of this city." "You are an example of what is possible," he said, "when, in the face of tragedy and in the face of hardship, good people come together to lend a hand, and, brick by brick, block by block, neighborhood by neighborhood, you build a better future."[49]

The president talked about the fried chicken he had eaten for lunch, at Willie Mae's Scotch House in Tremé. Willie Mae's had flooded when the levees broke, but with the help of volunteer labor and $200,000 in donations from across the country, the restaurant had reopened less than two years later. The restaurant's proprietor, Willie Mae Seaton, had been born in rural Mississippi. She moved to New Orleans during World War II, when her husband got a job at the Higgins Shipyard. After several years as a taxi driver and a dry cleaner, she got her beautician's license and opened a beauty parlor. Then, in 1957, she turned the parlor into a bar. She started frying chicken for her patrons. It gained renown as perhaps the best fried chicken in the world. In 2005, she won a prestigious James Beard Award. The bronze medal was one of the few possessions she took with her when she evacuated. Seaton died ten years after the flood, on September 18, 2015, at the age of ninety-nine. She lived just long enough to have the first African American president visit her restaurant and, later that day, reflecting on its restoration, to assert, "The country decided America could not afford to lose such an important place."[50]

Across the city, the population was 390,711, down 93,963 from what it had been in 2000. The white population had decreased by 8,689, or 7 percent. The African American population had decreased by 91,741, or 28 percent. One out of every ten white New Orleanians lived in poverty, while more than three out of every ten African Americans did, rates essentially unchanged since before the storm. By one measure, New Orleans had the second highest income inequality of any city in the country.[51] The median income for white families was $62,074; for African American families it was $26,819. In St. Bernard Parish, the population was 45,439, down 21,790, or 32 percent.[52]

Before he concluded his speech, Obama observed that America was "going to see more extreme weather events as the result of climate change." He asserted that New Orleans was "becoming a model for the nation when it comes to disaster response and resilience." Depending on who was asked, that was either a heartening or dispiriting proposition. Nearly eight in ten white New Orleanians surveyed during the summer of 2015 said Louisiana had "mostly recovered," while nearly six in ten African American New Orleanians said it had "mostly not recovered." Asked "how much efforts to rebuild New Orleans . . . have done to help people like you," two-thirds of white people and people above the poverty line answered "some" or "a lot," while half of African Americans and people below the poverty line answered "not too much" or "nothing at all." White people were more than twice as likely as African Americans to say that their quality of life had improved since the flood, while African Americans were more than three times more likely than white people to report that their lives had gotten worse.[53] Ten years on, Katrina could seem like one of the great Rorschach tests in modern American history, less a window than a mirror. But these were not competing interpretations of the same picture so much as they were different experiences of the same country.

One of America's most closely held myths is that the arc of the moral universe bends toward justice. We call times when things get worse disasters, setting them aside as unfortunate exceptions so that they do not dam up the flow of history, which we imagine runs inexorably toward progress. We dismiss the people who are damaged in much the same way. Having done so, it is traditional to conclude a story with a happy ending. But treating Katrina as history, accepting its hurt as our own, makes that conclusion impossible. The consolation of a happy ending would be an assault on the memory of the dead. Instead, we owe them, and ourselves, an honest measurement of the distance between what was, and what might have been. That reckoning, the historian's art, gives weight to loss and substance to hope.

Back in 2006, an interviewer had asked Malik Rahim what he imagined New Orleans would be in 2015, a decade after Hurricane Katrina. He said it was likely to be "the most progressive city in the world." He said it would be a "city of great opportunity," "environmentally clean," home to a "progressive . . . black hospital," and universities full of local students. Tourists would continue to flock to the city, he predicted, "because everybody's going to want to come here to see just what we were able to accomplish." "I have great hopes for New Orleans," Rahim asserted that day in 2006, "and I have great hope for America."[54]

Rahim could be forgiven if his vision seemed utopian. The interview was recorded at the Common Ground Collective, which Rahim had helped to found. Nearby, volunteers were busy gutting houses, operating a free health clinic, providing free legal services, remediating toxic soil, and making plans to plant marsh grasses in the wetlands—all things the government had thus far declined or failed to do, but that Rahim and his team were achieving. The volunteers there that day represented only a small percentage of the thousands of people, black and white, from near and far, that already had passed through his door, drawn by Common Ground's "solidarity not charity" ethos, eager to help New Orleans realize the dream of becoming a beloved community. Rahim had started the effort with fifty dollars. Anything seemed possible.

But Rahim's life experiences would not have allowed him to varnish difficult truths. A Vietnam War veteran, and former head of security for the New Orleans chapter of the Black Panther Party, Rahim had long advocated for armed African American self-defense. He had been involved in a shootout with the police and had spent years in prison for armed robbery.[55] In the days after the hurricane, he had encountered the bullet-ridden bodies of his neighbors lying in the streets of Algiers. "I watched them become bloated and torn apart by dogs," Rahim said. These were not victims of the storm or the levee failures—Algiers had not flooded—but of white vigilantes, also his neighbors, operating as a lynch mob.[56]

The interviewer asked Rahim if he thought that the repaired and just New Orleans he imagined a decade hence would become a reality. "Yes, indeed," he answered, his voice rising. "Yes, indeed." Rahim did not remain committed to the possibility of a better future despite his lifetime of struggle, but rather because of it. "We have no other choice," Rahim explained. "Because if it doesn't happen, we're going to destroy ourselves."[57]

NOTES

Abbreviations

ACEDL	US Army Corps of Engineers Digital Library
AMC	Acadiana Manuscripts Collection, Edith Garland Dupré Library, University of Louisiana-Lafayette
AP	Associated Press
BNOBC	Bring New Orleans Back Commission
BRA	*Baton Rouge Advocate*
CBO	Congressional Budget Office
CD	*Chicago Defender*
CDBG	Community Development Block Grants
EKL	Louisiana and Special Collection, Earl K. Long Library, University of New Orleans
FEMA	Federal Emergency Management Agency
FHA	Federal Housing Administration
FIRM	Flood Insurance Rate Map
HOLC	Home Owners Loan Corporation
HUD	Department of Housing and Urban Development
ILIT	Independent Levee Investigation Team
IPET	Interagency Performance Evaluation Task Force
LLMVC	Louisiana and Lower Mississippi Valley Collections, Louisiana State University Libraries
LPVHPP	Lake Pontchartrain and Vicinity Hurricane Protection Project
LRA	Louisiana Recovery Authority
LRC	Louisiana Research Collection, Howard-Tilton Memorial Library, Tulane University
LW	*Louisiana Weekly*
MRGO	Mississippi River–Gulf Outlet
NFIP	National Flood Insurance Program
NOG	*New Orleans Gambit*
NOI	*New Orleans Item*
NOPL	New Orleans Public Library
NOS	*New Orleans States*
NOSI	*New Orleans States-Item*

NOTP   *New Orleans Times-Picayune*
NYT   *New York Times*
OIG   Department of Homeland Security's Office of Inspector General
PG   *Plaquemines Gazette*
SBV   *St. Bernard Voice*
SOHP   Southern Oral History Program, Southern Historical Collection, Wilson
        Library, University of North Carolina at Chapel Hill
ULI   Urban Land Institute
USACE   US Army Corps of Engineers
VA   US Department of Veterans Affairs
WP   *Washington Post*
WSJ   *Wall Street Journal*

Introduction

1. For Burrwood, see R. Christopher Goodwin, Kenneth R. Jones, Debra M. Stayner, and Galloway W. Selby, *Evaluation of the National Register Eligibility of Burrwood, Plaquemines Parish, Louisiana* (New Orleans: R. Goodwin & Associates, Inc., 1985), in the Louisiana State Library, Baton Rouge, LA. For wind speed, see Isaac Cline, *Storms, Floods and Sunshine: A Book of Memoirs* (New Orleans: Pelican Publishing Company, 1945), 158. For the Eads jetties, see John M. Barry, *Rising Tide: The Great Mississippi Flood of 1927 and How It Changed America* (New York: Simon & Schuster, 1997), 78–92.

2. Isaac M. Cline, "The Tropical Hurricane of September 29, 1915 in Louisiana," *Monthly Weather Review* 43, no. 9 (1915): 459 (for the barometer) and 456 (for "intense"). For precipitation, see George G. Earl, *The Hurricane of Sept. 29th, 1915, and Subsequent Heavy Rainfalls,* report to the Sewerage and Water Board of New Orleans (October 14, 1915), 15, in the City Archives, Louisiana Division, NOPL.

3. For deaths, see Cline, "Tropical Hurricane," 465. For damage, see "Gulf Coast Loss Reaches Millions," *NYT,* October 2, 1915, p. 17. For Jean Saint Malo, see Gwendolyn Midlo Hall, *Africans in Colonial Louisiana: The Development of Afro-Creole Culture in the Eighteenth Century* (Baton Rouge: Louisiana State University Press, 1992), 213–232. For the steeple, see "Vieux Carre in Direct Path of Hurricane Weathers Storm with Very Small Damage," *NOTP,* September 30, 1915, p. 3. For the flood, *Thirty-Second Semi-Annual Report of the Sewerage and Water Board of New Orleans, LA* (New Orleans: Sewerage and Water Board, 1915), 63, in the City Archives, Louisiana Division, NOPL.

4. "'Storm Proof!' The Record Shows Orleans," *NOI,* September 30, 1915, p. 10. For the mayor, "Storm Over, City Emerges Victor," *NOI,* September 29, 1915, p. 1. For "safe to say," Earl, *The Hurricane of Sept. 29th,* 17–18.

5. US Army Corps of Engineers, *Hurricane Study: History of Hurricane Occurrences along Coastal Louisiana* (New Orleans: New Orleans District, 1972), 1, 12–23.

6. Earl, *Hurricane of Sept. 29th,* 17. On urban growth, see Harvey Molotch, "The City as Growth Machine: Toward a Political Economy of Place," *American Journal of Sociology* 82, no. 2 (September 1976): 309–332.

7. Original Pinettes Brass Band, "Ain't No City," 2014, YouTube video, https://www.youtube.com/watch?v=2bIF7VHY_jg.

8. On New Orleans's twentieth-century image, see Kevin Fox Gotham, *Authentic New Orleans: Tourism, Culture, and Race in the Big Easy* (New York: New York University Press, 2007); Lynnell L. Thomas, *Desire and Disaster in New Orleans: Tourism, Race, and Historical Memory* (Durham: Duke University Press, 2014); Anthony J. Stanosis, *Creating the Big Easy: New Orleans and the Emergence of Modern Tourism, 1918–1945* (Athens: University of Georgia Press, 2006); J. Mark Souther, *New Orleans On Parade: Tourism and the Transformation of the Crescent City* (Baton Rouge: Louisiana State University Press,

2006); and Louise McKinney, *New Orleans: A Cultural History* (New York: Oxford University Press, 2006).

9. On draining wetlands, see Craig E. Colten, *An Unnatural Metropolis: Wresting New Orleans from Nature* (Baton Rouge: Louisiana State University Press, 2005). For a map indicating the extent of the Katrina flood and "media era of construction of buildings per block as of 1939," see map titled "Threatened Historical Architecture" in Richard Campanella, *Bienville's Dilemma: A Historical Geography of New Orleans* (Lafayette: Center for Louisiana Studies, 2008), (map section, no page number). See also Peirce F. Lewis, *New Orleans: The Making of an Urban Landscape* (1976; Charlottesville: University of Virginia Press, 2018); Craig E. Colten, ed., *Transforming New Orleans and Its Environs: Centuries of Change* (Pittsburgh: University of Pittsburgh Press, 2000); Ari Kelman, *A River and Its City: The Nature of Landscape in New Orleans* (Berkeley: University of California Press, 2003); and Kelman, "Boundary Issues: Clarifying New Orleans's Murky Edges," *Journal of American History* 94, no. 3 (December 2007): 695–703.

10. The Katrina flood line limned the contours of the city as it stood in the 1890s, before the backswamp had been drained enough to begin significant residential construction off the highest ground near the Mississippi River. But because most houses constructed into the 1910s were raised above the street grade on piers, generally speaking, they were not inundated by the comparatively low flood waters that reached them in 2005. Thus, I use 1915 as an informed but approximate average date of construction for the oldest homes that experienced significant flooding in 2005, based in part on analyses I conducted with Richard Campanella, drawing on a post-Katrina damage survey created by the Federal Emergency Management Agency and City inspectors (https://data.nola.gov/Archived /Post-Katrina-Damage-Assessment/aned-jbk9/data), the US Army Corps of Engineers Interagency Performance Evaluation Task Force's "First Floor Survey" (ArcMap GIS data in author's possession), and 1940 Census data on age of home construction.

11. My argument here is informed by Kai T. Erikson, *Everything in Its Path: Destruction of Community in Buffalo Creek* (1978; New York: Simon & Schuster, 2006).

12. "Katrina's Racial Storm," *Chicago Tribune,* September 8, 2005. For a similar effort to put Katrina in the context of a Deep South that has been "the American storm center of social schism and human liberation for more than three centuries," see Clyde Woods, "Katrina's World: Blues, Bourbon, and the Return to the Source," *American Quarterly* 61, no. 3 (September 2009): 427–453 (quotation on p. 429).

13. The African American population in 2000 was 323,392. US Census for 2000. There is substantial uncertainty about the city's population in 2005. The US Census Bureau's postcensal estimate for 2005, based on projections forward from 2000, was 453,726. The Bureau's intercensal estimate for 2005, based on projections backward based on the 2010 Census, was 494,294. In other words, the Census Bureau initially believed that the city had lost approximately 30,000 people in the half-decade before the flood, then revised its count to suggest that New Orleans had in fact gained 10,000 people over the same time period. Because of the gulf between the two numbers, I rely on the comparatively definitive 2000 count; by necessity, I use the intercensal estimate for 2015, which counts 231,651 African Americans in New Orleans. For 2015, see US Census Bureau, Population Division, "Annual Estimates of the Resident Population by Sex, Race, and Hispanic Origin for the United States, States, and Counties: April 1, 2010 to July 1, 2017" (June 2018), https://factfinder.census.gov/bkmk/table/1.0/en/PEP/2017/PEPSR6H /0500000US22071?slice=Year~est72015.

14. George W. Bush, "Address to the Nation on Hurricane Katrina Recovery from New Orleans, Louisiana," September 15, 2005, in *Weekly Compilation of Presidential Documents* 40, no. 37 (US Government Printing Office, September 19, 2005), 1409.

15. William Shakespeare, *Julius Caesar,* Act I, Scene 2.

16. Andy Horowitz, "Don't Repeat the Mistakes of the Katrina Recovery," *NYT,* September 14, 2017. On "states of emergency," see Giorgio Agamben, *State of Exception* (Chicago: University of Chicago Press, 2008). On resilience, see Lawrence J. Vale and

Thomas J. Campanella, *Resilient City: How Modern Cities Recover from Disaster* (New York: Oxford University Press, 2005).

17. On American exceptionalism and Katrina, see Ron Eyerman, *Is This America?: Katrina as Cultural Trauma* (Austin: University of Texas Press, 2015), although I disagree that Katrina represented a "staggering blow to the myth of American exceptionalism," because many African Americans had never believed in such a myth, and many white Americans believed they remained protected (p. 130).

18. Neil Smith, "There's No Such Thing as a Natural Disaster," *Understanding Katrina: Perspectives from the Social Sciences,* Social Science Research Center (June 11, 2006), https://items.ssrc.org/understanding-katrina/theres-no-such-thing-as-a-natural-disaster/.

19. Although I believe there are justifiable reasons to distinguish the places where Katrina's flood was a direct result of the failure of the Army Corps's hurricane protection system, rather than a storm surge, I regret my participation in the continuing elision of Mississippi, Alabama, and the other places where Hurricane Katrina mattered. On putting the "narrative of metropolitan growth within a broader regional context," see Andrew Needham, *Power Lines: Phoenix and the Making of the Modern Southwest* (Princeton: Princeton University Press, 2014), 10.

20. "City Cut Off from Rest of World," *NOI,* September 29, 1915, p. 1.

21. For "tragedy," see Bush, "Address to the Nation on Hurricane Katrina Recovery," 1405. For "factors," see David Alexander, "Symbolic and Practical Interpretations of the Hurricane Katrina Disaster in New Orleans," *Understanding Katrina: Perspectives from the Social Sciences* (June 11, 2006), https://items.ssrc.org/understanding-katrina/symbolic-and -practical-interpretations-of-the-hurricane-katrina-disaster-in-new-orleans/. It was also likely a product of many scholars working to publish "instant history" after the storm. Lawrence N. Powell, "What Does American History Tell Us about Katrina and Vice Versa?" *Journal of American History* 94, no. 3 (December 2007): 863–876 (quotation on p. 876).

22. John C. Burnham, "A Neglected Field: The History of Natural Disasters," *Perspectives on History,* April 1, 1988. Among the most important exceptions is Ted Steinberg, *Acts of God: The Unnatural History of Natural Disaster in America* (Oxford: Oxford University Press, 2000).

23. For a review of disaster research in sociology, see Kathleen J. Tierney, "From the Margins to the Mainstream? Disaster Research at the Crossroads," *Annual Review of Sociology* 33 (2007): 503–525. For a review of the outpouring of research on Katrina as early as 2008, see Kai Erikson and Lori Peek, eds., *Hurricane Katrina Research Bibliography* (Social Science Research Council, April 2008).

24. Charles Fritz, "Disaster," in Robert K. Merton and Robert A. Nisbet, eds., *Contemporary Social Problems: An Introduction to the Sociology of Deviant Behavior and Social Disorganization* (New York: Harcourt, Brace & World, Inc., 1960), 651–694 ("liberation" on p. 683; "clean break" on p. 692).

25. Rebecca Solnit, *A Paradise Built in Hell: The Extraordinary Communities that Arise in Disaster* (New York: Viking, 2009), 7.

26. Sandi Zellmer and Christine Klein, *Mississippi River Tragedies: A Century of Unnatural Disaster* (New York: New York University Press, 2014), 5.

27. Although the sentiment is much older, one useful point of origin for this argument is geographer Gilbert White's assertion that "floods are acts of God, but flood losses are largely acts of man." White, "Human Adjustment to Floods: A Geographical Approach to the Flood Problem in the United States" (PhD dissertation, University of Chicago, 1942), 2. The most forceful contemporary expression is Steinberg, *Acts of God.*

28. James Hansen et al., "Ice Melt, Sea Level Rise and Superstorms: Evidence from Paleoclimate Data, Climate Modeling, and Modern Observations that 2°C Global Warming Could Be Dangerous," *Atmospheric Chemistry and Physics* 16 (2016): 3761–3812.

29. Steinberg, *Acts of God,* 211.

30. For example, Harold Kushner, *When Bad Things Happen to Good People* (New York: Random House, 1981).

31. Michele Landis Dauber, *The Sympathetic State: Disaster Relief and the Origins of the American Welfare State* (Chicago: University of Chicago Press, 2013), 15.

32. "Nature's Revenge," *NYT*, August 30, 2005, p. A18. Michiko Kakutani, "Katrinaworld: Somewhere Between Nature's Fury and Man's Incompetence," *NYT*, May 16, 2006, p. E1 (for "hubris.")

33. I have avoided trying to fit Katrina into the existing taxonomy of disaster—natural, man-made, slow, chronic, technological, environmental, or otherwise; it has features of all of those things. I similarly have avoided using terms such as response or recovery with the technical precision common to some in the field, because one of my main goals was to discover, instead, what these concepts meant to the people I wrote about. For efforts to define these terms, see, for example, Enrico L. Quarantelli, ed., *What Is a Disaster?: Perspectives on the Question* (New York: Routledge, 1998), and Greg Bankoff, *Cultures of Disaster: Society and Natural Hazard in the Philippines* (New York: Routledge, 2003), esp. 3.

34. For the related idea that disasters often are perceived as "instruments of progress," see Kevin Rozario, *The Culture of Calamity: Disaster and the Making of Modern America* (Chicago: University of Chicago Press, 2007). For disasters as "isolated misfortunes," see also Kenneth Hewitt, "The Idea of Calamity in a Technocratic Age," in *Interpretations of Calamity*, ed. Kenneth Hewitt (Boston: Allen & Unwin, 1983), 3–32.

35. "Kai Erikson in Conversation with Andy Horowitz," Tulane University, October 26, 2015, https://www.youtube.com/watch?v=5Bsj-x205Q8.

36. Jeremy Alford and Allen Johnson Jr., "Re-Defining 'Katrina,'" *NOG*, February 19, 2008.

37. Norman Maclean, *Young Men and Fire* (Chicago: University of Chicago Press, 1992), 46–47.

1. How to Sink New Orleans: Controlling Floods, Oil, and States' Rights, 1927–1965

1. William A. Read, "Louisiana Place Names of Indian Origin," 1927, reprinted in George Riser, ed., *Louisiana Place Names of Indian Origin: A Collection of Words* (Tuscaloosa: University of Alabama Press, 2008), 42–43. I am grateful to Ken Carleton for his assistance on this point.

2. For Riche's parents, see "Popular Gardner Dies at Son's Home," *NOTP*, February 26, 1917, p. 9; and "Love in Court," *NOTP*, July 15, 1905, p. 5. For Atakapa-Ishak people, see Fred B. Kniffen, "Preliminary Report on the Indian Mounds and Middens of Plaquemines and St. Bernard Parishes," in H. V. Howe, ed., *Louisiana Geological Survey Bulletin* 8 (New Orleans: Louisiana Department of Conservation, 1936): 407–422. On Francophone Louisiana, see Carl Brasseaux, *French, Cajun, Creole, Houma: A Primer on Francophone Louisiana* (Baton Rouge: Louisiana State University Press, 2005). On racial classification, see Virginia R. Dominguez, *White by Definition: Social Classification in Creole Louisiana* (New Brunswick: Rutgers University Press, 1994).

3. On the Yugoslavian community, see Milos M. Vujnovich, *Yugoslavs in Louisiana* (Gretna, LA: Pelican Publishing Company, 1974); and Frank M. Lovrich, "The Dalmatian Yugoslavs in Louisiana," *Louisiana History* 8, no. 2 (Spring 1967): 149–164.

4. Harnett T. Kane, *Deep Delta Country* (New York: Duell, Sloan & Pearce, 1944), xvi. The population also included people from Italy, the Philippines, and Canada.

5. "Spanish Transcription of Videotaped Oral History Interviews and Ethnographic Documentation of Isleños Lifeways," JELAF 4518, Box 6, Jean Lafitte National Historical Park and Preserve Archival Collection, Addendum 3, Mss. 294, EKL. For Isleños, see also Gilbert C. Din, *The Canary Islanders of Louisiana* (Baton Rouge: Louisiana State University Press, 1988).

6. "Governor's Proclamation," *NOTP*, April 27, 1927, p. 1. See also John M. Barry, *Rising Tide: The Great Mississippi Flood of 1927 and How It Changed America* (New York: Simon & Schuster, 1997).

7. "Fifty Join with City, State in Pledging Good Offices," *NOTP*, April 27, 1927, p. 1.

8. Robert W. Kelley, untitled photograph, June 2, 1955, in the LIFE Photo Archive, hosted by Google, http://images.google.com/hosted/life/63f1d9c106ed8f6c.html.

9. Robert W. Kelley, untitled photograph, June 2, 1955, in the LIFE Photo Archive, http://images.google.com/hosted/life/2e1dc833eebf97b0.html.

10. Harnett T. Kane, "Dilemma of the Crooner-Governor," *NYT Magazine*, January 1, 1961, p. 31 ("czar"). Roy Reeds, "'Hard-Headed' Residents of Perez's Parish Tell How They Clung to Life in the Hurricane," *NYT*, September 15, 1965, p. 32 ("fiefdom"). Richard Austin Smith, "Oil, Brimstone, and Judge Perez," *Fortune*, March 1958, p. 145. On Perez, see Glen Jeansonne, *Leander Perez: Boss of the Delta* (Jackson: University Press of Mississippi, 1977), "judge" on p. 29. See also James Conaway, *Judge: The Life and Times of Leander Perez* (New York: Alfred A. Knopf, 1973). My account of Perez's dealings is also informed by the twenty-part series by David Baldwin in the *NOI* in June 1950; and by Tyler Priest, "Technology and Strategy of Petroleum Exploration in Coastal and Offshore Gulf of Mexico," "Claiming the Coastal Sea: The Battles for the 'Tidelands,' 1937–1953," and "Auctioning the Ocean: The Creation of the Federal Offshore Leasing Program, 1954–1962," all in Diane Austin et al., *History of the Offshore Oil and Gas Industry in Southern Louisiana, Volume I: Papers on the Evolving Offshore Industry*, OCS Study MMS 2008-042 (New Orleans: US Department of the Interior, Minerals Management Service, Gulf of Mexico OCS Region, 2008), 11–36 (for "Technology"), 67–92 (for "Claiming"), and 93–116 (for "Auctioning").

11. William F. Buckley Jr. and Leander Perez, "The Wallace Movement," *Firing Line* no. 95, April 15, 1968 (New Orleans, LA), transcript, p. 6.

12. Brady R. Couvillion et al., "Land Area Change in Coastal Louisiana from 1932 to 2010," US Geological Survey Scientific Investigations Map 3164 (United States Geological Survey, 2011); Clare D'Artois Leeper, "Louisiana Places: Empire," Baton Rouge *Sunday Advocate*, September 13, 1970, reprinted in *Louisiana Places: A Collection of Columns from the Baton Rouge Sunday Advocate, 1960–1974* (Baton Rouge: Legacy Publishing Company, 1976), 89.

13. Amy Wold, "Washed Away," *BRA*, April 29, 2013.

14. *Louisiana's Comprehensive Master Plan for a Sustainable Coast* (Baton Rouge: Louisiana Coastal Protection & Restoration Authority, 2012), 82–83. Between 1884 and 2002, "the long-term average erosion rates for the Plaquemines barrier shoreline were –23.1 feet per year." Shea Penland et al., "Changes in Louisiana's Shoreline: 1855–2002," *Journal of Coastal Research* 44 (Spring 2005): 7–39 (quotation on p. 33).

15. For the argument that oil extraction has made Louisiana a "sacrifice zone," see Craig E. Colten, "An Incomplete Solution: Oil and Water in Louisiana," *Journal of American History* 99, no. 1 (June 2012): 91–99.

16. On the rise of modern conservatism in the South in the context of the New Deal order, see Ira Katznelson, *Fear Itself: The New Deal and the Origins of Our Time* (New York: Liveright Publishing, 2013); Nancy Maclean, "Southern Dominance in Borrowed Language: The Regional Origins of American Neoliberalism," in Jane L. Collins et al., eds., *New Landscapes of Inequality: Neoliberalism and the Erosion of Democracy in America* (Santa Fe: School for Advanced Research Press, 2008), 21–38; Bruce Schulman, *From Cotton Belt to Sunbelt: Federal Policy, Economic Development, and the Transformation of the South, 1938–1980* (Oxford: Oxford University Press, 1991); Matthew Lassiter, *The Silent Majority: Suburban Politics in the Sunbelt South* (Princeton: Princeton University Press, 2006); Bethany Moreton, *To Serve God and Wal-Mart: The Making of Christian Free Enterprise* (Cambridge: Harvard University Press, 2010); Elizabeth Tandy Shermer, *Sunbelt Capitalism: Phoenix and the Transformation of American Politics* (Philadelphia: University of Pennsylvania Press, 2013). Louisiana may have distinctive contingencies but does not represent a generic exception to national trends. See Matthew D. Lassiter and Joseph Crespino, eds., *The Myth of Southern Exceptionalism* (New York: Oxford University Press, 2009).

17. Joseph Crespino, *Strom Thurmond's America* (New York: Hill and Wang, 2012), 8–9.

18. William Leuchtenburg, *The White House Looks South: Franklin D. Roosevelt, Harry S. Truman, Lyndon B. Johnson* (Baton Rouge: Louisiana State University Press, 2005), 198.

19. "Rainach Tells Stand on Pay," *NOTP*, November 21, 1959, p. 14.

20. A. J. Liebling, *The Earl of Louisiana* (Baton Rouge: Louisiana State University Press, 1961), 154.

21. For "Every Man," see T. Harry Williams, *Huey Long* (New York: Alfred A. Knopf, 1970), 262. For "Utopia," see J. Ben Meyer, *The Land of Promise* (Buras, LA: Plaquemines Parish Library, 1975), no page numbers, typescript in the Louisiana Collection, State Library of Louisiana, Baton Rouge, LA.

22. The seminal work on the capture theory of regulation is George J. Stigler, "The Theory of Economic Regulation," *The Bell Journal of Economics and Management Science* 2, no. 1 (Spring 1971): 3–21.

23. For the debate over the causes of coastal erosion, see Tyler Priest and Jason P. Theriot, "Who Destroyed the Marsh? Oil Field Canals, Coastal Ecology, and the Debate over Louisiana's Shrinking Wetlands," *Economic History Yearbook* 2 (2009): 69–80. See also Jason P. Theriot, "Building America's Energy Corridor: Oil & Gas Development and Louisiana's Wetlands" (PhD dissertation, University of Houston, 2011).

24. Lou Block, "Delta Road, near New Orleans, LA," photograph, 1939. In the Farm Security Administration / Office of War Information Collection, Prints and Photographs Division, Library of Congress, Washington, DC, http://www.loc.gov/pictures/item/2011645340. Obituary of Emile Riche, *NOTP*, November 9, 1962, p. 2.

25. Kane, *Deep Delta Country*, 197.

26. "City to Feel Relief from Levee Breach in 48 Hours," *NOTP*, April 30, 1927, pp. 1–2.

27. "Refugee Caravan Winds Way as St. Bernard Folk Carry Belongings to City," *NOTP*, April 28, 1927, p. 1. For 10,000 evacuees, see Barry, *Rising Tide*, 347.

28. Barry, *Rising Tide*, 257.

29. Lawrence Powell, *The Accidental City: Improvising New Orleans* (Cambridge: Harvard University Press, 2012), 1–2.

30. Daniel Walker Howe, *What Hath God Wrought: The Transformation of America, 1815–1848* (New York: Oxford University Press, 2007), 9. The song quotation is from Jimmy Driftwood, "The Battle of New Orleans," 1959.

31. For "Queen City," see *The Picayune's Guide to New Orleans* (New Orleans: The Picayune, 1900), 194. On cities and their agricultural hinterlands, see William Cronon, *Nature's Metropolis: Chicago and the Great West* (New York: W. W. Norton, 1992).

32. Thomas Jefferson to Governor William C. C. Claiborne, July 7, 1804, in James P. McClure, ed., *The Papers of Thomas Jefferson Volume 44: July to November 1804* (Princeton: Princeton University Press, 2019), 53.

33. With apologies to Fred Siegel, *The Future Once Happened Here: New York, D.C., L.A., and the Fate of America's Big Cities* (New York: Free Press, 1997).

34. On the value of the slave trade, see Walter Johnson, *River of Dark Dreams: Slavery and Empire in the Cotton Kingdom* (Cambridge: Harvard University Press, 2013).

35. On changes in southern agriculture and demographics, see Jack Temple Kirby, *Rural Worlds Lost: The American South, 1920–1960* (Baton Rouge: Louisiana State University Press, 1986). For quarters, see Jane Pharr, "The Administration of Federal Relief in Plaquemines Parish" (MA thesis, Tulane University, 1938), 10.

36. "Bank Will Move in New Building," *NOTP*, November 29, 1927, p. 6. After the 1927 flood, the Orleans Levee District commissioners considered removing the levees from the entire east bank of Plaquemines Parish beneath Caernarvon. See "Levee Removal in Plaquemines Opposed by Jury," *NOTP*, July 14, 1927, p. 6. On wetlands, see Ann Vileisis, *Discovering the Unknown Landscape: A History of America's Wetlands* (Washington, DC: Island Press, 1997); David C. Miller, *Dark Eden: The Swamp in Nineteenth-Century American Culture* (Cambridge: Cambridge University Press, 1989); and Anthony Wilson, *Shadow and Shelter: The Swamp in Southern Culture* (Jackson: University Press of Mississippi, 2006).

37. The swamps had also been seen as unhealthy. See Craig E. Colten, *An Unnatural Metropolis: Wresting New Orleans from Nature* (Baton Rouge: Louisiana State University Press, 2005), 32–38.

38. *Report of the Register and Receiver of the Land Office at New Orleans,* H.R. Doc. No. 55, 24th Cong., 1st Sess. (1836), 77.

39. An Act to aid the State of Louisiana in draining the swamp lands therein, ch. 87, 9 Stat. 352 (March 2, 1849). Similar subsequent bills in 1850 and 1860 distributed wetlands in other states; not all of the land was transferred at once, and the ten-million-acre figure is the eventual total for Louisiana. US Geological Survey, *National Water Summary on Wetland Resources* (Washington, DC: US Government Printing Office, 1996), 21.

40. An Act to aid the State of Louisiana in draining the swamp lands therein, ch. 87, 9 Stat. 353 (March 2, 1849). At the same time, "[t]he fact that the federal government transferred the lands to the state reflected a realization that the federal government, and thus the country as a whole, stood to benefit from land reclamation on the lower Mississippi." Colten, *Unnatural Metropolis,* 30.

41. Carolyn Ramsey, "Rats to Riches," *Saturday Evening Post,* May 8, 1943, p. 78. For a profile of one such planter family, see David O. Whitten, "Rural Life along the Mississippi: Plaquemines Parish, Louisiana, 1830–1850," *Agricultural History* 58 (July 1984): 477–487.

42. An act to create a new levee district, to be known and styled the Buras Levee District, Louisiana Act 18 (1894); An act to create the Grand Prairie Levee District and the Board of Commissioners therefor, Louisiana Act 24 (1898).

43. Donald W. Davis, *Washed Away? The Invisible Peoples of Louisiana's Wetlands* (Lafayette: University of Louisiana at Lafayette Press, 2010). US Census for 1900.

44. Lyle Saxon, *Lafitte the Pirate* (1930; Gretna, LA: Pelican Publishing Company, 1999), 38. On Progressives, see Glenda E. Gilmore, ed., *Who Were the Progressives?* (New York: Palgrave, 2002). On maroon communities, see Herbert Aptheker, "Maroons Within The Present Limits of the United States," *The Journal of Negro History* 24, no. 2 (April 1939): 167–184; Gwendolyn Midlo Hall, *Africans in Colonial Louisiana: The Development of Afro-Creole Culture in the Eighteenth Century* (Baton Rouge: Louisiana State University Press, 1995), 203–207; and Powell, *Accidental City,* 236–240.

45. Archie M. Smith, *Report of Levee Examining Committee* (New Orleans: Orleans Levee District, 1926), 9, in the Louisiana State Archive, Baton Rouge, LA.

46. Percy Viosca Jr., *Flood Control in the Mississippi Valley in its Relation to Louisiana Fisheries* (New Orleans: Louisiana Department of Conservation, 1927), 16. Barry, *Rising Tide,* 159, 167–168. This may have been the first spillway constructed on the Mississippi. See "New West Flank Oiler at Harang Area Completed," *NOTP,* September 18, 1938, p. 17.

47. "Act of Donation by Narcise Cosse, Sr. to Board of Trustees for the Point Pleasant Cemetery," July 23, 1921. Scan of document in author's possession. See also "Board to Move Entire Villages in River Project," *NOTP,* May 19, 1925, pp. 1, 3.

48. An act to reduce the flood levels of the Mississippi River and to better protect the City of New Orleans from danger of overflow by the high waters of the Mississippi River, Louisiana Act 99 (1924).

49. Smith, *Report of Levee Examining Committee.* Board of Commissioners of the Orleans Levee District, *Historical Perspective Bohemia Spillway, 1924–2000* (2000), in the State Library of Louisiana, Baton Rouge, LA; "Spillways Plan in Plaquemines Is Recommended," *NOTP,* June 19, 1924, p. 3; "Spillway Step Taken," *NOTP,* June 13, 1925, p. 5; "New Pointe a la Hache Outlet Ready to Divert Mississippi Flood Water," *NOTP,* March 13, 1926, p. 3; and "Keep Bohemia Open," *NOTP,* June 19, 1952, p. 12 for details about size and costs of the spillway.

50. "Appraisers Glad Job Is Finished," *NOTP,* June 14, 1925, p. B-9.

51. Benjamin T. Waldo to Guy L. Deano, March 31, 1926. For the backswamp, see Benjamin T. Waldo to Guy L. Deano, August 16, 1926. Both in Box 4, O'Keefe Papers, NOPL.

52. Benjamin T. Waldo to Fred J. Grace, April 6, 1926. In Box 4, O'Keefe Papers, NOPL.

53. H. J. Chatterton, "The Muskrat Fur Industry of Louisiana," *Journal of Geography* 43, no. 5 (May 1944): 193–194.

54. Ramsey, "Rats to Riches," 78. See also Carlton Beals and Abel Plenn, "Louisiana Skin Game," *The Nation,* December 25, 1935, p. 738.

55. Donald W. Davis, "Trainasse," *Annals of the Association of American Geographers* 66 (September 1976): 349–359 (quotation on p. 355).

56. Jeansonne, *Leander Perez,* 32–61.

57. "Government Asked to Rebuild Dykes for Lower Coast," *NOTP,* December 14, 1915, p. 5.

58. Jeansonne, *Leander Perez,* 11. "Even Break in Plaquemines," *NOTP,* March 24, 1916, p. 5.

59. "Two Are Named Judges in Twenty-Ninth District," *NOTP,* December 9, 1919, p. 20; "Judge Perez Not Afraid of Attempt to Oust Him," *NOTP,* January 14, 1920, p. 10. For the concealed weapon charge, see "Jurist Asserts Ouster Program Is Political Plot," *NOTP,* October 11, 1923, pp. 1, 3. For the Klan, see "'Klan Block' in Legislature Marshaling Great Strength," *NOTP,* November 18, 1923, p. 1. See also H. P. McCall, "Political War in St. Bernard Growing Hotter," *NOTP,* November 18, 1923, p. 1.

60. "Break at Poydras Saves River Town," *NOTP,* May 13, 1922, p. 4. "Refugees Need Continued Care," *NOTP,* June 20, 1922, p. 7. "St. Bernard Judge Directs Action Against Liquor Runners and Speeders," *NOTP,* April 27, 1921, p. 7 ("easy mark"). "Dymond Gives Lie to Perez in Ouster Case," *NOTP,* October 12, 1923, pp. 1, 17.

61. "Michel Denies Perez, Meraux Figure in Deal," *NOTP,* April 14, 1926, p. 3.

62. Jeansonne, *Leander Perez,* 32–61. "Trappers Muster 1000 Men for War," *NOTP,* November 17, 1926, p. 1. Bryan M. Gowland, "The Delacroix Isleños and the Trappers' War in St. Bernard Parish," *Louisiana History* 44, no. 4 (Autumn 2003): 411–441; Beals and Plenn, "Louisiana Skin Game," 738–740; Ramsey, "Rats to Riches," 14–15, 78, 80; Carolyn Ramsey, "Louisiana's Fabulous Muskrat Marshland," *The Progressive,* February 12, 1945, p. 8. On trappers' efforts to secure access to the Bohemia Spillway, specifically, see "Two Bidders Seek Trapping Rights," *NOTP,* June 5, 1928, p. 27.

63. For enclosure, see E. P. Thompson, *The Making of the English Working Class* (New York: Pantheon Books, 1964), 218; and J. Crawford King, "The Closing of the Southern Range: An Exploratory Study," *Journal of Southern History* 48, no. 1 (February 1982): 53–70.

64. Viosca Jr., *Flood Control in the Mississippi Valley,* 16. See also Kane, *Deep Delta Country,* 178; Chatterton, "Muskrat Fur Industry," 191; and Edward J. Kammer, "A Socio-Economic Survey of the Marshdwellers of Four Southeastern Louisiana Parishes" (PhD dissertation, Catholic University, 1941), 92.

65. Beals and Plenn, "Louisiana Skin Game," 739. On narratives of community decline, see Thomas Bender, *Community and Social Change in America* (New Brunswick: Rutgers University Press, 1978). On "island communities," see Robert Wiebe, *The Search for Order, 1877–1920* (New York: Hill & Wang, 1966).

66. "Since the Black Pearl Was Found in the Oyster," *NOTP,* June 19, 1952, p. 12. With apologies to Jed Clampett, whose ballad was written by Paul Henning.

67. Theriot, "Building America's Energy Corridor," 27–64. For Gulf Oil's Grand Prairie dome in Plaquemines, see also "The Irrepressible Marsh Buggy," *Louisiana Conservation Review* 7 (Winter 1938–1939): 11. Bernard L. Krebs, "Magic Ring of Salt Domes Circles City with Liquid Wealth," *NOTP,* April 7, 1929, p. 22.

68. An act to authorize Parish School Boards in the State of Louisiana to execute oil, gas and mineral leases on any lands belonging in whole or in part to said School Boards, and to fix the terms and conditions of such leases, Louisiana Act 20 (1922). See also Brady Michael Banta, "The Regulation and Conservation of Petroleum Resources in Louisiana, 1901–1940" (PhD dissertation, Louisiana State University, 1981), 469. (Banta cites "Acts of Louisiana, 1928, p. 62.") On how human consumption creates value out of nature's capital, see Cronon, *Nature's Metropolis,* 148–151.

69. For the spillway, see "Levee Board Gets Oil Lease Bids," *NOTP,* May 9, 1928, p. 20; and "Texas Firm Soon to Begin Drilling on Spillway Land," *NOTP,* November 9, 1928, p. 15. For St. Bernard, see "Great Oil Field for New Orleans Area Predicted," *NOTP,* April 7, 1929, p. 27.

70. "Magic Ring of Salt Domes," *NOTP,* April 7, 1929, p. 22.

71. Paul S. Galtsoff et al., *Effects of Crude Oil Pollution on Oysters in Louisiana Waters,* US Department of Commerce, Bureau of Fisheries, Bulletin no. 18 (Washington, DC: Government Printing Office, 1935), 144.

72. "Our Parish and Paper," *PG*, September 28, 1928, p. 1.

73. There were 109 permits issued by 1939 according to Kammer, "Socio-Economic Survey of the Marshdwellers," 159. For oil development in Plaquemines, see also Priest, "Technology and Strategy," 11–36; Donald W. Davis, "Louisiana Canals and Their Influence on Wetland Development" (PhD dissertation, Louisiana State University, 1973).

74. "Louisiana's Most Richly Endowed Parish," *NOTP*, August 23, 1959, sec. 7, p. 13.

75. A joint resolution proposing an amendment to paragraph (k) of Section 14 of Article XIV of the Constitution of the State of Louisiana . . . , Louisiana Act 143 (1932). An act to authorize any parish to assume the outstanding bonded debt of road district . . . , Louisiana Act 164 (1932).

76. Jeansonne, *Leander Perez*, 62–73. Williams, *Huey Long*, 369, 400–402. "The Other Amendments," *NOTP*, November 6, 1932, p. 20 (for "complies").

77. David Baldwin, "Millionaire Perez Makes Hefty Fees," *NOI*, June 26, 1950, pp. 1, 14. William A. Friedlander (of the Subcommittee on Administration of the Internal Revenue Laws, Committee on Ways and Means, House of Representatives) to John E. Tobin, March 5, 1953. In the folder labeled "Material on Perez," Box 1073, Hale and Lindy Boggs Papers, Manuscripts Collection 1000, LRC.

78. "The 1 / 8 royalty was the minimum royalty required to be reserved in connection with a mineral lease by a political subdivision of Louisiana pursuant to 1928 La. Acts No. 66." In *Plaquemines Parish Commission Council v. Delta Development Corporation, Inc. et al.*, 502 So. 2d 1042 (Supreme Court of Louisiana no. 86-C-0950, 1987).

79. Friedlander to Tobin, March 5, 1953. See also Baldwin, "Millionaire Perez Makes Hefty Fees," 1, 14; and Jeansonne, *Leander Perez*, 74–84.

80. "Morrison Cites Plans to Punish Guilty in State," *NOTP*, December 23, 1939, p. 7 (for "abolish"). "Perez Slashes Noe Candidates in Plaquemines," *NOTP*, October 21, 1939, p. 1 (for "to hell").

81. US Census Bureau, "Louisiana Population of Counties by Decennial Census: 1900 to 1990."

82. Kane, *Deep Delta Country*, 258. Kammer, "Socio-Economic Survey of the Marshdwellers," 86.

83. Kammer, "Socio-Economic Survey of the Marshdwellers," 160–161. Since the nineteenth century, trappers had dredged "trainasses" through the marsh, small canals for their pirogues, but in comparison to mechanical dredging, the effects have been small. Furthermore, fur trappers had tended to observe local practical and ethical practices for limiting the effects of their canals. See Davis, "Trainasse," 349–359, esp. 355.

84. Lynn M. Alperin, *History of the Gulf Intracoastal Waterway* (National Waterways Study, US Army Engineer Water Resources Support Center, Institute for Water Resources; January 1983), 16.

85. Davis, "Louisiana Canals," 124, 156. "Field Operations in Louisiana's Marshes," *The Oil and Gas Journal*, July 11, 1955, p. 122 (for "huge circle").

86. For salt water intrusion, see Oliver A. Houk, "Land Loss in Coastal Louisiana: Causes, Consequences, and Remedies," *Tulane Law Review* 58 (October 1983): 1–167, esp. 39–40, and 35 for wave action. "Types of Wetlands," *America's Wetland Foundation*, http://www .americaswetlandresources.com/wildlife_ecology/plants_animals_ecology/wetlands /TypesofWetlands.html (for "cattails"); see also Richard Joel Russell, "Flotant," *Geographical Review* 32, no. 1 (January 1942): 74–98. For boat types, see Theriot, "Building America's Energy Corridor," 43. For wave action, see Houk, "Land Loss in Coastal Louisiana," 35.

87. Kane, *Deep Delta Country*, 148. Richard Joel Russell, "Physiography of Lower Mississippi River Delta," in State of Louisiana Department of Conservation, *Lower Mississippi River Delta: Reports on the Geology of Plaquemines and St. Bernard Parishes* (New Orleans: Department of Conservation Louisiana Geological Survey, 1936), 3–199, quotation on p. 164. For the suggestion that Russell was first, see Houk, "Land Loss in Coastal Louisiana," 10.

88. Penland et al., "Changes in Louisiana's Shoreline," 10. See also James P. Morgan and Philip B. Larimore, "Changes in the Louisiana Shoreline," *Gulf Coast Association of Geological Societies Transactions* 7 (1957): 303–310.

89. Russell, "Physiography of the Lower Mississippi River Delta," 61. The subsiding coastline was also partly the result of draining hydrocarbons from the earth, which created pockets that let the land sink under its own weight. See US Department of the Interior, US Geological Survey, "Wetland Subsidence, Fault Reactivation, and Hydrocarbon Production in the U.S. Gulf Coast Region," Fact Sheet FS-091-01 (January 9, 2013), http://pubs.usgs.gov/fs/fs091-01/index.html.

90. Houk, "Land Loss in Coastal Louisiana," 13. "This is an estimate from *natural* causes," Houk writes in note 35. His source is Dag Nummedal, "Future Sea Level Changes Along the Louisiana Coast," in D. F. Boesch, ed., *Proceedings of the Conference on Coastal Erosion and Wetland Modification in Louisiana: Causes, Consequences, and Options* (Washington, DC: US Fish & Wildlife Service, 1982), 164–176, esp. 165 and 171. For sediment load, see Robert H. Meade and John A. Moody, "Causes for the Decline of Suspended-Sediment Discharge in the Mississippi River System, 1940–2007," *Hydrological Processes* 24, no. 1 (January 2010): 3549.

91. Barry, *Rising Tide,* 166 (for river floods) 19–92 (for Eads and jetties). On river levees, see Colten, *Unnatural Metropolis,* 32. For the Flood Control Act of 1936, see also Joseph L. Arnold, "The Evolution of the 1936 Flood Control Act" (Fort Belvoir, VA: Office of History, US Army Corps of Engineers, 1988); and Karen O'Neill, *Rivers By Design: State Power and the Origins of U.S. Flood Control* (Durham: Duke University Press, 2006). For "the abyss," see Sherwood M. Gagliano et al., "Deterioration and Restoration of Coastal Wetlands," *Coastal Engineering Proceedings* 12 (1970): 1767–1781 (quotation on 1770).

92. Houk, "Land Loss in Coastal Louisiana," 11, citing "Senate and House Commission on Natural Resources," Legislature of Louisiana, Report on Special Projects for Coastal Louisiana, 1981. For the French Quarter, see Powell, *The Accidental City,* 4. For the conundrum of flood control, see William Darby, *A Geographical Description of the State of Louisiana* (New York: James Olmstead, 1817), 63; and Colten, *Unnatural Metropolis,* 17.

93. Percy Viosca Jr., "Louisiana Wet Lands and the Value of their Wild Life and Fishery Resources," *Ecology* 9 (April 1928): 216–229 ("civilization" on 227; "golden egg" on 229).

94. Louisiana Editors Association, *South Louisiana and the Beautiful Gulf Coast* (New Orleans: Louisiana Editors Association, 1937).

95. Williams, *Huey Long.* Robert D. Leighninger Jr., *Building Louisiana: The Legacy of the Public Works Administration* (Jackson: University Press of Mississippi, 2007). David S. Painter, "Oil and the American Century," *Journal of American History* 99, no. 1 (June 2012): 24–39.

96. William Leuchtenburg, *Franklin D. Roosevelt and the New Deal, 1932–1940* (New York: Harper and Row, 1963). For "messiah," see Arthur M. Schlesinger Jr., *The Age of Roosevelt: The Politics of Upheaval, 1935–1936* (New York: Houghton Mifflin, 1960), 42.

97. David Baldwin, "The Enormous Power of Leander Perez," *NOI,* June 14, 1950, pp. 1, 14 (for "vast mineral wealth"). Lester Velie, "Kingfish of the Dixiecrats," *Collier's,* December 17, 1949, p. 71 (for "welfare state").

98. Meyer, "The Land of Promise." For more on Meyer, see "Plaquemines Figure J. Ben Meyer Dies," *NOTP,* May 9, 1986.

99. Jeansonne, *Leander Perez,* 121–141. For rumors, see "Perez Control of Grand Prairie Board is Denied," *NOTP,* March 14, 1940, p. 4.

100. Petition, in Folder 107-2 ("E. F. Lehmann file"), Series V, in the Herman Lazard Midlo Collection, MSS 107, EKL.

101. "Perez," *NOSI,* February 15, 1941, p. 2.

102. Smith, "Oil, Brimstone, and 'Judge' Perez," 154 and 144 (for "demijohn").

103. Robert Sherrill, *Gothic Politics in the Deep South: Stars of the New Confederacy* (New York: Grossman Publishers, 1968), 15.

104. For an account of the dispute, see Garry Boulard, *The Big Lie: Hale Bogs, Lucille May Grace, and Leander Perez* (Gretna, LA: Pelican Publishing, 2001).

105. Memorandum from William A. Friedlander to John E. Tobin, Counsel, February 20, 1953. In the folder entitled "Material on Perez," Box 1073, Hale and Lindy Boggs Papers.

106. William Link, *Paradox of Southern Progressivism, 1880–1930* (Chapel Hill: University of North Carolina Press, 1997), 3 (for "despised"). Liebling, *Earl of Louisiana,* 121 (for "da feds").

107. Sherrill, *Gothic Politics in the Deep South*, 13. Crespino, *Strom Thurmond's America*, 78–80.

108. Gregory Blaine Miller, "Louisiana's Tidelands Controversy: *The United States of America v. State of Louisiana* Maritime Boundary Cases," *Louisiana History* 38, no. 2 (Spring 1997): 203–221 (quotation on 205).

109. A bill declaring lands under territorial waters of the continental United States to be a part of the public domain, S. 2164, 75th Cong., 3rd Sess. (1938). Tyler Priest, "Claiming the Coastal Sea," esp. 68.

110. Miller, "Louisiana's Tidelands Controversy," 205–206.

111. Priest, "Claiming the Coastal Sea," 73.

112. Miller, "Louisiana's Tidelands Controversy," 206 (for "Policy") and 207. Truman's actions might be seen as part of an "ocean enclosure movement." Lewis Alexander, "The Ocean Enclosure Movement: Inventory and Prospect," *San Diego Law Review* 20, no. 3 (1983): 561–594.

113. Priest, "Claiming the Coastal Sea," 74–75. For Kerr-McGee, see Tyler Priest, "Extraction Not Creation: The History of Offshore Petroleum in the Gulf of Mexico," *Enterprise & Society* 8, no. 2 (June 2007): 227–267, quotation on 237.

114. William J. Dodd, *Peapatch Politics: The Earl Long Era in Louisiana Politics* (Baton Rouge: Claitor's Publishing Division, 1991), 81.

115. Glenda E. Gilmore, *Defying Dixie: The Radical Roots of Civil Rights, 1919–1950* (New York: W. W. Norton, 2008), 419.

116. Priest, "Claiming the Coastal Sea," 80. Dodd, *Peapatch Politics*, 87.

117. Dodd, *Peapatch Politics*, 87.

118. Dodd, *Peapatch Politics*, 87–88. Jeansonne, *Leander Perez*, 166–167.

119. Dodd, *Peapatch Politics*, 87–91; Jeansonne, *Leander Perez*, 178–180.

120. Clinton C. Blackwell, "State Dems Plan to Fight," *Biloxi Daily Herald*, February 13, 1948, p. 1. For oil companies' "secret" support of state control, see Priest, "Auctioning the Ocean," 100–101.

121. Thomas L. Stokes, "Democratic Politics in Louisiana Explained by Character of 'Boss,'" *St. Petersburg Times*, October 25, 1948, p. 4. See also Thomas L. Stokes, "The Dixiecrats and Special Interests," *St. Petersburg Times*, August 25, 1949, p. 8.

122. Thomas Sancton, "White Supremacy-Crisis or Plot?" *The Nation*, July 24, 1948, pp. 95–97.

123. United States v. Louisiana, 339 U.S. 699 (1950), "marginal sea" at 704; Priest, "Claiming the Coastal Sea," esp. 76–79 (Daniel on p. 79).

124. Miller, "Louisiana's Tidelands Controversy," 209–220; Priest, "Claiming the Coastal Sea," 88–89; Priest, "Auctioning the Ocean," 93–105; Dodd, *Peapatch Politics*, 77 (for "disaster").

125. Penland, "Changes in Louisiana's Shoreline," 9–10. The study was Morgan and Larimore, "Changes in the Louisiana Shoreline," 303–310.

2. Help!: Hurricane Betsy and the Politics of Disaster in the Lower Ninth Ward, 1965–1967

1. Lucille Duminy, interview by Nilima Mwendo, November 19, 2003, interview 4700.1685, transcript, p. 36, LLMVC.

2. John E. Rousseau, "25,000 Homeless Being Cared For In Many Evacuation Centers," *LW*, September 18, 1965, p. 1.

3. In the Lower Ninth Ward, 6,285 homes and 175 commercial establishments "suffered generally severe flood damages." Another 6,350 homes were flooded in the Upper Ninth, also as a result of Industrial Canal breaches. See US Army Engineer District, New Orleans, *Report on Hurricane Betsy, 8–11 September 1965 in the U.S. Army Engineer District, New Orleans* (1965), 27–28. For other descriptions of infrastructure damage, see De Laureal Engineers, Inc., *Survey and Evaluation of Hurricane Betsy Damage* (New Orleans: City of New Orleans, Department of Streets, 1965); and Sewerage and Water Board of New Orleans, *Report on Hurricane Betsy, September 9–10, 1965* (New Orleans, 1965), both in the City Archives, Louisiana Division, NOPL.

4. "State's Death Toll Mounting," *NOTP*, September 13, 1965, p. 1. For reports of people drowning in attics, see John E. Rousseau, "Postman Describes Harrowing Ordeal," *LW*, September 18, 1965, p. 1.

5. "Statement of Hale Boggs . . . Before the House Committee on Public Works," October 13, 1965, p. 3, Folder 34, Box 998, Hale and Lindy Boggs Papers, Mss. 1000, LRC. Betsy set a hurricane record for the most insurable losses to property, although most losses in the Lower Ninth Ward were caused by flooding, which was not covered by insurance. See "Insurance Industry Sees Record Hurricane Lost," *NYT*, September 15, 1965, p. 32. The Red Cross called it "the most devastating tropical storm ever to strike the American mainland." "American Red Cross Disaster Action," p. 1, Folder 6, Box 306, Edwin Willis Papers, Collection 46, AMC.

6. Lyndon Johnson, "Remarks Upon Arrival at New Orleans Municipal Airport," September 10, 1965, transcript, in the Lyndon Baines Johnson Library and Museum at the University of Texas-Austin, a division of the National Archives and Records Administration (LBJ), published online at http://www.lbjlibrary.net/collections/quick-facts/lyndon -baines-johnson-hurricane-betsy/lbj-new-orleans-hurricane-betsy.html. See also "Johnson Visits City, Promises Swift Help," *NOTP*, September 11, 1965, p. 1.

7. "Forty years of debt . . . ," Handbill announcing Betsy Flood Victims meeting, June 6, 1966, Folder 2, Box 1, Elizabeth Rogers Collection, Mss. 176, EKL.

8. US House of Representatives, Committee on Public Works, 89th Cong., 1st Sess., *Hurricane Betsy Disaster of September 1965: Hearings before the Special Subcommittee to Investigate the Areas of Destruction of Hurricane, September 25–26, 1965* (Washington, DC: US Government Printing Office, 1965), 26.

9. "Hurricane Inquiry Imperative," *LW*, October 23, 1965.

10. For the influence of disasters on welfare policy during the New Deal, see Michele Landis Dauber, *The Sympathetic State: Disaster Relief and the Origins of the American Welfare State* (Chicago: University of Chicago Press, 2013).

11. Kristina Ford, *The Trouble with City Planning: What New Orleans Can Teach Us* (New Haven: Yale University Press, 2010), 2.

12. Along with the important exceptions cited later in this chapter, see also Craig E. Colten, *Perilous Place, Powerful Storms: Hurricane Protection in Coastal Louisiana* (Jackson: University of Mississippi Press, 2009); and Todd Shallat, "In the Wake of Betsy," in Craig E. Colten, ed., *Transforming New Orleans and Its Environs: Centuries of Change* (Pittsburgh: University of Pittsburgh Press, 2000), 121–137.

13. For example, see "A bill granting to the State of Louisiana a quantity of the public lands within the same, for the construction of a canal between the Mississippi River and Lake Pontchartrain," H.R. 455, 20th Cong. (February 24, 1829).

14. Thomas Ewing Dabney, *The Industrial Canal and Inner Harbor of New Orleans* (New Orleans: Board of Commissioners of the Port of New Orleans, 1921), 40.

15. Lawrence Powell, *The Accidental City: Improvising New Orleans* (Cambridge: Harvard University Press, 2012), 67. For New Orleans's physical expansion and development, see Craig E. Colten, *An Unnatural Metropolis: Wresting New Orleans from Nature* (Baton Rouge: Louisiana State University Press, 2005); Ari Kelman, *A River and Its City: The Nature of Landscape in New Orleans* (Berkeley: University of California Press, 2003); Peirce F. Lewis, *New Orleans: The Making of an Urban Landscape* (1976; Charlottesville: University of Virginia Press, 2018); and Richard Campanella, *Bienville's Dilemma: A Historical Geography of New Orleans* (Lafayette: Center for Louisiana Studies, 2008).

16. Colten, *Unnatural Metropolis*, 77–106. The pumps also helped combat yellow fever, in the context of Progressive Era sanitary reforms.

17. The September 19, 1947, storm and flood killed fifty-one people and caused $100 million in damages in New Orleans. Raymond B. Seed et al. [i.e., the Independent Levee Investigation Team (ILIT)], *Investigation of the Performance of the New Orleans Flood Protection Systems in Hurricane Katrina on August 29, 2005*, Vol. 1 (Berkeley: National Science Foundation, 2006), 11, 22, 26.

18. US Census for 1940 and 1960. I use census tract 8 to stand for Holy Cross, although I assume that the presence of white people in census tract 9 in the 1940 census (before it was divided into smaller tracts) reveals a statistical measure that does not line up perfectly with what residents considered to be the neighborhood boundaries. After Betsy, the Urban League's statistical profile of the Lower Ninth Ward included only census tracts 9A, 9B, 9C, and 9D, but not 7 or 8, as constituting the Lower Ninth neighborhood. *A Report on the Hurricane Betsy Disaster and the Urban League's Involvement* (New Orleans: Urban League of Greater New Orleans, September 30, 1965), 1, Box 117, Community Services Collection, EKL. Of the 8,637 housing units counted in 1960 census tracts 7, 8, 9A, 9B, 9C, and 10, 61.9 percent had been constructed since 1940, and 36.1 percent since 1950. See also Juliette Landphair, "Sewerage, Sidewalks, and Schools: The New Orleans Ninth Ward and Public School Desegregation," *Louisiana History* 40, no. 1 (Winter 1999): 35–62, esp. 35–40; Juliette Landphair, "'The Forgotten People of New Orleans': Community, Vulnerability, and the Lower Ninth Ward," *Journal of American History* 94, no. 3 (December 2007): 837–845; and Alexandra L. Giancarlo, "The Lower Ninth Ward: Resistance, Recovery, and Renewal" (MA thesis, Louisiana State University, 2011).

19. US Census of 1940 and 1960.

20. Lewis, *New Orleans,* 50–51.

21. US Census for 1960. According to the 1960 Census, 77 percent of nonwhite families in tract 7, 8, and 9(A,B,C,D) earned more than $2000 in 1959, compared to 70 percent in all of Orleans Parish; 60 percent of nonwhite families in the Lower Ninth earned more than $3,000 in 1959, compared to 50 percent in all of Orleans Parish; and roughly 41 percent of nonwhite families in the Lower Ninth earned more than $4,000 compared to 36 percent in all of Orleans Parish. See US Census Bureau, Family Income (Nonwhite Families), 1960. Prepared by Social Explorer.

22. Duminy, November 19, 2003, pp. 2–3, 9–10. Dolores and Raymond Parker, interview by Nimila Mwendo, December 2, 2003, interview 4700.1688, transcript, p. 10, LLMVC.

23. In 1960, 38 percent of African Americans in the Lower Ninth had lived in the same house in 1955, and 3 percent had moved to their current house from somewhere outside of Orleans Parish, meaning that nearly 62 percent of African American residents in 1960 had moved from somewhere else in New Orleans to the Lower Ninth in the previous five years. US Census Bureau, Residence in 1955 (Nonwhite Population) and Year Moved Into Unit (Nonwhite Occupied Housing Units), 1960. Prepared by Social Explorer.

24. Ida Belle Joshua, interview by Nilima Mwendo, November 20, 2003, interview 4700.1684, transcript, p. 3 ("afraid of debt"), 13 ("thriving"), 14 ("with a dream" and "with a hope"), 9 ("property owners."), LLMVC. The Magnolia extension was approved under the 1949 Federal Housing Act, a hallmark of President Harry Truman's "Fair Deal" agenda. See Martha Mahoney, "Law and Racial Geography: Public Housing and the Economy in New Orleans," *Stanford Law Review* 42, no. 5 (May 1990): 1251–1290, esp. 1276. On the post–World War II desire for a new house, see Kenneth Jackson, *Crabgrass Frontier: The Suburbanization of the United States* (New York: Oxford University Press, 1985). On how government policies encouraged new construction and class and race stratification in new neighborhoods, see Lizabeth Cohen, *A Consumer's Republic: The Politics of Mass Consumption in Postwar America* (New York: Knopf, 2003), 195–256.

25. Jason Berry, *Up From the Cradle of Jazz: New Orleans Music Since World War II* (New York: Da Capo Press, 1992), 29–39; Rick Coleman, *Blue Monday: Fats Domino and the Lost Dawn of Rock n' Roll* (New York: Da Capo Press, 2006), 16–20, 34. "Fats Domino's $200,000 Home," *Ebony,* July 1960, pp. 115–122 (quotation on p. 119).

26. To be sure, the policies and application of the GI Bill were often racist, and most African American veterans were denied the bill's benefits. See David H. Onkst, "'First a Negro . . . Incidentally a Veteran': Black World War Two Veterans and the G.I. Bill of Rights in the Deep South, 1944–1948," *Journal of Social History* 31, no. 3 (Spring 1998): 517–543. For decades of Ninth Ward protest against inadequate city services, see Landphair, "Sewerage, Sidewalks, and Schools," 35–62. Beginning in 1955, Leontine Luke led the Ninth Ward

Civic and Improvement League to advocate for "streets, lights, police protection, and better schools." Kim Lacy Rogers, *Righteous Lives: Narratives of the New Orleans Civil Rights Movement* (New York: New York University Press, 1993), 18–19 (quotation on p. 19).

27. The case was Bush v. Orleans Parish School Board, US Supreme Court, 364 U.S. 500 (1960).

28. On school desegregation, see Glen Jeansonne, *Leander Perez: Boss of the Delta* (Jackson: University Press of Mississippi, 1977), 253–270; "A Hero Among Us: The Civil Rights Movement Through the Eyes of a Child," E-Newsletter of the LSU School of Dentistry (February 2, 2011); Adam Fairclough, *Race & Democracy: The Civil Rights Struggle in Louisiana, 1915–1972* (Athens: University of Georgia Press, 1999); and Liva Baker, *The Second Battle of New Orleans: The Hundred-Year Struggle to Integrate the Schools* (New York: Harper Collins Publishers, 1996).

29. Kari Frederickson, *the Dixiecrat Revolt and the End of the Solid South, 1932–1968* (Chapel Hill: University of North Carolina Press, 2001), 158–62. On massive resistance, see Jason Ward, *Defending White Democracy: The Making of a Segregationist Movement and the Remaking of Racial Politics, 1936–1965* (Chapel Hill: University of North Carolina Press, 2011); and Numan Bartley, *The Rise of Massive Resistance: Race and Politics in the South During the 1950s* (Baton Rouge: Louisiana State University Press, 1999). There were important distinctions among Louisiana's white Democratic politicians, and some of their positions changed over time. Hale Boggs, for example, who signed the Southern Manifesto in 1956, supported the Voting Rights Act in 1965.

30. "Schiro Announces Platform," *NOTP*, September 3, 1965, p. 1. On Schiro, see Edward F. Haas, *Mayor Victor H. Schiro: New Orleans in Transition, 1961–1970* (Jackson: University Press of Mississippi, 2014).

31. Kent Germany, "The Politics of Poverty and History: Racial Inequality and the Long Prelude to Katrina," *Journal of American History* 94 (December 2007): 743–751 (statistic on p. 744).

32. Kent Germany, *New Orleans After the Promises: Poverty, Citizenship, and the Search for the Great Society* (Athens: University of Georgia Press, 2007), 24.

33. Arnold Hirsch, "New Orleans: Sunbelt in the Swamp," in Richard M. Bernard and Bradley R. Rice, eds., *Sunbelt Cities: Politics and Growth Since World War II* (Austin: University of Texas Press, 1983), 100–137, esp. 109–111.

34. Some of these men also belonged to a similar Mardi Gras krewe called Comus. John M. Barry, *Rising Tide: The Great Mississippi Flood of 1927 and How It Changed America* (New York: Simon & Schuster, 1997), 211–258. On "Share Our Wealth," see T. Harry Williams, *Huey Long* (New York: Alfred A. Knopf, 1970), 676–706.

35. Michael P. Smith, "Behind the Lines: The Black Mardi Gras Indians the New Orleans Second Line," *Black Music Research Journal* 14, no. 1 (Spring 1994): 43–73. On second line parades, see also Helen A. Regis, "Second Lines, Minstrelsy, and the Contested Landscapes of New Orleans Afro-Creole Festivals," *Cultural Anthropology* 14, no. 4 (November 1999): 472–504. For a general history of mutual aid societies, David T. Beito, *From Mutual Aid to the Welfare State: Fraternal Societies and Social Services, 1890–1967* (Chapel Hill: University of North Carolina Press, 2000).

36. Lyndon B. Johnson, "speech at the Jung Hotel, New Orleans, LA," October 9, 1964, https://millercenter.org/the-presidency/presidential-speeches/october-9-1964-speech-jung -hotel-new-orleans. See also Lyndon B. Johnson, "Remarks at the University of Michigan," May 22, 1964, https://millercenter.org/the-presidency/presidential-speeches/may-22 -1964-remarks-university-michigan; and Germany, *New Orleans After the Promises*.

37. Christian Roselund and Brian Marks, "Louisiana Petro-Populism and Public Services in the City of New Orleans," paper presented at the Workshop on the Political Economy of New Orleans, Tulane University (September 2010), 21–22. On schools, see also Baker, *Second Battle of New Orleans;* and Donald E. DeVore and Joseph Logsdon, *Crescent City Schools: Public Education in New Orleans, 1841–1991* (1991; Lafayette: University of Louisiana at Lafayette Press, 2012). On Charity Hospital, see John E. Salvaggio, *New Orleans' Charity Hospital: A Story of Physicians, Politics, and Poverty* (Baton Rouge: Louisiana State University Press, 1992).

38. Germany, "The Politics of Poverty and History," 748.

39. "Life Begins at Forty," *LW,* September 18, 1965, p. 6. On the civil rights movement in 1960s Louisiana, see Rogers, *Righteous Lives,* and Fairclough, *Race & Democracy.*

40. "List of Officers and Initial Committee," Committee for Progressive Action for the Lower Ninth Ward (undated, probably fall, 1965), Folder 995, Box 95, Community Services Council of New Orleans Collection, Mss. 34, EKL.

41. Joshua, November 20, 2003, pp. 7 and 54.

42. Bruce Schulman, *From Cotton Belt to Sunbelt: Federal Policy, Economic Development, and the Transformation of the South, 1938–1980* (Oxford: Oxford University Press, 1991), 34.

43. On "maximum feasible participation," and the Economic Opportunity Act of 1964, see Lillian B. Rubin, "Maximum Feasible Participation: The Origins, Implications, and Present Status," *The ANNALS of the American Academy of Political and Social Science* 385, no. 1 (September 1969): 14–29.

44. "Betsy Turns Northwest," *NOTP,* September 3, 1965, p. 1.

45. "Big Hurricane Stalls in Atlantic," *NOTP,* September 6, 1965, p. 1.

46. James McLean, "Gov. McKeithen Briefed on Hurricane Betsy Move," *NOTP,* September 9, 1965, p. 7.

47. By that point, the storm had already caused extensive damage in the Caribbean. "Wide Hurricane Watch as Betsy Moves in Gulf," *NOTP,* September 9, 1965, p. 1.

48. "Thousands Flee Flood Threat as Hurricane Slams into N.O.," *NOTP,* September 10, 1965, p. 1.

49. Duminy, November 19, 2003, pp. 14–15 ("just a storm" on 14). See also "9th Warders All Agree/No Evacuation Warning Given for Area," *LW,* September 25, 1965, pp. 1, 9.

50. Joshua, November 20, 2003, pp. 14–15 (quotation on 15).

51. Joshua, November 20, 2003, pp. 16 (first quotation) and 17 (subsequent quotations).

52. US Army Engineer District, *Report on Hurricane Betsy,* 8. Thomas R. Forrest, *Hurricane Betsy, 1965: A Selective Analysis of Organizational Response in the New Orleans Area,* Historical and Comparative Disaster Series #5 (Newark: University of Delaware Disaster Research Center, 1979), 8–16. For the official meteorological account of the storm, see US Weather Bureau, *Hurricane Betsy, August 27-September 12, 1965: Preliminary Report with Advisories and Bulletins Issued* (Washington, DC: US Weather Bureau, 1965).

53. Joshua, November 20, 2003, p. 20.

54. Joshua, November 20, 2003, pp. 20–22.

55. Duminy, November 19, 2003, pp. 19–20.

56. Duminy, November 19, 2003, pp. 19–21. The New Orleans *Times-Picayune* reports a Red Cross bus provisioning some Ninth Ward shelters with food, but not until 3:30 in the morning, after the Duminys had fled the shelter. Jules Fogel, "Storm Coverage Harrowing," *NOTP,* September 11, 1965, p. 6.

57. "Hurricane Flood Raises Toll to 50," *NYT,* September 12, 1965, p. 1.

58. Duminy, November 19, 2003, pp. 21–22.

59. Duminy, November 19, 2003, pp. 7, 24–25.

60. Dorothy Prevost, interview by Nilima Mwendo, December 2, 2003, interview 4700.1686, transcript, pp. 17, 50, LLMVC.

61. Joshua, November 20, 2003, pp. 32–33. For other accounts of the explosion, see Parker, December 2, 2003, pp. 51–52; Marguerite Guette to Mayor Schiro, "Inter-Office Memorandum," September 21, 1965, Folder 6, Box S65-13, Victor H. Schiro Papers, NOPL; hereinafter "Schiro Papers"; and Edward F. Haas, "'Don't Believe Any False Rumors . . .': Mayor Victor H. Schiro, Hurricane Betsy, and Urban Myths," *Louisiana History* 45, no. 4 (Autumn 2004): 463–468, esp. 465–466. Beyond these individual accounts, there is no evidence that anybody purposely breached the Industrial Canal floodwalls.

62. Lucy Thomas, interview by Nilima Mwendo, December 10, 2003, interview 4700.1687, transcript, p. 25, LLMVC.

63. J. Francis Pohlhaus to Horace C. Bynum, September 21, 1965. Quoted in Haas, "Don't Believe Any False Rumors . . . ," 466.

64. Haas, "Don't Believe Any False Rumors . . . ," 468.

65. Sewerage and Water Board, *Report on Hurricane Betsy*, 21–25. Thomas R. Forrest, "Hurricane Betsy: A Selective Analysis of Organizational Response" (Working Paper #7, Disaster Research Center, Ohio State University, December 1970), 10. All quotations are from Forrest's report, although the broader account is drawn from both. Forrest's report suggests that Army Corps personnel assisted the Sewerage and Water Board; the Sewerage and Water Board's account describes using an Army Corps vehicle but does mention the specific intervention of Army Corps officials. The accounts otherwise are basically similar. Colten made reference in 2007 to claims that the Army Corps "had opened gates in the floodwall along the Industrial Canal, creating a flood that inundated their homes," but Forrest's 1970 report suggests more definitive evidence that rather closing the gates exacerbated the flood. Craig E. Colten, "Environmental Justice in a Landscape of Tragedy," *Technology in Society* 29, no. 2 (April 2007): 173–179 (quotation on 175).

66. Haas, "Don't Believe Any False Rumors . . . ," 464 (for "crazy"). For 1927, see "Governor's Proclamation," *NOTP*, April 27, 1927, p. 1; and Barry, *Rising Tide*, 213–258.

67. The speech was on March 16, 1965. Keith M. Finley, *Delaying the Dream: Southern Senators and the Fight against Civil Rights, 1938–1965* (Baton Rouge: Louisiana State University Press, 2008), 293.

68. "Engineers See Flood Factors," *NOTP*, September 14, 1965, p. 1. After Betsy, the "Citizens Committee for Hurricane Flood Control" warned the Army Corps that the Mississippi River–Gulf Outlet "would form a funnel, channeling all hurricane surges and wind driven water into the Intracoastal Waterway and Industrial Canal." Kenneth LeSieur to Thomas Bowen, "Re: 1962 Master Plan for Hurricane Flood Control," November 24, 1965, in the ACEDL, https://usace.contentdm.oclc.org/digital/collection/p16021coll2/id/915. See also William R. Reudenburg, Robert B. Gramling, Shirley Laska, and Kai Erikson, *Catastrophe in the Making: The Engineering of Katrina and the Disasters of Tomorrow* (Washington, DC: Island Press, 2009), esp. 91. For the St. Bernard lawsuit, see Graci v. United States, 5th Circuit, 456 F.2d 20 (1971).

69. For a comparable argument, see Ari Kelman, "Even Paranoids Have Enemies: Rumors of Levee Sabotage in New Orleans's Lower Ninth Ward," *Journal of Urban History* 35, no. 5 (July 2009): 627–639.

70. Neil Smith, *Uneven Development: Nature, Capital, and the Production of Space* (New York: Blackwell, 1984).

71. Carl Lindahl, "Legends of Hurricane Katrina: The Right to Be Wrong, Survivor-to-Survivor Storytelling, and Healing," *Journal of American Folklore* 125, no. 496 (Spring 2012): 139–176.

72. Duminy, November 19, 2003, p. 15. An early estimate reported that there were fifty-two killed in the storm, thirty-one in New Orleans, and "between 75 and 80 percent of the dead are Negroes." John E. Rousseau, "25,000 Homeless Being Care for in Many Evacuation Centers," *LW*, September 18, 1965, p. 1.

73. US House of Representatives, 89 Cong., 1 Sess., *Southeast Hurricane Disaster Relief Act of 1965*, Rep. No. 1164 to accompany H.R. 11539, October 20, 1965, Folder 1, Box 55, Boggs Papers.

74. "Flood Death Toll Mounts," *NOTP*, September 13, 1965, p. 3.

75. "Parish by Parish Damage List," *NOTP*, September 15, 1965, p. 17.

76. For "refugees," see Forrest, *Hurricane Betsy, 1965* (1979), 9. For 260,000 evacuees and state-wide and national statistics, see Office of Emergency Planning, *Hurricane Betsy: Federal Action in Disaster* (Washington, DC: US Government Printing Office, 1966), 2.

77. All quotations from Russell Long and Edwin Willis to Lyndon Johnson, audio recording of telephone conversation, September 10, 1965. Published online at the Presidential Recordings Program, Miller Center of Public Affairs, University of Virginia, Charlottesville, VA, https://millercenter.org/the-presidency/educational-resources/lbj-and-senator-russell-long-on-hurricane-betsy. See also "Tree Damages Sen. Long Home," *NOTP*, September 11, 1965, p. 2.

78. Long, Willis, and Johnson, phone conversation recording. See also David Remnick, "High Water," *New Yorker*, October 3, 2005, pp. 48–57.

79. Johnson, "Remarks Upon Arrival at New Orleans Municipal Airport." See also "Johnson Visits City, Promises Swift Help," *NOTP*, September 11, 1965, p. 1.

80. McKeithen as quoted by Schiro, minutes of mayoral meeting with department heads, September 11, 1965, Folder 1, Box S65-12, Schiro Papers.

81. Edward F. Haas, "Victor H. Schiro, Hurricane Betsy, and the 'Forgiveness Bill,'" *Gulf Coast Historical Review* 6 (1990): 66–90, esp. 72–73 ("here to help" on 73); "President Johnson Requests Water After Visiting Shelter," transcript, September 10, 1965, LBJ (for "water"); "Johnson Visits City, Promises Swift Help," *NOTP*, September 11, 1965, p. 1; "President Johnson Speaks to Hurricane Victim William Marshall," transcript, September 10, 1965, LBJ; President's Daily Diary for September 10, 1965, http://www.lbjlibrary.net/collections/daily-diary.html, LBJ.

82. Prevost, December 2, 2003, pp. 25–26 (quotation on 26). On Sunday, there were nearly 4,000 people at the shelter, which Prevost referred to by an earlier name, the Port of Embarkation. See "Shelters Open as of 11:30 p.m. Sunday," memo, September 13, 1965, p. 2, Folder 1, Box S65-12, Schiro Papers.

83. Don Hughes, "Storm Refugees Formed into Bustling Community," *NOTP*, September 16, 1965, p. 4. For "14,000," see Walter Rogers and Elizabeth Rogers, "Riding the Nightmare Express," 1965, p. 14, Box 1, Elizabeth Rogers Collection, Mss. 176, EKL.

84. The Disaster Relief Act of 1950, Pub. L. 81-875, 64 Stat. 1109 (1950). See also Congressional Research Service, *After Disaster Strikes: Federal Programs and Organizations,* report to the Committee on Government Operations (Washington, DC: US Government Printing Office, 1974); and David A. Moss, "Courting Disaster?: The Transformation of Federal Disaster Policy since 1803," in Kenneth A. Froot, ed., *The Financing of Catastrophic Risk* (Chicago: University of Chicago Press, 1999), 307–362, esp. 315.

85. The Red Cross was afforded special status in the 1950 Disaster Act, which directed agencies to "cooperate to the fullest extent possible with . . . the American National Red Cross." "President Promises Help," *NOTP*, September 11, 1965, p. 3; "Relief Assured, Mayor Reports," *NOTP*, September 11, 1965, p. 2; "LA. Guard Role in Storm Cited," *NOTP*, September 13, 1965, p. 6; "Guard Working in Storm Area," *NOTP*, September 14, 1965, pp. 2–7; Joseph A. Lucia, "Relief Funds Available to Ravaged Areas Today," *NOTP*, September 13, 1965, pp. 2–6.

86. "Loan Program Official in N.O." *NOTP*, September 13, 1965, p. 11; Carolyn Kolb, "Financial Aid for Stricken Is Available," *NOTP*, September 14, 1965, p. 1; "Union Urges Federal Help Be Outlined," *NOTP*, September 14, 1965, p. 3; "List of Aid Steps Growing," *NOTP*, September 15, 1965, pp. 3–18; and James McLean, "Briefing on U.S. Aid Held for Officials," *NOTP*, September 15, 1965, p. 1.

87. Lyndon Johnson to Victor Schiro, telegram, September 12, 1965, Folder 4, Box S65-13, Schiro Papers.

88. "Thank You, Mr. President," *NOTP*, September 13, 1965, p. 12. Edwin E. Willis, "Extension of Remarks," September 13, 1965, Folder 3, Box 306, Willis Papers.

89. "Betsy a Big One But Wound Not Deep," *NOTP*, September 11, 1965, p. 8. "All Big Stores to Open Today," *NOTP*, September 11, 1965, p. 1. "Major Tourist Facilities Reported Nearly Normal," *NOTP*, September 15, 1965, p. 2.

90. Minutes from mayoral meeting with city department heads, September 27, 1965, pp. 4–5, Folder 1, Box S65-12, Schiro Papers.

91. "Flood Death Toll Mounts," *NOTP*, September 13, 1965, p. 3.

92. Minutes from mayoral meeting with city department heads, September 24, 1965, p. 4, Folder 1, Box S65-12, Schiro Papers. I could not locate a definitive statement on when the flood was fully drained from the Lower Ninth; the absence of such notice itself is telling.

93. New Orleans Police Department Press Release, September 15, 1965, p. 1, Folder 1, Box S65-12, Schiro Papers.

94. Duminy, November 19, 2003, p. 39.

95. For "shot on sight," see Jack McGuire to Victor Schiro, September 10, 1965, Box 9, Victor H. and Margaret G. Schiro Papers, Manuscripts Collection 1001, LRC. New Orleans Police

Department press release, September 15, 1965, Folder 1, Box S65-12, Schiro Papers. On "looting," see also Rebecca Solnit, *A Paradise Built in Hell: The Extraordinary Communities that Arise in Disaster* (New York: Viking, 2009), 21, 237–238; and Carl Lindhal, "Legends of Hurricane Katrina: The Right to Be Wrong, Survivor-to-Survivor Storytelling, and Healing," *Journal of American Folklore* 125, no. 496 (Spring 2012): 139–176, esp. 151. Schiro lifted the restrictions on entering the Ninth Ward sometime after City Council member Philip Ciaccio wrote a letter arguing that "repairmen have been turned back at check points leading to an almost impossible situation." See Ciaccio to Schiro, September 21, 1965, in Folder 6, Box S65-13, Schiro Papers.

96. Dick Aronson to Albert G. Rosenberg, October 12, 1965, Folder 995, Box 95, Community Services Collection, EKL.

97. Duminy, November 19, 2003, pp. 27–30, 34–35 ("taking care" on 26).

98. "Nightmare of Betsy Clings to New Orleans," *CD*, September 18, 1965, pp. 1–2 (quotations on 2). See also "9th Warders All Agree: No Evacuation Warning Given for Area," *LW*, September 25, 1965, p. 1. Forrest describes some confusion in trying to apply Civil Defense provisions for a "man-made" disaster to this "natural disaster" context. See Forrest, *Hurricane Betsy, 1965* (1979), 44.

99. James H. Gillis, "Flood Barrier, McKeithen Aim," *NOTP*, September 15, 1965, p. 1.

100. Stanley Taylor, "Hebert Strongly Disagrees with Dr. Teller's Charges," *LW*, September 25, 1965, p. 7.

101. "Eyes Intent on Hurricane Betsy," *NOSI*, September 9, 1965, p. 10. See also Forrest, *Hurricane Betsy, 1965* (1979), 7.

102. Gillis, "Flood Barrier . . ." *NOTP*, September 15, 1965, p. 1. On blaming nature, see Ted Steinberg, *Acts of God: The Unnatural History of Natural Disaster in America* (Oxford: Oxford University Press, 2000).

103. Johnson, "Remarks Upon Arrival at New Orleans Municipal Airport." See also "Johnson Visits City, Promises Swift Help," *NOTP*, September 11, 1965, p. 1.

104. Office of Emergency Planning, *Hurricane Betsy*, 1.

105. Taylor, "Hebert Strongly Disagrees," *LW*, September 25, 1965, p. 7.

106. Rogers and Rogers, "Riding the Nightmare Express," p. 14. On Rogers, see also Joseph Mamone, "Labor's Loves Lost: The Lives and Activism of Walter and Elizabeth Rogers" (MS thesis, University of New Orleans, 1998).

107. Mamone, "Labor's Loves Lost," 30. Geneva Griffith, "Lagniappe," *Cameron Parish Pilot*, May 2, 1958.

108. "Fellow Flood Sufferers," September 20, 1965, Folder 2, Box 1, Elizabeth Rogers Collection. Rogers had already been taking notes on supposed eyewitness accounts of the levee bombing before September 20. See her notebook, Box 1, Folder 1, Elizabeth Rogers Collection.

109. Rogers and Rogers, "Riding the Nightmare Express," p. 17.

110. Although the hearings were mentioned in advance in the newspaper, Rogers was still in an emergency shelter at the time. She asserted few Ninth Ward residents heard in advance about the hearings and for years, she called them "secret hearings." "Hear about the secret hearings on 'Betsy' problems held in New Orleans last September without inviting us," June 5, 1966, Folder 2, Box 1, Elizabeth Rogers Collection.

111. "Profiteering Reported in New Orleans; Storm Refugees Growing Restive," *NYT*, September 13, 1965, p. 19.

112. Committee on Public Works, *Hurricane Betsy Disaster of September 1965*, 8–11 (first quotation on p. 8; second and third quotation on p. 9; fourth quotation on p. 11).

113. Committee on Public Works, *Hurricane Betsy Disaster of September 1965*, p. 80 (Schiro quotation) and p. 132 (Director of Public Works quotation).

114. S. 2591, 89th Cong., 1st Sess. (1965). Haas argues that Schiro and Johnson pressured a reluctant Long into introducing the bill. See Haas, "Victor H. Schiro, Hurricane Betsy, and the 'Forgiveness Bill,'" 82.

115. Although Congress had passed the National Flood Insurance Act in 1956, it had never been implemented. Flood insurance was not available to Americans at the time Betsy hit. Flood insurance was debated at the Committee on Public Works hearings but was not actually enacted until after 1968.

116. Committee on Public Works, *Hurricane Betsy Disaster of September 1965,* 23.

117. Committee on Public Works, *Hurricane Betsy Disaster of September 1965,* 76.

118. "Hebert Lashes At Exploiters," *NOTP,* September 27, 1965, p. 9.

119. Haas, "Victor H. Schiro, Hurricane Betsy, and the 'Forgiveness Bill,'" 83–84.

120. Unsigned to Victor Schiro, telegram, October 22, 1965, Folder 1, Box S65-12, Schiro Papers; US House of Representatives, 89 Cong., *Calendars of the United States House of Representatives and History of Legislation: Final Edition* (Washington, DC, 1967), 162; Southeast Hurricane Disaster Relief Act of 1965, Pub. L. No. 89-339, 79 Stat. 1301 (November 8, 1965). Boggs had introduced the bill as H.R.11539 on October 12.

121. "Funds Dry Up Expected to Hit Negro Businesses Hard," *Chicago Daily Defender,* November 4, 1965, p. 19.

122. "Betsy Flood Victims Demand Spillway Pay and World Peace," petition submitted to Russell Long, June 1966, Folder 2, Box 1, Elizabeth Rogers Collection.

123. BFV Press Release, June 23, 1966, Folder 2, Box 1, Elizabeth Rogers Collection.

124. Duminy, November 19, 2003, pp. 44 (for trailers) and 45 (for grants).

125. Leander H. Perez to Robert E. Jones, September 22, 1965, in *Hurricane Betsy Disaster of September 1965,* 84.

126. Joshua, November 20, 2003, pp. 27 (first two quotations) and 33 (third quotation).

127. For example, see BFV to George Fallon, July 6, 1966; BFV to Victor Schiro, September 17, 1966; and BFV to New Orleans City Council, August 18, 1966, all in Folder 2, Box 1, Elizabeth Rogers Collection.

128. Rogers note, undated, Folder 2, Box 1, Elizabeth Rogers Collection.

129. O. C. W. Taylor, "La. Hurricane Victims Seek Urban Renewal Aid from U.S," *CD,* January 14, 1967, p. 34 (for "neglected" and "insufficient"); "Hurricane Victims Vow to Integrate Housing," *CD,* January 28, 1967, p. 30 (for "middle-class members").

130. Joshua, November 20, 2003, 34.

131. "Mixed Group from La. Goes to D.C. For Housing Aid," *CD,* February 11, 1967, p. 3. Members of the New Orleans City Council also attended, along with Albert W. Dent, A. P. Tureaud, and representatives of the Urban League.

132. "Hurricane Victims Vow to Integrate Housing," *CD,* January 28, 1967, p. 30. The Ninth Ward did eventually get urban renewal funding, but not until after 1967. See Germany, *New Orleans After the Promises.*

133. Edward George Sr. to Hale Boggs, December 17, 1966, Folder 9, Box 732, Boggs Papers.

134. Henry Glapion to Lyndon Johnson, Victor Schiro, et al., October 20, 1965, Folder 1, Box S65-12, Schiro Papers.

135. Joshua, November 20, 2003, pp. 24–26; Duminy, November 20, 2003, p. 32.

136. "Statement of Hale Boggs . . . Before the House Committee on Public Works," October 13, 1965, p. 7, Folder 34, Box 998, Boggs Papers.

137. Walter and Elizabeth Rogers, "Betsy Flood," *The Movement,* April 1967, p. 2.

138. Duminy, November 20, 2003, p. 32.

139. For an analogous case, see Pete Daniel, *Lost Revolutions: The South in the 1950s* (Chapel Hill: University of North Carolina Press, 2000), 7–90.

140. Joshua, November 20, 2003, p. 50.

3. The New New Orleans: Louisiana Grows and Shrinks, 1967–2005

1. "Bataan Defenders Forced Back Again," *NYT,* April 8, 1942, p. 1.

2. "Housing Needs Outlined to Congressmen," *NOS,* April 9, 1942, pp. 1, 4.

3. "Housing Needs Outlined to Congressmen," *NOS,* April 9, 1942, p. 4. Congressman Frank Boykin made the comment earlier in the day, at the Congressional hearing. A "Spot-check

survey of war housing needs" conducted by the private National Committee on the Housing Emergency estimated that New Orleans needed 20,000 to 30,000 dwelling units. See US House of Representatives, Committee on Public Works, 77 Cong., 2 Sess. *Hearings on H.R. 7312 A Bill to Increase by $600,000,000 The Amount Authorized to Be Appropriated for Defense Housing Under The Act of October 14, 1940, As Amended* (Washington, DC, 1942), 133.

4. "Sites for Housing Projects," *SBV,* April 25, 1942, p. 1.

5. Gentilly Terrace Company, "Gentilly Terrace, Where Homes Are Built on Hills" (no date, ca. 1910), 5.

6. Richard Campanella, *Geographies of New Orleans: Urban Fabrics Before the Storm* (Lafayette: Center for Louisiana Studies, 2006), 46. See also Soil Conservation Service, "Soil Survey of Orleans Parish, Louisiana" (US Department of Agriculture, 1989), 42–45; Virginia R. Burkett, David B. Zilkoski, and David A. Hart, "Sea-Level Rise and Subsidence: Implications for Flooding in New Orleans, Louisiana," in *U.S. Geological Survey Subsidence Interest Group Conference: Proceedings of the Technical Meeting, Galveston, Texas, November 27–29, 2001* (Austin, TX: US Geological Survey, 2003): 63–70; Richard Campanella, *Delta Urbanism: New Orleans* (Chicago: American Planning Association, 2010), 130.

7. "It is not a coincidence," a *New York Times* editorial asserted, for example, "that many of those hard-hit, low-lying areas have had poor and predominantly African American residents." "Hard Decisions for New Orleans," *NYT,* January 14, 2006, p. A14. "The most glaring feature of their circumstance suggests that Katrina's survivors lived in concentrated poverty—they lived in poor neighborhoods, attended poor schools, and had poor paying jobs that reflected and reinforced a distressing pattern of rigid segregation." Michael Eric Dyson, *Come Hell or High Water: Hurricane Katrina and the Color of Disaster* (New York: Basic Civitas, 2006), 6.

8. On environmental racism, see in Commission for Racial Justice, *Toxic Wastes and Race in the United States: A National Report on the Racial and Socio-Economic Characteristics of Communities with Hazardous Waste Sites* (New York: United Church of Christ, 1987); Robert D. Bullard, *Dumping in Dixie: Race, Class, and Environmental Quality* (Boulder: Westview, 1990); Bullard, Paul Mohai, Robin Saha, and Beverly Wright, *Toxic Wastes and Race at Twenty, 1987–2007: A Report Prepared for the United Church of Christ Justice & Witness Ministries* (Cleveland: The United Church of Christ, 2007); Laura Pulido, "A Critical Review of the Methodology of Environmental Racism Research," *Antipode* 28, no. 2 (1996): 142–159; Pulido, "Geographies of Race and Ethnicity II: Environmental Racism, Racial Capitalism and State-Sanctioned Violence," *Progress in Human Geography* 41, no. 4 (August 2017): 524–533; and Dorceta E. Taylor, *The Environment and the People in American Cities, 1600s–1900s: Disorder, Inequality, and Social Change* (Durham: Duke University Press, 2009).

9. Martin Luther King Jr., "Where Do We Go From Here?" speech to the Southern Christian Leadership Conference, Atlanta, Georgia, August 16, 1967, in Clayborne Carson and Kris Shepard, eds., *A Call to Conscience: The Landmark Speeches of Dr. Martin Luther King, Jr.* (New York: Warner Books, 2001), 196.

10. On the creation of racial inequalities in the twentieth-century metropolis, see, for example, Kenneth Jackson, *Crabgrass Frontier: The Suburbanization of the United States* (Oxford: Oxford University Press, 1985); Thomas Sugrue, *The Origins of the Urban Crisis: Race and Inequality in Postwar Detroit* (Princeton: Princeton University Press, 1996); Lizabeth Cohen, *A Consumers' Republic: The Politics of Mass Consumption in Postwar America* (New York: Knopf, 2003); Kevin M. Kruse and Thomas J. Sugrue, eds., *The New Suburban History* (Chicago: University of Chicago Press, 2006); Robert O. Self, *American Babylon: Race and the Struggle for Postwar Oakland* (Princeton: Princeton University Press, 2003); and Matthew D. Lassiter and Kevin M. Kruse, "Bulldozer Revolution: Suburbs and Southern History since World War II," *Journal of Southern History* 75, no. 3 (August 2009): 691–706.

11. On the complications of flood vulnerability, see Chapter 4, and also Christina Finch, Christopher T. Emrich, and Susan L. Cutter, "Disaster Disparities and Differential

Recovery in New Orleans," *Population and Environment* 31, no. 3 (March 2010): 179–202. Although I quibble with these scholars' "social vulnerability index," I agree that lower socioeconomic status does not account for the extent of the flood.

12. According to FEMA Flood and Damage Assessments, of a total population of 67,229, 64,955 residents of St. Bernard Parish—nearly 97 percent—experienced flood damage during Katrina. Thomas Gabe, Gene Falk, and Maggie McCarty, *Hurricane Katrina: Social-Demographic Characteristics of Impacted Areas,* CRS Report no. RL33141 (Washington, DC: Congressional Research Service, November 4, 2005), 9. Other estimates were lower: a later FEMA estimate, tabulated differently, suggested that 80.6 percent of occupied housing units in St. Bernard suffered flood damage. Nonetheless, this still amounted to a higher percentage than Orleans Parish, which was estimated to have seen 71.5 percent of its occupied housing units damaged. Office of Policy Development and Research, *Current Housing Unit Damage Estimates, Hurricanes Katrina, Rita, and Wilma,* Data from FEMA Individual Assistance Registrants and Small Business Administration Disaster Loan Applications (Washington, DC: US Department of Housing and Urban Development, February 12, 2006), 16.

13. St. Bernard Parish was 92.5 percent white and 7.3 percent black according to the 1960 US Census, and 88.3 percent white and 7.6 percent black according to the 2000 US Census. According to the 2000 US Census, median housing income in 1999 dollars for Orleans Parish was $27,133 and $35,939 for St. Bernard Parish.

14. The exceptions prove the rule: the African American neighborhoods that endured the worst flooding, such as those in eastern New Orleans, were occupied largely by middle-class homeowners.

15. A statistical analysis of the flood-damaged population suggesting that "the odds of living in a damaged area were . . . much greater for blacks, renters, and poor people," also showed that across the region, roughly the same number of non-Hispanic whites as blacks lived in damaged areas (294,000 versus 295,000), and that "the number of persons in" damaged areas "above the poverty line was much larger than the number of poor persons." John R. Logan, *The Impact of Katrina: Race and Class in Storm-Damaged Neighborhoods* (Providence: Brown University Spatial Structures in the Social Sciences Institute, 2005), 7. Ira Katznelson, *Fear Itself: The New Deal and the Origins of Our Time* (New York: W. W. Norton, 2013), 16.

16. Robert K. Merton, "The Unanticipated Consequences of Purposive Social Action," *American Sociological Review* 1, no. 6 (December 1936): 894–904, quotation on 903.

17. Home Owners' Loan Act of 1933, Pub. L. No. 73-43, 48 Stat. 128 (June 13, 1933).

18. Amy Hillier, "Redlining and the Home Owners' Loan Corporation" (PhD dissertation, University of Pennsylvania, 2001), 1–2. Jackson, *Crabgrass Frontier,* 196–197.

19. Division of Research and Statistics, Federal Home Loan Bank Board, "Summary of Economic, Real Estate, and Mortgage Survey and Security Area Descriptions of New Orleans, LA," April 28, 1939, pp. 1A–2A. In the City Survey File, 1935–1940, Box 88, folder "New Orleans #2," (450/68/5/01), Records of the Federal Home Loan Bank Board, Record Group 195, National Archives at College Park, College Park, MD.

20. Samuel R. Cook and Alec C. Morgan, "Report of Re-Survey New Orleans, Louisiana for the Division of Research and Statistics, Home Owners' Loan Corporation, Washington, D.C.," April 28, 1939, p. 42. In the City Survey File, 1935–1940, Box 67, folder "New Orleans, LA Re-survey Report" (450/68/4/5), Records of the Federal Home Loan Bank Board, Record Group 195, National Archives.

21. "Residential Security Map for the City of New Orleans," ca. 1935. In the City Survey File, 1935–1940, Box 127, Records of the Federal Home Loan Bank Board, 1933–1940, Record Group 195; National Archives at College Park, College Park, MD. For integrated neighborhoods, see Peirce F. Lewis, *New Orleans: The Making of an Urban Landscape* (1976; Charlottesville: University of Virginia Press, 2018), 50. The 1930 US Census reported that 28.3 percent (129,632) of Orleans Parish residents were black; 71.6 percent (328,446) were classified as white.

22. Cook and Morgan, "Report of Re-Survey New Orleans," 42.

23. For "tremendous expenditures" and cost estimates, see Cook and Morgan, "Report of Re-Survey New Orleans," 4–5. See also Division of Research and Statistics, "Survey of Economic, Real Estate, and Mortgage Finance Conditions in New Orleans, Louisiana" (Washington, DC: Federal Home Loan Bank Board, 1939), p. 6. In the City Survey File, 1935–1940, Box 67, folder "New Orleans, LA Re-survey Report" (450/68/4/5), Records of the Federal Home Loan Bank Board, Record Group 195, National Archives.

24. "Summary of Economic, Real Estate, and Mortgage Survey and Security Area Descriptions of New Orleans, LA," April 28, 1939, n.p. (described as "Part of Lakeview, New Orleans, La."). In the City Survey File, 1935–1940, Box 88, folder "New Orleans #2" (450/68/5/01).

25. Division of Research and Statistics, "Survey of Economic, Real Estate, and Mortgage Finance Conditions in New Orleans, Louisiana," 1.

26. Benjamin D. Maygarden et al., *National Register Evaluation of New Orleans Drainage System, Orleans Parish, Louisiana,* prepared for the US Army Corps of Engineers, report number COEMVN/PD-98/09 (November 1999), esp. 17–30. The statistics reprinted on p. 29 are from Martin Behrman, *New Orleans: A History of Three Great Public Utilities— Sewerage, Water, and Drainage: and Their Influence Upon the Health and Progress of a Big City,* speech before convention of League of American Municipalities, Milwaukee, WI, September 29, 1914 (Brandao Print, 1914), 5. See also Craig E. Colten, *An Unnatural Metropolis: Wresting New Orleans from Nature* (Baton Rouge: Louisiana State University Press, 2005), 77–107, esp. 105 for the argument that "rational engineering principles [overcame] racist tendencies of Jim Crow" in the distribution of new municipal public works.

27. Division of Research and Statistics, "Survey of Economic, Real Estate, and Mortgage Finance Conditions in New Orleans, Louisiana," 1.

28. H. W. Gilmore, "The Old New Orleans and the New: A Case for Ecology," *American Sociological Review* 9, no. 4 (August 1944): 385–394 (quotation on 394).

29. "How Much of City Is Below Sea Level?" *NOI,* April 13, 1948, p. 12.

30. Colten, *Unnatural Metropolis,* 99. See also Forrest E. Laviolette, "The Negro in New Orleans," in Nathan Glazer and Davis McEntire, eds., *Studies in Housing & Minority Groups: Special Research Report to the Commission on Race and Housing* (Berkeley: University of California Press, 1960), 110–134.

31. "Residential Security Map for the City of New Orleans." The French Quarter and Central Business District are not rated.

32. Homer Hoyt, *The Structure and Growth of Residential Neighborhoods in American Cities* (Washington, DC: US Government Printing Office, 1939), 116. To be sure, it is not clear what direct economic impact the ratings ultimately had. In New Orleans, HOLC made less than 2 percent of its loans in A areas, and 9 percent in "B" areas, "while nearly 45 percent were made to 'C' . . . areas and 38 percent [to] 'D' areas," suggesting that lower rated areas may have been more likely to receive HOLC loans. Nonetheless, the HOLC survey reveals how the government understood the city: when it came to property values, federal real estate experts understood the risk of an African American neighbor to be worse than the risk of a flood. For claims about the importance of the HOLC surveys, see Jackson, *Crabgrass Frontier,* 195–203. For the argument that HOLC's maps were not widely circulated, see Hillier, "Redlining and the Home Owners' Loan Corporation," esp. p. 51 for statistics on loans in New Orleans.

33. "Housing Needs Outlined to Congressmen," *NOS,* April 9, 1942, p. 4. For "swashbuckling," see John Morton Blum, *V Was for Victory: Politics and American Culture During World War II* (New York: Harcourt Brace & Company, 1976), 110. On Higgins, see Paul Neushul, "Andrew Jackson Higgins and the Mass Production of World War II Landing Craft," *Louisiana History* 39, no. 2 (Spring 1998): 136–166; and Jerry E. Stahan, *Andrew Jackson Higgins and the Boats that Won World War II* (Baton Rouge: Louisiana University Press, 1994). A similar process had already occurred on new land constructed on the shores of Lake

Pontchartrain, ostensibly for flood control, in the 1920s. "Perhaps the most astonishing thing about the Lakefront development was the way in which expensive public land was summarily and casually converted to private ownership." Lewis, *New Orleans*, 69.

34. "Demand for Home Greatly Increasing," *SBV*, April 4, 1942, p. 1.

35. For FHA subsidies, see "Green Aces," advertisement, *SBV*, March 6, 1943, p. 3. For drainage, see "Large Tract Is Purchased for New Subdivision in Arabi," *SBV*, November 18, 1944, p. 1. For "down payment," see "Green Aces," advertisement, *SBV*, March 1, 1947, p. 3.

36. "Plan Parish Improvements," *SBV*, October 25, 1941, p. 1. "Route 61 Extension to U.S. 90 Will Be Paved," *SBV*, March 13, 1943, p. 1.

37. "Campaign of Extermination to Be Waged on Mosquitoes. U.S. Public Health Department at Head," *SBV*, May 1, 1943, p. 1. "Long-Term Leases for at Least 10 Parish Farm Families Sought," *SBV*, October 25, 1941, p. 1.

38. "Bus Line in Parish Is Development Factor," *SBV*, January 17, 1942, p. 1.

39. "Appropriation Asked for Dredging Bayou LaLoutre," *SBV*, May 8, 1943, p. 1; "Improve of St. Bernard Bayous Is Wanted," *SBV*, October 26, 1946, p. 1. "Movement on Foot to Boost Seafood Industry," *SBV*, May 24, 1947, p. 1. On "second nature" and the construction of natural advantage, see William Cronon, *Nature's Metropolis: Chicago and the Great West* (New York: W. W. Norton, 1992), 56–57.

40. US Census for 1940 and 1950. "St. Bernard Villages Fast Developing into Towns," *SBV*, April 26, 1947, p. 1.

41. US Census for 1960. In 1975, looking back on the previous quarter century, a New Orleans tax assessor mused that "we are missing a generation in the older areas" of the city because when veterans returned home, "they could not get a mortgage in Central City, the Irish Channel, the Lower Garden District. So they went to Gentilly," and to the suburbs. Quoted in Ralph E. Thayer, *The Evolution of Housing Policy in New Orleans (1920–1978)* (New Orleans: Institute for Government Studies, Loyola University, 1979), 69.

42. "Many Homes Now Dot Territory Along Bayou Terre aux-Boeufs in St. Bernard," *SBV*, May 18, 1946, p. 1. On the New Deal order, see, for example, Steve Fraser and Gary Gerstle, eds., *The Rise and Fall of the New Deal Order, 1930–1980* (Princeton: Princeton University Press, 1989); William E. Leuchtenburg, *Franklin D. Roosevelt and the New Deal: 1932–1940* (New York: Harper & Row, 1963); and Alan Brinkley, *The End of Reform: New Deal Liberalism in Recession and War* (New York: Alfred A. Knopf, 1995).

43. "Local VA Office Reports on Loans," *NOTP*, December 26, 1954, sec. 5, p. 1.

44. "Street Lights Ceremony," *SBV*, December 9, 1950, p. 6. "Chalmette Vista, Inc., Offers to Donate Land For High School," *SBV*, July 18, 1952, p. 1.

45. "Enlarge Kaiser Plant," *SBV*, May 26, 1951, p. 1; "Facilities of Kaiser Aluminum & Chemical Plant at Chalmette," *SBV*, December 14, 1951, p. 5. "Kaiser Pays $314,909.66 in Taxes," *SBV*, January 15, 1960, p. 1.

46. "Anent the Kaiser Plant," *SBV*, February 10, 1961, p. 1.

47. On the double-edged sword of the New Deal, see, for example, Katznelson, *Fear Itself*; Patricia Sullivan, *Days of Hope: Race and Democracy in the New Deal Era* (Chapel Hill: University of North Carolina Press, 1996); and Glenda Elizabeth Gilmore, *Defying Dixie: The Radical Roots of Civil Rights, 1919–1950* (New York: W. W. Norton, 2008).

48. "River Bend Estate Sold to Negro Club," *SBV*, June 25, 1954, p. 1. "New Orleans Club Buys $250,000 Estate," *Jet*, July 1, 1954, p. 21. "Abandon Plans for Negro Club at Poydras," *SBV*, August 13, 1954, p. 1. "Report to the People by Gov. Robert Kennon," *SBV*, July 16, 1954, p. 2.

49. Adam Fairclough, *Race & Democracy: The Civil Rights Struggle in Louisiana, 1915–1972* (Athens: University of Georgia Press, 1999), 251.

50. "Presidential General Election, Louisiana, 1960 All Counties," *CQ Voting and Elections Collection* (Washington, DC: CQ Press, 2018), http://library.cqpress.com/elections /avg1960-1LA2.

51. US Census for 1940, 1950, 1960.

52. Forrest E. LaViolette and Joseph T. Taylor, "Negro Housing in New Orleans," draft, Special Research Report to the Commission on Race and Housing (Berkeley, September 1957), 46, LRC.

53. For the nascent environmentalism of the post-WWII suburbs, see Adam Rome, *The Bulldozer in the Countryside: Suburban Sprawl and the Rise of American Environmentalism* (Cambridge: Cambridge University Press, 2001).

54. "Kaiser Aluminum Will Spend $6,000,000 to Put an End to Smoke Problem in Chalmette," *SBV*, January 14, 1955, p. 1. "Refinery Resumes Normal Operations as Strike Is Settle Last Sunday Evening," *SBV*, July 3, 1953, p. 2. "To Pump Fresh Water in Violet Canal Decided at Meeting of Parish Officials," *SBV*, November 13, 1953, p. 1. "Says Taste of Water Due to Oil in River," *SBV*, July 8, 1955, p. 1.

55. "Trappers Say Fresh Water in Marshes Will Bring Back Rats," *SBV*, February 6, 1953, p. 1.

56. "Engineer Says It Would Cost $4,632.00 for Poydras Syphon," *SBV*, February 27, 1953, p. 1.

57. "Shell Beach Totally Destroyed by Hurricane Sunday Night," *SBV*, September 28, 1956, p. 1.

58. "Schindler Writes Congressman Hebert Asking Aid in 'Securing Advantages,'" *SBV*, May 24, 1957, p. 1.

59. On the MRGO's history, see William R. Feudenburg, Robert B. Gramling, Shirley Laska, and Kai Erikson, *Catastrophe in the Making: The Engineering of Katrina and the Disasters of Tomorrow* (Washington, DC: Island Press, 2009), 70–89.

60. Lytle Brown, Major General, Chief of Engineers, "Letter from the Chief of Engineers, United States Army, transmitting Report of the Board of Engineers for Rivers and Harbors on Review of Reports Heretofore Submitted on Mississippi River–Gulf Outlet and New Orleans Industrial Canal," H.R. Doc. No. 46, 71 Cong., 2d Sess. (June 11, 1930), 3 (p. 8 for port lobbying). R. F. Fowler, *Reexamination of the Outlets of the Mississippi River Including Advisability of Reimbursing Owners for Cost of the Industrial Canal, Louisiana* (New Orleans: US Engineer Office, New Orleans, LA, September 14, 1929), 8.

61. "Flood Control Given Priority," *NOTP*, October 13, 1944, pp. 1, 5.

62. For the cost-benefit analysis, see *Mississippi River–Gulf Outlet*, H.R. Doc. No. 245, 82d Cong., 1st Sess. (October 1, 1951), esp. pp. 14–15 and 26; and Freudenberg et al., *Catastrophe in the Making*, 82. For congressional authorization, see An Act to Authorize Construction of the Mississippi River–Gulf outlet, Pub. L. No. 84-455, 70 Stat. 65 (March 29, 1956).

63. "What a Blessing It Would Be!" *SBV*, July 20, 1946, p. 1. "Industrial Canal Tunnel," *SBV*, May 2, 1952, p. 1.

64. "Tidewater Channel Committee," *SBV*, December 28, 1956, p. 1.

65. "Schindler Writes Congressman Hebert Asking Aid in 'Securing Advantages,'" *SBV*, May 24, 1957, p. 1. The letter suggests that the FHA was withholding loans to parts of the parish it saw as flood prone.

66. Peter Delevett, "Shy Landowner Has Keys to St. Bernard," *NOTP*, August 27, 1990, p. A1. Lynne Jensen, "Joseph Meraux, Landowner in St. Bernard, Is Dead at 69," *NOTP*, March 22, 1992, p. B4.

67. "Tide Water Channel Committee Appointed," *SBV*, September 20, 1957, p. 1.

68. "Is St. Bernard Parish Doomed," *SBV*, November 15, 1957, p. 1 (for "cause" and "sacrifice"); "Is St. Bernard Parish Doomed," *SBV*, November 22, 1957, p. 1 (for 1927); "Is St. Bernard Parish Doomed," *SBV*, November 29, 1957, p. 1; "Is St. Bernard Parish Doomed," *SBV*, December 6, 1957, p. 1; "Is St. Bernard Parish Doomed," *SBV*, December 13, 1957, p. 1; "Is St. Bernard Parish Doomed," *SBV*, December 20, 1957, p. 1.

69. "Offer Channel Builders Free Rights-of-Way," *NOS*, December 11, 1957, p. 5.

70. "Ground Is Broken for Gulf Channel," *NOS*, December 10, 1957, pp. 1, 4; "Helpful Explosion for World Trade," *NOTP*, December 10, 1957, p. 12. Freudenberg et al., *Catastrophe in the Making*, 84.

71. "Tidewater Channel Committee of St. Bernard Police Jury Reports," *SBV*, April 4, 1958, pp. 1, 8.

72. Henry 'Junior' Rodriguez, deposition transcript, April 30, 2008, p. 95, In Re Katrina Canal Breaches Consolidated Litigation, US District Court, Eastern District of Louisiana, Civil Action No. 05-4182.

73. Sherwood Gagliano, deposition transcript, May 1, 2008, pp. 57–59, In Re Katrina Canal Breaches Consolidated Litigation, US District Court, Eastern District of Louisiana, Civil Action No. 05-4182.

74. Charles George "Pete" Savoye, deposition transcript, March 5, 2008, pp. 39–40 (for "crawfish"), 61 (for "disappeared"), 40 (for cypress trees), 51 (for "would raise"), In Re Katrina Canal Breaches Consolidated Litigation, US District Court, Eastern District of Louisiana, Civil Action No. 06-2268.

75. Several St. Bernard residents sued the federal government, alleging that the MRGO was responsible for the Betsy flood; they lost their suit. See Graci v. United States 456 F.2d 20 (5th Circuit, 1971).

76. US Army Corps of Engineers, "Fact Sheet: Mississippi River Gulf Outlet," May 12, 2004, p. 5; quoted in G. Paul Kemp, *Mississippi River Gulf Outlet Effects on Storm Surge, Waves and Flooding During Hurricane Katrina*, July 11, 2008, p. 29, expert report submitted for Norman Robinson et al v. United States of America, US District Court, Eastern District of Louisiana, Civil Action No. 06-2268.

77. Gagliano, deposition transcript, May 1, 2008, pp. 114–115.

78. Cornelia Carrier, "Enlarged River Channel Is Urged," *NOTP*, August 31, 1973, p. 21.

79. Savoye, deposition, March 5, 2008, pp. 52 (for "dying" and committee), 54–56 (for "bitch").

80. Savoye, deposition, March 5, 2008, p. 71.

81. The project was authorized by "An Act to authorize an examination and survey of the coastal and tidal areas of the eastern and southern United States, with particular reference to areas where severe damages have occurred from hurricane winds and tides," Pub. L. No. 84-71, 69 Stat. 140 (1955). The plan is described in US Army Engineer District, New Orleans, *Interim Survey Report, Lake Pontchartrain, Louisiana and Vicinity* (New Orleans, November 21, 1962), in the ACEDL, https://usace.contentdm.oclc.org/digital/collection/p16021coll2/id/904. See also *Lake Pontchartrain and Vicinity, Louisiana: Letter from the Secretary of the Army*, H. R. Doc. No. 231, 89th Cong., 1st Sess. (1965).

82. US House of Representatives, Committee on Public Works, *The Hurricane Betsy Disaster of September 1965: Report of the Special Subcommittee to Investigate Areas of Destruction of Hurricane Betsy*, House Committee Print No. 24, 89th Cong., 1st Sess. (Washington, DC: US Government Printing Office, 1965), 8.

83. An Act Authorizing the Construction, Repair, and Preservation of Certain Public Works on Rivers and Harbors for Navigation, Flood Control, and For Other Purposes, Pub. L. No. 89-298, 79 Stat. 1073 (October 27, 1965).

84. Colten reports the size as 101,700 acres. Craig. E. Colten, *Perilous Place, Powerful Storms: Hurricane Protection in Coastal Louisiana* (Jackson: University Press of Mississippi, 2009), 56.

85. US Army Engineer District, New Orleans, *Interim Survey Report*, 24 (for first quotations), C-2 (for "essentially complete"). For the Committee on Public Works, see *The Hurricane Betsy Disaster of September 1965*, 10.

86. US Army Engineer District, New Orleans, *Interim Survey Report*, 40 (for "high level"), 38 (for "front"), 41–42 (for 11.5 feet), 54 (for $79.8 million), ii (for "the establishment"). The high-level plan, the Corps believed, would cost $100 million, significantly more than the barrier plan, and would take "much longer" to build (p. 30). In March 1967, the Corps incorporated new data from Hurricane Betsy and raised design standards for the floodwalls along the Industrial Canal from thirteen to fourteen feet (p. 38); see also Colten, *Perilous Place*, 53. The $79.8 million figure included $64,703,000 for the Lake Pontchartrain barrier plan, and $15,143,000 for the Chalmette area, which the Army Corps itemized separately.

87. US Army Engineer District, New Orleans, *Interim Survey Report*, 50 (for "intangible benefits"), 15 (for population growth estimates), 49 (for economic growth).

88. Douglas Woolley and Leonard Shabman, *Decision-Making Chronology for the Lake Pontchartrain and Vicinity Hurricane Protection Project, Final Report for the Headquarters, U.S. Army Corps of Engineers* (Alexandria, VA: US Army Corps of Engineers, Institute for Water Resources, 2008), 2–37 (for projections). Colten, *Perilous Place,* 51–65 (for progress), 67 (for the new regulatory regime).

89. Colten, *Perilous Place,* 69–71. US Army Corps of Engineers, "The Lake Pontchartrain, Louisiana, and Vicinity Hurricane Protection Project," public hearing, Saturday, February 22, 1975, New Orleans, LA, transcript, pp. 172–178 (for the Audubon Society representative), 250–253 (for Fontenot), in the ACEDL, https://usace.contentdm.oclc.org /digital/collection/p16021coll2/id/958. For the Corps's cost-benefit ratio, see US Army Engineer District, New Orleans, *Final Environmental Statement, Lake Pontchartrain, Louisiana, and Vicinity Hurricane Protection Project* (New Orleans: US Army Engineer District, New Orleans, 1974), no page number (cover page); and Colten, *Perilous Place,* 66.

90. "The Lake Pontchartrain, Louisiana, and Vicinity Hurricane Protection Project," public hearing transcript, 238–243.

91. US District Court, Eastern District of Louisiana, "Order," Save Our Wetlands, Inc. v. Early Rush et al., Civil Action No. 75-3710, 424 F. Suppl. 354 (December 7, 1976), p. 375. US District Court, Eastern District of Louisiana, "Order," *Save Our Wetlands v. Rush,* December 30, 1977. See also Thomas O. McGarity and Douglas A. Kysar, "Did NEPA Drown New Orleans? The Levees, the Blame Game, and the Hazards of Hindsight," *Cornell Law Faculty Publications,* Paper 51, 2006, pp. 16–18; and Colten, *Perilous Place,* 72.

92. US Army Corps of Engineers, New Orleans District, *Lake Pontchartrain, Louisiana, and Vicinity Hurricane Protection Project, Reevaluation Study, Volume I, Main Report and Final Supplement I to the Environmental Impact Statement* (New Orleans: US Army Corps of Engineers, New Orleans District, July 1984), 2 (for "feasible") and 132–135. For 23 percent, see Colten, *Perilous Place,* 84.

93. For One Shell Square, see Richard Campanella, *Time and Place in New Orleans: Past Geographies in the Present Day* (Gretna, LA: Pelican Publishing Company, 2002), 171.

94. US Army Corps of Engineers, "FY 2006 Appropriation: Construction, General—Local Protection (Flood Control), Lake Pontchartrain and Vicinity," 69 (for costs) and 74 (for refinement).

95. Federal Flood Insurance Act of 1956, Pub. L. No. 84-1016, 70 Stat. 1078 (August 7, 1956). For the history of the National Flood Insurance Program, see Scott Gabriel Knowles and Howard C. Kunreuther, "Troubled Waters: The National Flood Insurance Program in Historical Perspective," *Journal of Policy History* 26, no. 3 (2014): 327–353, esp. 332.

96. Committee on Public Works, *The Hurricane Betsy Disaster of September 1965,* 18.

97. An Act to Provide Assistance to the States of Florida, Louisiana, and Mississippi for the Reconstruction of Areas Damaged by the Recent Hurricane, Pub. L. No. 89-339, 79 Stat. 1301 (November 8, 1965).

98. US Task Force on Federal Flood Control Policy, *A Unified National Program for Managing Flood Losses,* H. R. Doc. No. 465, 89th Cong., 2nd Sess. (1966) 34. On White, see Robert E. Hinshaw, *Living with Nature's Extremes: The Life of Gilbert Fowler White* (Boulder: Johnson Books, 2006).

99. US Task Force on Federal Flood Control Policy, *Unified National Program,* 14 (for "acts of God," which in the original is written "acts of Good"), and 21–32.

100. US Department of Housing and Urban Development, *Insurance and Other Programs for Financial Assistance to Flood Victims: A Report from the Secretary of the Department of Housing And Urban Development to the President, As Required by the Southeast Hurricane Disaster Relief Act of 1965* (Washington, DC: US Government Printing Office, 1966), ix.

101. The National Flood Insurance Act became Title XIII of the Housing and Urban Development Act of 1968, Pub. L. No. 90-448, 82 Stat. 476 (August 1, 1968). See also Knowles and Kunreuther, "Troubled Waters," 336.

102. Title 24-Housing and Housing Credit, Chapter VII-Federal Insurance Administration, Department of Housing and Urban Development, Subchapter B-National Flood Insurance Program, Miscellaneous Amendments to Subchapter, section 1911.52, *Federal Register* 34, no. 116 (June 18, 1969): 9558. For the rate itself, see Joe Massa, "Flood Insurance Solution Is Brought Closer by Act," *NOTP*, June 27, 1969, p. 5.

103. Housing and Urban Development Act of 1968, section 1362, Pub. L. No. 90-448, 82 Stat. 558. Between 1979 and 1994, the NFIP purchased approximately 1,400 flooded properties for approximately $52 million. American Institutes for Research, *A Chronology of Major Events Affecting the National Flood Insurance Program*, report to FEMA (December 2005), p. 28, https://www.fema.gov/media-library-data/20130726-1602-20490-7283/nfip_eval _chronology.pdf.

104. For a taxonomy of the NFIP's initial attempts at mitigation, see also Rutherford H. Platt, *Disasters and Democracy: The Politics of Extreme Natural Events* (Washington, DC: Island Press, 1999), 77.

105. "Metairie Chosen for U.S. Flood Insurance Program," *NOTP*, June 21, 1968, p. 1. "Violet Area Will Get HUD Flood Policies," *NOTP*, April 12, 1970, p. 3–12.

106. Emile Lafourcade Jr., "Flood Insurance Program Termed Injurious to Area," *NOTP*, August 14, 1970, pp. 1, 3.

107. American Institutes for Research, *A Chronology of Major Events Affecting the National Flood Insurance Program*, 16.

108. Flood Disaster Protection Act of 1973, Pub. L. No. 93-234, 87 Stat. 975 (December 31, 1973). During hearings on the 1973 bill, legislators questioned whether the 100-year floodplain was too lenient a standard for mandatory purchase, since according to one study, more than 60 percent of flood damages over the previous fifteen years had been caused by less likely floods. Again, in 1979, the General Accounting Office (GAO) suggested that "the appropriateness of the 100-year flood plain as a national standard" be reevaluated. Yet the standard stood. Henry Eschwege, director, US GAO, to Patricia Roberts Harris, Secretary of Housing and Urban Development, CED-79-58, March 22, 1979, pp. 11–12, https://www.gao.gov/assets/130/125962.pdf.

109. Erwann O. Michel-Kerjan, "Catastrophe Economics: The National Flood Insurance Program," *Journal of Economic Perspectives* 24, no. 4 (Fall 2010): 399–422, esp. 402–403.

110. For example, Comptroller General of the United States, *National Flood Insurance: Marginal Impact on Flood Plain Development, Administrative Improvements Needed*, CED-82-105 (Gaithersburg, MD: US General Accounting Office, August 16, 1982), 7.

111. Quoted in Platt, *Disasters and Democracy*, 82.

112. US House of Representatives, *Report of the Bipartisan Task Force on Disasters*, December 14, 1994, p. 1.

113. The NFIP "worked to sever risk from space." Steinberg, *Acts of God*, xxiv.

114. "WDSU Salutes Anchor Norman Robinson, Announces Date of Final Newscast," *WDSU*, May 16, 2014, https://www.wdsu.com/article/wdsu-salutes-anchor-norman -robinson-announces-date-of-final-newscast/3370776.

115. For the argument that "[b]lack economic opportunity, rather than white flight, dramatically transformed the racial composition of many New Orleans East neighborhoods," see Mickey Lauria, "A New Model of Neighborhood Change: Reconsidering the Role of White Flight," *Housing Policy Debate* 9, no. 2 (1998): 395–424, quotation on 395. See also Souther, "Suburban Swamp," 216.

116. Norman Robinson et al v. United States of America, et al., US District Court, Eastern District of Louisiana, Docket No. 06-CV-2268, trial transcript, April 22, 2009, morning session, p. 643.

117. For topographical estimates for New Orleans East (5.8 feet below sea level as a neighborhood average, and 7.06 below sea level for the Robinsons), see US District Court, Eastern District of Louisiana, "Findings of Fact and Conclusions of Law," Document 19415, *In Re Katrina Canal Breaches*, November 18, 2009, pp. 56–57. Robinson's previous home was on Westbend Parkway. See *Robinson v. United States*, trial transcript, April 22, 2009, morning

session, p. 617. For the flood zone there, see National Flood Insurance Program, Flood Insurance Rate Map, Orleans Parish, Louisiana, Community Panel number 2252030036B, revised January 6, 1978, p. 36. For Mayo Boulevard, see National Flood Insurance Program, Flood Insurance Rate Map, Orleans Parish, Louisiana, Community Panel number 2252030021B, January 6, 1978, p. 21. For the description of Robinson's house, see *Robinson v. United States*, trial transcript, April 22, 2009, morning session, p. 643.

118. 1970 Census Bureau data for tracts 17.7 through 17.13; and 2000 Census Bureau data for tracts 17.20 through 17.42. For flood zones and elevations, see National Flood Insurance Program, "Flood Insurance Rate Maps, Orleans Parish, Louisiana," map revised January 6, 1978, community panel numbers 225203 0001–0040. From 1970 to 2000, the New Orleans East population grew from 44,526 to 96,363.

119. According to the 2000 US Census, 23.96 percent of African American New Orleanians lived in eastern New Orleans north of the Intracoastal Canal. A higher percentage lived in eastern New Orleans writ large, including the Lower Ninth Ward. On African American suburbanization, see Andrew Wiese, *Places of Their Own: African American Suburbanization in the Twentieth Century* (Chicago: University of Chicago Press, 2004).

120. Department of Housing and Urban Development, Federal Insurance Administration, "FIA Flood Insurance Rate Maps," 220870000 08-16, effective August 31, 1973. According to the US Census, the population of St. Bernard was 51,185 in 1970 and 67,229 in 2000.

121. National Flood Insurance Program, "Flood Insurance Rate Map, St. Bernard Parish, Louisiana," map revised May 1, 1985, community panel number 225204 0290 B.

122. *Robinson v. United States*, trial transcript, April 21, 2009, volume 2, afternoon session, pp. 450–498, esp. 454 for "dollhouse," and 493 for $115,000.

123. According to a study by Donald Powell for the White House. Jeffrey Meitrodt and Rebecca Mowbray, "After Katrina, Pundits Criticized New Orleans, Claiming Too Many Residents Had No Flood Insurance. In Fact, Few Communities Were Better Covered," *NOTP*, March 19, 2006, p. 1. For sea level in 2000, see Campanella, *Delta Urbanism*, 170.

124. Coastal Wetlands Planning, Protection and Restoration Act, Pub. L. No. 101-646, 104 Stat. 4778 (November 29, 1990), 4784 (for "no net loss") and 4782 (for "net ecological").

125. "Doing the Right Thing," *NOTP*, April 1, 1991, p. B6.

126. Quoted in US District Court, Eastern District of Louisiana, "Orders and Reasons," Document 18212, *In Re Katrina Canal Breaches*, 627 F. Supp. 2d 656 (March 20, 2009), at 663.

127. Louisiana Coastal Wetlands Conservation and Restoration Task Force and the Wetlands Conservation and Restoration Authority, *Coast 2050: Toward a Sustainable Coastal Louisiana* (Baton Rouge: Louisiana Department of National Resources, 1998), 1–2, 31 (for one million acres).

128. Louisiana Coastal Wetlands Conservation, *Coast 2050*, 88–90.

129. St. Bernard Parish Council Resolution 12–98.

130. US Army Corps of Engineers, "Habitat Impacts of the Construction of the MRGO, prepared by the USACE for the Environmental Sub-committee to the MRGO Technical Committee," December 1999, quoted in John Day, Mark Ford, Paul Kemp, and John Lopez, *Mister Go Must Go: A Guide for the Army Corps' Congressionally-Directed Closure of the Mississippi River Gulf Outlet* (December 4, 2006), p. 7, https://saveourlake.org/wp-content/uploads/PDF-Documents/our-coast/MRGOwashpresfinalreport12-5-06.pdf.

131. John McQuaid and Mark Schleifstein, "Evolving Danger," *NOTP*, June 23, 2002, p. J12.

132. Savoye, deposition, March 5, 2008, 66–67, 76–77.

133. For seventy square miles, see Gagliano, deposition, May 1, 2008, pp. 120–121. A federal court estimated 19,559 acres, or thirty square miles, of land loss as a direct result of the MRGO. US District Court, Eastern District of Louisiana, "Findings of Fact and Conclusion at Law," Document 19415, *In Re Katrina Canal Breaches*, November 18, 2009, pp. 41 (for 2,000 feet), 38 (for thirty square miles).

134. Michael Grunwald and Manuel Roig-Franzia, "Awaiting Ivan in the Big Uneasy," *WP*, September 15, 2004, p. A1. For Hurricane Pam, see Innovative Emergency Management, "Southeast Louisiana Catastrophic Hurricane Functional Plan, Draft," August 6, 2004,

FEMA BPA HSFEHQ-04-A-0288, Task Order 001, p. 105. For prominent descriptions of a hurricane hitting New Orleans, see Mark Fischetti, "Drowning New Orleans," *Scientific American,* October 2001, pp. 77–85; Joel K. Bourne, "Gone with the Water," *National Geographic* 206 (October 2004): 89–92, 96, 99, 101–102, 104–105; and John McQuaid and Mark Schleifstein's five-part series in the *Times-Picayune* in June 2002, published under the title, "Washing Away." For the Coalition to Restore Coastal Louisiana's role, see Louisiana Coastal Wetlands Conservation, *Coast 2050,* 12.

135. Rodriguez, deposition, April 30, 2008, 180.
136. *Robinson v. United States,* trial transcript, April 20, 2009, morning session, p. 95.

Part II

1. Elizabeth Mullener, "Go Ahead On," *NOTP,* August 27, 2006, p. D-4; Brett Duke, "Help Us, Please," photograph, *NOTP,* September 2, 2005, p. 1.
2. "HELP US, PLEASE," *NOTP,* September 2, 2005, p. 1.
3. See, for instance, the CNN Katrina archive: http://edition.cnn.com/SPECIALS/2005 /katrina/archive/. On how the image of the flood "departed from the normative script of US exceptionalism," see Inderpal Grewal, *Saving the Security State: Exceptional Citizens in Twenty-First-Century America* (Durham: Duke University Press, 2017), 33–58, quotation on 37.
4. Mullener, "Go Ahead On," D-4; Susan Saulny, "5,000 Public Housing Units in New Orleans Are To Be Razed," *NYT,* June 15, 2006; Katy Reckdahl, *The Long Road from C.J. Peete to Harmony Oaks* (National Housing Institute, 2013), 5, http://www.nhi.org/research /3570/harmony_oaks/.
5. According to the Housing Authority of New Orleans, the development "received moderate damage from Hurricane Katrina," including debris about the site and damage to the roof, but "interior damage is minimal" and no flood damage was reported in any of the housing units (flood damage was reported at the community center). See "HANO— Preliminary Redevelopment Plan," April 2006, p. 33, in US House of Representatives, Committee on Financial Services, 110th Cong., 1st Sess., *Federal Housing Response to Hurricane Katrina: Hearing before the Committee on Financial Services* (Washington, DC, 2007), 241. Later sources suggest that "Hurricane Katrina's flood waters severely damaged C. J. Peete," but provide few details. See "HUD Awards $20 Million to Revitalize Aged C.J. Peete Public Housing Development in New Orleans," HUD News Release, March 20, 2008, http://archives.hud.gov/news/2008/pr08-041.cfm.
6. Charles Babington, "Some GOP Legislators Hit Jarring Notes in Addressing Katrina," *WP,* September 10, 2005.
7. Robert K. Merton, "The Self-Fulfilling Prophecy," *The Antioch Review* 8, no. 2 (Summer 1948): 193–210. Baker had, in fact, long been engaged politically with public housing.

4. Do You Know What It Means to Miss New Orleans?: Hurricane Katrina, August–September 2005

1. Richard D. Knabb, Jamie R. Rhome, and Daniel P. Brown, *Tropical Cyclone Report, Hurricane Katrina, 23–30 August 2005* (Miami: National Hurricane Center, 2011), 1.
2. Knabb, Rhome, and Brown, *Tropical Cyclone Report,* 1–3.
3. "Blanco's State of Emergency letter to President Bush," *NOTP,* August 27, 2005.
4. For Plaquemines Parish, see US House of Representatives, *A Failure of Initiative: Final Report of the Select Bipartisan Committee to Investigate the Preparation for and Response to Hurricane Katrina* (Washington, DC: US Government Printing Office, 2006), 112. For St. Bernard, see US Senate, *Hurricane Katrina: A Nation Still Unprepared, Special Report of the Committee on Homeland Security and Governmental Affairs* (Washington, DC: US Government Printing Office, 2006), 245.
5. Michael Grunwald and Manuel Roig-Franzia, "Awaiting Ivan in the Big Uneasy," *WP,* September 15, 2004, p. A1. For Nagin's declaration, see Assistant to the President for

Homeland Security and Counterterrorism, *The Federal Response to Hurricane Katrina: Lessons Learned*, (Washington, DC: The White House, 2006), 26. According to the 2000 Census, 130,896 people lived below the poverty rate, or 27.9 percent of the population.

6. National Hurricane Center, "Hurricane Katrina Advisory Number 19," August 27, 2005, http://www.nhc.noaa.gov/archive/2005/pub/al122005.public.019.shtml.

7. Statement of Max Mayfield, *Hearing on Hurricane Katrina: Predicting Hurricanes: What We Knew About Katrina and When,* Hearing Before the Select Bipartisan Committee to Investigate the Preparation for and Response to Hurricane Katrina, US House of Representatives, 109th Cong., September 22, 2005, quoted in US House of Representatives, *Failure of Initiative*, 70.

8. Knabb, Rhome, and Brown, *Tropical Cyclone Report*, 3.

9. National Weather Service, "Urgent Weather Message," New Orleans, Louisiana, August 28, 2005. For Ricks, see Brian Williams, "The Weatherman Nobody Heard," NBC News, September 15, 2005.

10. Ray Nagin, remarks at press conference, August 28, 2005, quoted in US House of Representatives, *Failure of Initiative*, 110. For the president's later claim that "no one predicted the levees would break," see George W. Bush, *Decision Points* (New York: Crown, 2010), 316.

11. For 430,000 cars, see Brian Wolshon, "Evacuation Planning and Engineering for Hurricane Katrina," *The Bridge* 36, no. 1 (Spring 2006): 27–34, esp. 31. For 1 million evacuees, see US Senate, *Nation Still Unprepared*, 244. For contraflow and 1.2 million evacuees, see US House of Representatives, *Failure of Initiative*, 64 (for contraflow and 1.2 million evacuees), 112 (for Plaquemines). For St. Bernard, see US Senate, *Nation Still Unprepared*, 245.

12. Jeff Smith, Deputy Director of the Louisiana Office of Homeland Security and Emergency Preparedness, testified that approximately 62,000 people were "rescued off of rooftops and out of water," while another 78,000 were evacuated from the Superdome, the Convention Center, the "cloverleaf" overpass on I-10 in Jefferson Parish, and from various points in St. Bernard Parish. Of these 140,000 people whom the government assisted in leaving the metropolitan area after the storm, the majority were from Orleans Parish. See "Testimony of Colonel Jeff Smith to the House Select Committee to Investigate the Preparation and Response to Hurricane Katrina," December 14, 2005, pp. 5–6, http://web.archive.org/web/20051227033153/http://katrina.house.gov/hearings/12_14_05/smith_121405.doc. For "refuge of last resort," see US Senate, *Nation Still Unprepared*, 155.

13. Knabb, Rhome, and Brown, *Tropical Cyclone Report*, 3, 8.

14. "Transcript for September 4," *Meet the Press*, NBC, September 5, 2005, http://www.nbcnews.com/id/9179790/#.U3TpLsbsKgE.

15. Raymond B. Seed et al. (i.e., "the Independent Levee Investigation Team," or "ILIT"), *Investigation of the Performance of the New Orleans Flood Protection Systems*, Vol. 1 (National Science Foundation, 2006), xxi (for "catastrophically") and xxiv (for "large number"). For "filling the bowl," see Mark Schleifstein and John McQuaid, "The Big One," *NOTP*, June 23, 2002. See also McQuaid and Schleifstein, *Path of Destruction: The Devastation of New Orleans and the Coming Age of Superstorms* (New York: Little, Brown and Company, 2006). For fifty levee breaches, see US Army Corps of Engineers Interagency Performance Evaluation Task Force (IPET), *Performance Evaluation of the New Orleans and Southeast Louisiana Hurricane Protection System*, Vol. 1 (US Army Corps of Engineers, 2009), 3.

16. Thomas Gabe, Gene Falk, and Maggie McCarty, *Hurricane Katrina: Social-Demographic Characteristics of Impacted Areas*, CRS report no. RL33141 (Washington, DC: Library of Congress, 2005), 7–13 (quotation on 13). These Congressional Research Service damage estimates are based on "FEMA flood and damage assessments and Census 2000 data" and "provide a rough approximation" (p. 3). According to a different FEMA account, 79,918

occupied housing units in New Orleans suffered "severe damage," and 26,405 units
suffered "major damage," out of a total of 188,251 occupied housing units in the parish. In
St. Bernard, FEMA estimated 13,748 units as severely damaged, and 5,938 as suffering
major damage, out of 25,123 total units. See US Department of Housing and Urban
Development, Office of Policy Development and Research, *Current Housing Unit Damage
Estimates: Hurricane Katrina, Rita, and Wilma* (February 12, 2006), https://www.huduser
.gov/publications/pdf/GulfCoast_Hsngdmgest.pdf. The 77 percent figure for Orleans
Parish includes all land area; for the estimate that 61 percent of New Orleanians lived in
areas that saw sustained flooding, see Richard Campanella, "An Ethnic Geography of
New Orleans," *Journal of American History* 94, no. 3 (December 2007): 704–715, esp. 714.
For more than 51 percent destroyed, see Timothy F. Green and Robert B. Olshansky,
"Rebuilding Housing in New Orleans: The Road Home Program after the Hurricane
Katrina Disaster," *Housing Policy Debate* 22, no. 1 (2012): 75–99, esp. 93.

17. US Senate, Committee on Homeland Security and Governmental Affairs, 111 Cong., 2
Sess., *Five Years Later: Lessons Learned, Progress Made, and Work Remaining from Hurricane
Katrina* (Washington, DC: US Government Printing Office, 2011), 49.

18. On the New Orleans drainage system, see Craig E. Colten, *An Unnatural Metropolis:
Wresting New Orleans from Nature* (Baton Rouge: Louisiana State University Press, 2005).
For Old Metairie, see Michelle Krupa, "Old Metairie Still Flooded," *NOTP*, Sep-
tember 6, 2005.

19. A statistical analysis of the flood-damaged population suggesting that "the odds of living
in a damaged area were . . . much greater for blacks, renters, and poor people," also
showed that across the region, roughly the same number of non-Hispanic whites as blacks
lived in damaged areas (294,000 versus 295,000), and that "the number of persons in"
damaged areas "above the poverty line was much larger than the number of poor persons."
John R. Logan, *The Impact of Katrina: Race and Class in Storm-Damaged Neighborhoods*
(Providence: Brown University Spatial Structures in the Social Sciences Institute, 2005),
7. See also Campanella, "An Ethnic Geography of New Orleans."

20. For narrative accounts of the days following the storm, see Jed Horne, *Breach of Faith:
Hurricane Katrina and the Near Death of a Great American City* (New York: Random
House, 2006); *When the Levees Broke: A Requiem in Four Acts,* directed by Spike Lee
(HBO, 2006) DVD; Christopher Cooper and Robert Block, *Disaster: Hurricane Katrina
and the Failure of Homeland Security* (New York: Henry Holt and Company, 2006); and
Dan Baum, *Nine Lives: Death and Life in New Orleans* (New York: Spiegel and Grau,
2009), esp. Part III. For a narrative account of the storm in St. Bernard Parish, see Ken
Wells, *The Good Pirates of the Forgotten Bayous* (New Haven: Yale University Press, 2008).

21. Joan Brunkard, Gonza Namulanda, and Raoult Ratard, "Hurricane Katrina Deaths,
Louisiana, 2005," *Disaster Medicine and Public Health Preparedness* 2, no. 4 (De-
cember 2008): 215–223. There is also debate about what it means to have died "during
Katrina." In other words, it is a debate over the definition of disaster. Some scholars have
suggested that the number of Katrina-related deaths is much higher than the CDC
estimated. Kevin U. Stephens Sr. et al., "Excess Mortality in the Aftermath of Hurricane
Katrina: A Preliminary Report," *Disaster Medicine and Public Health Preparedness* 1, no. 1
(July 2007): 15–20. In 2012, with access to additional records, the Louisiana Department of
Health reported that there were 1,115 Katrina-related deaths in Louisiana, including 769 in
Orleans Parish and 132 in St. Bernard Parish. Poppy Markwell and Raoult Ratard,
"Deaths Directly Caused by Hurricane Katrina," Louisiana Department of Health (2012),
http://ldh.la.gov/assets/oph/Center-PHCH/Center-CH/stepi/specialstudies
/2014PopwellRatard_KatrinaDeath_PostedOnline.pdf.

22. Although the updated 2012 Louisiana Department of Health report increased the number
of Katrina-related deaths in Orleans Parish to 769, the racial demographics remained
essentially the same: 68 percent were African American and 29 percent were white.
Markwell and Ratard, "Deaths Directly Caused by Hurricane Katrina," 4. For the
argument that "results do not directly support claims that African Americans were more

likely to become fatalities," see Sebastiaan N. Jonkman, Bob Masskant, Ezra Boyd, and Marc Lloyd Levitan, "Loss of Life Caused by the Flooding of New Orleans After Hurricane Katrina: Analysis of the Relationship Between Flood Characteristics and Mortality," *Risk Analysis* 29, no. 5 (2009): 676–698, quotation on 685. See also Logan, "The Impact of Katrina," 7.

23. Elizabeth Mullener, "Go Ahead On," *NOTP*, August 27, 2006, D-1 and D-4 (Perkins quotations on D-4). The *Washington Post* reported there were as many as 20,000 people at the Convention Center. For that estimate and "pronounced dead," see Wil Haygood and Ann Scott Tyson, "'It Was as If All of Us Were Already Pronounced Dead,'" *WP*, September 15, 2005.

24. For "we need," see Joby Warrick, Spencer S. Hsu, and Anne Hull, "Blanco Releases Katrina Records," *WP*, December 4, 2005. For 500 buses, see US Senate, *Nation Still Unprepared*, 69. For Brown, see Lisa Myers, "Critics Question FEMA Director's Qualifications," *NBC News*, September 4, 2005.

25. Paul Morse, "President George W. Bush Looks Out Over the Devastation in New Orleans," photograph, August 31, 2005, https://georgewbush-whitehouse.archives.gov /news/releases/2005/08/images/20050831_p083105pm-0117jas-515h.html. For evacuating the Superdome, see US Senate, *Nation Still Unprepared*, 70. For Memorial, see Sheri Fink, *Five Days at Memorial: Life and Death in a Storm-Ravaged Hospital* (New York: Crown Publishers, 2013).

26. For O'Brien, see "City of New Orleans Falling Deeper Into Chaos and Desperation," transcript, CNN.com, September 2, 2005. For Nagin, see "Mayor to Feds: 'Get off your asses,'" transcript of WWL radio interview, CNN.com, September 2, 2005.

27. US Senate, *Nation Still Unprepared*, 71.

28. Fink, *Five Days at Memorial*, esp. 230 for forty-five deaths.

29. For "heck of a job," see George W. Bush, "Remarks on the Aftermath of Hurricane Katrina in Mobile, Alabama," September 2, 2005, in *Weekly Compilation of Presidential Documents* 41, no. 35 (US Government Printing Office, September 5, 2005), 1339. For the resignation, see "FEMA Director Brown Resigns," CNN.com, September 12, 2005. For "remained stranded," see US Senate, *Nation Still Unprepared*, 71.

30. Tania Ralli, "Who's a Looter? In the Storm's Aftermath, Pictures Kick Up a Different Kind of Tempest," *NYT*, September 5, 2005. Van Jones, "Black People 'Loot' Food . . . White People 'Find' Food," *Huffington Post*, September 1, 2005.

31. Wolf Blitzer, "The Situation Room," CNN, September 1, 2005.

32. For "the situation," see "The Man-Made Disaster," *NYT*, September 2, 2005. For "dark streets," see *CNN Reports: Katrina—State of Emergency* (Kansas City: CNN, 2005), 75. For "snake pit," see Maureen Dowd, "United States of Shame," *NYT*, September 3, 2005. For Fox, MSNBC, and Compass, see David Carr, "More Horrible than Truth: News Reports," *NYT*, September 19, 2005. For "animalistic state," see US House of Representatives, *Failure of Initiative*, 248. For "eating corpses," see Randall Robinson, "New Orleans," *Huffington Post*, September 2, 2005.

33. For "elite panic" after Katrina, see Rebecca Solnit, *A Paradise Built in Hell: The Extraordinary Communities that Arise in Disaster* (New York: Viking, 2009), esp. 231–304. See also Kathleen Tierney, Christine Bevc, and Eric Kuligowski, "Metaphors Matter: Disaster Myths, Media Frames, and Their Consequences in Hurricane Katrina," *The Annals of the American Academy of Political and Social Science* 604 (March 2006): 57–81, esp. 57–61. For the argument that looting is "very rare and in many cases almost nonexistent in American-type communities," see Enrico L. Quarentelli, "Conventional Beliefs and Counterintuitive Realities," *Social Research* 75, no. 3 (Fall 2008): 873–904 (quotation on 883). Quarentelli does not clarify what he means by "American-type communities." For the Hobbesian state of nature, see Thomas Hobbes, *Leviathan* (1651), chapter 13, "Of the Natural Condition of Mankind."

34. The Louisiana National Guard confirmed six deaths inside the Superdome: "four died of natural causes, one overdose and another jumped to his death in an apparent suicide," and

another four outside. The state's official count lists seven fatalities at the Superdome. The discrepancy likely refers to how people outside of the building were classified. Brian Thevenot and Gordon Russell, "Rape. Murder. Gunfights.," *NOTP,* September 26, 2005, pp. A-1, 4–5 (National Guardsmen quotations on A-4). Brunkard et al., "Hurricane Katrina Deaths, Louisiana, 2005," 5. For the 2004 murder total, see Mark J. VanLandingham, "Murder Rates in New Orleans, LA, 2004–2006," *American Journal of Public Health* 97, no. 9 (September 2007): 1614–1616, statistic on p. 1614.

35. "Military Due to Move in to New Orleans," CNN.com, September 2, 2005. Horne, *Breach of Faith,* 121. Sabrina Shakman, Tom Jennings, Brendan McCarthy, Laura Maggi, and A. C. Thompson, "New Orleans Cops Say They Got Orders Authorizing Them to Shoot Looters in the Chaos After Hurricane Katrina," *NOTP,* August 25, 2010.

36. A. C. Thompson, Brendan McCarthy, and Laura Maggi, "In New Orleans, Chaos in the Streets, and in Police Ranks, Too," *ProPublica,* December 12, 2009. It is not clear whether the deaths attributable to police shootings were counted in the records of "Katrina-related" deaths. For McCann, see A. C. Thompson, Brendan McCarthy, and Laura Maggi, "Did New Orleans SWAT Cops Shoot an Unarmed Man?" *ProPublica,* December 15, 2009. For Glover, see A. C. Thompson, "Body of Evidence," *ProPublica,* December 19, 2008; and A. C. Thompson, "Judge Hands Out Tough Sentences in Post-Katrina Killing by Police," *ProPublica,* March 31, 2011. For Brumfield, see A. C. Thompson, Brendan McCarthy, Laura Maggi, and Gordon Russell, "Police Shooting After Katrina," *NOTP,* December 14, 2009. For the Danziger Bridge, see "Law and Disorder: Danziger Bridge," *ProPublica,* http://www.propublica.org/nola/case/topic/case-six. For Perkins, see Mullener, "Go Ahead On," D-1 and D-4.

37. Nicholas Riccardi, "After Blocking the Bridge, Gretna Circles the Wagons," *Los Angeles Times,* September 16, 2005. See also Arnold R. Hirsch and A. Lee Levert, "The Katrina Conspiracies: The Problem of Trust in Rebuilding an American City," *Journal of Urban History* 35, no. 2 (January 2009): 207–219.

38. Malik Rahim, "This Is Criminal," *Bay View,* September 2, 2005. For Rahim's role in the Black Panther Party, see Orissa Arend, *Showdown in Desire: The Black Panthers Take a Stand in New Orleans* (Fayetteville: University of Arkansas Press, 2009). For the argument that during Katrina "the black citizens of the Big Easy . . . were treated by the rest of us as garbage," see Michael Eric Dyson, *Come Hell or High Water: Hurricane Katrina and the Color of Disaster* (New York: Basic Civitas Books, 2007), 14.

39. Lisa de Moreas, "Kanye West's Torrent of Criticism, Live on NBC," *WP,* September 3, 2005. Kalamu ya Salaam, "A Superdome System of Thought" (2005), video of performance, September 30, 2005, Bowery Poetry Club, New York, NY, https://www.indybay.org/olduploads/kalamu_live_at_bowery_poetry_club.mov.

40. Dorothy Moye, "The X-Codes: A Post-Katrina Postscript," *Southern Spaces,* August 26, 2009. "The resulting movement of 50,000 National Guard and 22,000 active-duty troops in response to Katrina was the largest deployment of military capability within the United States since the Civil War." US Senate, *Nation Still Unprepared,* 476. For "worst thing," see Mullener, "Go Ahead On," D-4. For the diaspora, see Matthew Ericson, Archie Tse, and Jodi Wolgoren, "Storm and Crisis; Katrina's Diaspora," *NYT,* October 2, 2005; Gordon Russell, "New Orleans, 77054," *NOTP,* October 28, 2005, p. 1; Lynn Weber and Lori Peek, eds., *Displaced: Life in the Katrina Diaspora* (Austin: University of Texas Press, 2012), esp. Jessica W. Pardee, "Living through Displacement: Housing Insecurity among Low-Income Evacuees," pp. 63–78; and Narayan Sastry and Jesse Gregory, "The Location of Displaced New Orleans Residents in the Year After Hurricane Katrina" (Washington, DC: Center for Economic Studies, 2012), 12–19.

41. Jean Rhodes et al., "The Impact of Hurricane Katrina on the Mental and Physical Health of Low-Income Parents in New Orleans," *American Journal of Orthopsychiatry* 80, no. 2 (April 2010): 237–247, esp. 237, 241.

42. Shaila Dewan and Janet Roberts, "Louisiana's Deadly Storm Took Strong as Well as the Helpless," *NYT,* December 18, 2005. On Cherrie, see also LaKisha Michelle Simmons,

"'Justice Mocked': Violence and Accountability in New Orleans," *American Quarterly* 61, no. 3 (September 2009): 477–498. For a rumination on the counterfactual, see Rebecca Solnit, "Nothing Was Foreordained," in Solnit and Rebecca Snedeker, eds., *Unfathomable City: A New Orleans Atlas* (Oakland: University of California Press, 2013), 127–132.

43. The poll was conducted September 6–7. *Huge Racial Divide Over Katrina and Its Consequences* (Washington, DC: Pew Research Center for People & The Press, 2005). See also "Two-In-Three Critical of Bush's Relief Efforts," September 8, 2005, http://www.people-press.org/2005/09/08/two-in-three-critical-of-bushs-relief-efforts/. On African American tendencies to understand questions about racism as structural, and white tendencies to understand these questions as individual, see Paul Frymer, Dara Z. Strolovitch, and Dorian T. Warren, "New Orleans Is Not the Exception: Re-Politicizing the Study of Racial Inequality," *DuBois Review* 3, no. 1 (2006): 37–57, esp. 42–43; and Andrew Diamond, "Naturalizing Disaster: Neoliberalism, Cultural Racism, and Depoliticization," in Romain Huret and Randy J. Sparks, eds., *Hurricane Katrina in Transatlantic Perspective* (Baton Rouge: Louisiana State University Press, 2014), 81–99, esp. 89.

44. Ari Kelman, "Even Paranoids Have Enemies: Rumors of Levee Sabotage in New Orleans's Lower 9th Ward," *Journal of Urban History* 35, no. 5 (July 2009): 627–639. For Dyan French Cole, see Lisa Byers, "Were the Levees Bombed in New Orleans? Ninth Ward Residents Give Voice to a Conspiracy Theory," NBCNews.com, December 7, 2005. See also Alan H. Stein and Gene B. Preuss, "Oral History, Folklore, and Katrina," in Chester W. Hartman and Gregory D. Squires, eds., *There Is No Such Thing as a Natural Disaster: Race, Class, and Hurricane Katrina* (New York: Routledge, 2006), 37–58.

45. John M. Barry, *Rising Tide: The Great Mississippi Flood of 1927 and How It Changed America* (New York: Simon & Schuster, 1997). For the argument that trauma is more profound when people believe their misfortune was caused by human decisions rather than a so-called "act of God," see J. Steven Picou, Brent K. Marshall, and Duane A. Gill, "Disaster, Litigation, and the Corrosive Community," *Social Forces* 82, no. 4 (June 2004): 1493–1522, esp. 1495–1496. See also Kai T. Erikson, *Everything in Its Path: Destruction of Community in Buffalo Creek* (1978; New York: Simon & Schuster, 2006); Kai Erikson, *A New Species of Trouble: The Human Experience of Modern Disasters* (New York: W. W. Norton, 1994); and William R. Freudenburg, "Contamination, Corrosion and the Social Order: An Overview," *Current Sociology* 45, no. 3 (July 1997): 19–39.

46. For "helplessness," see Bush, *Decision Points*, 310.

47. For Chertoff, see Soledad O'Brien, "Interview with Homeland Security Secretary Michael Chertoff," September 1, 2005, CNN.com. For Brown, see "FEMA Chief: Victims Bear Some Responsibility," CNN.com, September 1, 2005.

48. According to the 2000 Census, 27.3 percent of households in Orleans Parish did not have a vehicle, including 15.3 percent of white alone households, 34.8 percent of black alone households, and 18.1 percent of Asian alone households. For a study showing that "nearly half of the estimated 110,000 people who remained in New Orleans did so because they did not believe the storm would be as bad as forecast," see Timothy J. Haney, James R. Elliott, and Elizabeth Fussell, "Families and Hurricane Response: Evacuation, Separation, and the Emotional Toll of Hurricane Katrina," in David L. Brunsma, David Overfelt, and Steven J. Picou, eds., *The Sociology of Katrina: Perspectives on a Modern Catastrophe* (Lanham: Roman & Littlefield, 2007), 71–90. See also Lynn Weber and Lori Peek, "Documenting Displacement," in Weber and Peek, eds., *Displaced,* 1–20 ("nearly half" on 2).

49. Nicole M. Stephens et al., "Why Did They 'Choose' to Stay? Perspectives of Hurricane Katrina Observers and Survivors," *Psychological Science* 20, no. 7 (July 2009): 878–886. For an analogous example, see Kathryn Marie Dudley, *Debt and Dispossession: Farm Loss in America's Heartland* (Chicago: University of Chicago Press, 2007), esp. 45.

50. Roger Yu, "Evacuees Can Get $2,000 per Household from FEMA," *USA Today*, September 7, 2005.

51. Jeff Duncan, "SWAMPED," *NOTP*, September 25, 2005, pp. A-1, A-26.

52. For standard project hurricane, see *Lake Pontchartrain and Vicinity, Louisiana: Letter from the Secretary of the Army*, H. R. Doc. No. 231, 89th Cong., 1st Sess. (1965), 46. The authorization was "An Act Authorizing the construction, repair, and preservation of certain public works on rivers and harbors for navigation, flood control, and other purposes," Pub. L. No. 89-298, 79 Stat. 1077 (October 27, 1965). Although the meteorological understanding of what storms were "reasonably characteristic of the region" changed over time—making the initial analyses based on the 1959 Standard Project Hurricane inadequate and obsolete—the Army Corps did not update its design criteria accordingly. See Ivor Van Heerden et al. ("Team Louisiana"), *The Failure of the New Orleans Levee System During Hurricane Katrina*, a report prepared for Secretary Johnny Bradberry, Louisiana Department of Transportation and Development (December 18, 2006), iv–v. Nonetheless, elements of the levee system that failed to meet even the Army Corps's own standards are sufficient to account for the flood, because levees designed for even that lower standard, properly constructed, should have overtopped but not collapsed, which would have substantially limited the extent of the flood. "The storm surge and wave loading at the eastern flank of the New Orleans flood protection system was not vastly greater than design levels, and the carnage that resulted owed much to the inadequacies of the system as it existed at the time of Katrina's arrival." ILIT, *Investigation of the Performance*, 15-1–15-2.

53. For "arrogance," see Robert G. Bea, "Reflections on the Draft Final USACE IPET Report," June 2, 2006, in Heerden et al., *The Failure of the New Orleans Levee System*, Appendix 6 (no page numbers). For "incompetence," see US District Court, Eastern District of Louisiana, "Orders and Reasons," Document 10984, In Re Katrina Canal Breaches Consolidated Litigation, Civil Action No. 05-4182 (January 30, 2008), 44.

54. For "system," see IPET, *Performance Evaluation*, I-127.

55. In November 2009, federal judge Stanwood Duval found that much of the flooding in St. Bernard Parish and the Lower Ninth Ward was caused by the Army Corps's negligence. *In Re Katrina Canal Breaches*, 647 F. Supp. 2d 644 (E.D. La. 2009). The 5th Circuit Court of Appeals reversed the ruling, although the legal question did not pertain directly to whether the Corps was negligent, but rather, whether the Corps was liable for damages under federal law. ILIT asserted that "[n]o one organization, agency or group of individuals had a monopoly on their contribution to this disaster. Federal government (including the Congress), the Corps of Engineers, local government and local oversight agencies (including the local Levee Board and the local Water and Sewerage Board), and outsourced engineering firms all contributed." Nonetheless, ILIT noted that "the local levee board lacked the resources and funding to mount serious review of the Federal plans and designs, and the mandate to challenge problems that should have been apparent at early stages." ILIT, *Investigation of the Performance*, 8-44–8-45 (for "no one") and 8-48 (for "local levee board").

56. ILIT, *Investigation of the Performance*, xx–xxi, 2-6-2-7 (attributing the delay in finishing to the failure of a Congressional appropriation since 1994–1995 and explaining their collapse), and 6–21 (for cost savings). For Louisiana's official investigation of the levee failures, which was conducted by experts at Louisiana State University, see Van Heerden et al., *The Failure of the New Orleans Levee System*. For the 1978 guidelines, see US Army Corps of Engineers, "Engineering and Design: Design and Construction of Levees," Manual No. 1110-2-1913 (March 31, 1978) as described in Van Heerden et al., *The Failure of the New Orleans Levee System*, vii, which also notes that the New Orleans District "did not follow standard engineering practice or Corps guidance" when it decided to forgo erosion protection.

57. ILIT, *Investigation of the Performance*, xxii. The Corps also acknowledged that "the structures failed catastrophically prior to water reaching design elevations." See IPET, *Performance Evaluation*, I-3. Nonetheless, "Team Louisiana" argued that the failure of the Industrial Canal floodwalls may also be attributable to overtopping scouring the eastern side of the levees. See Van Heerden et al., *The Failure of the New Orleans Levee System*, 67.

58. For "daggers," see ILIT, *Investigation of the Performance*, xxiii. For "heavy storms," see J. D. Rogers, "Development of the New Orleans Flood Protection System prior to Hurricane Katrina," *Journal of Geotechnical and Geoenvironmental Engineering* 134, no. 5 (May 2008): 602–617, quotation on 611.

59. Craig. E. Colten, *Perilous Place, Powerful Storms: Hurricane Protection in Coastal Louisiana* (Jackson: University Press of Mississippi, 2009), 77–78, 125–127.

60. For example, US Army Corps of Engineers, New Orleans District, *Lake Pontchartrain, Louisiana, and Vicinity Hurricane Protection Project, Reevaluation Study, Volume I, Main Report and Final Supplement I to the Environmental Impact Statement* (New Orleans: US Army Corps of Engineers, New Orleans District, July 1984), 70–71, describes both raising floodwalls and constructing floodgates as viable solutions. The Water Resource Development Act of 1990 and the Energy and Water Development Act of 1992 made the outfall canals part of the hurricane protection system, and therefore within the purview of the Army Corps of Engineers. The test the Army Corps relied on regarding how deep to anchor floodwalls was the E-99 Sheet Pile Wall Field Load Test Report, which was conducted in 1985 and published in June 1988. J. David Rogers, G. Paul Kemp, H. J. Bosworth, and Raymond B. Seed, "Interaction Between the US Army Corps of Engineers and the Orleans Levee Board Preceding the Drainage Canal Wall Failures and Catastrophic Flooding of New Orleans in 2005," *Water Policy* 17, no. 4 (August 2015): 707–723. For the argument—made earlier by the same authors, with less evidence on hand—that residential development limited the Corps's ability to properly anchor the floodwalls, and attributing the drainage canal breaches in part to the squabble among local agencies, see ILIT, *Investigation of the Performance*, 8-11–8-13. See also Colten, *Perilous Place*, 77–78.

61. ILIT, *Investigation of the Performance*, 3-1 (for 4–5 feet).

62. For 70 percent, see IPET, *Performance Evaluation of the New Orleans and Southeast Louisiana Hurricane Protection System: Draft Final Report*, Vol. 1 (June 1, 2006), I-7. The final, 2009 version of the IPET report did not disaggregate the outfall canal breaches from the failures on the Industrial Canal; see IPET, *Performance Evaluation*, I-124. For 80 percent, see ILIT, *Investigation of the Performance*, xxiii.

63. Knabb, Rhome, and Brown, *Tropical Cyclone Report*, 9.

64. IPET, *Performance Evaluation*, I-28. The Corps estimated that in May 2005, the project was 90 percent complete in Orleans Parish, 70 percent complete in Jefferson Parish, and 90 percent complete in St. Bernard Parish (p. I-28). See also Douglas Woolley and Leonard Shabman, *Decision-Making Chronology for the Lake Pontchartrain and Vicinity Hurricane Protection Project, Final Report for the Headquarters, U.S. Army Corps of Engineers* (Alexandria, VA: US Army Corps of Engineers, Institute for Water Resources, 2008).

65. For the Corps's estimate, see IPET, *Performance Evaluation*, 2009, I-3. Team Louisiana argued that the Corps overestimated the effect of rainfall on total flood levels, thereby understating the effect of the breaches. Van Heerden et al., *The Failure of the New Orleans Levee System*, 42–44. For ILIT, see Bea, "Reflections on the Draft Final USACE IPET Report."

66. The land loss figure is as of 1998. Sherwood M. Gagliano, "Faulting, Subsidence and Land Loss in Coastal Louisiana," in *Coast 2050: Toward a Sustainable Coastal Louisiana, The Appendices* (Baton Rouge: Louisiana Department of Natural Resources, 1999), figure 3–7 (no page number). For marsh, see Ivor van Heerden and Mike Bryan, *The Storm: What Went Wrong and Why During Hurricane Katrina* (New York: Penguin, 2006), 169; and Oliver Houk, "Retaking the Exam: How Environmental Law Failed New Orleans and the Gulf Coast South and How It Might Yet Succeed," *Tulane Law Review* 81 (2006–2007): 1059–1083, esp. 1065.

67. For the MRGO, see US District Court, Eastern District of Louisiana, "Findings of Fact and Conclusion at Law," Document 19415, *In Re Katrina Canal Breaches*, November 18, 2009, p. 38. See also Bob Marshall, "Plans Didn't Account for Area's Subsidence," *NOTP*, May 1, 2006.

68. Federal Emergency Management Agency, Federal Insurance Administration, "Projected Impact of Relative Sea Level Rise on the National Flood Insurance Program," October 1991, p. 6 (for "no need"), 9 (for "highest"), and 25 (for "near term"). Congress had ordered the study in the Defense Production Act Amendment of 1989, Pub. L. No. 101-137, 103 Stat. 824 (November 3, 1989).

69. Van Heerden et al., *The Failure of the New Orleans Levee System*, viii.

70. ILIT, *Investigation of the Performance*, 3–19.

71. Gagliano, "Faulting, Subsidence and Land Loss in Coastal Louisiana," figure 3–20 (no page number).

72. IPET, *Performance Evaluation*, II-77. For "museum," see Van Heerden et al., *The Failure of the New Orleans Levee System*, viii.

73. Heerden and Bryan, *The Storm*. John Schwartz, "Ivor van Heerden's 'Storm' Draws Fire at L.S.U.," *NYT*, May 30, 2006. Katz, Marshall & Banks, LLP, "Hurricane Katrina Whistleblower Ivor van Heerden Files Wrongful Termination Lawsuit against LSU," press release, February 10, 2010, https://www.kmblegal.com/news/hurricane-katrina -whistleblower-ivor-van-heerden-files-wrongful-termination-lawsuit-against-lsu. "Developments Relating to Association Censure," *Academe* 99, no. 3 (May–June 2013): (no page numbers). Bill Lodge, "Van Heerden, LSU Reach Settlement," *BRA*, February 13, 2013. Bill Lodge, "Fired LSU Professor Releases Emails in Levee Case," *BRA*, February 17, 2013. Mark Schleifstein, "LSU Spent Nearly $1 Million on Legal Fight Over Firing of Coastal Researcher Ivor van Heerden," *NOTP*, April 2, 2013.

74. The law states, "no liability of any kind shall attach to or rest upon the United States for any damage from or by floods or flood waters at any place." An act for the control of floods on the Mississippi River and its tributaries, and for other Purposes," Pub. L. No. 70-391, 45 Stat. 534 (May 15, 1928). The federal courts also denied some of the cases on the basis of the government's so-called discretionary function exception.

75. US District Court, Eastern District of Louisiana, "Orders and Reasons," Document 10984, *In Re Katrina Canal Breaches*, January 30, 2008, pp. 44–45.

76. The Fifth Circuit dismissed the remainder of the cases on September 24, 2012. *In Re Katrina Canal Breaches Litigation*, 696 F.3d 436 (5th Cir., 2012). In the final case, claimants argued that the Army Corps's failure to maintain the MRGO lowered property values in St. Bernard Parish and eastern New Orleans, and therefore violated Fifth Amendment protections against takings "without just compensation." See St. Bernard Parish Government v. United States, Nos. 2016-2301 and 2016-2373, 887 F.3d 1354 (Fed. Cir. 2018). The Supreme Court denied certiorari on January 7, 2019.

77. Henry "Junior" Rodriguez, deposition transcript, April 30, 2008, p. 243, *In Re Katrina Canal Breaches*.

78. Robert Travis Scott, "Mayor Again Puts Out Welcome Mat," *NOTP*, September 29, 2005, p. A1. "N.O. Fires 3,000 City Workers," *NOTP*, October 5, 2005. For the election, which included three referenda on neighborhood taxes, see State of Louisiana, Executive Department, Executive Order No. KBB 2005-36, "Delay of the October 15, 2005 Primary Election and the November 12, 2005 General and Proposition Election in the Parishes of Jefferson and Orleans," September 14, 2005. See also Mark Waller, "Jeff, Orleans Elections Postpone," *NOTP*, September 13, 2005.

79. For patina, see Shannon Dawdy, *Patina: A Profane Archaeology* (Chicago: University of Chicago Press, 2016), 1–4. Lee Boe, interview by Elizabeth Shelburne, June 2, 2006, interview U-0224, transcript, p. 13 (for "only description), 34 (for "powerful"), SOHP Collection. On losing belongings, see Erikson, *Everything in Its Path*, 177.

80. Vincanne Adams, *Markets of Sorrow, Labors of Faith: New Orleans in the Wake of Katrina* (Durham: Duke University Press, 2013), 69.

81. The first appropriation was Emergency Supplemental Appropriations Act to Meet Immediate Needs Arising From the Consequences of Hurricane Katrina, 2005, Pub. L. No. 109-61, 119 Stat. 1988 (September 2, 2005). The second appropriation was Second Emergency Supplemental Appropriations Act to Meet Immediate Needs Arising from the

Consequences of Hurricane Katrina, 2005, Pub. L. No. 109-62, 119 Stat. 1990 (September 8, 2005). Quotation and $2 billion per day is from "Congress Approves $52 Billion in Katrina Relief Funds," *PBS News Hour,* September 8, 2005.

82. For debris, see Elizabeth Royte, "Rough Burial," *On Earth* (Spring 2006), pp. 28–31; and Linda Luther, *Disaster Debris Removal After Hurricane Katrina: Status and Associated Issues,* CRS report no. RL3477 (Washington, DC: Library of Congress, 2008). For refrigerators, see Tom Varisco, *Spoiled: Refrigerators of New Orleans Go Outside in the Aftermath of Hurricane Katrina* (Tom Varisco Designs, 2005). For the landfill, which Nagin closed in August 2006 after intense political pressure, and facing a lawsuit from neighbors, see Leslie Eaton, "A New Landfill in New Orleans Sets Off a Battle," *NYT,* May 8, 2006; and Leslie Eaton, "New Orleans Mayor Closes a Disputed Landfill Used for Debris from Hurricane," *NYT,* August 16, 2006. On New Orleans's Vietnamese American community, see also Mark VanLandingham, *Weathering Katrina: Culture and Recovery among Vietnamese Americans* (New York: Russell Sage Foundation, 2017).

83. For "right to return," see Rachel E. Luft, "Beyond Disaster Exceptionalism: Social Movement Developments in New Orleans after Hurricane Katrina," *American Quarterly* 61, no. 3 (September 2009): 499–527 (quotation on 516). For science versus emotion, see Richard Campanella, *Bienville's Dilemma: A Historical Geography of New Orleans* (Lafayette: Center for Louisiana Studies, 2008), 344. For "rise again," see George W. Bush, "Address to the Nation on Hurricane Katrina Recovery from New Orleans, Louisiana," September 15, 2005, in *Weekly Compilation of Presidential Documents* 41, no. 37 (US Government Printing Office, September 19, 2005), 1405. For Elie, see Lolis Eric Elie, interview by Elizabeth Shelburne, May 28, 2006, interview U-0234, transcript, p. 16, SOHP Collection.

84. Charles Babington, "Hastert Tries Damage Control After Remarks Hit a Nerve," *WP,* September 3, 2005. Klaus Jacob, "Time for a Tough Question: Why Rebuild?" *WP,* September 6, 2005.

85. Malik Rahim, interview by Pamela Hamilton, May 23, 2006, interview U-0252, transcript, p. 45, SOHP Collection.

86. David Brooks, "Katrina's Silver Lining," *NYT,* September 8, 2005. "Barbara Bush Calls Evacuees Better Off," *NYT,* September 7, 2005. For a similar argument, repeated a decade later, see Malcom Gladwell, "What Social Scientists Learned from Katrina," *New Yorker,* August 24, 2015.

87. For "party's over," see Matthias Gebauer, "New Orleans after Katrina: Will the Big Easy Become White, Rich and Republican?" *Spiegel Online International,* September 20, 2005. For "completely different," see Christopher Cooper, "Old-Line Families Escape Worst of Flood and Plot the Future," *WSJ,* September 8, 2005.

88. Edward L. Glaeser, "Should the Government Rebuild New Orleans, or Just Give Residents Checks?" *The Economists' Voice* 2 (2005): 1–6, esp. 3 (for "insuring the people") and 6 (for "silver lining"). See also Daniel T. Rodgers, *Age of Fracture* (Cambridge: Harvard University Press, 2012).

89. Joseph A. Schumpeter, *Capitalism, Socialism & Democracy* (1942; London: George Allen & Unwin, 1976), 83. See also Kevin Rozario, *The Culture of Calamity: Disaster and the Making of Modern America* (Chicago: University of Chicago Press, 2007), esp. 84–86.

90. For "state of nature," see Hirsch and Levert, "The Katrina Conspiracies," 208. For "social stratigraphy," see Dawdy, *Patina,* 40–47.

91. Lance Hill, "Orland on the Bayou," September 16, 2005, http://web.archive.org/web/20150107234916/http://www.southerninstitute.info/commentaries/?m=200509. Suncere Ali Shakur, interview by Pamela Hamilton, May 26, 2006, interview U-0255, transcript, pp. 1–6 (quotation on 3), SOHP Collection. On Common Ground, which recruited more than 10,000 volunteers in the first year following the flood, see Sue Hilderbrand, Scott Crow, and Lisa Fithian, "Common Ground Relief," in South End Press Collective, ed., *What Lies Beneath: Katrina, Race, and the State of the Nation* (Cambridge: South End Press

Collective, 2007), 80–99. For the second line, see Shaila Dewan, "With the Jazz Funeral's Return, the Spirit of New Orleans Rises," *NYT,* October 10, 2005.

92. Lori Rodriguez and Zeke Minaya, "HUD Chief Doubts New Orleans Will Be as Black," *Houston Chronicle,* September 29, 2005.

5. Rebuilding the Land of Dreams: 2005–2015

1. Kalamu ya Salaam, "Foreword: Know the Beginning Well and the End Will Not Trouble You," in Taylor Sparrow, *A Problem of Memory: Stories to End the Racial Nightmare* (Portland, OR: Eberhardt Press, 2007), 14–18 (quotation on 18). For Salaam's post-flood experiences, see Kalamu ya Salaam, interview by Joshua Guild, June 5, 2006, interview U-0264, transcript pp. 5–6, SOHP Collection. For "land of dreams," see Spencer Williams, "Basin Street Blues," song, 1928, and Randy Newman, "Land of Dreams," song, 1988; see also Nick Spitzer, "Rebuilding the Land of Dreams with Music," in Eugenie L. Birch and Susan M. Wachter, *Rebuilding Urban Places After Disaster: Lessons from Hurricane Katrina* (Philadelphia: University of Pennsylvania Press, 2006), 305–382. For synthetic, narrative accounts of New Orleans after Hurricane Katrina, see Gary Rivlin, *Katrina: After the Flood* (New York: Simon & Schuster, 2015); Daniel Wolff, *The Fight for Home: How (Parts of) New Orleans Came Back* (New York: Bloomsbury, 2012); and Roberta Brandes Gratz, *We're Still Here Ya Bastards: How the People of New Orleans Rebuilt Their City* (New York: Nation Books, 2015).

2. Lawrence N. Powell, "New Orleans: An American Pompeii?" lecture delivered at the University of Michigan, September 29, 2005, reprinted in Reinhold Wagnleitner, ed., *Satchmo Meets Amadeus* (Innsbruck, Austria: StudienVerlag, 2006), 142–156.

3. That rationale explains why, more than a decade after the flood, the Department of Homeland Security's Office of Inspector General (OIG) criticized New Orleans's use of $2.05 billion in FEMA funds to repair the city's water infrastructure. "The infrastructure was old and in poor condition even before the hurricanes," the OIG asserted. If the city's water pipes needed repair before the storm, the OIG argued, that is how federal disaster policy ought to have left them afterward. Department of Homeland Security, Office of Inspector General, *FEMA Should Disallow $2.04 Billion Approved for New Orleans Infrastructure Repairs,* OIG-17-97-D (Washington, DC), July 24, 2017. As I describe elsewhere, the moral valence for large firms is more nebulous: disaster relief policies are meant to profit them. The question is how much.

4. Figures are drawn from the 2000 US Census and 2015 US Census American Community Survey. For Lakeview in 2000, I use Census tracts 55, 56.01, 56.02, 56.03, 56.04, 76.03, and 76.04. For Lakeview in 2015, I use Census tracts 55, 56.01, 56.02, 56.03, 56.04, 76.04, and 76.06. For the Lower Ninth Ward in 2000 and 2015, I use Census tracts 7.01, 7.02, 8, 9.01, 9.02, 9.03, 9.04.

5. Kalima Rose, Annie Clark, and Dominque Duval-Dlop, "A Long Way Home: The State of Housing Recovery in Louisiana," *PolicyLink Equity Atlas* (2008), 47.

6. Robert Travis Scott, "Mayor Again Puts Out Welcome Mat," *NOTP,* September 29, 2005, p. 1. Gary Rivlin, "New Orleans Forms a Panel on Renewal," *NYT,* October 1, 2005. See also Rivlin, *Katrina,* 136–138. Signaling both the scale of the task at hand, the lack of coordination to address it, the New Orleans City Council also created an eleven-member "Advisory Committee on Hurricane Recovery" in September, which did not meet until January. FEMA, too, developed a recovery plan under its Emergency Support Function #14 process, although it had little influence or impact.

7. Gary Rivlin, "A Mogul Who Would Rebuild New Orleans," *NYT,* September 29, 2005.

8. "Nature's Revenge," *NYT,* August 30, 2005. For the urban planning debate, see Richard Campanella, *Bienville's Dilemma: A Historical Geography of New Orleans* (Lafayette: Center for Louisiana Studies, 2008), 344–350; Karl F. Seidman, *Coming Home to New Orleans: Neighborhood Rebuilding After Katrina* (New York: Oxford University Press, 2013), 20–34; Robert B. Olshansky and Laurie Johnson, *Clear as Mud: Planning for Rebuilding of New*

Orleans (Washington, DC: American Planning Association, 2010); and Carol M. Reese, Michael Sorkin, and Anthony Fontenot, eds., *New Orleans Under Reconstruction: The Crisis of Planning* (New York: Verso, 2014).

9. Martha Carr, "Panel Will Advise on Rebirth of N.O.," *NOTP*, October 28, 2005, p. 1. Martha Carr, "Citizens Pack Rebirth Forum," *NOTP*, November 15, 2005, p. Metro-1 for quotations. For "resided," see Campanella, *Bienville's Dilemma*, 345. For "just a fact," see "Harsh Urban Renewal in New Orleans," *AP*, October 12, 2005.

10. Urban Land Institute, *New Orleans, Louisiana: A Strategy for Rebuilding* (Washington, DC: ULI, 2006), 37–49 (Zone C on p. 46, Zone A on p. 45).

11. Rivlin, *Katrina*, 176.

12. Frank Donze, "Don't Write Us Off, Residents Warn," *NOTP*, November 29, 2005, p. 1.

13. For "all neighborhoods," see City Council Resolution No. M-05-590, December 15, 2005. See also Bruce Eggler, "No Neighborhood Left Behind, Council Vows," *NOTP*, December 17, 2005, p. 1. For the City Council's planning process, see City Council Resolution No. M-05-592, December 15, 2005. The resulting "City of New Orleans Neighborhoods Rebuilding Plan" was released in October 2006 and was sometimes called the "Lambert Plan" because the process was directed by the consulting firm Lambert Advisory. For Morial, see Gordon Russell and Frank Donze, "Officials Tiptoe Around Footprint Issue," *NOTP*, January 8, 2006, p. 01.

14. Bring New Orleans Back Commission, Urban Planning Committee, *Action Plan for New Orleans: The New American City* (January 11, 2006), (no page numbers).

15. For green dots, see "Plan for the Future," *NOTP*, January 12, 2006, p. 1. For Tobias, see Michelle Krupa, "Many Areas Marked for Green Space After Hurricane Katrina Have Rebounded," *NOTP*, August 23, 2010.

16. "A Responsible Plan," *NOTP*, January 15, 2006, p. 6.

17. Manuel Roig-Franzia, "Hostility Greets Katrina Recovery Plan," *WP*, January 12, 2006.

18. James Dao, "In New Orleans, Smaller May Mean Whiter," *NYT*, January 22, 2006, p. 1. For "worst fears," see Manuel Roig-Franzia, "Hostility Greets Katrina Recovery Plan," *WP*, January 12, 2006. Shakur, interview by Pamela Hamilton, pp. 3–4. John R. Logan, *The Impact of Katrina: Race and Class in Storm-Damaged Neighborhoods* (Providence: Brown University Spatial Structures in the Social Sciences Institute, 2005), 16. Logan projected that New Orleans would become a majority white city; his report noted that the disparate racial impacts did not extend to other areas flooded by broken levees. See also James Dao, "Study Says 80% of New Orleans Blacks May Not Return," *NYT*, January 27, 2006.

19. The survey, commissioned by the Louisiana Recovery Authority, was conducted between February 15 and April 30, 2006. Collective Strength, *2006 South Louisiana Recovery Survey: Citizen and Civic Leader Research Summary of Findings* (Baton Rouge: Louisiana Recovery Authority Support Foundation, 2006), 12.

20. Stephanie Grace, "Big Decisions Shape Recovering City," *NOTP*, August 22, 2010. On grassroots planning and recovery efforts, see also Seidman, *Coming Home to New Orleans*, and Emmanuel David, *Women of the Storm: Civic Activism after Hurricane Katrina* (Urbana: University of Illinois Press, 2017). For "all hell," see Stephanie Grace, "Will Plan Lift the Curse of the Green Dot?" *NOTP*, April 1, 2007, p. 7. For ACORN, see Mike Davis, "Who Is Killing New Orleans?" *The Nation*, March 23, 2006. For "Broadmoor Lives," see Campanella, *Bienville's Dilemma*, 347. For weekends, see Frank Donze, "Young Leadership Council to Relaunch 'Proud to Call It Home' Slogan," *NOTP*, November 10, 2010.

21. Bertha Irons, interview by Elizabeth Shelburne, May 26, 2006, interview U-0236, transcript, p. 35, SOHP Collection. Vien The Nguyen, interview by Elizabeth Shelborne, May 22, 2006, interview U-0247, transcript, p. 35, SOHP Collection. Jerrelyn Jessup Madere, interview by Megan Pugh, May 31, 2006, interview U-0241, transcript, p. 15, SOHP Collection.

22. Lance Hill, "How White People Elected Ray Nagin," *LW*, May 21, 2006. Ray Nagin, speech at New Orleans City Hall, January 16, 2006; transcript at "full video of Nagin's

chocolate city speech," WWLTV.com, April 28, 2010. For the election, see State of Louisiana, Executive Department, "Delay of the Qualifying Period and the February 4, 2006 and March 4, 2006 Elections in the Parish of Orleans," Executive Order No. KBB 2005-96, December 9, 2005. State of Louisiana, Executive Department, "Rescheduling the Qualifying Proposition, Primary, and General Elections in the Parish of Orleans," Executive Order No. KBB 2006-2, January 24, 2006. For 80 percent, see Adam Nossiter, "Voters Re-Elect Nagin as Mayor in New Orleans," *NYT,* May 21, 2006, p. A1.

23. For "plan by default," see Adam Nossiter, "Sparing Houses in New Orleans Spoils Planning," *NYT,* February 5, 2006, pp. 1, 22. Rivlin, *Katrina,* 219. Beginning in the fall of 2006, working with support from the Rockefeller Foundation, the Clinton-Bush Katrina Fund, and the Greater New Orleans Foundation, the city developed the "Unified New Orleans Plan," which served as the official recovery plan, and fulfilled the Louisiana Recovery Authority's requirement that every parish have a comprehensive recovery plan in place in order to receive CDBG funds. The Unified New Orleans Plan had a projected cost of approximately $14.4 billion but received limited funding for implementation.

24. Kevin Fox Gotham and Miriam Greenberg, *Crisis Cities: Disaster and Redevelopment in New York and New Orleans* (New York: Oxford University Press, 2014), ix. To be sure, the Gulf Opportunity Zone, which created tax incentives for development in damaged neighborhoods, fits those descriptions. See Gulf Opportunity Zone Act of 2005, Pub. L. No. 109-135, 119 Stat. 2577 (December 21, 2005). On neoliberalism, see also George Lipsitz, "Learning from New Orleans: The Social Warrant of Hostile Privatism and Competitive Consumer Citizenship," *Cultural Anthropology* 21, no. 3 (August 2006): 451–468; Cedric Johnson, ed., *The Neoliberal Deluge: Hurricane Katrina, Late Capitalism, and the Remaking of New Orleans* (Minneapolis: University of Minnesota Press, 2011); and Naomi Klein, *The Shock Doctrine: The Rise of Disaster Capitalism* (New York: Picador, 2008).

25. See also Clyde Woods, *Development Drowned and Reborn: The Blues and Bourbon Restorations in Post-Katrina New Orleans* (Athens: University of Georgia Press, 2017), and Jordan Camp and Laura Pulido's analysis of Woods's critique of disaster capitalism at pp. xxiii–xxiv.

26. Louisiana Katrina Reconstruction Act, S. 1765, 109th Cong., 1st Sess. (2005). For "brazen," see Michael Grunwald and Susan B. Glasser, "Louisiana Goes After Federal Billions," *WP,* September 26, 2005. See also Carl Hulse, "Louisiana Lawmakers Propose $250 Billion Recovery Package," *NYT,* September 23, 2005. For the influence of lobbyists on the proposal, see Alan C. Miller and Ken Silverstein, "Lobbyists Advise Katrina Relief," *Los Angeles Times,* October 10, 2005.

27. Hurricane Katrina Recovery, Reclamation, Restoration, Reconstruction and Reunion Act of 2005, H.R. 4197, 109th Cong., 1st Sess. (2005), introduced November 2, 2005. For quotations, see Sec. 2; for the 2015 goal, see Sec. 1202.

28. Baker's bill, the Louisiana Recovery Corporation Act, H.R. 4100, 109th Cong., 1st Sess. (2005), was introduced on October 20, 2005. Senators Landrieu and Vitter introduced companion legislation in the Senate on December 21, 2005, as the Hurricane Katrina Response Act, S. 2172. For support, see, for example, *H.R. 4100, The Louisiana Recovery Corporation Act,* Hearing Before the Committee on Financial Services, Serial No. 109-64, US House of Representatives, 109th Cong., 1st Sess., November 17, 2005 (see p. 32 for Jay Batt's "hodge-podge" quotation); and also Adam Nossiter, "A Big Government Fix-It Plan for New Orleans," *NYT,* January 5, 2006. For Powell, see Bill Walsh, "White House Against Baker Bailout Bill," *NOTP,* January 25, 2006, p. 1.

29. Bruce R. Linsday and Jarden Conrad Nagel, *Federal Disaster Assistance after Hurricanes Katrina, Rita, Wilma, Gustav, and Ike,* CRS report no. R43139 (Washington, DC: Library of Congress, 2013). For $75 billion, see Allison Plyer, "Facts for Features: Katrina Impact," The Data Center, August 26, 2016, https://www.datacenterresearch.org/data-resources /katrina/facts-for-impact/. The $120.5 figure does not include claims paid through the National Flood Insurance Program, which amounted to approximately $16.3 billion. "Significant Flood Events," Federal Emergency Management Agency, https://www.fema .gov/significant-flood-events. Roughly $76 billion of the $120.5 billion went to Louisiana.

Bruce Alpert, "$120 Billion in Katrina Federal Relief Wasn't Always Assured," *NOTP*, August 21, 2015. At the same time, "Congress offset Gulf relief with over $40 billion worth of cuts in Medicaid, food stamps and student loans. . . . Treasury Secretary John Snow refused to guarantee New Orleans municipal bonds, forcing Mayor Nagin to lay off 3,000 city employers [*sic*] just when the city needed them the most." Julian Bond, "In Katrina's Wake: Racial Implications of the New Orleans Disaster," *Journal of Race & Policy* (May 2007): 1–24, quotation on 22 (citing Davis, "Who Is Killing New Orleans?"). FEMA also rejected the Louisiana's initial efforts to use Hazard Mitigation Grant Program funds to acquire flooded properties. See US Government Accountability Office, *Gulf Coast Disaster Recovery: Community Development Block Grant Program Guidance to States Need to Be Improved*, Report to the US Senate Committee on Homeland Security and Governmental Affairs, GAO report no. 09-541 (June 2009), 22–23.

30. Statement of Derrell Cohoon, in *Katrina and Contracting: Blue Roof, Debris Removal, Travel Trailer Cast Studies, Hearing Before the Federal Financial Management, Government Information, and International Security Subcommittee*, S. Hrg. 109–743, 109th Cong., 2nd Sess., New Orleans, LA (April 10, 2006), p. 116. See also Statement of Patrick J. Fitzgerald, pp. 11 (for "markups"), and 30 (for Scalise).

31. Vincanne Adams, *Markets of Sorrow, Labors of Faith: New Orleans in the Wake of Katrina* (Durham: Duke University Press, 2013). On subcontracting, see also Gordon Russell and James Varney, "From Blue Tarps to Debris Removal, Layers of Contractors Drive Up the Cost of Recovery, Critics Say," *NOTP*, December 29, 2005, p. 1; and L. Elaine Halchin, "Hurricane Katrina Contracting: Subcontracting Tiers," Congressional Research Service Memo to the Senate Committee on Homeland Security and Governmental Affairs, Subcommittee on Federal Financial Management, Government Information, and International Security, March 29, 2006, in *Katrina and Contracting*, 143–149.

32. The first appropriation, for $11.5 billion, was the Department of Defense, Emergency Supplemental Appropriations to Address Hurricanes in the Gulf of Mexico, and Pandemic Influenza Act, 2006, Pub. L. No. 109-148, 119 Stat. 2680 (December 30, 2005). The second appropriation, for $5.2 billion, was Emergency Supplemental Appropriations Act for Defense, the Global War on Terror, and Hurricane Recovery, 2006, Pub. L. No. 109-234, 120 Stat. 418 (June 15, 2006). See also US Government Accountability Office, *Gulf Coast Disaster Recovery*, 4–5; and Eugene Boyd, *Community Development Block Grant Funds in Disaster Relief and Recovery*, CRS report no. RL33330, September 11, 2011. Pub. L. No. 109-148 appropriated $11.5 billion total in CDBG funds but required that "no State shall receive more than 54 percent of the amount provided," limiting the amount that Louisiana received, even though Louisiana received more than 54 percent of hurricane damage. Pub. L. No. 109-234 included a similar, although less draconian, limit, pre-venting any state (read: Louisiana) from receiving more than $4.2 billion. The limit, which ensured that funds would not be allocated proportionally with damage, was likely instituted at the insistence of Mississippi Senator Thad Cochran, Chairman of the Senate Appropriations Committee. See Sheila Crowley, "Where Is Home? Housing for Low-Income People After the 2005 Hurricanes," in Chester Hartman and Gregory D. Squires, eds., *There Is No Such Thing as a Natural Disaster: Race, Class, and Hurricane Katrina* (New York: Routledge, 2006), 121–166, esp. 145.

33. An Act Making Appropriations for the Department of Defense for the Fiscal Year Ending September 30, 2008, and for Other Purposes, Pub. L. No. 110-116, 121 Stat. 1295 (November 13, 2007). This appropriation brought a measure of parity to the CDBG allocations: Louisiana contained 67 percent of damaged housing units, and with this appropriation, received a total of 68 percent of CDBG funds. See US Government Accountability Office, *Gulf Coast Disaster Recovery*, 5–6.

34. "Louisiana Recovery Authority," Executive Order no. KBB 2005-63, October 17, 2005.

35. Laura Maggi, "Small Group Has Recovery Power," *NOTP*, January 23, 2006, p. 1.

36. Leslie Eaton, "Hurricane Aid Flowing Directly to Homeowners," *NYT*, July 17, 2006; Leslie Eaton, "Slow Home Grants Stall Progress in New Orleans," *NYT*, November 11, 2006.

37. The Louisiana bill was A concurrent resolution to approve The Road Home Housing Programs Action Plan Amendment for Disaster Recovery Funds . . . Senate Concurrent Resolution no. 63, Regular Session 2006 (May 10, 2006). HUD approved the plan on May 30, 2006. See "Jackson Approves Louisiana's $4.6 Billion 'Road Home Program,'" May 30, 2006, HUD No. 06-058.

38. Louisiana Recovery Authority, *Substantial Changes and Clarifications to Action Plan Amendment No. 1 for FY 2006, CDBG Disaster Recovery Funds, Action Plan Amendment for Disaster Recovery Funds* (Baton Rouge: Louisiana Division of Administration, 2006).

39. Homeowners who lived in Special Flood Hazard Areas but had not purchased flood insurance sacrificed 30 percent of the maximum award. See Louisiana Recovery Authority, *Substantial Changes and Clarifications to Action Plan Amendment No. 1 for FY 2006*, p. 9.

40. The Road Home program did include $892.7 million for "Workforce and Affordable Rental Housing Programs," but the funds went to developers seeking to build affordable housing, rather than to residents directly. "Jackson Approves Louisiana's $4.6 Billion 'Road Home Program,'" May 30, 2006, HUD No. 06-058 According to the 2000 Census, 51.2 percent of New Orleanians lived in rented housing units.

41. Davida Finger, "Stranded and Squandered: Lost on the Road Home," *Seattle Journal for Social Justice* 7, no. 1 (2008): 59–100. For "No. 1," see Laura Maggi, "Companies Seek Ethics Opinions," *NOTP*, June 2, 2006, p. 12. For "green light," and July 2006, see Eaton, "Hurricane Aid Flowing Directly to Homeowners." For late August, see Laura Maggi, "Company Chosen to Take the Wheel for Road Home," *NOTP*, June 10, 2006, p. 4.

42. Louisiana Department of Health and Hospitals, *2006 Louisiana Health and Population Survey, Survey Report, January 17, 2007* (New Orleans: Louisiana Public Health Institute, 2007), 2. The population survey had a 9.6 percent margin of error. The population for the West Bank is from the US Census for 2000. Among people who had lived in New Orleans before the storm and continued to live there a decade later, one study suggested that 50 percent of people returned within a year, a number that included 70 percent of whites but only 42 percent of African Americans. Gender mattered too: the study showed that 77 percent of white men returned within a year, compared to only 34 percent of African American women. Michael Henderson, Belinda Davis, and Michael Climek, *Views of Recovery Ten Years After Katrina and Rita* (Baton Rouge: LSU Manship School of Mass Communication, Reilly Center for Media & Public Affairs, August 25, 2015), 7.

43. In September 2006, 52 schools were open. Boston Consulting Group, *The State of Public Education in New Orleans* (Greater New Orleans Education Foundation, June 2007), 15. For Entergy and the Sewerage and Water Board, see Amy Liu, *Building a Better New Orleans: A Review of and Plan for Progress One Year after Hurricane Katrina* (Washington, DC: The Brookings Institution, 2006), quotation on 34. For trailers, see J. David Stanfield, ed., *The Challenges of Sudden Natural Disasters for Land Administration and Management: The Case of the Hurricane Katrina in New Orleans* (Nairobi: United Nations Human Settlements Program, 2008), 39–40. For formaldehyde, which was found at dangerous levels in 83 percent of trailers tested in one study, see Spencer S. Hsu, "FEMA Knew of Toxic Gas in Trailers," *WP*, July 20, 2007. For "horrible unending," see David Winkler-Schmit, "Call to Action," *NOG*, March 14, 2006.

44. State of Louisiana, Division of Administration, Office of Community Development, "The Road Home Week 26 Situation & Pipeline Report," January 2, 2007, p. 1. See also Jeffrey Meitrodt, "Understaffed and Overwhelmed," *NOTP*, January 28, 2007, p. 1; David Hammer, "Audit Finds Uneven Road," *NOTP*, April 3, 2007, p. 1; Stanfield, ed., *The Challenges of Sudden Natural Disasters*, 59.

45. Some of the reforms for which the Citizens' Road Home Action Team advocated were adopted by the state and ICF, including allowing homeowners to submit post-flood appraisals that estimated the pre-flood values of their houses, and allowing the state to pay homeowners even if they had appealed their initial grant award. "A Constructive Approach," *NOTP*, December 27, 2006, p. 6. A resolution to direct the vision of

administration, office of community development, to immediately cancel the state contract with ICF Emergency Management Services, LLC, and procure new contractors . . . , Louisiana House Resolution No. 17, Second Extraordinary Session, 2006 (December 15, 2006). Rivlin reports the vote as 97-1, but the *Official Journal of the House of Representatives of the State of Louisiana* records the vote as 98-0 with four abstentions on p. 73. See Rivlin, *Katrina*, 313. Senator Mary Landrieu held critical hearings on the Road Home Program in May 2007. See Committee on Homeland Security and Governmental Affairs, *The Road Home? An Examination of the Goals, Costs, Management, and Impediments Facing Louisiana's Road Home Program: Hearing before the Ad Hoc Subcommittee on Disaster Recovery*, US Senate, 110th Cong., 1st Sess., May 24, 2007.

46. Leslie Eaton, "Louisiana Sets Deadline for Storm Damage Claims," *NYT*, May 31, 2007, p. A13. In November 2007, Congress appropriated an addition $3 billion for the Road Home program to cover an unanticipated number of applicants, roughly 163,000. Leslie Eaton, "$3 Billion More Set for Hurricane Rebuilding," *NYT*, November 7, 2007, p. A23. On March 16, 2007, the program shifted from "incremental disbursement of funds" to "lump-sum payments." See US Government Accountability Office, *Gulf Coast Disaster Recovery*. For a description of the revised "lump-sum" program guidelines, see Louisiana Recovery Authority, *Action Plan Amendment 14 (First Allocation)—Road Home Homeowner Compensation Plan* (Baton Rouge: Louisiana Division of Administration, May 14, 2007). Blanco believed the Bush administration vetoed her version of the program as a plot to hurt Democrats. For that, and for details on the failure of the Road Home to enable homeowners to raise their homes out of the floodplain, see David Hammer, "Examining Post-Katrina Road Home Program," *The Advocate*, August 23, 2015.

47. Amy Liu and Nigel Holmes, "An Update on the State of New Orleans," *NYT*, August 28, 2007. Adam Nossiter, "Largely Alone, Pioneers Reclaim New Orleans," *NYT*, July 2, 2007. The New Orleans East population estimate is for May 2007. See Susan Saulny, "Aching for Lost Friends, but Rebuilding with Hope," *NYT*, July 2, 2007.

48. For the murder rate, see Brendan McCarthy and Laura Maggi, "Killings Bring the City to Its Bloodied Knees," *NOTP*, January 5, 2007, p. 1. For the parade, see Stacey Plaisance, "New Orleans Residents March on City Hill," *AP*, January 11, 2007. The *Times-Picayune* estimated that there were 3,000 people in attendance. Laura Maggi, "Enough!—Thousands March to Protest City's Alarming Murder Rate," *NOTP*, January 12, 2007, p. 1.

49. State of Louisiana, Division of Administration, Office of Community Development, *The Road Home Week 113 Situation & Pipeline Report* (January 20, 2009), 2 (for number of closings) and 5 (for grant amounts). Some observers suggested that ICF's calculation of the value of the grants it distributed included operating costs incurred by ICF itself, including over $2 million in annual bonuses to the company's executives. Adams, *Markets of Sorrow*, 84. While the implication was that subcontracting to a private corporation would create efficiency, some suggested ICF's fees must have exceeded the 5 percent cap on administrative costs that would otherwise have applied to CDBG funding. See Stanfield, ed., *The Challenges of Sudden Natural Disasters*, 126. Because of the nature of ICF's contract, however, it is difficult to tell how the company apportioned their funds.

50. Erwann O. Michel-Kerjan, "Catastrophe Economics: The National Flood Insurance Program," *Journal of Economic Perspectives* 24, no. 4 (Fall 2010): 399–422, statistics on 400.

51. Christina Finch, Christopher T. Emrich, and Susan L. Cutter, "Disaster Disparities and Differential Recovery in New Orleans," *Population and Environment* 31, no. 4 (March 2010): 179–202.

52. Adam Nossiter, "After Fanfare, Hurricane Grants Leave Little Mark," *NYT*, August 30, 2008. See also US Government Accountability Office, *Gulf Coast Disaster Recovery*. For "bureaucratic failure," see Adams, *Markets of Sorrow*, 74–97, quotation on 89.

53. For the estimate of 6,234 cases of heir property in New Orleans, see Richard Kluckow, "The Impact of Heir Property on Post-Katrina Housing Recovery in New Orleans" (MA thesis, Colorado State University, 2014), esp. p. 34. See also Meitrodt, "Understaffed and Overwhelmed," p. 1; Hammer, "Audit," p. 1; Stanfield, ed., *The Challenges of Sudden*

Natural Disasters, 59; Adams, *Markets of Sorrow,* 74–97; and Leslie Eaton, "HUD Institutes Changes to Speed Storm Repairs," *NYT,* April 7, 2007.

54. According to the lawsuit filed by the Greater New Orleans Fair Housing Action Center, before the flood, in nearly every New Orleans neighborhood where African Americans owned at least 60 percent of the homes, the median home value was less than $150,000, whereas in nearly every neighborhood were white people owned at least 80 percent of the homes, the median home value was more than $150,000. Similarly, 80 percent of African American homeowners in New Orleans owned homes with a market value of less than $100,000—marking the upper-bound of their potential grant awards—compared to only 33 percent of white homeowners. "Complaint for Declaratory and Injunctive Relief," Document 1, Greater New Orleans Fair Housing Action Center et al. v. United States Department of Housing and Urban Development et al., US District Court for the District of Columbia, Civil Action No. 08-01938, November 12, 2008, p. 11.

55. This data refers to the 84,114 closed Road Home applications as of June 26, 2008. Kalima Rose, Annie Clark, and Dominque Duval-Dlop, "A Long Way Home: The State of Housing Recovery in Louisiana," *PolicyLink Equity Atlas* (2008), 42–43, 47–48. See also Timothy F. Green and Robert B. Olshansky, "Rebuilding Housing in New Orleans: The Road Home Program after the Hurricane Katrina Disaster," *Housing Policy Debate* 22, no. 1 (2012): 75–99, esp. 92–95. A smaller study conducted with Road Home data through 2010 showed gaps that were substantially wider for all groups: a $53,560 gap across Louisiana, for example, between damage estimates and insurance and grant settlements. The study also suggested that homeowners in Mississippi got larger CDBG grants, compared to actual damage, than did homeowners in Louisiana. See Jonathan Spader and Jennifer Turnham, "CDBG Disaster Recovery Assistance and Homeowners' Rebuilding Outcomes Following Hurricanes Katrina and Rita," *Housing Policy Debate* 24, no. 1 (2014): 213–237, esp. 222.

56. "Plaintiffs' Memorandum and Points of Authorities in Support of their Motion for a Temporary Restraining Order and a Preliminary Injunction," Document 50-1, *Greater New Orleans Fair Housing Action Center v. US Department of Housing and Urban Development,* June 2, 2010, p. 14. Katy Reckdahl, "2 Lead Plaintiffs in Road Home Discrimination Suit Will Get Nothing from $62 Million Settlement," *NOTP,* July 18, 2011. Previously, in November 2007, the LRA had announced additional compensation grants of up to $50,000 for homeowners with incomes of less than 80 percent of the area's median income; then, facing pressure from Randolphs' suit, in October 2009, the LRA lifted the $50,000 cap, which meant that four years after the storm, homeowners with lower incomes became eligible for the full cost of repairs up to $150,000. The new policy enabled some 13,000 homeowners to receive an additional $470 million in grants. But the additional funding did nothing to help the Randolphs—and over 9,000 other applicants in New Orleans alone—who made more than 80 percent of the median income. For the $50,000 grants, which were initially called "Affordable Compensation Loans," see Louisiana Recovery Authority, *Further Changes and Clarifications to Road Home Program (Amendment No. 7)* (Baton Rouge: Louisiana Division of Administration, November 30, 2006). On lifting the cap, see Louisiana Recovery Authority, *Proposed Action Plan Amendment 39: Removal of Affordable Compensation Grant Cap* (Baton Rouge: Louisiana Division of Administration, 2009). The amendment was submitted to HUD October 12, 2009, and approved January 28, 2010. See also "Settlement Agreement," *Greater New Orleans Fair Housing Action Center v. US Department of Housing and Urban Development,* June 2011, pp. 1–2, https://www.hud.gov/sites/documents/ROADHOMESETTLEMENT.PDF.

57. "Plaintiff's Memorandum," *Greater New Orleans Fair Housing Action Center v. US Department of Housing and Urban Development,* 24. For "no legitimate reason," see "Memorandum Opinion," Document 61, *Greater New Orleans Fair Housing Action Center v. US Department of Housing and Urban Development,* July 6, 2010, p. 8. See also Michael A. Fletcher, "A Tale of Two Recoveries," *WP,* August 27, 2010; and David Hammer, "Road Home's Grant Calculations Discriminate Against Black Homeowners, Federal

Judge Rules," *NOTP*, August 16, 2010. For the settlement, see Greater New Orleans Fair Housing Action Center, "State Amends Problematic Hurricane Relief Program," July 7, 2011, http://www.gnofairhousing.org/2011/07/07/state-ammends-problematic-hurricane -relief-program/. For the Randolphs, see Reckdahl, "2 Lead Plaintiffs."

58. State of Louisiana, Division of Administration, Office of Community Development, *The Homeowner Assistance Program: Situation & Pipeline Report #470, September 2017* (October 2, 2017), 1 (for 54 percent) and 11 (other calculations by the author). Unsurprisingly, homeowners who took the buyout option in New Orleans tended to live in parts of the city with the greatest flood damage. See Green and Olshansky, "Rebuilding Housing in New Orleans," 86–89.

59. Liu, *Building a Better New Orleans*, 11–15. For "insufficient funds," see Louisiana Recovery Authority, *The Road Home Housing Programs: Action Plan for the Use of Disaster Recovery Funds* (Baton Rouge: Louisiana Division of Administration, ca. January–June, 2006), 18. See also Louisiana Recovery Authority, *Clarifications to the Road Home Affordable Rental Housing Action Plan Amendment for Disaster Recovery Funds, Amendment 11* (Baton Rouge: Louisiana Division of Administration, February 9, 2006); and Louisiana Recovery Authority, *Action Plan Amendment # 18 (First Allocation): Modifications to Workforce and Affordable Rental Housing Programs* (Baton Rouge: Louisiana Division of Administration, November 28, 2007).

60. David Hammer, "Road Home Rental Program to Get Fresh Start," *NOTP*, April 15, 2009. Despite changes to the program, as of December 31, 2010, the Small Rental Property Program had distributed less than $331 million statewide. Louisiana Recovery Authority, *CDBG Katrina/Rita Program Appropriations, Allocations and Expenditures for 2011* (n.d. ca. 2012), https://www.doa.la.gov/OCDDRU/Reports/KR_Expenditures/KR_Expenditures _2011.pdf. For 39 percent increase, see Liu, *Building a Better New Orleans*, 12.

61. An ordinance to establish a moratorium on the re-establishment and development of any multi-family dwellings in St. Bernard Parish throughout the disaster recovery period, Saint Bernard Parish Ordinance no. 632-11-05, November 1, 2005. For related by blood, see An ordinance to prohibit the rental, lease, loan or certain other occupancy of single family residences in R-1 zones, St. Bernard Parish Ordinance no. 670-09-06, September 19, 2006. For 93 percent, see Hannah Adams, "Fair Housing Center Calls on St. Bernard Parish to Repeal Discriminatory Ordinance," Greater New Orleans Fair Housing Action Center press release, September 22, 2006, http://www.gnofairhousing .org/2006/09/22/fair-housing-center-calls-on-st-bernard-parish-to-repeal -discriminatory-ordinance-ordinance-may-ban-non-white-renters/. In March 2006, the Council had put a moratorium on renting out single-family homes, which it repeated in December. An ordinance to preserve the integrity of single family dwelling neighbor-hoods by placing a moratorium on single family homes becoming rental properties . . . , St. Bernard Parish ordinance no. 643-03-06, March 7, 2006. An ordinance repealing ordinance no. 643-03-06 . . . , Saint Bernard Parish ordinance no. 693-12-06, De-cember 5, 2006. For continued limits on rental housing, see An ordinance to amend ordinance 670-09-06 . . . , Saint Bernard Parish ordinance no. 697-12-06, December 19, 2006; and An ordinance placing a moratorium on all R-3, (Multiple-Family Residen-tial), and/or any housing developments . . . , Saint Bernard Parish ordinance no. 905-09-08, September 16, 2008. For "going to bring," see Campbell Robertson, "A Battle Over Low-Income Housing Reveals Post-Hurricane Tensions," *NYT*, October 4, 2009, p. A16.

62. The judge also ruled that it ran afoul of the terms of the Consent Order put in place after the blood relative law. "Orders and Reasons," Greater New Orleans Fair Housing Action Center and Wallace Rodrigue v. St. Bernard Parish and St. Bernard Parish Council, US District Court, Eastern District of Louisiana, Civil Action no. 06-7185, 641 F. Supp. 2d 563 (E. D. La. 2009), March 25, 2009. For the original consent order, see "Consent Order," Document 104, Greater New Orleans Fair Housing Action Center v. Saint Bernard Parish, February 20, 2008.

63. Office of Public Affairs, "Justice Department Charges St. Bernard Parish, Louisiana for Limited Rental Housing Opportunities for African-Americans," Department of Justice, January 31, 2012. Marlene Theberge, "Fair Housing Center Announced $900,000 Settlement Agreement with St. Bernard Parish," Greater New Orleans Fair Housing Action Center, May 10, 2013. For "true freedom," see Robertson, "Battle Over Low-Income Housing."

64. Calculations by the author based on 2000 and 2010 Census data.

65. Calculations by the author based on 2000 and 2010 Census Tract data for Orleans Parish Census Tracts 7.02 and 9.01 and St. Bernard Parish Census Tract 303.

66. Martha Mahoney, "Law and Racial Geography: Public Housing and the Economy in New Orleans," *Stanford Law Review* 42, no. 5 (May 1990): 1251–1290, esp. 1268–1281. HANO boasted that New Orleans was, in fact, the first city to receive Wagner Act funds for public housing. See Margaret C. Gonzalez-Perez, "A House Divided: Public Housing Policy in New Orleans," *Louisiana History* 44, no. 4 (Autumn 2003): 443–461, esp. 455. Ralph Thayer asserted that in 1970, New Orleans had more public housing units "per capita than any other American city." Thayer, *The Evolution of Housing Policy in New Orleans (1920–1978)* (New Orleans: Institute for Governmental Studies, Loyola University, 1979), 92. On public housing in New Orleans, see also John Arena, *Driven From New Orleans: How Nonprofits Betray Public Housing and Promote Privatization* (Minneapolis: University of Minnesota Press, 2012).

67. HUD regulations required one-for-one replacements from 1979 to 1986; in 1987, Congress passed the Housing and Community Development Act which made one-for-one replacement law. In its HUD appropriations bill for 1996, Congress gave HUD the authority to waive the requirement. Congress fully repealed the one-for-one replacement requirement with the Quality Housing and Work Responsibility Act of 1998. See US General Accounting Office, *Public Housing: Funding and Other Constraints Limit Housing Authorities' Ability to Comply With One-for-One Rule*, report no. RCED-95-78 (March 3, 1995).

68. For 1,510, see Arena, *Driven from New Orleans*, xxxiv. For St. Thomas data, see Bill Quigley and Sarah H. Godchaux, "Locked Out and Torn Down: Public Housing Post Katrina," https://billquigley.wordpress.com/2015/06/08/locked-out-and-torn-down-public-housing-post-katrina-by-bill-quigley-and-sara-h-godchaux/. HUD began managing HANO in 2002, when the local agency was put in federal receivership for mismanagement, but the shift in control did not represent a change in direction, because federal policy called for the end of traditional public housing across the country.

69. Sources differ on the peak number of public housing units in New Orleans. For example, Arena lists 14,591, of which 2,331 were at scattered sites, but does not give a date. Arena, *Driven from New Orleans*, xxxiv. Gotham and Pardee list 13,681, of which 1,419 were in scattered sites, as total units constructed. Jessica W. Pardee and Kevin Fox Gotham, "HOPE VI, Section 8, and the Contradictions of Low-Income Housing Policy," *Journal of Poverty* 9, no. 2 (2005): 1–21, esp. 14. Bullard and Wright count 13,694 units of conventional public housing in 1996. Robert D. Bullard and Beverly Wright, "Race, Place, and the Environment in Post-Katrina New Orleans," in Bullard and Wright, eds., *Race, Place, and Environmental Justice After Hurricane Katrina* (Boulder: Westview Press, 2009), 19–48, esp. 28. For 2005 numbers, see Housing Authority of New Orleans, "Post-Katrina Frequently Asked Questions," April 2006, reproduced in *Federal Housing Response to Hurricane Katrina: Hearing Before the Committee on Financial Services US House of Representatives*, Serial no. 110-1, 110th Cong., 1st Sess. February 6, 2007, p. 222. The same source reports, "HANO had an allocation of 9,400 Housing Choice Vouchers pre Katrina, with 8,981 vouchers utilized and another 700 issued to individuals searching for units." Before the storm, HUD reported that there were 8,250 families on New Orleans's waiting list for public housing, and 16,102 families were on the waiting list for Section 8. US Department of Housing and Urban Development, "PHA Plans: 5 Year Plan for Fiscal Years 2001–2005, Annual Plan for Fiscal Year Beginning 10/2003," pp. 8–9, reproduced in *Federal Housing Response to Hurricane Katrina*, 219.

70. HANO described "minor flooding" at C. J. Peete, 12 inches of flooding at Lafitte, 24 inches of flooding at Cooper (although HUD also noted that 300 units there had "sustained no unit flooding and little wind damage"), and "significant flood and sustained damage" at St. Bernard. In the next sentence, HUD described "complete devastation" at the Florida and Desire, noting that "based on preliminary reports," these complexes "may require complete demolition"—implying that all of the other developments were repairable. See Housing Authority of New Orleans, "Post-Katrina Frequently Asked Questions," April 2006, 224–225. Another April 2006 HANO report noted "interior damage is minimal" at C. J. Peete and described flooding only to the Community Center. See "C. J. Peete Housing Development," reproduced in *Federal Housing Response to Hurricane Katrina*, 241. For 3,077, see Katy Reckdahl, "B.W. Cooper Housing Site's Slow March to Rebirth Reaches Finish Line," *NOTP*, May 5, 2012.

71. "Statement of Gloria Williams, Tenant," *Solving the Affordable Housing Crisis in the Gulf Coast Region Post-Katrina, Part I, Field Hearing Before the Subcommittee on Housing and Community Opportunity of the Committee on Financial Services, US House of Representatives,* Serial no. 110-5, 110th Cong., 1st Sess., February 22, 2007, pp. 61–62. In December 2005, Congress directed HUD "within the extent feasible," to "preserve all [public and subsidized] housing." Pub. L. No. 109-148, sec. 901, 119 Stat. 2680 at 2781.

72. For Jackson, see Lori Rodriguez and Zeke Minaya, "HUD Chief Doubts New Orleans Will Be as Black," *Houston Chronicle,* September 29, 2005. For Baker, see Babington, "Some GOP Legislators Hit Jarring Notes in Addressing Katrina." For Thomas, see James Varney, "HANO Wants Only Working Tenants," *NOTP,* February 21, 2006, p. 1. For Williams, see "Statement of Gloria Williams," 61–62. For the fence, see Gwen Filosa, "Public Housing Still Empty," *NOTP,* April 9, 2006, p. 1. HUD previously asserted it would "make repairs to units that were previously occupied" at C. J. Peete, B. W. Cooper, and Lafitte. Housing Authority of New Orleans, "Post-Katrina Frequently Asked Questions," April 2006, p. 225. For officials, see Jordan Flaherty, "Floodlines: Preserving Public Housing in New Orleans," *Race, Poverty & the Environment* (Fall 2010): 61–65.

73. Pamela Mahogany, interview by Joshua Guild, June 4, 2006, interview U-0243, transcript, pp. 14–15, SOHP Collection. For "steal," see Phyllis Jenkins, quoted in Susan Saulny, "Clamoring to Come Home to New Orleans Projects," *NYT,* June 6, 2006. For supporting demolition, see Reckdahl, "B.W. Cooper." For "bomb," see Bertha Irons, May 26, 2009, p. 35.

74. "UN Experts Call for Protection of Housing Rights of Hurricane Katrina Victims," *UN News,* February 28, 2008. For National Trust, see Richard Moe to Alphonso Jackson, December 6, 2006, reprinted in *Federal Housing Response to Hurricane Katrina,* 266. For right of return, see "Prepared Statement of Judith A. Browne-Dianis," February 6, 2007, in *Federal Housing Response to Hurricane Katrina,* 181–190.

75. "Declaration of David Martinez," Yolanda Anderson, et al., v. Alphonso Jackson, et al., US District Court, Eastern District of Louisiana, Civil Act No. 06-3298, October 23, 2006. For a similar assertion from an architect, see "Declaration of John E. Fernandez," *Yolanda Anderson v. Jackson,* October 23, 2006. Housing Authority of New Orleans, "Preliminary Recovery Plan for the Redevelopment and Repair of Public Housing Properties Summary," June 4, 2006, p. 24. All in *Federal Housing Response to Hurricane Katrina,* 258–262 (for Martinez), 263–265 (for Fernandez), and 236 (for HANO).

76. US Department of Housing and Urban Development, "HUD Outlines Aggressive Plan to Bring Families Back to New Orleans' Public Housing," news release, June 14, 2006, reproduced in *Federal Housing Response to Hurricane Katrina,* 227–288. Susan Saulny, "5,000 Public Housing Units in New Orleans Are to Be Razed," *NYT,* June 15, 2006. For the argument that the destruction of public housing constituted a form of asset stripping from African Americans, see Clyde Woods, "Les Misérables of New Orleans: Trap Economics and the Asset Stripping Blues," *American Quarterly* 61, no. 3 (September 2009): 769–792.

77. William C. Thorson [HUD's HANO receiver] to Orlando J. Cabrera [Assistant Secretary for Public and Indian Housing], email, July 21, 2006. See also "Statement of Judith A.

Browne-Dianis, Co-Director, Advancement Project." Thorson also urged an associate to "take photos of the worst of the worst parts," and to reprint *Times-Picayune* articles about "murders at Iberville. . . . the idea being that reopening lafite as before would create another iberville." William C. Thorson to Jeffrey Riddel, August 4, 2006. All in *Federal Housing Response to Hurricane Katrina*, 256–257 (for Thorson to Cabrera), 123–124 (for Browne-Dianis), and 240 (for Thorson to Riddel). For Thorson's appointment, see Gwen Filosa, "Top HANO Officials Replaced," *NOTP*, April 14, 2006, p. 1.

78. Gulf Coast Hurricane Housing Recovery Act of 2007, H.R. 1227, 110th Cong., 1st Sess. (2007), Sec. 202 and Sec. 203. The bill was introduced on February 28, 2007, and passed on March 21, 2007. The accompanying Senate bill, S. 1668, was introduced on June 20, 2007, and was referred to the Senate Committee on Banking, Housing, and Urban Affairs. The Congressional Budget Office estimated that fully rehabilitating 5,000 public housing units in New Orleans would cost $667 million, although the score was not based on direct inspection of housing conditions. Congressional Budget Office, "Cost Estimate for H.R. 1227," April 30, 2007, https://www.cbo.gov/sites/default/files/110th-congress-2007-2008 /costestimate/hr122700.pdf. For Johnigan, see "Statement of Donna Johnigan, Tenant," *Solving the Affordable Housing Crisis in the Gulf Coast Region Post-Katrina, Part I*, 62–63. David Vitter, "Housing Recovery Act Endangers Reform," *NOTP*, October 6, 2007, p. 7. Johnigan's efforts prompted developers to keep 350 "interim" apartments standing and occupied at B. W. Cooper, until new buildings were available to tenants; activism among former Cooper residents also prompted some residents to be hired to work on the construction. See Katy Reckdahl, "B.W. Cooper."

79. Adam Nossiter and Leslie Eaton, "New Orleans Council Votes for Demolition of Housing," *NYT*, December 21, 2007. "New Orleans Police Taser, Pepper Spray Residents Seeking to Block Public Housing Demolition," *Democracy Now*, December 21, 2007. See also Bill Quigley, *Storms Still Raging: Katrina, New Orleans and Social Justice* (New York: BookSurge, 2008). For "demagogues" and "washed away," see Gwen Filosa, "Live Updates on Demolition Vote from Council Chambers," *NOTP*, December 19, 2007.

80. Rick Jervis, "New Orleans' Homeless Rate Swells to 1 in 25," *USA Today*, March 16, 2008. A study that winter suggested that 86 percent of the city's homeless population had lived in the city before the storm, and that 60 percent said their homelessness was "due to Katrina." UNITY of Greater New Orleans, "Claiborne Encampment Survey Results," February 28, 2008, http://unitygno.org/wp-content/uploads/2010/07/Claiborne EncampmentSurvey.pdf.

81. Larry Blumenfeld, "Mardi Gras Indian Chiefs Stand Spectacular, Tall, and Proud," *Village Voice*, February 26, 2008. For Lewis, see Geraldine Wyckoff, "Jerod 'Big Chief Rody' Lewis," *LW*, December 9, 2013; and Jay Mazza, "Big Chief Rody, R.I.P." *The Vinyl District*, December 5, 2013. "The percent of very low-income renters in Orleans Parish who were cost burdened increased significantly from 2007 to 2008." Allison Plyer et al., *Housing Production Needs: Three Scenarios for New Orleans* (New Orleans: Greater New Orleans Community Data Center, November 2009), 7.

82. For Section 8 housing vouchers, which were supposed to aid former public housing tenants, but were difficult to use because of complicated regulations and discrimination in the private market, see Katy Reckdahl, "Section 8 Loophole Thwarts Evacuees Hoping to Return," *NOTP*, July 5, 2008; *Housing Choice in Crisis: An Audit Report on Discrimination against Housing Choice Voucher Holders in the Greater New Orleans Rental Housing Market* (New Orleans: Greater New Orleans Fair Housing Action Center, November 2009), 8; and Stacy Seicshnaydre and Ryan C. Albright, *Expanding Choice and Opportunity in the Housing Choice Voucher Program* (New Orleans: The Data Center, July 8, 2015), 2–4.

83. Katy Reckdahl, "Back to the Big Four," *NOTP*, August 21, 2011, p. 1. Reckdahl, "New C.J. Peete Complex Is Solid, Shiny—But Not as Social, Some Residents Say." "Statement of Gloria Williams, Tenant," 61. For thirteen families in May 2012, see Reckdahl, "B.W. Cooper." For Lewis, see Wyckoff, "Jerod 'Big Chief Rody' Lewis." By 2015, HANO had only opened 1,829, and fewer than half of those had public housing–level rents. Katy

Reckdahl, "10 Years After Katrina, New Orleans Public Housing Still in Limbo," *Next City,* June 15, 2015.

84. Louisiana Revised Statue 46:6, "Admission to State-Supported Charity Hospitals," as quoted in Kenneth Brad Ott, "The Closure of New Orleans' Charity Hospital After Hurricane Katrina: A Case of Disaster Capitalism" (MA thesis, University of New Orleans, 2012), 60. The law was changed by Act 906 of 2003 to means-test eligibility at 200 percent of the federal poverty level and uninsured.

85. For uncompensated care costs, see *Health Challenges for the People of New Orleans: The Kaiser Post-Katrina Baseline Survey* (Kaiser Family Foundation, July 2007), 45. Allen Toussaint, "Charity's Always There," song, Warner Tamerlane Music / Marsaint Music Inc., 1987. John E. Salvaggio, *New Orleans' Charity Hospital: A Story of Physicians, Politics, and Poverty* (Baton Rouge: Louisiana State University Press, 1992), 276.

86. On the building, see Robert D. Leighninger, *Building Louisiana: The Legacy of the Public Works Administration* (Jackson: University Press of Mississippi, 2007), 138–148. For critiques of the vision, see for example, Woods, "Les Misérables of New Orleans," esp. 785; and Anne M. Lovell, "Reformers, Preservationists, Patients, and Planners: Embodied Histories and Charitable Populism in the Post-Disaster Controversy over a Public Hospital," in Romain Huret and Randy J. Sparks, eds., *Hurricane Katrina in Transatlantic Perspective* (Baton Rouge: Louisiana State University Press, 2014), 100–120. The Louisiana Health Care Authority had recommended a new building in 1991, and Charity had briefly lost its accreditation from the Joint Commission in 1994, in part because of building code violations, although the 1991 report also praised the "Louisiana Model" of indigent care. Louisiana Health Care Authority, *Strategic Plan: Report to the Louisiana Legislature* (March 15, 1991), as described in Ott, "The Closure of New Orleans' Charity Hospital," 38. In 2002 the Joint Commission on Accreditation of Healthcare Organizations had encouraged Charity's leadership to "strongly consider seeking from the state a more modern facility to improve patient safety, environmental safety, patient privacy and infection control." Joint Commission of Healthcare Organizations, *Joint Commission on Accreditation of Healthcare Organizations Official Accreditation Decision Report: Medical Center of Louisiana at New Orleans,* December 13, 2002, quoted in Federal Emergency Management Agency, "Draft Programmatic Environmental Assessment for Site Selection," Veterans Affairs Medical Center (VAMC) and Louisiana State University Academic Medical Center of Louisiana (LSU AMC), October 2008, pp. 2–9.

87. Adams Project Management, *Site and Facility Master Plan Consolidation of Charity and University Hospitals* (2005), quoted in Ott, "The Closure of New Orleans' Charity Hospital," 69. For the 2013 projection, see Jared E. Munster, "They Took My Bedroom: A Case Study of Eminent Domain in New Orleans" (PhD dissertation, University of New Orleans, 2012), 204. For decent care, see Katy Reckdahl, "Who's Caring?" *NOG,* October 7, 2003.

88. Kiersta Kurtz-Burke, remarks at "The Katrina Disaster Now" program at Tulane University, November 17, 2005, videorecording in author's possession. The estimate of 1,200 people is Kurtz-Burke's and is also the figure used by the *Times-Picayune,* but other figures vary widely. James Aiken, the Medical Director for Emergency Preparedness, Medical Center of Louisiana, estimated that there were 400 patients at Charity, nine of whom died. US Senate, *Hurricane Katrina: A Nation Still Unprepared, Special Report of the Committee on Homeland Security and Governmental Affairs* (Washington, DC: US Government Printing Office, 2006), 406. The House investigation described the evacuation—of 200 patients from Charity and 167 from University Hospital, with three fatalities—as having taken place on the afternoon of September 1. US House of Representatives, *A Failure of Initiative: Final Report of the Select Bipartisan Committee to Investigate the Preparation for and Response to Hurricane Katrina* (Washington, DC: US Government Printing Office, 2006), 286. *CNN* reported that the evacuation occurred on September 2. "Patients Finally Rescued from Charity Hospital," CNN.com, September 3, 2005. For 1,200, see also Jan Moller, "New Charity May Rise in Katrina's Wake," *NOTP,* September 15,

2005. For snipers, see "Sniper Fire Halts Hospital Evacuation," CNN.com, September 1, 2005. See also *A Failure of Initiative*, 285. For Smithburg, see Jan Moller, "Charity Evacuation Begins," *NOTP*, September 1, 2005.

89. The Robert T. Stafford Disaster Relief and Emergency Assistance Act, Pub L. 100-707, 102 Stat. 4689 (November 23, 1988), amending the Disaster Relief Act of 1974, Pub. L. No. 93-288, 88 Stat. 143 (May 21, 1974). For the so-called 50 percent rule, see 44 CFR 206.226(f), 55 FR 2217 (January 23, 1990) at 2309. See also US Government Accountability Office, *Hurricane Katrina: Status of the Health Care System in New Orleans and Difficult Decisions Related to Efforts to Rebuild It Approximately 6 Months After Hurricane Katrina,* GAO report no. 06-576R, (March 28, 2006), 4.

90. "We're trying to show and convince FEMA this damage was done by the storm," the director of Louisiana's Office of Facility Planning and Control, who was in charge of negotiating with FEMA, explained. Richard Webster, "Special Treatment: Reopening Charity Hospital's First Three Floors Possible," *New Orleans City Business,* July 23, 2007. Quoted in Ott, "The Closure of New Orleans' Charity Hospital," 95.

91. FEMA noted some additional repair costs might become evident. FEMA, "Response of the Federal Emergency Management Agency to Arbitration Request of the Louisiana Facility Planning and Control, State of Louisiana," September 30, 2009, pp. 12–18. For LSU's figures, see Adams, "Executive Summary Excerpted from Emergency Facilities Assessment, University and Charity Hospitals, New Orleans, Louisiana, for LSU Health Sciences Center," November 2005, p. 4.1. Adams noted that the entire replacement cost, including "site development, demolition, professional fees and other soft costs," would be $632.6 million.

92. For example, an assessment conducted as part of an effort to place the building on the National Register of Historic Places found that "deferred maintenance, and a building that was never formally mothballed, but was only closed-in without providing for air circulation" created "the greatest physical threat." Earth Search, Inc., "National Register of Historic Places, Registration Form, Charity Hospital of New Orleans," submitted December 8, 2010, pp. 7–8.

93. Ott, "The Closure of New Orleans' Charity Hospital," 76–77, 181. Alex Glustrom, director, "Big Charity: The Death of America's Oldest Hospital," documentary film, 2014. Military officials and doctors involved in cleaning up the hospital believed that Charity was ready to accept patients again less than a month after the hurricane. Roberta Berthelot, "The Army Response to Hurricane Katrina," September 10, 2010, https://www.army.mil/article /45029/the_army_response_to_hurricane_katrina; George Flynn, "'Charity' Suffers Long: Emergency Medicine Revives the Spirit of Centuries-Old New Orleans Institution," *Annals of Emergency Medicine* 48, no. 3 (September 2006): 309–311; Cain Burdeau, "Honoré: Ex-La. Governor Halted Hospital Reopening," *AP,* July 14, 2009. Lolis Eric Elie, "City Needs Charity to Return," *NOTP,* March 24, 2006, p. 1.

94. Kaiser Family Foundation, *Health Challenges for the People of New Orleans,* esp. 1–4. For 3,500, see Jan Moller, "Charity Plan Calls for Shift in Services," *NOTP,* November 9, 2005, p. 5. For the field hospital, see Jan Moller, "LSU Field Hospital's Days Are Numbered," *NOTP,* January 21, 2006, p. 3. For 500 patients per day, see Jan Moller, "LSU Will Open Clinic in New Orleans Centre," *NOTP,* February 22, 2006, p. 5. For Elmwood, see Jan Moller, "Trauma Center to Be in Elmwood," *NOTP,* February 9, 2006, p. 4. LSU announced that it intended to reopen a trauma center with limited inpatient services in New Orleans, at University Hospital, but construction delays and difficulties hiring staff postponed the opening until late November 2006, well over a year after the hurricane. Jan Moller, "Staff to Reopen Hospital Scarce," *NOTP,* September 22, 2006, p. 2. See also John Pope, "Damage to Charity Minor, Protestors Say," *NOTP,* June 9, 2006, p. 1. Uninsured patients were also being treated at several other hospitals that had reopened across the region.

95. Kaiser Family Foundation, *Health Challenges for the People of New Orleans,* 1–3, 53, 13. For suicides, see Susan Saulny, "A Legacy of the Storm: Depression and Suicide," *NYT,* June 21, 2006, p. A1.

96. Before the flood, across the region, there had been 462 psychiatric beds; in September 2006, there were 190. Bill Walsh and Jan Moller, "When Needed Most, Psych Services Gone," *NOTP*, September 5, 2006, p. 1. The forty-bed count for Charity's CIU is from Kaiser Family Foundation, *Health Challenges for the People of New Orleans*, 45. For PTSD at University, see Lisa Mills et al., "Post-Traumatic Stress Disorder in an Emergency Department Population One Year After Hurricane Katrina," *Journal of Emergency Medicine* 43, no. 1 (July 2012): 76–82. For PTSD in schools, see Lisa H. Jaycox et al., "Children's Mental Health Care following Hurricane Katrina: A Field Trial of Trauma-Focused Psychotherapies," *Journal of Trauma and Stress* 23, no. 2 (April 2010): 223–231. For "number one cause," see American College of Emergency Physicians, *Emergency Medicine One Year After Hurricane Katrina* (August 2006), 3; quoted in Ott, "The Closure of New Orleans' Charity Hospital," 86.

97. For stillbirths, see Sammy Zahran et al., "Maternal Exposure to Hurricane Destruction and Fetal Mortality," *Journal of Epidemiological Community Health* 68, no. 8 (August 2014): 760–766. The pre-Katrina mortality rate was 62.17 deaths per 100,000 population; from January to June 2006, the rate was 91.37 deaths per 100,000 population. This data, the authors concluded, "supports the civilian population's suspicions about the enduring health consequences of the hurricane." Stephens Sr. et al., "Excess Mortality in the Aftermath of Hurricane Katrina," 15–20. For "aftermath," see Saulny, "A Legacy of the Storm: Depression and Suicide."

98. For the process of site selection and assembling the property for the medical center, see Munster, "They Took My Bedroom," 196–233. Charity's section of the medical center comprised thirty-seven acres; seventy acres is the figure for the entire complex, including the VA and associated construction. For the site inventory, see Federal Emergency Management Agency, "Programmatic Environmental Assessment, Site Selection VAMC and LSU AMC," October 2008, pp. 3–69. It is likely that fewer people lived in the area in 2006, when the plan was first proposed, than did in 2008, when FEMA conducted its site assessment. The Environmental Assessment itemizes how many of the parcels were commercial, residential, occupied, or vacant.

99. Jan Moller, "LSU and VA Collaborate to Rebuild N.O. Health Care," *NOTP*, February 23, 2006, p. 1. For the VA hospital, see Department of Veterans Affairs, *Report to Congress on Planning for Re-Establishing a VA Medical Center in New Orleans* (February 28, 2006), p. 7 for 2004, https://www.va.gov/oca/CMRs/Unique/Main_Report_Final_c.pdf.

100. Coleman Warner, "Protestors Dispute Charity Closing," *NOTP*, March 26, 2006, p. 1. On the People's Hurricane Relief Fund and community-based efforts to provide health care, see Rachel E. Luft, "Beyond Disaster Exceptionalism: Social Movement Developments in New Orleans After Hurricane Katrina," *American Quarterly* 61, no. 3 (September 2009): 499–527.

101. New Orleans City Council, Resolution no. 06-143 (April 6, 2006); A concurrent resolution to urge and request the governor . . . to use a portion of the Medical Center of New Orleans (Big Charity Hospital) to provide medical services . . . , Louisiana House Concurrent Resolution no. 89, Regular Session, 2006 (April 19, 2006). For the independent assessment, see RMJM Hillier, *Medical Center of New Orleans, Charity Hospital, Feasibility Study* (Foundation for Historical Louisiana, August 20, 2008), 5. Jan Moller, "LSU Unveils Plan for Medical Complex," *NOTP*, May 18, 2006, p. 1. LSU unveiled more details at a June 19, 2006, news conference, including announcing that the footprint would be bounded by South Claiborne, Tulane, South Galvez, and Canal Streets, and that $625 million had been allocated for the VA. See John Pope and Jan Moller, "State, VA Map Plan for Medical Complex," *NOTP*, June 20, 2006, p. 1.

102. In January 2006, the Bring New Orleans Back Commission's Health and Social Services Committee had argued that New Orleans's "ultimate objective" should be "to eliminate a two-tiered system of health and delivery." The BNOBC urged the city to pursue universal health care and ability to use Medicare and Medicaid anywhere, not just at Charity Hospital. Bring New Orleans Back Health and Social Services Committee, *Report and*

Recommendations to the Commission (January 18, 2006), n.p. For PricewaterhouseCoopers, see PricewaterhouseCoopers, *Report on Louisiana Healthcare Delivery and Financing System,* delivered to the Louisiana Recovery Authority (April 2006), esp. pp. 6, 13. See also Adam Nossiter, "Dispute Over Historic Hospital for the Poor Pits Doctors Against the State," *NYT,* December 17, 2005.

103. In June 2006, the LRA approved the call for a new hospital building in New Orleans but did not endorse the broader call for eliminating the statewide charity system writ large. Moller, "LSU Unveils Plan," p. 1. For the debate between Blanco and Vitter, see Jan Moller, "Vitter, Blanco, Reach Deal on Hospital," *NOTP,* February 22, 2007, p. 1.

104. US Department of Veterans Affairs, "VA and Louisiana State University Announce Site Selections for New Orleans Medical Center Projects," press release, November 25, 2008. Adam Nossiter, "New Orleans Hospitals Plan Angers Preservationists," *NYT,* November 25, 2008, p. A21. For Road Home data, see Bill Barrow, "State Expropriation for New Hospital Includes Those Who Rebuilt After Katrina," *NOTP,* November 29, 2009. The majority of displaced Road Home recipients ($2.7 million worth of grants) were on the VA, rather than the UMC, side of the development. The City Council had issued a moratorium on building permits in the proposed project site in November 2007. Munster, "They Took My Bedroom," 217. The National Trust later sued the Department of Veterans Affairs and FEMA in a failed attempt to stop demolition. Bill Barrow, "Preservation Group Sues to Block Hospital Projects," *NOTP,* May 1, 2009.

105. Kate Moran, "Lawsuit Filed to Reopen Charity Hospital," *NOTP,* January 18, 2008. Allen Johnson Jr., "Save Charity—The Protest Price Is Right," *NOG,* September 8, 2009.

106. The American Recovery and Reinvestment Act of 2009, Pub. L. No. 111-5, 123 Stat. 115 (February 17, 2009); the arbitration process is described in sec. 601. See also Bill Barrow, "Sen. Mary Landrieu, Obama Administration Tout New Arbitration Rules for Charity Hospital, Other Recovery Projects," *NOTP,* August 6, 2009. For the argument that "Katrina is the wedge that opened the door for Democrats," see Melissa Harris-Perry and James Perry, "Obama's Debt to New Orleans," *The Nation,* March 12, 2009.

107. US House of Representatives, Committee on Transportation and Infrastructure, *Post-Katrina Disaster Response and Recovery: Evaluating Federal Emergency Management Agency's Continuing Efforts in the Gulf Coast and Response to Recent Disasters,* Hearing before the Subcommittee on Economic Development, Public Buildings, and Emergency Management, 111th Cong, 1st Sess., February 25, 2009 (Washington, DC: US Government Printing Office, 2009), 109 (for "blessed") and 111 (for $25M). On Jindal, see Adam Nossiter, "In Louisiana, a Test Case in Using Huge Federal Aid," *NYT,* April 4, 2009, p. A16.

108. US Civilian Board of Contract Appeals, "In the Matter of State of Louisiana, Facility Planning and Control," CBCA 1741-FEMA, January 27, 2010. Kevin Sack, "Louisiana Wins in Bid for Money for Hospital," *NYT,* January 28, 2010, p. A14.

109. I am inspired here by Stephen Hilger's 2012 photograph, "Footprint." Reprinted in Matthew Leifheit, "A Love Song for New Orleans," *Aperture,* March 14, 2017; see also Andru Okun, "The Last Days of Lower Mid-City," *NOG,* March 13, 2017. For twenty-seven blocks, see, New Orleans Preservation Timeline Project, "Site Clearing in Mid-City Begins for New Hospital Sites," Tulane School of Architecture, April 1, 2010, http://architecture.tulane.edu/preservation-project/timeline-entry/1419. For Thurman, see Cain Burdeau, "New Orleans Neighborhood Survives Katrina But Not Urban Renewal," *AP,* December 10, 2010. In 42 percent of the cases, the state expropriated the property by means of eminent domain. Munster, "They Took My Bedroom," 228–229. In September 2010, Landrieu announced a $3.2 million plan to move eighty-one historic houses, mostly from the VA Hospital side of the site. Two years later, only twenty-eight houses had been restored. The *Times-Picayune* reported that "the city has spent $808,500 to move houses that it would eventually destroy." Richard A. Webster, "Program to Move Homes from LSU-VA Hospital Site, Rehab Them, Remains in Disarray," *NOTP,* November 26, 2012.

110. For Landrieu, see Michelle Krupa and Frank Donze, "Mayor Mitch Landrieu Says, 'The World Deserves a Better New Orleans,'" *NOTP,* May 3, 2010. For "substantially younger,"

see the Henry J. Kaiser Family Foundation, *New Orleans Five Years After the Storm: A New Disaster Amid Recovery* (August 2010), 3. For "Cinderella," see Joel Kotkin, *Sustaining Prosperity: A Long Term Vision for the New Orleans Region* (New Orleans: Greater New Orleans, Inc., February 2014), 3.

111. For Perry, see Michael A. Fletcher, "Uneven Katrina Recovery Efforts Often Offered the Most Help to the Most Affluent," *WP*, August 27, 2010. For the survey, see Kaiser Family Foundation, "New Orleans Five Years After the Storm," 8. For poverty rates, see Allison Plyer, Nihal Shrinath, and Vicki Mack, *The New Orleans Index at Ten: Measuring Greater New Orleans' Progress toward Prosperity* (New Orleans: The Data Center, July 2015), 9.

112. For vacant homes, see Allison Plyer, *Population Loss and Vacant Housing in New Orleans Neighborhoods* (New Orleans: Greater New Orleans Community Data Center, February 5, 2011), 4. For people living in abandoned buildings, see UNITY of Greater New Orleans, *Search and Rescue Five Years Later: Saving People Still Trapped in Katrina's Ruins* (August 2010), 3, https://unitygno.org/wp-content/uploads/2010/08/UNITY_AB-Report _August2010.pdf. For population changes, see "Census Population Change by Parish, 2000–2010," graph accompanying Michelle Krupa, "New Orleans Neighborhoods that Suffered Worst Flooding Lost Most Residents, Census Data Show," *NOTP*, February 6, 2011. The graph does not totally support the text of the article. According to 2000 and 2010 Census data, the St. Bernard population had fallen from 67,229 to 35,897.

113. The 2000 Census counted 135,956 white people and 325,947 African Americans in New Orleans. The 2010 Census counted 113,428 white people and 206,871 African Americans.

114. Kaiser Family Foundation, *New Orleans Five Years After the Storm*, 19–20.

115. For worries, see Kaiser Family Foundation, *New Orleans Five Years After the Storm*, 19–20. For "we didn't close," see Gwen Filosa, "Supreme Court Hears Oral Arguments in Charity Hospital Cast," *NOTP*, May 5, 2009. In 2013, Governor Jindal transferred management of the New Orleans hospital, and others in the Charity system across the state, from LSU to a private, not-for-profit operator called LCMC Health. While LCMC Health would continue to serve indigent patients in New Orleans—"subject to the receipt of required funding," its contract stipulated—it would also cater to patients with private insurance. The new model aspired for a "patient mix" that could provide new revenue for the hospitals. Abby Goodnough, "Hospital Is Replaced, With Hope of Preserving Its Mission," *NYT*, August 1, 2015, p. A12.

116. The estimated total cost for the new Department of Veterans Affairs Hospital was $1.035 billion. David Wise, "VA Construction: VA's Actions to Address Cost Increases and Schedule Delays at Major Medical-Facility Projects," Testimony Before the Committee on Veterans' Affairs, House of Representatives, GAO-15-332T, January 21, 2015, p. 3. The estimated total cost for the new University Medical Center was $1.063 billion. Jacobs [program management firm], *New Facilities for the University Medical Center, New Orleans, Louisiana, Monthly Report March 2015*, prepared for the Division of Administration, Facility Planning and Control, State of Louisiana (March 2015), 1.

117. For UMC, see Rebecca Catalanello, "University Medical Center Opens to First Patients," *NOTP*, August 1, 2015. For the VA, see Kevin Litten, "Long Awaited, Long Delayed: New Orleans VA Hospital Finally Opens," *NOTP*, November 18, 2016. For DeBlieux, see Goodnough, "Hospital Is Replaced." For Kurtz-Burke, see Kurtz-Burke, remarks at "The Katrina Disaster Now."

118. Bush, *Decision Points*, 308–332.

119. There was a $20.9 million federal grant available specifically to support charter schools in New Orleans. "Gov. Kathleen Blanco Issues Call for Special Legislative Session," press release, November 1, 2005. On school reform in New Orleans, see also Sarah Carr, *Hope Against Hope: Three Schools, One City, and the Struggle to Education America's Children* (New York: Bloomsbury Press, 2013); Luis Mirón, Brian R. Beabout, and Joseph L. Boselovic, eds., *Only in New Orleans: School Choice and Equity Post-Hurricane Katrina* (Rotterdam: Sense Publishers, 2015); Adrienne Dixson, "Whose Choice?: A Critical Race Perspective on Charter Schools," in Cedric Johnson, ed., *The Neoliberal Deluge*, 130–151; Andre Perry

and Michael Schawm-Baird, "School by School: The Transformation of New Orleans Public Education," in Amy Liu, Ronald V. Anglin, Richard M. Mizelle Jr., and Allison Plyer, eds., *Resilience and Opportunity: Lessons from the U.S. Gulf Coast after Katrina and Rita* (Washington, DC: Brookings Institution Press, 2011), 31–44.

120. For school population, see State of Louisiana, Department of Education, "Student Enrollment & Demographics," n.d. (ca. 2015). For test scores, see the Cowen Institute for Public Education Initiatives, *Transforming Public Education in New Orleans: The Recovery School District, 2003–2011* (New Orleans: Tulane University, 2011), 1. For "intellectual slavery," see John Hainkel, quoted in "Many 'Elephants of School Change," *BRA*, June 24, 2003. For corruption, see Brian Thevenot, "Schools Sweep Indicts 11 More," *NOTP*, December 17, 2004, p. 1. On corruption and mismanagement, see also Peter F. Burns and Matthew O. Thomas, *Reforming New Orleans: The Contentious Politics of Change in the Big Easy* (Ithaca: Cornell University Press, 2015), 62–78.

121. Seventy-seven percent of students enrolled in New Orleans's public schools were eligible for free or reduced price lunch (across the city, 40 percent of children lived below the poverty line). Boston Consulting Group, *The State of Public Education in New Orleans*, 8. Douglas N. Harris, "The Post-Katrina New Orleans School Reforms: Implications for National School Reform and the Role of Government" (Educational Research Alliance for New Orleans, 2013), 11–12. For the graduation rate, see Douglas N. Harris, "Good News for New Orleans," *Education Next* 15, no. 4 (Fall 2015): 8–15, statistic on 10.

122. Cowen Institute, *Transforming Public Education in New Orleans*, 3–4.

123. The Bush administration, meanwhile, had proposed a $488 million plan to give evacuated students vouchers to attend private schools, which would have been the "largest federal school voucher program ever." Nick Anders, "Bush Proposes Private School Relief Plan," *WP*, September 17, 2005. For Blanco's order, see State of Louisiana Executive Order No. KBB 2005-58, October 7, 2005. For the West Bank, see Steve Ritea, "Orleans Board Makes 13 Schools Charters," *NOTP*, October 8, 2005, p. 1. After Rev. Arthur Wardsworth sued, Judge Nadine Ramsey—calling the plan, "a disguised back-door attempt to push through a pre-hurricane agenda while the citizens of this city are displaced throughout the country"—stayed the decision because it violated an open meetings law, the board voted to approve it again on October 28. Catherine Gewertz, "Judge Calls Halt to New Orleans' Charter School Plan," *Education Week*, October 26, 2005, p. 3. See also Catherine Gewertz, "Judge Rules New Orleans Board Must Revote on Charters," *Education Week*, November 2, 2005, p. 15.

124. An act . . . to provide for the transfer of certain schools to the Recovery School District . . . , Louisiana Act 35, First Extraordinary Session of 2005. An act . . . to provide for a definition of a failed school . . . , Louisiana Act 9, Regular Session of 2003 initially set a threshold SPS of 45 for four years, which the legislature raised to 60 in 2004. The state average, which Act 35 established as the new threshold for failure, was 87.4. Dixson, "Whose Choice?" 134. For "silver lining," see Erik W. Robelen, "Louisiana Eyes Plan to Let State Control New Orleans Schools," *Education Week*, November 4, 2005. Sources differ on how many schools were controlled by OPSB at the start of the 2005 academic year, and how many were transferred to BESE and then to RSD. I draw the numbers I use here from the plan the Recovery School District presented to the State Legislature in June 2006. Recovery School District, "Legislatively Required Plan," June 7, 2006, pp. 12 (for RSD schools) and 14 (for OPSB schools), http://web.archive.org/web/20060618125304/http://www.louisianaschools.net/lde/uploads/8932.doc.

125. The Board had eight members elected by geographic districts to serve for four-year terms, and three at large members appointed by the governor and confirmed by the state senate. Laura Maggi, "State to Run New Orleans Schools," *NOTP*, November 23, 2005, p. 1. For the New Orleans delegation's objection, see Laura Maggi, "Senate Panel OKs School Takeover Bill," *NOTP*, November 11, 2005, p. 3.

126. Harris, "The Post-Katrina New Orleans School Reforms," 6. In January 2006, the Bring New Orleans Back Commission's Education committee largely endorsed the changes

augured by Act 35. The BNOBC committee included the Executive Director of Teach for America of Greater New Orleans, but no person who specifically represented the city's current teachers. Bring New Orleans Back Commission, Education Committee, "Rebuilding and Transforming: A Plan for World-Class Public Education in New Orleans," January 17, 2006. For "Thank you, Katrina" see Theo Emery, "The Big Easy's Next Test," *Time,* August 17, 2006.

127. Eddie Oliver, Oscarlene Nixon, and Mildred Goodwin v. Orleans Parish School Board, No. 2014-C-0329, Consolidated with No. 2014-C-0330, 156 So.3d (2014). For the layoff notice, see Danielle Dreilinger, "7,000 New Orleans Teachers, Laid Off After Katrina, Win Court Ruling," *NOTP,* January 16, 2014.

128. Jane Arnold Lincove, Nathan Barrett, and Katherine O. Strunk, *Did the Teachers Dismissed After Hurricane Katrina Return to Public Education?* (New Orleans: Education Research Alliance for New Orleans, May 31, 2017), 3. See also Kristen L. Buras, "The Mass Termination of Black Veteran Teachers in New Orleans: Cultural Politics, the Education Market, and Its Consequences," *The Educational Forum* 80, no. 2 (2016): 154–170.

129. Specifically, 22 percent of New Orleans teachers. For the estimate that, considering hurricane damage and normal attrition, "the combined effects of dismissal and reform . . . reduced the 2007 education employment of pre-Katrina New Orleans teachers by at least 16 percentage points," and 8–11 percentage points for the 2013 school year, see Lincove et al., *Did the Teachers Dismissed After Hurricane Katrina Return to Public Education?,* 4. For the racial impact, see Nathan Barrett and Douglas N. Harris, *Significant Changes in the New Orleans Teacher Workforce* (New Orleans: Education Research Alliance for New Orleans, August 24, 2015), 3.

130. For the estimate of several thousand "young urban rebuilding professionals," see Richard Campanella, "Gentrification and Its Discontents: Notes from New Orleans," *New Geography,* March 1, 2013. On New Orleans as "the Peace Corps with better food," see Campbell Robertson and Richard Fausset, "10 Years After Katrina," *NYT,* August 26, 2015; and Michael Tisserand, "The Charter School Flood," *The Nation,* September 10–17, 2007, p. 22. According to the American Community Survey, between 2011 and 2013, "New Orleans added nearly 10,000 college graduates under age 40." Ben Casselman, "Katrina Washed Away New Orleans's Black Middle Class," fivethirtyeight.com, August 24, 2015.

131. Cowen Institute for Public Education Initiatives, *The State of Public Education in New Orleans Five Years After Hurricane Katrina* (New Orleans: Tulane University, July 2010), 14 (for teaching experience) and 24 (for 60 percent). For degrees from local colleges, see Barrett and Harris, *Significant Changes in the New Orleans Teacher Workforce,* 4.

132. For Vallas, see Walter Isaacson, "The Greatest Education Lab," *Time,* September 6, 2007. See also Daniella Ann Cook, "Voices Crying Out from the Wilderness: The Stories of Black Educators on School Reform in Post Katrina New Orleans" (PhD dissertation, University of North Carolina-Chapel Hill, 2008), 73–76; and Tisserand, "The Charter School Flood," 23.

133. *Oliver v. Orleans Parish School Board.* Gwendolyn Ridgley, interview by Myrna Matherne, May 4, 2007, MSS 4700.1955, LLMVC. See also Gwendolyn Ridgley, obituary, *BRA,* October 19, 2012. For 32 years, see Kevin McGill, "Post-Katrina School Firings Wrongful," *AP,* June 20, 2012. For cancer, see Kari Dequine Harden, "7,500 Fired Teachers Take Their Case to U.S. Supreme Court," *LW,* March 16, 2015.

134. Harris, "Good News for New Orleans," 15.

135. For poverty, see Vicki Mack, *New Orleans Kids, Working Parents, and Poverty* (New Orleans: The Data Center, February 26, 2015). For other statistics, see Institute of Women and Ethnic Studies, *Emotional Wellness and Exposure to Violence: Data from New Orleans Youth Age 11–15* (2015), 3. On children's experience of Katrina, see also Alice Fothergill and Lori Peek, *Children of Katrina* (Austin: University of Texas Press, 2015).

136. "Prepared Statement of Linda Johnson," US Senate, Committee on Health, Education, Labor, and Pensions, *A Fresh Start for New Orleans' Children: Improving Education After*

Katrina: Hearing before the Subcommittee on Education and Early Childhood Development, 109th Cong., 2nd Sess., July 14, 2006, 11.

137. Adolph Reed, "Three Tremés," Nonsite.org, July 4, 2011. For "free market," see "Prepared Statement of Linda Johnson," 9. For "cruel optimism," see Lauren Berlant, *Cruel Optimism* (Durham: Duke University Press, 2011).

138. For 98 percent, see the Henry J. Kaiser Family Foundation, *Giving Voice to the People of New Orleans: The Kaiser Post-Katrina Baseline Survey* (May 2007), 57. The amendment was Louisiana Constitutional Amendment 3 of 2006. It consolidated local levee boards into the Southeast Louisiana Flood Protection Authority and created rules designed to insulate the board from political influence: most positions on the board now would require a degree in engineering or hydrology. Some criticized the changes, noting that it was the Army Corps's malfeasance, not local levee boards, that had caused the flood, and questioning whether engineers were equipped to make decisions that affected the fate of the city broadly. For Citizens for 1 Greater New Orleans, see Citizens for 1 Greater New Orleans, "Timeline," http://www.citizensfor1.com/library/CitizensFor1timeline.pdf; Charles C. Mann, "The Long, Strange Resurrection of New Orleans," *Fortune,* August 21, 2006, pp. 92–109; and Pamela Tyler, "The Post-Katrina, Semiseparate World of Gender Politics," *Journal of American History* 94, no. 3 (December 2007): 780–783. For criticisms, see for example Public Affairs Research Council of Louisiana, Inc., "Guide to the Constitutional Amendments, September 30, 2006 Ballot," September 2006. See also Adam Nossiter, "In Move to Change, Louisiana Will Consolidate Levee Boards," *NYT,* February 18, 2006.

139. For CPRA, see An act to . . . authorize and provide for the development and implementation of a comprehensive coastal protection plan . . . , Louisiana Act 8, First Extraordinary Session, 2005. For "make levees," see, for example, Liza Featherstone, "Make Levees, Not War," *The Nation,* September 25, 2005.

140. For "stronger than it has ever been," see George W. Bush, "Address to the Nation on Hurricane Katrina Recovery from New Orleans, Louisiana" September 15, 2005, in *Weekly Compilation of Presidential Documents* 41, no. 37 (US Government Printing Office, September 19, 2005), 1408. For "consider providing," see P. L. 109-148, 119 Stat. 2814. For the Corps report, see US Army Corps of Engineers, *Louisiana Coastal Protection and Restoration, LACPR Summary Report* (August 2009), S33–34. See also Bob Marshall, "New Orleans' Flood Protection System: Stronger than Ever, Weaker than It Was Supposed to Be," *The Lens,* May 15, 2014. For criticism, see National Research Council of the National Academies, *Final Report from the NRC Committee on the Review of the Louisiana Coastal Protection and Restoration (LACPR) Program* (Washington, DC: The National Academies Press, 2009).

141. A 500-year storm has a 6 percent chance of occurring over the course of a 30-year mortgage, and an 18 percent chance of coming each century. The Bush administration's "recovery czar" Donald Powell announced on March 30, 2006, that the new levees would not meet the NFIP standard. John Schwartz, "The Dilemma of the Levees," *NYT,* April 1, 2006, p. A12. FEMA confirmed that the new levees would not meet NFIP standards. Federal Emergency Management Agency, "Flood Recovery Guidance," April 12, 2006, https://www.fema.gov/pdf/hazard/flood/recoverydata/orleans_parish04-12-06.pdf.

142. The administration began to withdraw its support for Category 5 protection as early as November 2005. Spencer S. Hsu and Terence O'Hara, "A Bush Loyalist Tackles Katrina Recovery," *WP,* November 21, 2005. For "devil's bargain," see Mark Schleifstein, "New Orleans Area's Upgraded Levees Not Enough for Next 'Katrina,' Engineers Say," *NOTP,* August 18, 2015. See also Bob Marshall, "Rebuilt Levees Don't Meet Goal to Protect New Orleans Against Category 5 Hurricane," *The Lens,* August 19, 2015.

143. Water Resources Development Act of 2007, Pub. L. No. 110-114, sec. 7012, 121 Stat. 1041 at 1279. The same bill ordered the deauthorization of the Mississippi River–Gulf Outlet. For MRGO, see sec. 7013, 121 Stat. 1280. For 200-year storm, see *Lake Pontchartrain and Vicinity, Louisiana: Letter from the Secretary of the Army,* H. R. Doc. No. 231, 89th Cong., 1st Sess. (1965), 46. In 1978, the Corps described the Standard Project Hurricane as a

250-year event. See US Army Corps of Engineers, Mississippi Valley Division, "Lake Pontchartrain Hurricane Protection Project Level of Protection," June 1978, in the ACEDL, https://usace.contentdm.oclc.org/digital/collection/p16021coll2/id/1007.

144. Gulf Coast Civic Works Act, H.R. 4048, 110th Cong., 1st Sess. (2007).

145. The Corps never adopted a consistent way of referring to Hurricane Katrina's strength, describing it variously, for example, as a "low Category 5 event," a "400-year event," and a "200-year event, but [with] a surge . . . that was much greater than a 200-year event." For "low Category 5" and "400-year," see US Army Corps of Engineers, New Orleans District, *Louisiana Coastal Protection and Restoration, Final Technical Report, Structural Plan Component Appendix* (June 2009), 1. For "200-year," see Robert L. Van Antwerp, remarks at the Third Plenary of the 8th Religion Science and the Environment Symposium," October 23, 2009, New Orleans, Louisiana. Other accounts described Katrina's surge in Saint Bernard Parish as a 200-year event, and the surge on Lake Pontchartrain's south shore as a 150-year event. Schleifstein, "New Orleans Area's Upgraded Levees.'"

146. US Army Corps of Engineers, "INHC-Lake Borgne Surge Barrier," May 2015, https://www.mvn.usace.army.mil/Portals/56/docs/PAO/FactSheets/Fact%20Sheet%20update%2010_15/-IHNC-Lake%20Borgne%20Surge%20Barrier%20(May%202015).pdf. US Army Corps of Engineers, "Seabrook Floodgate Complex," August 2015, https://www.mvn.usace.army.mil/Portals/56/docs/PAO/FactSheets/Fact%20Sheet%20update%2010_15/Seabrook%20Floodgate%20Complex%20(August%202015).pdf. US Army Corps of Engineers, "Permanent Canal Closures & Pumps," March 2017, https://www.mvn.usace.army.mil/Portals/56/docs/PAO/PCCP%20March%202017%20fact%20sheet.pdf?ver=2017-03-14-112758-863. Louisiana officials unsuccessfully lobbied the Corps to strengthen the floodwalls that lined the drainage canals. See, for example, AECOM, *Permanent Protection System, Opinion of Probable Cost, Options 1, 2, and 2a,* Vol. 1, report prepared for the Sewerage and Water Board of New Orleans (May 2010). "My big overarching concern," Senator David Vitter told the Corps at a Congressional hearing, "is that we could be repeating a grave mistake of history." US Senate, *New Orleans Hurricane and Flood Protection and Coastal Louisiana Restoration,* 43. For armoring, see US Army Corps of Engineers, "HSDRRS [Hurricane & Storm Damage Risk Reduction System] Armoring," http://www.mvn.usace.army.mil/Missions/HSDRRS/Armoring/.

147. The funds were appropriated as follows: $2.083 billion in Pub. L. No. 109-148; $3.647 billion in Pub. L. No. 109–234; $1.325 billion in the US Troop Readiness, Veterans' Care, Katrina Recovery, and Iraq Accountability Appropriations Act, 2007, Pub. L. No. 110–28, 121 Stat. 112 (May 25, 2007); $5.761 billion the Supplemental Appropriations Act, 2008, Pub. L. No. 110–252, 122 Stat. 2323 (June 30, 2008); and $1.615 billion in the Consolidated Security, Disaster Assistance, and Continuing Appropriations Act, 2009, Pub. L. No. 110–329, 122 Stat. 3574 (September 30, 2008). See US Army Corps of Engineers, *Review Plan, Final Version, Implementation of Section 2035 of WRDA 2007 for the Greater New Orleans Hurricane and Storm Damage Risk Reduction System* (December 12, 2012), 4–5.

148. For the conclusion that, "while there is not a consensus on an acceptable risk to life criteria, the post-Katrina risk to life for New Orleans is relatively high" when "compared to other large-scale engineering systems" such as dams or nuclear plants, see A. Miller, S. N. Jonkman, and M. Van Ledden, "Risk of Life Due to Flooding in Post-Katrina New Orleans," *Natural Hazards and Earth System Sciences* 15 (2015): 59–73, esp. 71.

149. For the 500-year recommendation, see "Statement of Jeffrey Jacobs, Scholar, National Research Council and Study Director, Committee on New Orleans Regional Hurricane Protection Projects," US Senate, *New Orleans Hurricane and Flood Protection and Coastal Louisiana Restoration,* 47. For "too often," see US Army Corps of Engineers Interagency Performance Evaluation Task Force, *Performance Evaluation of the New Orleans and Southeast Louisiana Hurricane Protection System,* Vol. 1 (US Army Corps of Engineers, 2009), I-8.

150. The specific count from the 2011 study is 974 people, or 2,945 dead if the storm surge breached the levees. Richard J. Varuso, "USACE Levee Screening Tool," PowerPoint

presentation in author's possession, US Army Corps of Engineers, November 17, 2011, p. 30. I am grateful to Mark Schleifstein for sharing this with me. See also Mark Schleifstein, "New Orleans Area Levee System 'High Risk,' and 'Minimally Acceptable,' Corps Says," *NOTP*, May 22, 2018. For Graves, see John Schwartz and Mark Schleifstein, "Fortified but Still in Peril, New Orleans Braces for Its Future," *NYT*, February 24, 2018.

151. For accreditation, see US Army Corps of Engineers, "FEMA Accredits Hurricane and Storm Damage Risk Reduction System," press release, February 21, 2014. For 2009 FIRMs, see Chris Kirkham, "Long-Awaited FEMA Maps Give Residents Detailed Snapshot of Flood Risks," *NOTP*, February 5, 2009.

152. The city also feared plans in Congress to limit the federal subsidies for flood insurance premiums and instead charge actuarial rates for coverage, which would have imposed crippling costs on homeowners in Special Flood Hazard Areas. The plan was enacted with the Biggert-Waters Flood Insurance Reform Act of 2012, Pub. L. No. 112-141, 126 Stat. 916 (July 6, 2012), and repealed with the Homeowner Flood Insurance Affordability Act of 2014, Pub. L. No. 113–89, 128 Stat. 1020 (March 21, 2014). See also Andy Horowitz, "Could New Orleans Flood Again?" *NYT*, May 31, 2016, p. A21; and Bob Marshall, "Here's a FEMA Map that Actually Delivers Good News for New Orleans," *The Lens*, March 28, 2016. The city announced that the changes would affect nearly 85,000 policy holders. Kelsey Davis, "Mayor, City Officials to Discuss Benefits of New FEMA Flood Maps Friday," WDSU, April 8, 2016. In June 2016, there were 84,828 policies in force in New Orleans; in June 2017, there were 81,581. Richard Rainey, "New Orleans Saw Drop in National Flood Insurance Policies," *NOTP*, September 7, 2017.

153. Coastal Protection and Restoration Authority of Louisiana, *Louisiana Comprehensive Master Plan for a Sustainable Coast* (effective June 2, 2017), 74. Adjusted for inflation, the cost of the Coastal Master Plan was more than $91.7 billion. See Mark Davis, Harry Vorhoff, and John Driscoll, *Financing the Future: Turning Coastal Restoration and Protection Plans Into Realities: The Cost of Comprehensive Coastal Restoration and Protection* (New Orleans: Tulane Institute on Water Resources Law & Policy, 2014).

154. Benjamin Alexander-Block, "St. Bernard Voters Reject Levee Tax Again," *NOTP*, May 2, 2015. For the vote count of 1,272 to 1,785, see Louisiana Secretary of State, "Official Election Results, Results for Election Data: 5/2/2015, St. Bernard," https://voterportal.sos.la.gov/static/2015-05-02/resultsRace/44.

155. Peter Whoriskey, "Repairs Don't Allay Fears of Next Storm," *WP*, June 1, 2007.

156. Andy Horowitz, "Don't Repeat the Mistakes of the Katrina Recovery," *NYT*, September 14, 2017.

Epilogue: The End of Empire, Louisiana

1. For the waste weir, see Board of Levee Commissioners, Orleans Levee District, *Report of Levee Examining Committee, Plaquemines Parish East Bank Levee District* (New Orleans, 1926), in the Louisiana State Archives, Baton Rouge, LA. For the cemetery, see "Act of Donation by Narcise Cosse, Sr. to Board of Trustees for the Point Pleasant Cemetery," July 23, 1921, copy in author's possession.

2. "Simmons Wins 1st Place in State Muskrat Judging," *PG*, January 23, 1959, p. 3. Philip Simmons, interview by Andy Horowitz, July 12, 2010, interview R-0498, transcript, pp. 2–3, SOHP Collection.

3. For the resource curse, see Richard M. Auty, *Sustaining Development in Mineral Economies: The Resource Curse Thesis* (New York: Routledge, 1993); Terry Lynn Karl, *The Paradox of Plenty: Oil Booms and Petro-States* (Berkeley: University of California Press, 1997); and William R. Freudenburg and Robert Gramling, "Linked to What? Economic Linkages in an Extractive Economy," *Society & Natural Resources* 11, no. 6 (1998): 569–586. For an opposing view embedded in the memoir a former Freeport executive, see Gordon Cain, *Everybody Wins! A Life in Free Enterprise* (Philadelphia: Chemical Heritage Foundation, 2001). For cancer, see F. D. Groves et al., "Is There a 'Cancer Corridor' in

Louisiana?" *Journal of the Louisiana Medical Society* 48, no. 4 (April 1996): 155–165; and Barbara Allen, *Uneasy Alchemy: Citizens and Experts in Louisiana's Chemical Corridor Disputes* (Cambridge: The MIT Press, 2003). For BP, see BP, "4Q 2009 Results Presentation to the Financial Community," February 2, 2010, p. 1. For poverty rates, see US Census Bureau, "Poverty: 2009 and 2010," American Community Survey Briefs, October 2011, p. 2. For sea level, see Bob Marshall, "New Research: Louisiana Coast Faces Highest Rate of Sea-Level Rise Worldwide," *The Lens,* February 21, 2013.

4. Simmons, July 12, 2010, pp. 17 (for "survivor"), 12 (for "that wood").

5. Simmons, July 12, 2010, pp. 10–11. Between 1884 and 2002, "the long-term average erosion rates for the Plaquemines barrier shoreline were −23.1 feet per year." See Shea Penland et al., "Changes in Louisiana's Shoreline: 1855–2002," *Journal of Coastal Research* 44 (Spring 2005): 7–39. On the lived experience of coastal erosion, see also Davis, *Washed Away;* David M. Burley, *Losing Ground: Identity and Land Loss in Coastal Louisiana* (Jackson: University of Mississippi Press, 2010); Mike Tidwell, *Bayou Farewell: The Rich Life and Tragic Death of Louisiana's Cajun Coast* (New York: Vintage, 2004); and Shirley Laska et al., "At Risk: The Human, Community, and Infrastructure Resources of Coastal Louisiana," *Journal of Coastal Research* 44 (2005): 154–175.

6. "State, Corps Consider Opening Bonnet Carre Spillway to Keep Gulf Oil Spill at Bay," *NOTP,* May 5, 2010. For Simmons's cattle, see Cecil H. Yancy Jr., "Walking Through the Flood," *Mid South Farmer,* February 2008, p. 5.

7. Simmons, July 12, 2010, p. 16.

8. Isleño resident of St. Bernard Parish, interview by Jonathan West, November 3, 2006, quoted in West, "Negotiating Heritage: Heritage Organizations amongst the Isleños of St. Bernard Parish, Louisiana and the Use of Heritage Identity to Overcome to Isleño/Tornero Distinction" (MS thesis, University of New Orleans, 2009), 20. For Louisiana, the state nativity rate was 79.4 percent. For Orleans Parish, the rate was 77.4 percent. For Louisiana, see US Census Bureau, "Tape DP-2. Profile of Selected Social Characteristics: 2000, Geographic Area: Louisiana." For Orleans Parish, see US Census Bureau, "Table DP-2. Profile of Selected Social Characteristics: 2000, Geographic Area: Orleans Parish, Louisiana." For African American nativity in New Orleans and Atlanta, see James Dao, "In New Orleans, Smaller May Mean Whiter," *NYT,* January 22, 2006, p. 1.

9. "Thomas Jessen Adams, "New Orleans Brings It All Together," *American Quarterly* 66, no. 1 (March 2014): 245–256. For "soul kitchen," see Wynton Marsalis, "Saving America's Soul Kitchen," *Time,* September 19, 2005, p. 84. See also Tom Piazza, *Why New Orleans Matters* (New York: HarperCollins, 2005); and Roger D. Abrahams et al., *Blues for New Orleans: Mardi Gras and America's Creole Soul* (Philadelphia: University of Pennsylvania Press, 2006). On "sense of place," generally, see Irwin Altman and Setha Low, eds., *Place Attachment* (New York: Plenum Press, 1992); Dolores Hayden, *The Power of Place: Urban Landscapes as Public History* (Cambridge: MIT Press, 1995); and Yi-Fu Tuan, *Space and Place: The Perspective of Experience* (Minneapolis: University of Minnesota Press, 1977).

10. On New Orleans tourism, see Kevin Fox Gotham, *Authentic New Orleans: Tourism, Culture, and Race in the Big Easy* (New York: New York University Press, 2007); J. Mark Souther, *New Orleans On Parade: Tourism and the Transformation of the Crescent City* (Baton Rouge: Louisiana State University Press, 2006); Anthony J. Stanosis, *Creating the Big Easy: New Orleans and the Emergence of Modern Tourism, 1918–1945* (Athens: University of Georgia Press, 2006); and Lynnell Harris, *Desire and Disaster in New Orleans: Tourism, Race, and Historical Memory* (Durham: Duke University Press, 2014). For "own kind of truth," see Andy Horowitz, "The Complete Story of the Galveston Horror: Trauma, History, and the Great Storm of 1900," *Historical Reflections* 41, no. 3 (Winter 2015): 95–108, quoting from 105. For "know what it means," see "We Know What It Means to Miss New Orleans," *American Routes,* November 2, 2005.

11. Nick Spitzer, "*Mondé Creole:* The Cultural World of French Louisiana Creoles and the Creolization of World Cultures," in Robert Baron and Ana C. Cara, eds., *Creolization as*

Cultural Creativity (Jackson: University Press of Mississippi, 2011), 32–67, esp. 61 (for "chronically broken" and 55 (for Toussaint).

12. Ashley Morris, "Fuck You, You Fucking Fucks," November 27, 2005, http://ashleymorris .typepad.com/ashley_morris_the_blog/2005/11/fuck_you_you_fu.html. On Morris, see also Dave Walker, "Blogger Ashley Morris Provides Some of the Words for John Goodman's HBO 'Treme' Character," *NOTP,* April 9, 2010; and Chris Rose, "We'll Miss the Blogger Next Door," *NOTP,* April 15, 2008.

13. Philip Frazier, quoted in Nick Spitzer, "Rebuilding the 'Land of Dreams' with Music," in Eugenie Ladner Birch and Susan M. Wachter, eds., *Rebuilding Urban Places After Disaster: Lessons from Hurricane Katrina* (Philadelphia: University of Pennsylvania Press, 2006), 305–328, quotation on 326. On the debate over the first Mardi Gras after the flood, see Randy J. Sparks, "Why Mardi Gras Matters," in Romain Huret and Randy J. Sparks, eds., *Hurricane Katrina in Transatlantic Perspective* (Baton Rouge: Louisiana State University Press, 2014), 178–197. For Harrison, see Larry Blumenfeld, "Hard Listening in the Big Easy," *Village Voice,* April 18, 2006.

14. From 2008 to 2012, the average amount a New Orleans musician earned for a performance steadily declined, as did the average number of gigs she or he played per month; 40 percent of New Orleans musicians made less than $10,000 per year (the 2012 average was $17,800). Sweet Home New Orleans, *2012 State of the New Orleans Music Community Report* (August 2012), 4.

15. Jordan Hirsch, "End of the Line," *Slate,* August 25, 2015. See also Nick Spitzer, "Love and Death at Second Line," *Southern Spaces,* February 20, 2004.

16. Hirsch, "End of the Line." For the right to the city, see Henri Lefebvre, *Le Droit à la Ville,* 1968; Eleonore Kofman and Elizabeth Lebas, trans. and ed., *Henri Lefebvre: Writings on Cities* (Blackwell, 1996), 147–159.

17. "Complaint," Social Aid and Pleasure Club Task Force et al. vs. City of New Orleans, Louisiana et al., US District Court for the Eastern District of Louisiana, Civil Action No. 06-10057, Document 1, November 16, 2006, pp. 15–16. After negotiations, the NOPD lowered the fee to $3,760, which remained unaffordable to most clubs.

18. "Amended Consent Judgment," *Social Aid and Pleasure Club v. City of New Orleans,* Document 64, March 9, 2017.

19. "James, Kerwin," obituary, *NOTP,* October 5, 2007. John Swenson, "Obituary: Kerwin James (1972–2007)," *Offbeat Magazine,* November 2007. See also Matt Sakakeeny, "'Under the Bridge': An Orientation to Soundscapes in New Orleans," *Ethnomusicology* 54, no. 1 (Winter 2010): 1–27.

20. Campbell Robertson and Richard Fausset, "10 Years After Katrina," *NYT,* August 26, 2015. Katy Reckdahl, "Culture, Change Collide in Tremé," *NOTP,* October 3, 2007. Larry Blumenfeld, "Band on the Run in New Orleans," *Salon,* October 29, 2007. Red Cotton, "What Really Happened in Tremé the Night Musicians Were Arrested," *NOG,* September 28, 2012. In 2004, for example, 43 percent of New Orleans renters had housing costs considered unaffordable; by 2016, 51 percent did. Allison Plyer and Lamar Gardere, "The New Orleans Prosperity Index: Tricentennial Edition," *The Data Center,* April 11, 2018.

21. For one such critique, see Adolph Reed, "Three Tremés," Nonsite.org, July 4, 2011. On the importance of SAPCs and their members, see Frederick Weil, "The Rise of Community Organizations, Citizen Engagement, and New Institutions (full draft)," July 27, 2010, https://www.lsu.edu/fweil/lsukatrinasurvey/ReconstitutingCommunityDraftSummary .pdf; Frederick Weil, "Rise of Community Organizations, Citizen Engagement, and New Institutions," in Amy Liu, Roland V. Anglin, Richard Mizelle, and Allison Plyer, eds., *Resilience and Opportunity: Lessons from the U.S. Gulf Coast after Katrina and Rita* (Washington, DC: Brookings Institution Press, 2011), 201–219; and Nick Spitzer, "Learning from the Second Lines," *NOTP,* October 14, 2007.

22. On Mardi Gras Indian performance, see Joseph Roach, *Cities of the Dead: Circum-Atlantic Performance* (New York: Columbia University Press, 1996), 207; and George Lipsitz, "Mardi Gras Indians: Carnival and Counter-Narrative in Black New Orleans," *Cultural*

Critique 10 (Autumn 1988): 99–121. For police harassing Indians, see, for example, Katy Reckdahl, "Mardi Gras Indians Concerned About Police Antagonism," *NOTP,* March 8, 2009.

23.   Emily Chamlee-Wright and Virgil Henry Storr, "'There's No Place Like New Orleans': Sense of Place and Community Recovery in the Ninth Ward after Hurricane Katrina," *Journal of Urban Affairs* 31, no. 5 (2009): 615–634, survey on 629. For "fabric," see David Mildenberg, "Census Finds Hurricane Katrina Left New Orleans Richer, Whiter, Emptier," *Bloomberg,* February 3, 2011.

24.   For "comfortable," see Claudia Feldman et al., "After Katrina, Louisianans Have Left Their Mark on Houston," *Houston Chronicle,* August 29, 2010; see also Wade Goodwyn, "Some Katrina Evacuees Long for What They Lost," *All Things Considered,* August 27, 2010. For "die down," see Samuel H. Winston, "Street Soul," *NOG,* April 24, 2006. For "authentic mystery," see John Lomax, "Stealing the Show," *Houston Press,* October 19, 2006.

25.   Soul Rebels Brass Band, "No Place Like Home," recorded February 13, 2009, on Soul Rebels *No Place Like Home: Live from New Orleans* (2010). Spitzer, "Rebuilding the 'Land of Dreams' with Music," 305.

26.   "Tradition is the creation of the future out of the past." Henry Glassie, "Tradition," *Journal of American Folklore* 108, no. 430 (Autumn 1995): 395–412, quotation on 395. For "collectively self-authored," see Spitzer, "Rebuilding the 'Land of Dreams' with Music," 327.

27.   Matthew N. Peters et al., "Natural Disasters and Myocardial Infarction: The Six Years After Hurricane Katrina," *Mayo Clinic Proceedings* 89, no. 4 (April 2014): 472–477. For the quotation, see Blake Hanson, "Stress of Rebuilding Disrupted Heart Attack Timing, Tulane Study Says," *WDSU News,* March 18, 2014.

28.   Rose, "We'll Miss the Blogger Next Door." For "loved me back," see Ashley Morris, "Light at the End of the Tunnel," blog post, September 27, 2006, http://ashleymorris .typepad.com/ashley_morris_the_blog/2006/09/oyster_ashley_l.html.

29.   For "the worst," see Barack Obama, "Address to the Nation on the Oil Spill in the Gulf of Mexico," June 15, 2010, *Daily Compilation of Presidential Documents* No. 201000502 (Office of the Federal Register, National Archives and Records Administration), 1. There is no definitive measure of how much oil spilled. For the purposes of assessing damages under the Clean Water Act, Judge Carl J. Barbier of the Federal District Court in New Orleans ruled that 4 million barrels had spilled, but because BP had collected some of it, a total of 3.19 million barrels (or 134 million gallons) had been left in the Gulf. While BP argued that 3.26 million barrels had spilled, experts testifying for the federal government had offered estimates of 5 million barrels. John Schwartz, "Judge's Ruling on Gulf Oil Spill Lowers Ceiling on the Fine BP Is Facing," *NYT,* January 15, 2015. National Commission on the BP Deepwater Horizon Oil Spill and Offshore Drilling, *Deep Water: The Gulf Oil Disaster and the Future of Offshore Drilling* (Washington, DC: US Government Printing Office, 2011). For other accounts of the oil spill, see William R. Freudenburg and Robert Gramling, *Blowout in the Gulf: The BP Oil Spill Disaster and the Future of Energy in America* (Cambridge: MIT Press, 2010); Antonia Juhasz, *Black Tide: The Devastating Impact of the Gulf Oil Spill* (Hoboken: John Wiley and Sons, 2011); and Abraham Lustgarten, *Run to Failure: BP and the Making of the Deepwater Horizon Disaster* (New York: W. W. Norton & Company, 2012).

30.   Brian Stelter, "Cooper Becomes Loud Voice for Gulf Residents," *NYT,* June 17, 2010. Justin Gillis and Campbell Robertson, "On the Surface, Gulf Oil Spill Is Vanishing Fast," *NYT,* July 28, 2010, p. A1. The article did note that "concerns stay."

31.   Rick Jervis, "In The Gulf: Lives Forever in Recovery," *USA Today,* June 18, 2010. Kai Erikson, *A New Species of Trouble: The Human Experience of Modern Disasters* (New York: W. W. Norton, 1994), 20. Anne McClintock, "Slow Violence and the BP Oil Crisis in the Gulf of Mexico: Militarizing Environmental Catastrophe," *e-misférica,* Summer 2012, p. 9. See also Rob Nixon, *Slow Violence and the Environmentalism of the Poor* (Cambridge: Harvard University Press, 2011); Michelle Meyer Lueck and Lori Peek, "The Crude Awakening: Gulf Coast Residents Reflect on the BP Oil Spill and the 2010 Hurricane Season," in Lisa A. Eargle and Ashraf Esmail, eds., *Black Beaches and Bayous: The BP*

Deepwater Horizon Oil Spill Disaster (Lanham: University Press of America, 2012), 159–180. On the chronic stress called by so-called "technological disasters," see also Duane A. Gill and Steven Picou, "Technological Disaster and Chronic Community Stress," *Society & Natural Resources* 11, no. 8 (1998): 799–815.

32. Cherri Foytlin, interview by Andy Horowitz, July 6, 2010, interview R-0494, transcript, pp. 21–22, SOHP Collection.

33. "Findings of Fact and Conclusions of Law, Phase One Trial," In re: Oil Spill by the Oil Rig "Deepwater Horizon" in the Gulf of Mexico, on April 20, 2010, US District Court, Eastern District of Louisiana, case nos. 10-2771 and 10-4536, Document 13355, September 4, 2014, p. 152. The finding apportioned the blame 67 percent to BP, 30 percent to Transocean, and 3 percent to Halliburton. For misdemeanor charges, see "Former BP Rig Supervisor Found Not Guilty," *AP*, February 25, 2016.

34. The amount included a $5.5 billion civil penalty for violating the Clean Water Act, $8.1 billion for damages to natural resources, $4.9 billion for economic damages, $1 billion to resolve other claims made by local governments, and $1.3 billion to resolve other, smaller claims. US District Court for the Eastern District of Louisiana, "Consent Decree Among Defendant BP Exploration & Production Inc. ("BPXP"), the United States of America, and the States of Alabama, Florida, Louisiana, Mississippi, and Texas," *In Re Oil Spill by the Oil Rig "Deepwater Horizon,"* Document 15, April 4, 2016. See also US Department of Justice, "Deepwater Horizon, Proposed Consent Decrees," https://www.justice.gov/enrd/deepwater-horizon. The settlement did not include a 2012 class action settlement, or other lawsuits by individuals.

35. BP negotiated the settlement such that $15.3 billion (all but a $5.5 billion Clean Water Act penalty, which under federal law could have been as high as $13.7 billion) qualified as a tax deduction for the company. Mark Schleifstein, "No Tax Deduction of Settlement for BP," *NOTP*, November 19, 2015. Steven Mufson, "BP's Bill for Oil Spill Hits $61.6 Billion," *WP*, July 14, 2016. Given the finding of BP's "gross negligence," under the Clean Water Act, the company was liable to a fine of $4,300 per barrel, but it structured the settlement such that most of its payments were attributed to the natural resource damage assessment, which was tax deductible. In 2015, Louisiana exempted $196 million in state severance taxes, and $96 million in state petroleum products taxes, among other tax exemptions accrued by the oil and gas industry. Louisiana Department of Revenue, "State of Louisiana Tax Exemption Budget, 2016–2017," p. 9.

36. BP, "BP to Settle Federal, State and Local Deepwater Horizon Claims for up to $18.7 Billion With Payments to be Spread Over 18 Years," press release, July 2, 2015.

37. Nathaniel Rich, "The Most Ambitious Environmental Lawsuit Ever," *NYT Magazine,* October 2, 2014. Donald F. Boesch et al., "Scientific Assessment of Coastal Wetland Loss, Restoration and Management in Louisiana," *Journal of Coastal Research,* Special Issue no. 20 (1994): 1–103, esp. 5. The specific study referred to the period from 1955 through 1978, although it continued to be relied on as a definitive estimate. See also Ricardo A. Olea and James L. Coleman, Jr., "A Synoptic Examination of Causes of Land Loss in Southern Louisiana as Related to the Exploitation of Subsurface Geologic Resources," *Journal of Coastal Research* 30, no. 5 (2014): 1025–1044. For "15,000 km of canals," see John W. Day, Jr., "Restoration of the Mississippi Delta; Lessons from Hurricanes Katrina and Rita," *Science* 315, no. 5819 (March 23, 2007): 1679–1684. For land loss predictions, see Coastal Protection and Restoration Authority of Louisiana, *Louisiana Comprehensive Master Plan for a Sustainable Coast* (effective June 2, 2017), 74.

38. Coastal Protection and Restoration Authority, *Louisiana's Comprehensive Master Plan for a Sustainable Coast,* 129. See also Mark Davis, Harry Vorhoff, and John Driscoll, *Financing the Future: Turning Coastal Restoration and Protection Plans into Realities: The Cost of Comprehensive Coastal Restoration and Protection* (New Orleans: Tulane Institute on Water Resources Law & Policy, 2014).

39. Tyler Priest, "Claiming the Coastal Sea: The Battles for the 'Tidelands,' 1937–1953," in Diane Austin et al., *History of the Offshore Oil and Gas Industry in Southern Louisiana,*

Volume I: Papers on the Evolving Offshore Industry, OCS Study MMS 2008-042 (New Orleans: US Department of the Interior, Minerals Management Service, Gulf of Mexico OCS Region, 2008), 82 (amount extrapolated from 1995, when Priest estimates the loss at $27.63 billion). Louisiana did not receive any royalties or other payments for oil extraction that took place more than three miles from the state's eroding coastline until 1986, when changes in the law secured Louisiana 27 percent of revenues from between 3 and 6 miles offshore. From 1986 through 2005, the state received just over $1 billion, which it dedicated, by state constitutional amendment, to education. The Mineral Leasing Act of 1920 assigned 50 percent of oil royalties received by the federal government to the state from which the oil was extracted, but no royalties came to the Gulf states for offshore drilling until a 1978 amendment to the Outer Continental Shelf Lands Act of 1953 (Outer Continental Shelf Lands Act Amendments of 1973, Pub. L. No. 95-372, 92 Stat. 629, which passed September 18, 1978) required that offshore revenues be distributed in a "fair and equitable" manner to nearby states. After Louisiana sued, in 1985, Congress set the amount at 27 percent in with the Consolidated Omnibus Budget Reconciliation Act of 1985, Pub. L. No. 99-272, 100 Stat. 82 (April 7, 1986).

40. Gulf of Mexico Energy Security Act of 2006, Pub. L. No. 109-432, 120 Stat. 3000 (December 20, 2006). On August 5, 2010, Senator Landrieu introduced the Restoring Ecosystem Sustainability and Protection on the Delta Act, S. 3763, which would have secured Louisiana a larger share of offshore oil revenues immediately, rather than waiting until 2017. The bill was referred to the Committee on Energy and Natural Resources, but never received a vote.

41. Della Hasselle, "Louisiana Faces Unexpected Shortfall in Major Source of Funding for Coastal Protection," *The Lens,* October 18, 2017; Della Hasselle, "State Pulls Back on Coastal Restoration Projects Due to Shortfall in Oil and Gas Royalties," *The Lens,* December 14, 2017.

42. Julie Demansky, "Five Years After the BP Oil Spill, Gulf Coast Residents Say 'BP Hasn't Made Things Right," DeSmog, April 21, 2015, https://www.desmogblog.com/2015/04/21/five -years-after-bp-oil-spill-gulf-coast-residents-say-bp-hasn-t-made-things-right. Quotations from embedded video, Dean Blanchard, interviewed by Julie Dermansky, April 21, 2015. The lawsuit was *Board of Commissioners of the Southeast Louisiana Flood Protection Authority-East v. Tennessee Gas Pipeline Company, LLC et al.,* Civil District Court, Parish of Orleans, Louisiana, case no. 13-6911; once it moved to the US District Court, Eastern District of Louisiana, it became Civil Action no. 13-5410; on appeal to the US Court of Appeals, Fifth Circuit, it became case no. 15-30162. For Jindal, see Jeff Adelson, "Jindal Denounces Lawsuit Targeting Oil and Gas Firms," *The Advocate,* July 25, 2013. The legislation to kill the suit began as Louisiana Senate Bill 469, which passed and became Louisiana Act 544 of 2014, and then was found unconstitutional in *The Louisiana Oil & Gas Association, Inc. v. Honorable James D. "Buddy" Caldwell, In His Capacity as Attorney General of the State of Louisiana,* on October 31, 2014. The US Court of Appeals for the Fifth Circuit dismissed the Southeast Louisiana Flood Protection Authority's suit on March 3, 2017.

43. State of Louisiana, Coastal Protection & Restoration Authority, *Louisiana's Comprehensive Master Plan for a Sustainable Coast* (2012), 159 (for "relocation") and 175 (for "retreat").

44. On Ironton, see Tyronne Edwards, *The Forgotten People: Restoring a Missing Segment of Plaquemines Parish* (Xlibris, 2017), 193–200.

45. Michelle Bates Deakin, "Phoenix Rising," *UU World,* December 11, 2006, https://www .uuworld.org/articles/stub-7062. Zion Travelers Cooperative Center, http://www.ziontcc .com/home/.

46. Tyronne Edwards, public comment at Coastal Protection and Restoration Authority meeting, January 18, 2017, New Orleans, LA. Printed in Coastal Protection and Restoration Authority, *2017 Coastal Master Plan. Attachment G1: Public Hearing Transcripts* (April 2017), 200, http://coastal.la.gov/wp-content/uploads/2017/04/Attachment-G1 _FINAL_03.24.2017.pdf.

47. Tyronne Edwards, remarks at Tulane University, November 10, 2015, video recording in author's possession. For the diversion, see Coastal Protection and Restoration Authority, *Louisiana's Comprehensive Master Plan for a Sustainable Coast* (2017), 149.

48. Constitution of the State of Louisiana, adopted March 7, 1868. Edwards, remarks at Tulane University. "Asking me to sacrifice" is a phrase Edwards used in a conversation with the author on November 6, 2015, notes in author's possession.

49. Barack Obama, "Remarks on the 10th Anniversary of Hurricane Katrina in New Orleans, Louisiana," August 27, 2015, *Daily Compilation of Presidential Documents* No. 201500573 (Office of the Federal Register, National Archives and Records Administration), 2.

50. Obama, "Remarks on the 10th Anniversary of Hurricane Katrina," 5. For Seaton, see Todd A. Price, "Willie Mae Seaton of Willie Mae's Scotch House Dies at 99," *NOTP*, September 21, 2005. For $200,000 and evacuating, see Neda Ulaby, "In New Orleans, A Fried Chicken Institution Revived," *All Things Considered,* July 30, 2008.

51. The Asian population stayed the same, while the number of New Orleanians who called themselves Hispanic or Latino increased by 6,658. In New Orleans, 21,484 people reported being Hispanic or Latino, and 120,182 people reported being white alone, while 231,651 people reported being black or African American alone, and 11,528 people reported being Asian alone. See US Census Bureau, Population Division, "Annual Estimates of the Resident Population by Sex, Race, and Hispanic Origin for the United States, States, and Counties: April 1, 2010 to July 1, 2017." For poverty, see US Census Bureau, 2016 American Community Survey 1-Year Estimates, "Poverty Status in the Past 12 Months." For income inequality, see Marla Nelson, Laura Wolf-Powers, and Jessica Fisch, *Persistent Low Wages in New Orleans' Economic Resurgence: Policies for Improving Earnings for the Working Poor* (New Orleans: The Data Center, August 2015), 1. On population changes, see also Elizabeth Fussell, "The Long-Term Recovery of New Orleans' Population After Hurricane Katrina," *American Behavioral Scientist* 59, no. 10 (2015): 1231–1245.

52. US Census Bureau, 2015 American Community Survey 1-Year Estimates. See also Allison Plyer, Nihal Shrinath, and Vicki Mack, *The New Orleans Index at Ten: Measuring Greater New Orleans' Progress toward Prosperity* (New Orleans: The Data Center, July 2015). For St. Bernard Parish, see US Census Bureau, Population Division, "Annual Estimates of the Resident Population for Selected Age Groups by Sex for the United States, States, Counties, and Puerto Rico Commonwealth and Municipios: April 1, 2010 to July 1, 2017" (June 2018).

53. Obama, "Remarks on the 10th Anniversary of Hurricane Katrina," 6. For "mostly recovered," see Michael Henderson, Belinda Davis, and Michael Climek, *Views of Recovery Ten Years After Katrina and Rita* (Baton Rouge: LSU Manship School of Mass Communica- tion, Reilly Center for Media & Public Affairs, August 25, 2015), 5. For "people like you," see The Henry J. Kaiser Family Foundation, *New Orleans Ten Years After the Storm: The Kaiser Family Foundation Katrina Survey Project* (2015), 5. Among African Americans, 20 percent said their lives were better, and 36 percent said their lives were worse; among white people, 41 percent said their lives were better and 10 percent said their lives were worse. Henderson, Davis, and Climek, *Views of Recovery Ten Years After Katrina and Rita,* 10.

54. Malik Rahim, interview by Pamela Hamilton, May 23, 2006, interview U-0252, transcript, pp. 50–51, SOHP Collection.

55. On Rahim, and Common Ground, see Joshua B. Guild, "'Nobody Can Tell Me What We Can't Do': Malik Rahim, the Black Radical Tradition, and Struggles for Social Justice in New Orleans, 1970–2010," 2015, unpublished paper in author's possession. See also Rebecca Solnit, *A Paradise Built in Hell: The Extraordinary Communities that Arise in Disaster* (New York: Viking, 2009), 231–304.

56. Trymaine Lee, "Inquiries Give Credence to Reports of Racial Violence After Katrina," *NYT,* August 27, 2010, p. A9.

57. Rahim, May 23, 2006, p. 51.

ACKNOWLEDGMENTS

When I started working on this book, I knew that writing history involved telling other people's stories. I did not know, however, the extent to which writing history also involved building on other people's insights, grappling with other people's criticism, and if things are going really well, spending other people's money. This book's flaws reflect my own limits as a historian, but its achievements, such as they may be, reveal the wisdom and generosity of those around me.

Institutional support made it possible for me to write this book. I started this project while I was in graduate school, and a Henry S. McNeil Fellowship and a Helena P. Bulkley Fellowship in American History, both from Yale University, provided major funding for my education. The Yale Club of New Haven awarded me a scholarship six years in a row. The Archibald Hanna, Jr., Fellowship in American History at the Beinecke Rare Book and Manuscript Library, a Policy Fellowship from the Yale Institution for Social and Policy Studies, and the John Morton Blum Fellowship for Graduate Research in American History and Culture all supported various research endeavors. A Mrs. Giles Whiting Fellowship in the Humanities enabled me to spend a full year as a graduate student focused on writing. The New Orleans Center for the Gulf South at Tulane University awarded me a Global South Fellowship when I was a graduate student and a Monroe Fellowship after I joined the Tulane faculty. At Tulane, I also relied on generous support from the History Department and the School of Liberal Arts and enjoyed a productive residency at A Studio in the Woods. Finally, like alchemy, the Louisiana Board of Regents' Awards for Louisiana Artists and Scholars program transmuted a semester's leave granted by Tulane into an entire academic year of protected time for research and writing.

My research also was only possible because of the archivists and librarians at the Yale University Library, the Beinecke Rare Book and Manuscript Library, the Tulane University Library, the Louisiana Research Collection, the Amistad Research Center, the Hogan Jazz Archive, the Earl K. Long Library at the University of New Orleans, the Louisiana State University Library, the T. Harry Williams Center for Oral History, the Edith Garland Dupré Library at the University of Louisiana-Lafayette, the Frazar Memorial Library at McNeese State University, the Louisiana State Library, the Louisiana State Archive, the New Orleans Public Library, the Southern Historical Collection at the University of North Carolina, the Disaster Research Center at the University of Delaware, the US Army Corps of Engineers, the Library of Congress, and the US National Archives.

As I tried to make sense of what I found in those archives, I shared my work in progress at more than a dozen conferences, in several disciplines, on three continents. This book is much better for it. I am grateful to the academic institutions and professional organizations that facilitated those opportunities, and to all of the scholars who shared their time and expertise with me. I am grateful, as well, to the scholars who served as editors and anonymous reviewers for the articles I published on related topics in the *Journal of Southern History* and *Southern Cultures,* and appreciate those journals' permission to reproduce portions of those articles here. Chapter 2 is an edited and expanded version of "Hurricane Betsy and the Politics of Disaster in New Orleans's Lower Ninth Ward, 1965–1967," *Journal of Southern History* 70, no. 4 (November 2014): 893–934. Portions of the Epilogue were first published in "The BP Oil Spill and the End of Empire Louisiana," *Southern Cultures* 20, no. 3 (Fall 2014): 6–23.

The amazing Southern Oral History Program has supported my work for nearly two decades. The SOHP, the Louisiana State Museum, and the Beinecke Library enabled me to spend the summer of 2006 in New Orleans, asking people about the future of the city for a project we called "Imagining New Orleans." Jacquelyn Hall, Glenda Gilmore, Karen Leathem, and George Miles made it possible, and Maura Fitzgerald, Josh Guild, Pamela Hamilton, Megan Pugh, and Elizabeth Shelburne made it happen. The SOHP also enabled me to spend part of the summer of 2010 in Louisiana, interviewing people about their experiences of the BP oil spill. The people we interviewed for those projects are too many to list here, but some of their words are in this book, and their insights—and their generosity during difficult times—remain with me.

I am thankful for everyone at Harvard University Press who helped to produce this book, especially Robin Bellinger, who saw it through to the finish line. Three scholars read the entire manuscript at the behest of the press and offered truly helpful advice. Molly Roy made the maps. I will remain grateful to my editor, Thomas LeBien, for responding to my initial book proposal with the idea that I ought to write this book instead. If at any point you found yourself wishing that the book had a murkier narrative, three epigraphs at the start of every chapter, or 125 more pages, you may direct your criticism to Thomas.

Were I to list the people at Tulane who have helped me in various ways over the past years, this acknowledgments section would quickly become redundant with the university directory. I hope it suffices to say that I am indebted to my colleagues at Tulane, especially those in the History Department, the Environmental Studies program, at the ByWater Institute, and at the New Orleans Center for the Gulf South. In the same spirit, I say thank you to my classmates at Yale, and to my students, at Tulane and Yale, who have taught me more than they know.

The following people made specific, and often substantial, contributions to this project: Francesca Ammon, Rosanne Adderley, Tom Beller, David Blight, Chris Bonner, Josh Caffery, Michael Coenen, Craig Colten, Mark Davis, John Demos, Kate Dudley, Maura Fitzgerald, Bev Gage, Bruce Gray, Fabienne Gray, Peggy Gray, Josh Guild, Jacob Hacker, Leslie Harris, Mac Herring, Emerson Hilton, Jonathan Holloway, Rebecca Jacobs, Matt Jacobson, Alison Kanosky, Marcy Kaufman, Liz Kinsley, Carolee Klimchock, Scott Knowles, Robin Morris, Andrew Offenberger, Jen Parker, Paige Pemberton, Allison Plyer, Doug Rae, Katy Reckdahl, Jacob Remes, Edward Richards, Joe Roach, Elihu Rubin, Paul Sabin, Rebecca Snedeker, Randy Sparks, Nick Spitzer, Ted Steinberg, Tom Sugrue, John Szwed, Chloe Taft, Lauren Tilton, Caitlin Verboon, Carolyn Ware, Molly Worthen, Ruthie Yow, and Talya Zemach-Bersin. I am preemptively grateful to the people I may have inadvertently left off this list for not holding a grudge. I am particularly indebted to Larry Powell for giving me a trove of material, to Rich Campanella for looking at maps with me, and to Megan Pugh for sharpening my sentences. Liz Cohen, who convinced me to go to graduate school, read a draft of this manuscript and made transformative notes on nearly every page. I regret that space constraints prevent me from going on at great length about how important many of these people have been to this project, or from acknowledging the many other people who did not necessarily improve the book directly but who certainly improved its author.

Three mentors helped me to conceive of this project, and their influence endured through to the end. Johnny Faragher, who has the most finely calibrated bullshit detector I have ever encountered, kept me honest. Kai Erikson, the peerless scholar of disaster and community, helped me to see that the purpose of studying the humanities is to learn the practical art of being humane. And then there is Glenda Gilmore. Ever since I walked into her classroom on my first day of college, I have felt like she has been telling me secrets about my own country. She has helped me to orient my life around the power of empathy, the possibility of change, and the necessity of hope. In other words, Glenda Gilmore is the reason I am a historian.

Let me conclude by looking back toward an even earlier beginning. This history of my debts logically could have started in the bottom of the laundry wagon that, family legend has it, my great-grandparents used to escape a pogrom in Babruysk a century ago. After all, this book would not exist without that wagon, or the cunning of its temporary inhabitants. I am sure that none of my ancestors ever visited Louisiana, but I think they would have understood this place. They knew something about the courage and hope it takes to try to repair the world. And most of my people love to sing. I don't know how to put into words what I owe them, my grandmothers Mary and Zelda, my brother Jesse, my sister-in-law Gabby, my nephews Benji and Remy, my Aunt Nina, my Uncle Holland, and my cousins Matt, Jon, Lauren, Amy, Reece, Elliot, and Henry—and especially my parents Sidney and Gladys—except to say that every day I am aware of my inconceivable good luck: I was born into the best family.

Finally—and now I'm just bragging—I also married the best person. Among the many blessings she has bestowed upon me is making our miraculous daughters, Mira and Zelda, into sixth-generation New Orleanians. For that and for everything else, Sarah, I wrote this for you.

INDEX

Note: Page numbers in italic type indicate illustrations.